Bonnie and Clyde
A TWENTY-FIRST-CENTURY UPDATE

James R. Knight
with Jonathan Davis

EAKIN PRESS  Fort Worth, Texas

This work is dedicated to "Partners in Crime," an informal depression-era-out-laws Internet discussion and research group whose members include some of the best-informed people on the subject to be found anywhere. Many of them provided the inspiration, encouragement, and resources which made this book possible. There were also a few other experts who were willing to help a rookie learn the ropes. Thanks, guys. You know who you are.

Library of Congress Cataloging-in-Publication Data

Knight, James R.
    Bonnie and Clyde : a twenty-first-century update / James R. Knight
with Jonathan Davis.– 1st ed.
        p.   cm.
    Includes bibliographical references and index.
    ISBN 1-57168-794-7 (pb : alk. paper)
    1. Barrow, Clyde, 1909-1934. 2. Parker, Bonnie, 1910-1034.
3. Criminals–United States–Biography. I. Davis, Jonathan. II. Title
HV6245.K55 2003
364.15'52'092273–dc21   2003008509

Contents

Preface

There have always been outlaws.

For as long as there have been laws, instituted by some authority—God or man—there have been those who, for their own reasons, have chosen to break them. Whether it was David and his small gang of followers running from King Saul and living off the local population in southern Judea three thousand years ago, or Robin of Locksley and his merry men making life miserable for Prince John and the sheriff of Nottingham in twelfth-century England, or an ex-Confederate guerrilla named Jesse Woodson James putting his acquired skills in small-unit tactics to use against banks and railroad express cars, the lives of the men and women who have chosen to live outside the boundaries of society's rules have always held a kind of fascination for the rest of us. Add to that a pair of tragic, doomed, star-crossed lovers and the tale becomes irresistible.

The story of Clyde Chestnut Barrow and Bonnie Elizabeth Parker has all the elements of the classic outlaw tale—with a distinctive 1930s "Grapes of Wrath" kind of twist. It has a little Jesse James, only with Ford V-8s and automatic weapons; a little Robin Hood, only with poor sharecroppers, small-town banks, and Texas Rangers; and a little of Shakespeare's *Romeo and Juliet*, only with moonshine whiskey and told with a southwestern country twang. This is the stuff legends are made of. In Bonnie and Clyde's case, just as in all the others, the true story behind the legend is not only elusive but in many ways differs from the public perception.

Clyde Barrow and Bonnie Parker were front-page news for a few months in the early 1930s, and then they were killed by law enforcement officers under what some thought were suspicious circumstances. After that, they faded from the scene and the public memory for a while. By the time America had come through World War II, few people remembered—or cared—who Bonnie and Clyde were. From that low point, however, they began a slow comeback. Books and articles began to appear now and then—not serious research, but personal stories of people who had been involved with them. It took Hollywood to bring them back to the front page.

In September 1967, the movie *Bonnie and Clyde* opened. As history, it was only occasionally accurate, but at the box office, and as public relations for the outlaw couple, it was a success. Coming as it did in the middle of the turbulent sixties, a whole new generation of people who may not even have known their names now saw the couple as antiestablishment heroes. Some of that same feeling existed when Bonnie and Clyde were alive, but only among people who were not in their line of fire. More books and articles came along, and finally, in the last two decades of the century, serious historical research began to be done by a few authors.

As the twenty-first century begins, there are still a few left who remember Bonnie and Clyde, whose lives were touched by them for good or ill, and it has been my privilege to talk to some of them. Many of these people were a little puzzled at the attention paid to the bandit couple and surprised that anyone would still be interested in hearing about their experiences. By and large, they didn't see themselves as witnesses to history and didn't quite understand the excitement of today's researchers and collectors who pursue their stories and artifacts. One man took one of Clyde's homemade "whippit guns" (a semiautomatic shotgun cut down with a hacksaw) out of a car abandoned by the gang. Rather than see it as a historically significant weapon belonging to a famous outlaw, he sent it back to the factory to be completely redone. The sawed-off barrel and stock made it useless to him as a quail hunter!

Others were reluctant to talk about their experiences. For some families, there were painful things they would just as soon leave in the past. Others still feel a real fear concerning their associ-ation with the outlaw couple. Since most who told me their stories do so in spite of their misgivings of one kind or another, I've tried to honor their desire for anonymity in return for their trust in me.

Thanks to the work of people such as author John Neal Phillips, Barrow family friend, and my collaborator, Jonathan Davis, and many other private researchers, today it's possible to put together a clearer picture of the two young people who became the most famous outlaw couple of the twentieth century.

This book is certainly not the last word on the famous pair, just the next one. At this writing, a recently discovered manuscript, written by Blanche Barrow while she was in prison, is being edited and prepared for publication. When it becomes public, things in this book and others will surely have to be changed as we get Blanche's own version of her time with Bonnie and Clyde and we are able to fill in a few more pieces of the puzzle.

—James R. Knight
Franklin, Tennessee

Acknowledgments

This project began with a meeting, instigated by Sandy Jones, between myself and Jonathan Davis, in a hotel lobby in Fort Worth, Texas. Marie Barrow Scoma's stories of her early years, and the Barrow family's experiences during the time that Clyde Barrow was a wanted man, recorded by Mr. Davis, became the foundation for the early chapters of this book. As the story came to the point that the lives of the people involved entered the public record, however, the help of many other people became necessary.

After Bonnie and Clyde became public figures, the best and most detailed accounts of their exploits often came from the pages of small-town newspapers. These stories were written down within hours of the actual events and usually included interviews with participants who had no idea they were dealing with the Barrow Gang. Finding these stories was the trick, and without the librarians and volunteers in places like Storm Lake, Perry, Spencer, and Fort Dodge, Iowa; Marshall, Temple, Sherman, Eastland, Mabank, Kaufman, Denton, and Waco, Texas; Enid and Commerce, Oklahoma; Ruston, Louisiana; Joplin, Springfield, and Carthage Missouri; Fort Smith and Fayetteville, Arkansas; and several others, it would have been impossible. These folks were generous and helpful to an unknown researcher who, many times, was just a voice on the phone. Thank you all.

From the start, I knew that pictures were going to be an important part of the story, and the ones seen here came from several sources. The excellent facilities of the Dallas Public Library and the Texas Ranger Museum in Waco provided many of the classic but seldom seen images. Others came from private collections. I'd like to especially thank Sandy Jones, Bob Fischer, Renay Stanard, Rick Mattix, Pat McConal, Harrison Hamer, and Phillip Steele for the photographs they provided.

History is sometimes hard to recognize as you see it happening. The eyewitnesses provided a unique perspective, and I'd like to thank them all for the willingness to talk to a stranger—Roy Ferguson, whose car battery was almost stolen; Clemie Booker Methvin, who fed Clyde and a slightly drunk Bonnie supper and knew many of the people involved in Bienville Parish, Louisiana; Gladys Cartwright, who was shot in the hand; Velma Humphrey and Walter Patton Jr., who told me the story of the killing of their father and uncle, Henry Humphrey; and my mother, Hilda Farris Knight, and my uncle, William S. Farris, who saw Buck and W. D. Jones drive past their house.

Finally, there were several people who are authorities in this and related fields whom I went to for help more than once. I'd like to thank Sandy Jones, gangster artifacts collector and 1934 Ford V-8 expert; Jonathan Davis and Buddy Williams for issues pertaining to the Barrow family and Bonnie and Clyde in the Dallas area; Pat McConal for the

Eastham escape and Huntsville Prison details; Joe Bauske for the account of the death of W. D. Jones; Sid Underwood for his book on Raymond Hamilton; Brian Beerman for the Okabena robbery story; Rick Mattix and Mike Woltz for details concerning the Barrow gang in Iowa; Carroll Y. Rich for the tale of aftermath of the ambush in Arcadia, Louisiana; and Robert H. Russell for his grandfather's notes on the harboring trial.

Finally, for the overall story, I must thank John Neal Phillips. His benchmark work on Ralph Fults and Bonnie and Clyde was constantly open on my desk. The quality and depth of his research meant that, for some incidents in Bonnie and Clyde's life, there was literally no place else to go. In addition, he personally endured numerous questions, some serious and some foolish; answered many e-mails; and generally was a great help and encouragement. I believe his willingness to help another researcher in the same field is a measure of the well-deserved confidence he has in his own work. On the subject of Clyde Barrow, Bonnie Parker, and their families and associates, he is "the man."

INTRODUCTION
The Legend of Bonnie and Clyde

During the early autumn of 1934, a volume entitled *Fugitives: The Story of Clyde Barrow and Bonnie Parker*[1] appeared in bookstores across America. Bonnie and Clyde were two of the best-known individuals in the country at that time, due to the fact that their two-year odyssey of crime had reached a violent end on a stretch of rural Louisiana highway a few months earlier. In 1934 many of the best-known public figures in America were fugitives and wanted persons. Besides Bonnie and Clyde, it was the year of John Dillinger, "Pretty Boy" Floyd, "Baby Face" Nelson, Alvin Karpis, and the Barker gang, with their notorious "Ma." *Fugitives* was advertised as being written by Nell Barrow, Clyde's sister, and Emma Parker, Bonnie's mother, and compiled by Jan Fortune, a screenwriter.

In Dallas, sixteen-year-old Marie Francis eagerly awaited the publication of this account of the lives of the outlaw couple. She had been married to Joe Bill Francis for a few months, but her maiden name was Barrow. Clyde was her older brother. Marie, the youngest of the seven Barrow children, along with the rest of her family, had spent the last two years living the story. After all the media attention, police scrutiny, and just plain hype, Marie was hoping that this book would eradicate misconceptions. The Clyde Barrow and Bonnie Parker she knew weren't the depraved "mad-dog killers" portrayed in much of the news coverage that followed their two-year career.[2]

Marie had no part in the preparation of the new book, so she had to wait until it came out and read it like everyone else. When it did, she was in for a major disappointment. Marie thought the book was more fiction than fact. She was upset and confronted her sister Nell the next time she saw her. Nell said she was just as surprised as Marie about how the book turned out and hadn't said many of the things that appeared in *Fugitives* as Barrow family recollections. It was the same with the Parker family: Emma Parker denied having said what Jan Fortune attributed to her.

True Detective magazine had beaten *Fugitives* to the newsstands with its six-part series entitled "The Inside Story of Bonnie Parker and the Bloody Barrows." The publishers of *True Detective* already had much of the work done on the series and were ready to go to press as soon as they got word that Bonnie and Clyde had been captured or killed. Word came on May 23, 1934, and the first installment of "The Bloody Barrows" appeared in the June issue. Since the Barrow and Parker families deny being the source for a lot of the material in *Fugitives,* Ms. Fortune must have gotten it from somewhere else. The *True Detective* series was appearing at the time Fortune was preparing her draft of *Fugitives* and was about the only thing available at the time that attempted to cover the Barrows' whole two-year career.[3] Regardless of how the families felt about it, since it was the first full-length treatment of their lives, *Fugitives* (and, by extension, *True Detective*) became an authoritative and primary source for much of what has been written since about "the Barrow gang."

As inaccurate as Marie felt Ms. Fortune's book was, she believed that some of the works that followed it were even worse.[4] Marie noted that the people who have written about her brothers and family over the years didn't go to enough effort to find what she considered the real story, but just relied on those who had gone before them. Few of them actually knew the real people behind the headlines or, until recently, even contacted the Barrow or Parker families.[5]

Unfortunately, Marie Barrow and others over the years have left the impression that almost nothing in *Fugitives* can be trusted. Looking back, we can certainly spot many errors, but recent research has also shown that the book is more accurate—in some places—than previously believed.[6] Whatever is true about the accuracy of the story told in Jan Fortune's book, one thing is certain. It was the beginning of the legend of Bonnie and Clyde.

In September 1934, when *Fugitives* came out, the public image of the pair of outlaw lovers from Dallas was anything but glamorous. They had, after all, eluded and embarrassed lawmen in more than a dozen states for over two years. Nine policemen and three civilians were dead because of them in robberies, gunfights, and jailbreaks. When the couple was finally betrayed and died in a hail of bullets on a country road, many people thought that they got what they deserved.

Until *Fugitives* appeared, almost everything written about Bonnie and Clyde was from the point of view of the press and the authorities.[7] In the style of the journalism of the day, they were routinely pictured as depraved, bloodthirsty animals. The authorities certainly weren't interested in creating any public sympathy, and the press was glad to pick up on any rumor or lurid detail, no matter how outlandish. Times were hard, and those kinds of stories sold newspapers.

Fugitives, as disappointing as it was to the Barrows, was still the first attempt to tell the story from the family point of view. For the first time, you see Clyde as a normal kid who grew up on a farm, got started in petty crime as a teenager, and finally got caught. You then see him come out of two years in the brutal Texas prison system as a hard case with a hatred of the law, harassed by the local police and almost certain to turn back to crime. You also, for the first time, see Bonnie as a bright, loving, scrappy, headstrong, manipulative, spoiled, homesick girl who was married at fifteen, a deserted wife at seventeen, and a "bored to tears" waitress by nineteen. Then she met a young man who was different from the other boys who tried to date her, and she fell madly in love—having no idea where it would lead.

Many of the terrible things written about them in the papers were true. Places were robbed, men were killed, and families were deprived of husbands and fathers. While they were alive, it was easier to portray Bonnie and Clyde as entirely evil, bloodthirsty, amoral murderers. Now that they were dead, however, it became possible to begin to show them as complex, contradictory human beings instead of cartoon-character gangsters.

Bonnie and Clyde's image as nothing more than thieving, murdering white trash developed over two years. The swing of the pendulum to the other extreme of John Steinbeck–type folk heroes took a little longer. It was, more or less, completed by the 1967 release of the movie starring Warren Beatty as Clyde and Faye Dunaway as Bonnie. The movie was nominated for several Oscars, and 1930s clothes became the current fashion. *Playboy Magazine* even ran an interview with a former gang member, done by a Houston reporter. In many ways, though, the good-looking, good-natured, good-hearted, fast-shooting hillbillies of the 1967 movie were just as unreal as the cold-hearted killers of the 1934 newspapers.

Thankfully, the pendulum has moved back toward the middle. In the last twenty years, some authors have finally begun to research this famous outlaw couple with the level of scholarship that true historical figures deserve.

Using the recollections and family stories of Marie Barrow and other Barrow family members;

the best and most reliable of those accounts written at the time and over the years since; and new research that is still continuing, we will try to tell the story of Bonnie and Clyde as we know it today. They weren't just cold-blooded killers, and they weren't just innocent victims of circumstance. Like everybody else of their time and place, they blended good and bad, passion and indifference, fear and courage, hope and despair.

Depending on where you fit in their lives, Bonnie and Clyde could be your dearest son or daughter, your idolized brother or sister, your most faithful friend, or your worst enemy. Clyde could, literally, take presents to his mother on Christmas Eve, then help kill a young husband and father in his own front yard eighteen hours later. He would kill policemen who cornered him without hesitation, but then kidnap others, ride them around all night, joke with them, give them expense money, and let them go unharmed. He would steal money from banks, storekeepers, and service station attendants but faithfully return borrowed china and silverware to a lady at a takeout diner.

Bonnie was tiny, delicate, and cute, and she loved babies. She would get homesick and cry for her mother, paint her toenails, carry around a pet rabbit, read movie fan magazines, and write poetry, but she could also load a .45 automatic, slap around a woman prisoner, and drive a getaway car. She looked fragile, but she drank moonshine, smoked cigarettes (not cigars), and swore like a sailor. She lived out of the back seat of a Ford V-8 for months at a time and endured car wrecks, burns, and gunshot wounds without giving up. That's not to say that she was the kind of girl to suffer in silence, however. She and Clyde loved each other, but sometimes they fought intensely.

To affirm that Bonnie and Clyde had loyal, loving families and gave them love and trust in return does not change the fact that they also robbed banks and killed people. To point out that Clyde grew up during some of the hardest times our country has ever seen, was changed by a cruel and brutal prison system, and was harassed by local police doesn't excuse the fact that he chose the life of a criminal. Yet to get a sense of Bonnie and Clyde and their world, we have to look at both the good and the bad—as honestly as we can.

CHAPTER 1

The Barrow Family

In many of the pictures taken during his outlaw career, Clyde Barrow is dressed in a three-piece suit and looks like a prosperous young businessman. In fact, in one of his more successful robberies, he was at first mistaken for a bank examiner. But despite his polished image, Clyde Barrow, like many other southwestern outlaws of his time, was born and raised on a farm.

Clyde's father, Henry B. Barrow, was born January 10, 1874, the son of a Pensacola, Florida, shoemaker named James Barrow. Henry was a sickly child and was unable to go to school. He was subject to chills and fever, which the family, in later years, believed were caused by malaria-carrying mosquitoes in the Florida panhandle. Lack of schooling left Henry unable to read or write for the rest of his life, but his quick mind and ability with numbers shone through. Years later, when Henry ran his own business, he would do all the figures in his head. Sometime in the 1880s, after Henry's mother died, James Barrow decided to move his family to Grimes County, Texas.

Henry and his older brother Frank arrived in Texas when the West was still wild. Names like Sam Bass, "Wild Bill" Hickock, Ben Thompson, Billy the Kid, Jesse James, "Bat" Masterson, Wyatt Earp, "Doc" Holliday, Geronimo, Sitting Bull, Crazy Horse, "Long Haired Jim" Courtright, Luke Short, Belle Starr, and others were not relegated to history books but appeared in recent or current newspaper headlines. In spite of this, the move to Texas did Henry Barrow a world of good. Away from the swampy area in western Florida, his bouts of fever subsided and he grew into a healthy and strong young man.

There was nothing in Henry's early life to suggest the violence that would make his sons infamous, but he did cause his father to worry from time to time. Except for the occasional scuffle common to all growing boys, Henry was a rather peaceful fellow, but he loved fast horses and began to frequent the races. These were local affairs, held on Sundays, and very popular with the "sporting" society. They drew large crowds, and a lot of money changed hands. Henry's father viewed the racetrack as dangerous to a young man's character and strongly disapproved of Henry's attendance. By this time, however, Henry was about sixteen years old, and his interest in racehorses was soon to be replaced by something else.

Sometime in 1890, Henry Barrow left home. His father, Jim, had remarried and Henry now had two half-brothers, so he decided it was time to go out on his own. In those days, a strong young man, even with no schooling, could make his way in the world if he was willing to work, and Henry was determined to do just that. He moved northeast about 100 miles to the Nacogdoches area and got a job at a sawmill. There he found something to replace his love of horse races. Her name was Cumie T. Walker.

The Walker family had been in Nacogdoches County for several years, and Cumie lived on a farm with her parents and several brothers and sisters. She was almost a year younger than Henry, born November 21, 1874. The Walkers were strict about their daughter's upbringing, so no makeup or other worldly extravagances were permitted. Naturally, her dating was carefully controlled as well. The wildest party she had ever attended was probably a Baptist church social. In fact, it may well have been at church that Henry and Cumie met, since he had been raised in that denomination as well. Henry was one of Cumie's first beaus, and their courtship lasted about a year. On December 5, 1891, Henry B. Barrow and Cumie T. Walker were married at the home of Cumie's parents near the little community of Swift, Texas. Henry quit his job at the sawmill and rented a small farm, and the young couple settled in to raise a family.

Farming in Texas, or anywhere else in the West in the last few years of the nineteenth century, was a chancy proposition. If you were lucky with the weather and the insects and made a good crop, the market price for that crop was likely to be down. If the market was up, there might be a drought. Tenant farmers like the Barrows, who not only had to make a living but also pay rent on the land, were especially vulnerable to the swings of fortunes common in agriculture. Henry and Cumie were young, strong, and willing to work hard, so they managed to make a living, but they couldn't seem to get any money ahead. The first two Barrow children were born on the farm in Nacogdoches County—Elvin Wilson "Jack" Barrow, born June 20, 1894, and Artie Adell Barrow, born March 30, 1899—but by the turn of the century, the Barrows were on the move to what they hoped were greener pastures.

By 1903, Henry and Cumie were settled on a new rented farm in Milam County near the town of Jones Prairie. It was there that the next two children were born—Marvin Ivan "Buck" Barrow on March 14, 1903, and Nellie May Barrow on May 12, 1905.[1] A few years later, Henry decided to move north to Ellis County. Near the town of Telico, the Barrows made their last attempt to farm successfully. In Ellis County, the last three Barrow children were born: Clyde Chestnut Barrow on March 24, 1909, L. C. Barrow[2] on August 13, 1913, and Lillian Marie Barrow on May 27, 1918 (Marie was actually born in the town of Mabank, not Telico). Seven children had been born over a period of twenty-four years. Clyde's birth was attended by a midwife named Annie Curtis, the wife of H. A. Curtis of Telico. Mrs. Curtis also made Clyde his first baby dress. Actually, the Barrow clan was small for a farming family at the turn of the century. In those days, farming families were larger due both to the work that needed to be done and to the higher infant mortality rates in rural areas, where quality healthcare was seldom available. On the last count, the Barrows beat the odds. At a time when childhood diseases carried off hundreds of thousands of children—rich and poor—every year, all seven of Henry and Cumie's children lived to adulthood.

CHAPTER 2
Growing Up "Barrow"

Like all the information Marie Barrow had about her family up to this point, her descriptions of life on the Barrow farm in Ellis County, Texas, come from conversations with older members of her family and access to family records. She was only four years old when they moved to west Dallas.

The economy in Ellis County at the time of the First World War was founded on agriculture in general and cotton in particular. The biggest towns in the county were Waxahachie, the county seat, and Ennis, several miles to the east. Telico, where the Barrows lived, was a small community that provided for the basic needs of the all of the farming families in the surrounding area. There were a couple of dry goods stores, a blacksmithing establishment, and the Telico Cotton Gin, but no post office. The mail came out of Ennis with a rural carrier.

As in most communities in the South and Southwest, the dry goods store owners accommodated their farming clientele according to the annual cycle of planting and harvesting the cotton crop. The farming families purchased on credit what they needed while the cotton crop was growing in the fields during the spring and summer. In the autumn, they would, hopefully, pay off their accumulated bills with the proceeds from the sale of their cotton crop. Sometimes the store owners would buy the cotton crops themselves and deduct the amount of the purchase from their customers' tab. These stores were where the Barrows traded.

Beside the farms in the vicinity of Telico there was also a sand and gravel company, which operated two shifts every day. The men who worked there lived in railroad boxcars on the premises and ate their meals in a cook shack.

Social life in Telico centered around the church and the school. The Telico school was a frame building constructed around the turn of the century. The schoolgirls were required to sweep and clean the school building while the boys brought in wood for the stoves that heated it.

When the Barrow kids were growing up, they weren't seen as different from other children in the area. Clyde's early years seemed to have been those of a normal Texas farm boy.

Only one family story about their time at Telico portrays Clyde involved in any kind of trouble. As the story goes, Mr. Tims, a dry goods merchant, one day caught Clyde helping himself by reaching into a glass jar full of candy. After that, Mr. Tims made Clyde whistle every time he came into his store so he would know that Clyde didn't have his mouth full of candy. This peculiar arrangement only lasted a short while, until Mr. Tims decided that Clyde had learned his lesson.

Something that bothered Marie Barrow about accounts of the Barrow family was the idea that the children were always being "farmed out" to uncles and aunts all over southeastern Texas, even though this practice was not unusual among the

School picture taken about 1910—possibly in the Corsicana, Texas, area. The boy seated on the far left on the front row is Marvin Ivan "Buck" Barrow, age seven. In the second row, third from the right, leaning to her right to see over a boy's head, is Nell Barrow, age five. In the back row, the tall girl second from the right is Artie Barrow, age eleven.

—Courtesy Jonathan Davis

large, poor farm families of the time. While it's true that the Barrow children spent time with relatives, Marie didn't remember it as being forcibly "farmed out." She said that all the children enjoyed staying at their uncle's place. Clyde worked hard on the farm with his cousins, but it wasn't all work at Uncle Frank's. They went fishing with Uncle Frank's kids, and some of the older ones also went hunting. Looking back on it, Marie found it ironic that, although Clyde liked guns, he wasn't much of a hunter. She said Clyde didn't like to hunt animals but loved to go target shooting and "plinking." Clyde would later become well known for his obsessive target practicing.

Although Clyde showed an early interest in guns on Uncle Frank's farm, Marie didn't believe

he was "gun crazy." In fact, the only firearm she can recall Clyde personally owning before he went out on the road after his prison sentence was a lever-action 1892 Winchester rifle in .25-20 caliber, which he purchased in the late 1920s. Marie learned how to shoot with that rifle, and that particular gun remained in the possession of the Barrow family for close to seventy years. Clyde bought an old leather carrying case for the gun and carved his initials ("C. B.") in it. Recently, this rifle and leather case sold at auction for over $20,000. As a youngster, Clyde was interested in the firearms of the Old West, such as Colt six-shooters and Winchester rifles, just like most Texas boys.

Although farm work occupied part of the year, Clyde still attended school fairly regularly at two different locations. When he lived at his parents' farm, he went to school in that vicinity; when living at Uncle Frank's, he attended school at Corsicana. Clyde also attended services at the local Baptist churches wherever he was living. Marie even remembered Clyde being baptized at the little Baptist church near Eureka, Texas, in 1924.

All in all, Clyde's early years were primarily based in the country in both Ellis and Navarro counties. All aspects of his life, whether working on the farm or attending school and church, were typical of most other young men of his era and locale. If he had stayed down on the farm, the rest of his life might have taken a different turn. However, things changed for the Barrow family in the early 1920s, and these changes would alter the direction of Clyde's life—and not for the better.[1]

CHAPTER 3

The Move to Dallas

The stock market crash of October 1929 might have signaled the beginning of the Great Depression on Wall Street, but for the American farmer, hard times were already ten years old. After World War I ended, the agricultural industry of America was staggered when prices for farm commodities collapsed. Cotton had risen as high as fifty cents a pound during the war, and by 1918, farmers were borrowing money and planting it on every acre and fence row they could find. In November, the war ended, but the next spring and summer provided excellent weather and a huge harvest. Although there was cotton everywhere, the wartime demand was gone. Cotton prices fell by 90 percent to five cents a pound, and other commodities followed suit. Farmers at all levels were economically devastated, with the marginal operator, farming rented land, being hit the hardest.[1]

As if the collapse of commodity prices weren't enough, in 1920 the dreaded boll weevil appeared in Ellis County. What the national economy did not destroy, the weevil finished off. Many people just gave up on farming and headed toward the cities to try to make a living. Some, however, like the Barrows, tried to hang on. Henry supplemented what he made on the farm near Telico with wages from working at both the Telico Cotton Gin and the brickyard in Ennis, but even that wasn't enough. Soon he began to see the handwriting on the wall.

The economy wasn't the only thing that caused the Barrows to consider leaving the farm. By 1922, only the three youngest children were still at home. Marie was just a four-year-old, and the two youngest boys, L. C. and Clyde, were only nine and thirteen. They weren't going to be enough help, and Henry and Cumie were beginning to feel their forty-eight tough years. The fact was, it was getting too hard to make a crop, and even if you did, you couldn't make enough off it to live. In 1922 Henry and Cumie and the three youngest Barrows finally gave up and followed their older children to the big city.

The four older Barrow kids (Jack, Artie, Buck, and Nell) had already left home, and none of them stayed in Ellis County. If you wanted secure employment, comforts, and conveniences, you had to move to town. The nearest large city, Dallas, was just a few miles to the north, and that's where they all went. Now the rest of the family were following.

Jack and his wife were living on Forest Avenue in south Dallas, and he was running an automobile garage that he operated out of his house. They were already building a family and would eventually have four daughters. The two sisters, Artie and Nell, went into the beauty parlor business in downtown Dallas, with a shop located in the Sanger Hotel. Artie later became the first female barber in town. It was Buck's life that seemed to lack any kind of stability.

The Barrows certainly weren't the only farming

family to pull up stakes and relocate in the city. There was already a steady stream of economic refugees pouring into Dallas from all over central Texas. Since most of these urban immigrants had no place to stay when they first moved into Dallas, tent cities and shantytowns sprang up in many places.

When Henry and Cumie moved to Dallas, the two youngest children stayed with them, but Clyde began dividing his time between Dallas and Uncle Frank's farm. The Barrows' first residence in west Dallas was at the campgrounds, which were located close to the Texas and Pacific railroad tracks. There were already a lot of other farming families living there in tents and shanties when the Barrows arrived. It was pretty basic living. They weren't actually living under a viaduct as some versions relate, but the conditions were not much better.

Those years in west Dallas were tough. Government welfare and unemployment programs were unknown in those early decades of the twentieth century, but most able-bodied people, like Henry Barrow, probably wouldn't have taken it in any case. The only form of public assistance that they ever received was in the form of free bread, supplied by an anonymous benefactor, which was brought into the campground on a wagon. When things were extremely tight, this food was gratefully received by those who had nothing else to eat.

When the Barrow family first arrived at the west Dallas campground, Henry immediately began to earn money to support his family by what was referred to back then as "peddling," which meant the buying and selling of just about anything that might turn a profit. Henry began his peddling with a wagon and an old white horse that had been with the family for several years.

Henry Barrow's peddling activities were only done on a temporary basis to keep body and soul together. Marie remembers that they had to live in tents while her father arranged something more permanent. Before long, he began to build a small wooden house, which he intended to move to a permanent location. It was built as the accumulation of money and materials permitted, and it would be several years before it was actually moved off of the campground.

The Barrows' house contained only the barest essentials and consisted of just a few bedrooms. There was no kitchen, so Cumie had to cook and wash outside. Many people who are reading this account have undoubtedly seen the frequently published photo of the old Barrow filling station on the Eagle Ford Road in west Dallas. The structure built on the campground was moved to the Eagle Ford Road location first, and the filling station was added later. It would be eight or ten years after the move to Dallas before the service station was in full operation. Henry and Cumie's bedroom was at the front of this house. Marie's bedroom was across from her parents' room, and L. C.'s bedroom was behind hers. When Clyde came to the campground to stay with them, he shared L. C.'s room.

Even though they lived in what they considered a city environment, life was still hard. There were no nonessentials. At Christmastime, Cumie was able to get a few gifts, along with some apples and oranges, from the Salvation Army, and sometimes clothes as well. For most of the families on the campground, these kinds of things made a huge difference.

Chapter 4

Country Boys in the Big City

While the younger Barrow kids were growing up during the middle and late 1920s, the older brothers and sisters were making their way in the world. Jack and his wife were raising their family of four girls on Forest Avenue, and Nell and Artie continued with their beauty parlor business, but Buck's life seemed to be going from bad to worse.

In 1920, when he was seventeen, Buck married Margaret Heneger. Twins boys were born from this marriage, but one of the children died when he was five months old.[1] According to Mrs. Barrow, it wasn't long after the twin's death that Buck found a new girlfriend, named Pearl. Predictably, Margaret took a dim view of the situation, filed for divorce, and left, taking the surviving son.

In addition to indulging his eye for the ladies, Buck had other unfortunate habits. Back on the farm, Buck had begun raising fighting roosters and fighting dogs. After he moved to the city, Buck continued to keep them in west Dallas, and one of these fighting dogs caused some trouble for Marie. This particular dog was a ferocious pit bull so ill tempered that no one except Buck could even get close to it, but he sometimes tied it up at the side of his parents' house. One day Marie was outside playing ball. She got too close to this dog and it went after her. Luckily, she was not close enough for the dog to actually knock her down and maul her, but it did rip a large part of her dress. Henry and Cumie were already concerned about Buck's

involvement in dogfights and cockfights, so after this incident, Cumie banned all of Buck's animals from the premises.

Buck and his girlfriend Pearl married, and his parents hoped that his life would change for the better. It did look that way for a while, especially when a little girl was born. Unfortunately, the restlessness that seemed to be ingrained in his personality took over again, and his second marriage ended much like the first, with Pearl taking the little girl and leaving.[2]

Buck gravitated from job to job, but there always seemed to be something a little shady about whatever he did. Before he first got married, he was in the poultry business, buying and selling chickens. Unlike a cow, which you can brand, a "rustled" chicken is a lot harder to spot, which probably suited Buck just fine. Then he got involved in the peddling business with some other young men in west Dallas. He bought some brass at an extremely low price. Of course, he claimed he knew nothing about the source of the scrap metal. In fact, it turned out to be stolen, and the police were actively investigating the theft. The cops caught up with the purloined metal when Buck had it in his possession, and he was arrested. From that point on, the police began to keep an eye on Marvin "Buck" Barrow.

Marie Barrow said there was a marked difference in the personalities of her four brothers. Both

Buck and L. C. were more hot tempered and pugnacious than were Jack and Clyde. She didn't think her brothers ever really looked for trouble. It just seemed that Buck and L. C. were always there when it appeared. Of course, neither Buck nor L. C. believed in backing down.

While Buck was rambling around, Clyde was still moving between his parents' home on the campground and Uncle Frank's farm. Marie said that when their parents moved into Dallas, Clyde had finished the sixth grade, and it was during the years on the campground that she really got to know him. She was, of course, the "little sister"—nine years younger

than Clyde—and looked up to him. She remembers Clyde during this period of time as a completely good and normal brother, but, of course, she wasn't aware of everything he might have been doing.

Clyde and L. C. were the older brothers whom Marie really grew up knowing. Jack and Buck were already out on their own by the time she was aware of everybody. In fact, she was about the same age as a couple of Jack's daughters, although she was their aunt. Marie said that she and Clyde did a lot together during those years. There was even one time in the mid-1920s when they got seriously ill together with typhoid fever. The two kids—along

Children sitting on steps. This picture is from a collection of photos originally owned by Dorothy Anderson and was taken in west Dallas in the early 1920s. Dorothy Anderson is the girl third from the left on the top row. Nell Barrow is on the top row, far right. On the first row, second from the left, is L. C. Barrow. Fourth from the left is Clyde Barrow. In between the Barrow brothers is Walter Howard, a boyhood friend.

—Courtesy Jonathan Davis

Elvin W. "Jack" Barrow, in gag photo, 1913.
—Courtesy the Bob Fischer/Renay Stanard collection .

L. C. Barrow in gag photo, 1926.
—Courtesy Bob Fischer/Renay Stanard collection

"Buck" Barrow, on the right, in gag photo with unidentified friend, circa 1920.
—Courtesy the Bob Fischer/ Renay Stanard collection

with their father, who was also sick—were taken to Parkland Hospital.

One of Clyde's ambitions, during his teens, was to be a musician. He liked music, and his family thought he showed a real talent for it. He could play just about any instrument he picked up. Clyde could also sing and do a pretty good Charleston, which was the popular dance of the 1920s. Like many boys his age, Clyde was also fascinated with aviation. The pilots of that era seemed like heroes, and he used to go out to Love Field airport to watch the airplanes. Marie also remembers the old Bull Durham bags in which both Clyde and L. C. used to carry marbles. Like most boys of the time, both brothers loved the game.

When it came to school, Clyde and L. C. were typical west Dallas boys. Playing hooky was the neighborhood pastime. In the country, it was expected that farm children would take time off from school in order to help with the planting and harvesting and a lot of the work in between. This was understood by all parties involved, so absences were not particularly noted. If a child decided to take an extra day or two off in order to spend some time on his own, it wasn't considered anything to get excited about. In Dallas, however, the brothers found the attitude of the school authorities much more severe concerning absenteeism. Clyde and L. C. had to learn to keep an eye out for the truant officer when they decided the day was too nice to be spent within the confines of a classroom.

Even though the two boys were quickly learning how to get along in the big city, they soon found out that they weren't the only ones who were learning the system. Clyde, L. C., and little Marie were supposed to walk part of the way together before separating to go to their own schools, but Clyde and L. C. frequently had other plans. The brothers would go off on their own just as soon as they were outside their neighborhood, leaving little sister to go on to school by herself. To ensure that she wouldn't tell their mother, they tried to buy her off with a quarter, but Marie drove a hard bargain. She knew she had the upper hand, so, in addition to the quarter, she held out for "bicycle rights" from L. C., which meant that he had to agree to let her ride his bike whenever she wanted.

Even though, as a little sister, Marie couldn't have known all the people Clyde ran around with, she still believed that there was a lot of false information about whom he did and didn't know as he was growing up. Marie said that Clyde did not know either Floyd Hamilton or Raymond Hamilton during the 1920s, and that may or may not be true. In later years, Floyd Hamilton told stories about how he knew Clyde at the Cedar Valley School, but Marie contends that the only school Clyde ever attended in Dallas was Sidney Lanier.

Ted Hinton, the Dallas officer who was part of the posse that killed Bonnie and Clyde, said that he knew Clyde somewhat but that he was better acquainted with both Buck and Mr. and Mrs. Barrow. Marie remembers Ted as a good man who later helped members of her family but can't recall ever seeing him around much during those years. She doesn't remember Buck ever mentioning him and feels sure that he never came to visit her parents socially in the years before Clyde and Buck became wanted men.

Finally, Marie says Clyde never knew Bonnie Parker while he was growing up. The only connection between the two of them was indirect. One of Clyde's closest friends in west Dallas was named Clarence Clay. Clarence's sister later married a boy named Hubert "Buster" Parker, who was Bonnie's older brother. While the Clays and the Parkers may have had some contact, the Barrows and the Parkers did not.

Henry and Cumie Barrow and Marie Barrow Francis. Taken while they were traveling with Charles Stanley's "Crime Does Not Pay" show. Late 1934.

—Courtesy Marie Barrow Scoma and author Phillip W. Steele

Clyde Barrow with his two older sisters, Nell, left, and Artie, right. Probably taken about 1927.

—Courtesy Marie Barrow Scoma and author Phillip W. Steele

CHAPTER 5
The Great Divide

In 1934, Bonnie Parker wrote the following verse as part of her poem "The End of the Line " (later known as "The Story of Bonnie and Clyde"):

From Irving to West Dallas viaduct
Is known as the Great Divide,
Where the women are kin,
And the men are men,
And they won't stool on Bonnie and Clyde.

Of course, this verse was a bit of social commentary on the neighborhood where many of the kids who later became well-known fugitives were raised.

The west Dallas viaduct was indeed "Great Divide." In terms of actual geographical distance, west Dallas was only a couple of miles from the office buildings and businesses of downtown Dallas, but in socioeconomic terms, west Dallas was light-years away. In fact, the area of west Dallas, although it bore the name of the city, was not formally incorporated into the surrounding metropolis until the early 1950s, thirty years after the Barrow family moved into the area.

The area of west Dallas was actually county territory under the jurisdiction of the Dallas County Sheriff's Office, but this small detail didn't stop the Dallas city police from coming out and rounding up "the usual suspects" when a crime against property was committed in the city. The city police just automatically assumed that some

boy from west Dallas was probably involved in the robbery or burglary, and many times, of course, they were right. Marie Barrow, however, remembers west Dallas as a decent place that was a lot more civilized than it was generally given credit for being, and that crime there was a lot less plentiful than commonly believed. Not surprisingly, the police had a different opinion.

Times were hard, and the people who lived in the west Dallas area were realists; they knew that they were regarded as being from "the wrong side of the tracks." They looked out for one another and helped their neighbors when hard times or illness or death struck a family, and they also tended to close ranks against the police when they came looking for one of their own. The bad reputation of west Dallas in the early 1930s was such that one of its nicer nicknames was "Little Cicero," after Al Capone's neighborhood near Chicago. It was also known as "The Bog" and "The Devil's Back Porch."

By 1926, Clyde was seventeen years old and was spending most of his time in west Dallas. He had discovered girls, and he needed money if he was going to be able to dress well and take them out. Marie remembers Clyde first working at the Brown Cracker and Candy Company in Dallas for one dollar a day. He then moved on to Procter & Gamble, where he made better money—thirty cents an hour.[1] Clyde's third job was with the United Glass Company, where for two years he worked as a glazier.

Pay receipt from Procter & Gamble Manufacturing Company
signed by Clyde Barrow. It shows $18 pay for sixty hours' work—
thirty cents an hour.

—Courtesy Sandy Jones–
The John Dillinger Historical Society

*Eleanor Bee Williams, Clyde's girlfriend, with Clyde and his two
older sisters, Artie and Nell, circa 1927.*

—Courtesy Bob Fischer/Renay Stanard collection

For many years, the Barrow family kept in its possession a piece of Clyde's work during his period of employment at United Glass. It was a mirror with "EBW" inscribed on its handle, the initials of Clyde's first serious girlfriend. Her name was Eleanor Williams, and Clyde had made the mirror for her as a gift.[2] Whatever Clyde had been involved in before, his relationship with Eleanor brought about his first serious brush with the law. What follows represents Marie's version of the story:

Even though Clyde and Eleanor considered themselves secretly engaged, like all young lovers, they had a fight, and, a few days later, she went to east Texas to stay with relatives. Before long, Clyde was sorry and wanted to make up, so he devised a scheme to give Eleanor's mother a ride over to see the same relatives. Clyde didn't have a car to drive, but he managed to rent one under his own name and address, agreeing to return it on a specific date. Clyde and Eleanor's mother drove into east Texas, where there was a happy reunion between the three of them. Things were going so well that they stayed a little longer than expected. Meanwhile, the return time had passed, and the owner of the rented car reported it to the police as stolen. When Clyde and the two women returned to Dallas, they ran right into trouble. The matter was sorted out in short order and Clyde received no sentence once the authorities determined that no criminal intent was involved, but the Dallas police began to show an interest in Clyde.

So goes the story, as Marie told it in later years, but it didn't happen quite that way. Clyde did rent the car, but he didn't mention that he planned to take it out of town. That would have required a bigger deposit. When it became overdue, the agency contacted the Barrow family and were told the family's name in Broaddus, Texas, where Clyde had gone. Before long, the local sheriff's deputies were knocking on the door, asking for Clyde. Instead of trying to explain, Clyde ran away and hid, so they took the car and left. Eleanor's moth-

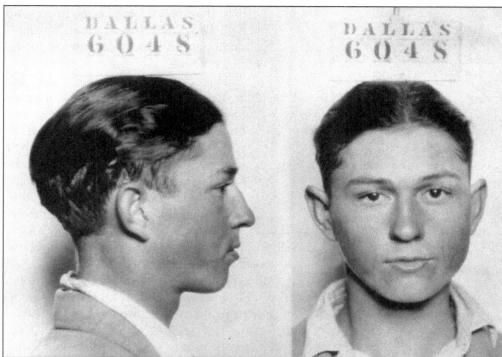

Mug shot of Clyde Chestnut Barrow, 17 years old. Taken following his arrest in Dallas, Texas, December 3, 1926, for auto theft.

—From the collections of the Texas/Dallas History and Archives Division, Dallas Public Library

Clyde Barrow and Eleanor Bee Williams, summer 1926. Eleanor is on Clyde's right, wearing the hat. The girl on Clyde's left is Lela Heslep, Eleanor's first cousin. Notice Clyde standing on the lower rail of the bridge so he won't seem shorter than the girls.

—Courtesy Shirley Chesney, daughter of Lela Heslep

er was not impressed with her prospective son-in-law, and so, if there ever had been an engagement, it was off.

Clyde hitchhiked back to Dallas and was arrested on December 3, 1926. It was at this point that the first and most often reproduced mug shot of Clyde Barrow was taken. It shows the seventeen-year-old with the Dallas number 6048 over his head. Since the rental agency got the car back, they eventually dropped the charges.[3] Clyde and Eleanor continued to see each other secretly for a while, but eventually their romance died out and Eleanor gave Clyde's mirror back to him. This mirror remained in his mother's wooden chest for well over six decades until it was recently sold at auction.

Clyde's second brush with the law occurred just after his arrest because of the rental car, but this affair also involved his older brother. Buck Barrow was still dealing in poultry on the side and told Clyde that he had the chance to get a carload of turkeys cheap—just in time for the holidays. Knowing that Clyde needed the money (or maybe wanting a partner), Buck offered to

MEMBERSHIP CARD

METROPOLITAN RECREATION CLUB

2506 ELM STREET
OF DALLAS, TEXAS

MR. *Clyde Barrow*

IS A MEMBER IN GOOD STANDING AND HIS DUES ARE PAID UP TO

192 9

METROPOLITAN RECREATION CLUB

By *Sam Kickwill*

SECRETARY

Membership card for the Metropolitan Recreation Club of Dallas, Texas, for 1929. Signed by Clyde Barrow.

—Courtesy Sandy Jones–The John Dillinger Historical Society

cut him in on the deal. Both these boys had long since become streetwise, so believing that they didn't suspect that the turkeys were stolen is very difficult, but that's the story they told.

If the two Barrow boys ever believed that the turkey deal was legitimate, the police told them otherwise when they were stopped and charged with possession of stolen goods. Clyde was released, and Buck, who took all the blame, was given what amounted to a slap on the wrist, but the incident confirmed the two brothers' place on the Dallas County Sheriff's list of suspected crimi-

nals. The police now began to pick up both Buck and Clyde regularly for questioning when anything happened in the city of Dallas.

Marie seemed to believe that her brothers were innocent victims of someone else's schemes. More likely, her brothers, twenty-three and seventeen years old, were into a lot more than their eight-year-old sister realized. Also, by telling this story, Marie gives at least some credibility to the book she denounced so often, since the story of the stolen turkeys appears there first—credited to her sister Nell. *Fugitives* also reports that Buck took the blame and served a week in jail.[4]

After the arrest in connection with the stolen turkeys, Clyde was not formally arrested for a number of months, although he was regularly picked up for questioning regarding what others had done. Clyde tried to continue with his regular jobs. After spending two years with the United Glass Company, he worked at the Bama Pie Company with his sister Nell's husband. Clyde's last regular job was with the A & K Top and Paint Shop. As far as Marie knew, Clyde never had any trouble with his jobs, was never suspected of stealing anything from any employer, and was never fired.

CHAPTER 6
Breaking into the Bigtime

Marie Barrow was nine years old in 1927. She didn't really understand all of the activity between the police and her two brothers, and her other siblings continued in their stable, law-abiding ways. Her sister Artie had a business going in Denison, Texas, where her husband worked for the local newspaper. Nell had gotten married to an orchestra leader, and Jack continued to raise his family on Forest Avenue.

Henry and Cumie were very concerned about the turn that events were taking with Clyde and Buck, but there was very little that they could do. They could only pray that things wouldn't get any worse. But in 1928 things did become worse for both of the brothers. According to Clyde's record, he was formally arrested in Fort Worth on February 22. The charge was described as "investigation," and the charges were dismissed, but that fact didn't give his parents any significant peace of mind.

On August 13, 1928, Buck Barrow was arrested in San Antonio on a charge of attempted car theft. Evidently, a policeman saw Buck walking down the street, carrying a small child and trying the door handles and ignition switches of parked cars. He finally selected a Whippet Roadster and was getting in when the officer confronted him. Buck ran but was captured. He was given a court date and released on bond but failed to appear. He was already under a suspended sentence from Waxahachie, so when he was later picked up, he was put in the county jail.[1]

Word of Buck's arrest reached his parents in Dallas, and they decided to go down to San Antonio and provide whatever moral support they could. Henry, Cumie, L. C., and Marie were still living at the campground, so a 270-mile trip was a big deal. They didn't have a car and couldn't afford to take a train, so the family made the trip by horse and wagon.

The wagon was pulled down to San Antonio by the white horse Marie's father used to move from the farm and pick up scrap metal. This same horse was later struck by a car crossing the west Dallas viaduct. The animal was run through by a piece of metal from that automobile, but it still managed to gallop all of the way back to the campground before it dropped dead. It wasn't all bad, though. Henry Barrow collected damages from the driver and bought himself a Model T automobile. Marie said that the Model T was the only car that her father ever drove in his life and was also the first automobile she ever learned to drive.

The Barrow family didn't travel down to San Antonio alone. They were accompanied by a Mrs. Jones and two of her three sons, William Daniel, always known as W. D., and Roy Lee. The older Jones boy was named Clyde. The Barrows knew the Jones family because they were living on the west Dallas campground too. Clyde Barrow and Clyde Jones were about the same age, L. C. and W. D. were friends, and Roy Lee and Marie were the youngest in each family. Four years later, W. D. Jones would beg to ride with Clyde Barrow, the famous outlaw.

Marie remembered the trip down to San Antonio very well. Not only did neither family have the money to afford any transportation by rail or automobile, none of them really had the money to afford the trip when traveling by horse and wagon either. They made their living expenses by picking cotton and doing other work on the farms along the way.

Henry Barrow was one of the best cotton pickers Marie ever saw. Picking cotton was very hard on his hands, though, and his fingernails would always come off after he'd been working for a long time. Ten-year-old Marie picked for one day, but when her sack was found to contain more twigs and leaves than cotton, it was unanimously agreed that she could do other tasks on these farms to earn extra money for the trip. All of the others in the Barrow-Jones traveling group continued to pick cotton. The money they earned bought food, which Mrs. Barrow and Mrs. Jones cooked over a campfire in heavy iron skillets.

The travelers finally made it to San Antonio, where the Barrows became involved in doing whatever they could to assist Buck, and the charge against him was dismissed on January 23, 1929.[2] Everyone was very relieved, and they all returned to Dallas afterward. The relief would not last long, however. There were a lot of things the Barrow family didn't know about Buck and Clyde's activities. In fact, it was just a matter of time until both the brothers would make enough mistakes for the law to catch up with them.

Within the Barrow family, there were several opinions as to the causes of Clyde's descent into a life of crime, and there probably was some truth to each of them. Clyde's mother thought it had begun when Clyde started associating with some "wayward women" around west Dallas. She believed that the girls demanded to be treated in a grander style than Clyde could afford by working regular jobs, so he turned to crime for the money to impress the ladies.[3]

Nell Barrow and her sister Marie emphasized Clyde's choice of companions as a big factor in his downfall. While this is undoubtedly true, the companion who may have been most responsible was Clyde's own brother. Later, when Buck was serving his time in prison, he would tell fellow prisoners about the many burglaries he and Clyde had pulled over the years—including some as far away as Atlanta, Georgia.[4] The stolen turkey flock in 1926 was probably not the first criminal partnership between the two brothers, and it certainly wasn't the last during the years 1926–29.

While Marie Barrow and her sister Nell saw their brother Buck as a victim of circumstances and didn't seem to blame him for Clyde's troubles, they did point to some of Clyde's friends.[5] One fellow whom Marie and Nell both felt strongly about was Frank Clause. They say that Clyde met him at one of his last jobs, but other sources say it was at the city jail.[6] Given Clause's vocation, the latter seems more likely. Frank Clause was a good-looking young man from the city of Dallas proper, not the "wrong side of the tracks" area that was Clyde's turf. He was also, in Marie Barrow's words, a professional "second-story man." He and Clyde were soon roommates, and beginning in early 1929, they joined some other local boys (probably including Buck) in a series of burglaries and house break-ins in Dallas, Lufkin, Hillsboro, and Waco, Texas.[7]

Ironically, Marie said that it was about this time that Buck came under the influence of the one person who could have made a big improvement in his life. After Buck and the family returned from San Antonio in early 1929, he began to date a girl in west Dallas. One night when Buck went over to this girl's house, he met an eighteen-year-old named Blanche, who happened to be visiting at the same time. After this accidental meeting, Buck dropped his current girlfriend. He had found the love of his life.

Iva Blanche Caldwell was born on New Year's Day, 1911, to Matthew Fountain Caldwell, age forty, and Lillian Bell Pond, age sixteen, of Garvin, Oklahoma.[8] Most popular accounts state that Blanche came from a farm in Missouri, but this was not the case.[9] At the time she met Buck, Blanche's father was still living in the McCurtain County,

Oklahoma, area, but her mother may have been in Missouri. Her parents had been separated for several years.

Marie Barrow knew Blanche from the time she and Buck met in 1929 until Blanche's death in 1988. The Barrow family always spoke very highly of Blanche, and Marie often said that if Buck had met Blanche earlier, things might have been different. Perhaps, but while Blanche was probably never directly involved in any of the robberies or an actual shooter in any of the gunfights, she was not the passive, innocent girl some have said. Even less was Blanche the terrified, screaming, hysterical little wife that her portrayal by Estelle Parsons in the 1967 movie would suggest. She and several other Barrow family members were present for some of the filming of the movie, and, afterward, Blanche sued the movie company for the way they portrayed her.[10]

Four years before her death, Blanche Barrow was interviewed by author John Neal Phillips about her time with Buck and Bonnie and Clyde. She made it clear that she was never forced to do anything. When she married Buck in 1931, she knew he had been married twice before, had two children, and was, at the

Blanche Caldwell Barrow
—Courtesy Marie Barrow Scoma and author Phillip W. Steele

time, an escaped convict.[11] She also freely admitted that from March 1930 until December 1931, when Buck was at large, she went with him on several robberies before convincing him to go back and finish his sentence. She may not have been particularly happy about the life she and Buck were leading, but, as she told Phillips, "Clyde never held a gun to my head. I was there because I wanted to

be, plain and simple."[12] Unfortunately, it was just a few months after Buck met Blanche that he and Clyde got into their first really serious trouble.

Jan Fortune's book, *Fugitives*, does offer some significant family information along with the errors the Barrow family correctly point out. According to Fortune, Nell actually came upon Clyde filing the motor numbers off a stolen car and went down-

Buck and Blanche Barrow with unidentified child—probably a young relative. Taken around the time of their marriage in McCurtain County, Oklahoma, July 3, 1931.
—Courtesy the Texas Ranger Hall of Fame and Museum, Waco, Texas

couldn't prove anything. Just after Thanksgiving, a road trip changed everything.

On November 29, 1929, Clyde, Buck, and a fellow named Sidney Moore left Dallas in a stolen vehicle headed northwest toward Wichita Falls. In the small town of Henrietta, Texas, they traded their Buick for a Ford and began to cruise around for a score. They located an unoccupied house, and the break-in went smoothly, but the take was disappointing. Clyde found some jewelry, which he shared with the other two, but very little cash.

On the way home to Dallas, someone had a bright idea. Since they were going through Denton, why not look for another opportunity? They arrived just after 1:00 A.M. and settled on the Motor Mark Garage on Oak Street. They forced the rear door and found a small safe inside. After a few unsuccessful tries to crack the safe where it was, they loaded it into the car and took it with them.

It was just past 2:00 A.M. when their luck ran out. A patrol car saw them and wondered what a strange car was doing out that time of the morning. When the police tried to pull them over, Clyde, who was driving, took off, but the chase didn't last long. Clyde took the corner from West Oak Street onto Piner too fast and broke the car's front axle on the curb. Now the men were afoot. Officer Clint Starr shot Buck Barrow through both legs, and Moore stopped and gave himself up, but Clyde kept right on running. He hid under a house all that day and then hitchhiked back home. The owner of the Motor Mark later said that the safe contained only about $30.[14] Buck and Sidney

town with him when the police picked him up for questioning. Nell explained that the police told her Clyde and Frank Clause were cracking safes but she didn't want to believe it.[13]

Clyde Barrow had been involved in burglary, safecracking, and car theft for at least three years by Thanksgiving 1929. The police had picked up Clyde and Buck on suspicion many times but

Moore were even caught trying to get rid of the jewelry from the Henrietta job.

On December 6, 1929, they were indicted, and the trial date was set for Tuesday the 17th. Buck and Sidney pled not guilty, and by noon they had rested their case—such as it was. The jury took just a few minutes to return a guilty verdict. Six days later, both were given four years, and on January 14, 1930, they were moved to the state prison at Huntsville.[15] Buck assumed full responsibility for the affair. He never implicated his younger brother in connection with what happened in Denton.

Clyde lay low in west Dallas for several weeks after he made his way home. To the family, he seemed thoroughly unnerved by what had happened. As far as they knew, the action in Denton represented the first time Clyde had ever been the subject of a police chase, an automobile crash, and officers' gunfire. They hoped the shock of Buck's arrest and sentence and his own brush with capture might cause Clyde to resolve to walk the straight and narrow way, and he did—for a few weeks.

Clyde began to return to his friends from earlier years. On the evening of January 5, 1930, he and old friend Clarence Clay went over to Clarence's sister's house for a visit. There were several other young people there that evening, including some of Clarence's in-laws. It was strictly a social gathering, just a group of friends and relatives getting together for an evening of fun and talk.[16] One of the guests happened to be the younger sister of Hubert "Buster" Parker, Clarence Clay's brother-in-law. Her name was Bonnie Thornton, and she was a nineteen-year-old blue-eyed blonde currently "estranged" from her husband of three years, who was in prison for robbery.[17] Before the night was out, Clyde Barrow was in love.

In spite of several other versions of the meeting of Bonnie and Clyde—including the one made famous in the 1967 film when Bonnie looks out her window and sees Clyde trying to steal her mother's car—Marie Barrow's version, given above, has the ring of truth because it is so utterly commonplace and elegant in its simplicity. A bored, lonely, young, out-of-work waitress, abandoned by her imprisoned husband, goes over to her brother's house and meets a charming young fellow. Nobody thought it was anything special. Nobody guessed where it would lead.

CHAPTER 7
Bonnie

Formal portrait of Bonnie Parker.
—From the collections of the Texas/Dallas History and Archives Division, Dallas Public Library

Bonnie Parker was born October 1, 1910, the second of three children, to Charles Parker and Emma Krause in Rowena, Texas, about 250 miles southwest of Dallas. Charles Parker had a good trade (he was a brick mason), and the family lived a good, quiet life centered around the First Baptist Church.[1] When Charles Parker died suddenly in 1914, Emma Parker was left with three small children to raise alone.[2] Fortunately, Emma's parents took them all in.

Frank and Mary Krause lived at 2908 Eagle Ford Road in west Dallas.[3] When Emma found a job, Grandma Mary looked after the kids while Emma was at work. In the book that Marie and the Barrow family denounce, Jan Fortune quotes Bonnie's mother and her cousin Bess as they tell stories about Bonnie's childhood, and it's hard to believe that it's all invention. The Bonnie they knew was a bundle of energy—and mischief—from the time she could stand. She was cute and attracted the boys, even in grade school. She could be utterly charming when it suited her, and, according to Bess, she was devoted to her mother.[4] Unfortunately, this devotion, which was real and lasted to the end of Bonnie's life, didn't keep Bonnie from playing on her mother's sympathy and manipulating her to get her own way. Later on, Bonnie would lie to her mother about many things as her relationship with Clyde deepened.

Bonnie arrived in west Dallas about eight years

before Clyde. She had lived there ever since she could remember, unlike the refugees from the farm country who began arriving in the early 1920s—people like the Barrows. There were oil refineries and foundries along Eagle Ford Road near Bonnie's grandfather's house, but the area took its name from the large Trinity-Portland Cement Company nearby. It was called Cement City.

Bonnie went to school in Cement City and, according to her cousin Bess, showed about equal parts talent and combativeness. Bess remembers Bonnie being a star pupil and winning a spelling contest and then, on the same page, tells how the two of them beat the living daylights out of two other girls who were stealing Bonnie's pencils.[5] Even if Fortune was guilty of embellishing her notes for the sake of a good story, Bonnie still emerges as a feisty, headstrong girl who was determined not to be pushed around and to have her way even if it meant a fight.

Bonnie had always had boyfriends while she was growing up, but when she met Roy Thornton, she fell in love. She was not quite sixteen when they married on September 25, 1926. Unfortunately, Bonnie and Roy were not a good match. Bonnie couldn't bear to be separated from her mother for long (a trait she and Clyde would share), and Roy, as it turned out, was a thief. Roy was already acquainted with many people Bonnie would come to know well—Raymond Hamilton and his brother Floyd, the Mace brothers (Fred Mace would marry Bonnie's younger sister, Billie Jean), and, of course, the Barrows.[6]

Bonnie and Roy set up housekeeping a couple of blocks from Emma, but for Bonnie, even that was too far. Bonnie was constantly crying to go back home to see her mother. After a while, it became a running joke. Roy finally gave up and they moved back in with Emma, but he found his own way to deal with the situation.[7] Beginning in August 1927, he would just disappear for several weeks at a time. When he left for the third time, around the first of December, Bonnie decided she was through with

Bonnie Parker (left), Roy Glenn Thornton, and a friend, Annie McLean. Taken around the time Bonnie and Roy were married—September 1926. Most versions of this picture show only Bonnie and Roy, but the original, shown here, includes the third person.

—Courtesy Sandy Jones–The John Dillinger Historical Society

him. She didn't see him again for over a year. When Roy finally showed up in January 1929, Bonnie told him it was over. Not long after that, he was arrested during a robbery at Red Oak, Texas, and sent to Huntsville for five years.[8]

With Roy gone, Bonnie had to go to work. Shortly after he left in December 1927, she got a job at Hargraves Cafe on Swiss Avenue and found that she had a talent for working with the public. Cute and full of life, she soon became a favorite with the customers. In early 1929, she moved downtown to Marco's on Main Street, near the courthouse. She was doing well in her new situation, but in October, the stock market crashed, and in November Marco's closed and Bonnie was out of a job.[9] Just after New Year's, Bonnie went over to her older brother's house and met the man who would change her life.

The Parkers

Emma Krause Parker and her three children. Probably taken in Rowena, Texas, near the time her husband died—1914.
          —Courtesy the Bob Fischer/Renay Stanard collection

Bonnie Parker, left, and her sister Billie Jean Parker Mace. Probably taken about 1930.
          —Courtesy Marie Barrow Scoma and author Phillip W. Steele

The Parker children about 1918. Left to right: "Buster," Bonnie, with a sucker in her mouth, and Billie Jean.
     —Courtesy the Bob Fischer/Renay Stanard collection

Emma Parker and her children somewhat later. Probably taken at Emma's parents' house on Eagle Ford Road in west Dallas: Billie Jean, standing by her mother, Bonnie, facing the camera, and Hubert "Buster" Parker.
          —Courtesy the Bob Fischer/Renay Stanard collection

CHAPTER 8
Busted

After Bonnie and Clyde met on that early-January evening, they quickly became an item. Bonnie's mother met her daughter's new boyfriend a couple of weeks later. She said he looked more like a student than the bandit he turned out to be. She was introduced to him in the kitchen, where he was wearing an apron and making hot chocolate—not a very threatening figure.[1]

Clyde continued to see Bonnie on into February while trying to keep out of sight of the cops. He hadn't been charged along with Buck and Sidney Moore, but he knew he was still "hot." About the second week in February, Clyde was visiting Bonnie at her mother's house and stayed until late in the evening. Some sources say he told Bonnie he was leaving town the next day, and Bonnie may have already known that the police were looking for him.[2] Bonnie's mother suggested that, since it was so late, Clyde should just stay over.

The Parker house, in February 1930, was a little crowded.[3] Emma Parker was living there with her two daughters, plus Billie Jean's husband, Fred Mace, and their young baby. That's why Clyde got the living room couch for the night. In the morning, Mrs. Parker fixed breakfast, saw Fred off to work, and let Clyde sleep in a little. The Barrow family always believed that the police found out through the grapevine that Clyde had started seeing Bonnie on a regular basis and began watching the Parker house for a chance to catch him. He was

still on the couch, wearing a pair of Bonnie's brother's pajamas, when they came to arrest him.[4]

Once in custody, Clyde found he was wanted in several places. From the Dallas jail, he was sent to Denton for the Motor Mark Garage job. He was kept there until the end of the month, but there was not enough evidence to convict him. Next in line was Waco, and that was a different situation. There, he was charged with several things relating to his activities with Frank Clause the year before. Whatever the evidence was, it convinced Clyde to plead guilty to seven counts of burglary and auto theft. He was given two years on each count but would be allowed to serve them concurrently. This may have been part of a deal for a guilty plea. He could be free and clear in twenty-four months. Clyde had been moved from the Dallas area to Waco on March 2, 1930, and the next day, his mother traveled there to be with him during the proceedings. Along with her went Bonnie Parker.[5]

According to Marie Barrow, the arrests of both Buck and Clyde devastated their mother. Not only were two of her sons in serious trouble, but now they had both been sentenced to substantial terms in the state prison system—known as one of the most brutal in the nation. The boys had been routinely picked up by the police, but they had never before been found guilty or sentenced to any jail terms.

Just before he was transferred to Huntsville from the Denton jail, Buck wrote a letter home. In this original letter, Buck's early lack of interest in schoolwork was apparent, as was the influence of movies and dime novels. The letter was dated January 12, 1930.

> Mr. and Mrs. H. B. Barrow
>
> My dear mother and father and all home folks,
>
> It is with pleasure that I send this letter to you in answer to your sweet letter which I received today. However, it grieves me to be compelled to send it to you from prison. Mother, the days drag on here now and it seems like six years since your tear-stained face looked into the jail here at me, your son. I can fully realize that if I had've heeded your and Father's kind, loving advice, I would not have been here on this dreary, lonesome day. Oh, mother, if God gives me one more chance I shall try to do the best that is in me to lead a worthwhile life in the future and to be a man that the people will respect and that my relatives will honor. I know the heartaches and sorrow that my crookedness has given to you and Father.
>
> Mother, tell B——— that I am going to whip her year [*sic*] down if she doesn't write me, and also tell Elvin to send me gloves when I get down on the farm, but don't send auto gloves for there are no cars to drive down there and send me two big red handkerchiefs also. This is all for this time. I send you all of my love.
>
> Your son, Buck Barrow.[6]

As a postscript, Buck included "All for my dear mother" with a whole line of "X's" afterward.

Buck's first letter from the Huntsville area, with its news of him being in the prison hospital, didn't reassure his mother. This letter was dated January 16, 1930.

> Dear Mother and all:
>
> Will write you a few lines to let you know that I have made the trip. Mother, I am in the hospital now and my legs are hurting pretty bad. It sure looks hard but I am going to take it.
>
> Mother, try to get me a furlough and don't

fail to write often and don't forget to tell Blanche to write me and to tell me all of the news that happens in the outside world. Send me some stamps and envelopes that I can write every day and I wish you would do the same. Mother, tell sister to send my shoes and send me some more pajamas because they burned mine up, but they will let me have some more now if you send them to me and tell her to help me all she can to get out on a parole or a furlough while you are so sick.

> I hope that the outside world don't forget me because I am in the walls.
>
> Goodbye Mother and don't worry—
> [signed] Marvin Barrow[7]

Buck's second letter also had a postscript: "Don't send me any tobacco but send me some money. Because they won't let any tobacco come in."

While Clyde was sitting in the Denton jail, Buck wrote his family another letter from prison. It was dated February 24, 1930, and was postmarked from Midway, Texas. In this letter Buck seemed to be adjusting to prison life. The letter reads as follows:

> My dear mother—
>
> I am sorry I have not written you sooner. I am well and hope you are the same. The guards and the Captain down here treat me awfully good. So I see no reason why I should not get along. You must write me often and with all of the good news. Tell Marie that I will send her something pretty when I get some money. My Captain's name is W. R. Crume and anything you want to write him for me will be all right. You ask me if I need anything—I am doing fine and don't need a thing, only lots of sweet letters from you, Mother Dear.
>
> Will close with all of my love to you—
> Your son Buck—
> Ferguson Farm, Midway, Texas[8]

Clyde hadn't gotten around to bringing his new girlfriend home before he was arrested, but once he was in jail, Bonnie became a regular visitor at the Barrows'. That was when Marie first met her. She said that Bonnie could be characterized as cute, even pretty when she fixed herself up.[9]

One question that naturally came up when Bonnie and Clyde got together was Bonnie's status as a married woman. Evidently, Bonnie discussed this with her mother (and with the Barrows as well on a few occasions, because Marie knew her feelings on the matter). Emma, Bonnie's mother, had encouraged her to divorce Roy Thornton—especially after he was sent to prison. By then, Roy had been gone for a long time, and Bonnie had decided in her own mind that she and Roy were through. That seemed to be enough for her. For some reason, she felt that, since she hadn't divorced him after he abandoned her, to divorce him now that he was locked up would be like kicking him when he was down. Besides, she told her mother, she wasn't interested in marrying anyone else.

Bonnie was just seventeen when Roy left for good, and she had been dating other men since then, even before Roy was "sent up." None of the dates were serious—until Clyde, and now that she had fallen head over heels for him, he was in jail too.[10] She couldn't just stay in Dallas and wait, so, when she found out that Cumie was going to Waco for Clyde's trial, she asked to go along.

According to Emma Parker, Bonnie was able to go to Waco because she had a cousin named Mary she could stay with free of charge. Cumie also stayed at Mary's house for a couple of days, but when Clyde pleaded guilty and was sentenced, she went back to Dallas.[11] Bonnie was determined to stay until Clyde was transferred to Huntsville. Until now, Bonnie Parker had been around—and fallen in love with—some shady characters, but she had not committed any crime herself. That was about to change.

CHAPTER 9

"You're the Sweetest Baby in the World to Me"

The Barrow family felt, when they read Buck's letter near the end of February, that he might be settling into the prison routine and would get out soon. Unfortunately, he did in fact get out. About two weeks after his February 24 letter, he stuck his head in the door of the Barrow home on Eagle Ford Road. He and another prisoner had escaped. Like many other events in the lives of the Barrow brothers that were played up and dramatized by the media, the real story of Buck's breakout was actually very simple. It certainly wasn't the classic 1930s escape from the big house with baying bloodhounds, machine-gun-wielding guards, and howling sirens.

During the first week of March, Buck was working as a trusty in the prison kitchen, his wounded legs keeping him from farm duties. He and another prisoner saw an opportunity to leave and simply walked out of the kitchen. Once outside, they got into one of the guard's cars and drove away, losing themselves in the maze of country roads and wooded areas around Huntsville.[1] All Buck's determination to go straight if given "one more chance" seemed to have been forgotten. Buck and the other inmate made their way to west Dallas from the prison farm in about five hours' time.

The first place Buck went, of course, was to his parents' home. Marie Barrow remembered that day very well. She said they heard someone walk up on the porch and open the door to the house. Buck stuck his head into the doorway, gave them a good-natured laugh, and then walked in, still in his prison clothes. Marie said they almost fainted. Except for Clyde, Buck was the last person they expected to see. In his letter of February 24, he had sounded so resigned to his situation.

Buck seemed to take the whole thing in stride as he told his flabbergasted parents about how he leisurely drove away from the Ferguson farm. Henry Barrow just smiled, shook his head, and said, "That's Buck." Cumie and Marie, while delighted to see him, were frightened by the circumstances under which this unexpected reunion took place.

Buck might have been happy to be home, but he was under no illusions about his situation either. He was there just long enough to reassure the family and to get out of his prison uniform. The other boy was still with him, and they were still using the guard's car. Buck changed out of his prison clothes and shoes and told his mother to burn them, but Marie later said she didn't. Then he and the other boy disappeared into the night, separating soon after leaving the Barrow house. Buck's fellow escapee was shortly captured and sent back to prison. Meanwhile, Buck picked up Blanche, and the two of them vanished.[2] The authorities would not see him again for twenty-one months. Buck's escape had been a spur-of-the-moment kind of thing. Clyde's would take a little more planning but would be much less successful.

On March 8, the same day Buck escaped, four new prisoners were put in the cell block at Waco. Three were first-time offenders. The fourth was William Turner. He had already been in prison, escaped, and been recaptured, and he was now up on a federal rap for robbing a post office. Turner was a local boy, and his parents still lived in Waco. He had an escape plan, but he needed outside help and began to ask around to see if any of the other inmates were interested in getting out. Clyde Barrow certainly was.

When Bonnie visited Clyde later that day, she was in for a shock. Clyde introduced his new friend and asked Bonnie if she would help them escape. The plan involved a gun at Turner's parents' house. Bonnie would have to get in the house while the Turners were away, take the gun, and smuggle it in to Clyde. When Bonnie agreed, Clyde slipped her a map that Turner had drawn showing the house and the location of the gun. At the bottom, Clyde had written, "You're the sweetest baby in the world to me."[3] With her cousin Mary as a rather unwilling accomplice, Bonnie drove to the address on the map—625 Turner Avenue—found the key where she had been told it would be, went in the house, and found the gun. She then concealed it under her clothes, went back to the jail, and passed it to Clyde. Until then, she had been a law-abiding girl in love with a criminal, but now she had stepped over the line.

The next day, another new prisoner arrived. Emory Abernathy was a burglar and bank robber. Both he and Turner were looking at serious time and knew it, so Abernathy was added to the group. On the evening of March 11, they made their move. Turner complained of an upset stomach and asked for a bottle of milk. When the milk was delivered, Turner jammed the door open with his body and Abernathy put the gun to the guard's head. Before the three of them left, they locked the guard in the cell with the remaining prisoners, who had decided against joining the break.

Clyde and his cronies were out of the cell; now they had to get out of the building. One floor down sat the turnkey, a man named Jones. The escaped trio got the drop on him and, after a little persuasion, had the keys to the outside. Jones managed to wing a few pistol shots at them as they ran down an alley. The shots missed, but they woke up the chief jailer, Glenn Wright, who had quarters in the building, and he and Jones began phoning the alarm to other cities. Of course, as soon as Clyde and his friends got away from the jail, they began to look for a car, and Mrs. J. M. Byrd was the unlucky victim. Her green Ford coupe was parked a few blocks away. It only took a few seconds to hot-wire it, and the three escapees were gone.

After passing the gun to Clyde, Bonnie and her cousin went back to Mary's house. They had been excited and anxious while doing their part, but now the real fear set in. The waiting was the hardest part: waiting to find out if the escape came off at all; if Clyde might get shot; if their part had been discovered by the police. Finally, the morning after the escape, it was all in the paper. Everything had gone as planned, nobody was hurt, and there wasn't a word about them. Only one thing went wrong: Clyde hadn't come for Bonnie like she had thought he would.

Bonnie planned to go home to Dallas late that evening, but she changed her mind when two men arrived at Mary's house and knocked on the door. The two girls weren't about to open the door to a couple of strangers, so they waited them out. The men sat in their car at the curb for a while and finally drove away. Afraid the law might be watching them now, Bonnie forgot about the bus or train and hitchhiked back to Dallas. Actually, the two men had been sent by Clyde to get Bonnie, but she didn't find that out until later.

Clyde and his two buddies put as many fast miles behind them as they could, leaving a trail of stolen cars through Texas, Missouri, and Illinois. Finally, from Nokomis, Illinois, Clyde sent Bonnie a telegram telling her he was all right and asking her to contact his mother and wait for him.[4]

CHAPTER 10
The Dumbbell Bandits

A week after they had broken out of the Waco jail, Barrow, Turner, and Abernathy were in Middletown, Ohio, just north of Cincinnati, and the trio needed money to finance a return trip to Texas. On the afternoon of March 17, 1930, they stopped at the Baltimore & Ohio depot, and Clyde went in and asked for a train schedule. He also cased the joint. The ticket agent, Bernard J. Krebs, must have recognized a suspicious character when he saw one, because he took down their license number (Indiana 163-439)—just in case. The three escapees spent the rest of the afternoon parked beside a canal.

Late that evening, they began making the rounds. They were later suspected of breaking into three service stations, finding a total of about $10. They denied this but confessed to breaking into the Gough-Lamb Cleaners on Charles Street. They also admitted that they finished up the night with the robbery of the Baltimore & Ohio Railroad office, where they got $57.97. Their getaway was successful until they turned onto the dirt roads of the Ohio countryside. Being unfamiliar with the area, the three fugitives got lost in the dark in short order. Finally, they stopped and slept for a while near Elk Creek on property owned by a family named Gentry. After sunrise, they accidentally drove back into Middletown, directly by the B&O depot they had just robbed. Even though they had license plates from four other states on hand, they were still using the ones Mr. Krebs had seen. What

had started out as a bad morning was about to get a lot worse.

Officers Harry Richardson and George Woody had been sent to investigate the break-in at the depot and were coming out of the railroad office with the license number in hand just as the boys drove by. No wonder the Waco newspaper would refer to them as "The Dumbbell Bandits." Within seconds, the chase was on through the streets of Middletown. When the police car closed in and ordered them to stop, the car turned onto Auburn Street and speeded up.[1] Officer Woody fired on the car. When they didn't stop, Woody fired again, and this time the car pulled over to the curb and the three men ran. Woody fired a third time at Clyde, who got away, as did Abernathy, but Officer Richardson chased Turner into an alley and captured him.

Abernathy was caught about an hour later on the east side of town, but Clyde hid under a house for almost five hours. About 1:00 P.M., he made a run for it, but he was spotted by another officer, Tom Carmody. Clyde led them on a merry chase on foot and then stole a car belonging to Orville Baird. Clyde might have had a chance except he turned up a dead-end street. With the police running up behind him, he drove up in someone's yard, jumped out, and tried to run again, but there was nowhere to go. Just before he was captured, he threw the gun Bonnie had given him into the Middletown Hydraulic Canal.

Clyde Barrow mug shot taken after his capture, March 18, 1930, in Middletown, Ohio, following his escape from the Waco, Texas, jail. He was six days short of his twenty-first birthday. When captured, Barrow claimed to be Robert Thomas of Indianapolis.

—Courtesy the Middletown, Ohio, Police Department

contact with the folks in Waco, so Clyde finally admitted he was the third man. The Middletown policemen received commendations for their good work, and by March 21, all three escapees were back in Waco.[2] On his arrival, Clyde found that he and Frank Clause had been implicated in the murder of Howard Gouge, a Houston man. Some "secret witness" had named Clyde and Frank, but this witness was later discredited and Clyde Barrow's first murder charge was dropped.[3]

Marie Barrow remembered that the Waco newspapers had a field day with this jailbreak, the local press referring to Clyde "Schoolboy" Barrow in some articles. The three boys were called "Baby Bandits" and "Baby Thugs," in addition to the "Dumbbell Bandits" because of the fiasco in Middletown, Ohio.[4]

Marie remembered reporters from Waco coming up to west Dallas to interview her parents, and that her mother had quite a bit to say in defense of her son. Cumie told the newsmen that Clyde was a good boy before he got involved with this Waco crowd through his acquaintance with Frank Clause. She said that Clyde's involvement in the escape was unnecessary, due to the fact that he hadn't gotten a severe sentence from his participation in the Clause-related burglaries. Even so, the family felt that, since Clyde's escape from the Waco jail had involved a gun, several counts of car theft, interstate flight, armed robbery, and forcible recapture, he had likely forfeited any consideration of leniency that he may have gotten from the court, and they were right.

At the police station, Turner and Abernathy confessed that they were escaped convicts, but they tried to run the story that Clyde was just a hitchhiker they had picked up. Clyde went along for a while, identifying himself as Robert Thomas of Indianapolis. Unfortunately, the Middletown police were already in

The judge in Waco, who had allowed Clyde to serve his seven two-year sentences concurrently, saw no humor in his jailbreak and ruled that he could now serve the whole fourteen years. Clyde's mother later took the case to the Texas Supreme Court, and eventually got the sentence reduced to the original two years.[5]

Marie also remembered that, after returning from Waco, Bonnie continued to frequently visit her family. In fact, when Clyde's mother was interviewed by some of the Waco newspaper reporters, Bonnie was there and her presence was noted in one of the printed accounts. Of course, they did not know that she was the one who had smuggled the gun into the Waco jail.

Clyde and Bonnie regularly wrote each other for several weeks after Clyde was returned to Waco, but then her initially frequent letters began to taper off somewhat as she began to get involved with other boyfriends in west Dallas. Her visits to the Barrow house also became more and more irregular as her interest in Clyde seemed to fade. Then her letters to Clyde and her visits to the Barrow house stopped altogether. Marie later found out that Bonnie's mother was pressuring her to end her relationship with Clyde due to his troubles with the law.[6]

Clyde was finally on his way to the Texas State Prison at Huntsville, but there would be one more delay. Just as Clyde was arriving at Waco the first time, the prison board stopped all new arrivals. Severe crowding was given as the reason, but there were more serious problems. Governor Dan Moody had toured the prison in January and pronounced the conditions "not fit for a dog."[7] A new general manager, Lee Simmons, was hired, and on April 12 he began accepting new inmates. All this time, Clyde sat in the Waco jail. His time came on April 21 when the prison system's famous transfer agent, Bud Russell, made a stop in Waco.[8]

When Clyde entered the state prison system, he was processed like anyone else. He was given number 63527 and required to fill out the standard questionnaire. It will come as no surprise that he wasn't entirely honest. He gave his birthdate as March 24, 1912, making him only eighteen instead of the actual twenty-one. He listed his middle name as "Champion" instead of the actual "Chestnut," an error that would follow him through the works of several authors, and he listed Bonnie as his wife, which would allow her to write him. On physical examination, he was found to be 5'5½" tall and 127 pounds. He had three tattoos: a heart and dagger with the initials "EBW" for his old girlfriend Eleanor B. Williams; a shield with "USN"; and a picture of a girl's head. He also said he didn't smoke, drink, or gamble.[9]

Clyde at first stayed at the main prison at Huntsville, known as "The Walls." One reason was that there were still more bench warrants out on him for other things. Every so often, he would be taken out and sent to some court or other, but none of the charges ever stuck. The last trip out was back to Waco. On the return trip, in Bud Russell's "one-way wagon," Clyde struck up a conversation with another prisoner. He had been told he was going to be sent to a place called Eastham Farm. He wondered if the other prisoner knew anything about it. It turned out that the other young fellow knew quite a bit about Eastham Farm, but nothing Clyde heard was good news.

CHAPTER 11
Hard Time: Eastham Farm

It was September 18, 1930, when Clyde began his ride back to Huntsville from the court in Waco, and the other prisoner with him was Ralph Fults. At nineteen, Ralph was almost two years younger than Clyde, but he had much more prison experience. As a boy, Ralph had spent several years in the State Juvenile Training School at Gatesville, Texas. As an adult, he had just spent ten months at Eastham Farm, Camp 1 (June 1929–April 1930), escaped from solitary with three other men, and stayed at large until September, when he was captured in St. Louis. Now Ralph and Clyde were headed back to Eastham, where they had special treatment for escapees, and where Clyde Barrow's criminal education was about to begin in earnest.[1]

Barrow and Fults' first stop was the main unit at Huntsville. Lee Simmons was the general manager of the whole operation, and W. W. Waid was the warden of "The Walls" unit. The prisoners stayed there only a few days and were then sent on to Eastham Camp 2, a few miles north of Huntsville near the town of Weldon. This camp was much the same as the older Camp 1, from which Fults had escaped, except there was no solitary at Camp 2. Instead, inmates were put outside in small sheet-iron boxes and the Texas sun did the rest. The buildings in which the prisoners were kept on the prison farms were not cellblocks like you would see on Alcatraz or at Leavenworth. These were dormitorylike arrangements with a big room full of bunk beds where the prisoners slept. There were no barred, individual cells, and meals were cooked and served outside.

As they arrived, Clyde got his first good look at a favorite punishment method of the guards. It was called "riding the barrel," and it was brilliantly, brutally simple. A man's hands were handcuffed behind him and he was made to stand on an upended pickle barrel. He was told to stand there until further notice. After several hours, his legs became tired and numb, and eventually he fell off. He was then beaten for "disobeying" and put back on the barrel. After a few cycles, his attitude was considered "adjusted." Clyde would have his turn on the barrel several times.

When Barrow and Fults first lined up for work, Clyde saw a demonstration of another method used to control the inmates. The farm manager walked up to the new group, picked out a prisoner at random, and clubbed him to the ground. Fults told Clyde this was known as a "tune-up" and was used to psychologically intimidate the others. This was Clyde's introduction to Eastham.[2]

One of the mandates Lee Simmons received when he took the job of general manager was to put the prison on a paying basis. For this to happen, agricultural production had to increase, so the workload on inmates had increased. Although the guards figured Clyde for a "city boy," he had grown up on farms and knew how to work cotton, but even experienced men were ground down by the back-breaking pace.

Not long after they arrived at Camp 2, Clyde also witnessed what happened to an escapee who was brought back. He and Fults were working around a woodpile when they were surrounded by guards with shotguns. Ralph, of course, knew what was coming. A trusty had already told him that the guards had drawn straws for the honor of giving him his "welcome home" beating. Some of the guards held their guns on Clyde while the others kicked and pistol-whipped Fults to the ground.[3] Fults told Clyde that this was what you got the first time. The second time you escaped and got caught, they killed you.[4] It was about this time that Clyde began talking about coming back, after they got out, raiding the farm, and freeing as many prisoners as they could. It was an idea that Clyde never abandoned.[5]

In addition to the regular guards, there were always additional mounted officers present when the men were working in the fields. They were meant to stay at a distance and were called "high riders." They were picked for their marksmanship, since, if a prisoner ran, it was their job to stop him—permanently. The high riders also had a sort of pastime. If an inmate began to lag behind or seem to be loafing, they would ride him down and trample him with their horse. Fults said that one of them tried this on Clyde, but, being raised with horses on the farm, he caught the reins and stopped the horse—and was almost shot for saving himself.[6] Fults also said that he and Clyde once managed to maneuver a tree they were cutting down so that it fell on another inmate known to be an informer. They were sure they had killed him, but he proved tougher than they thought and survived with only a concussion.[7]

A few days after the tree-felling incident, Clyde was suddenly transferred to Eastham Camp 1. Fults was sure it was because the authorities were concerned that he and Barrow were becoming too friendly. Even after the transfer, however, Ralph would occasionally hear how Clyde was doing, and he got to talk to him a few times when their work parties met. He says that it was at one of these meetings he first learned that Clyde had killed a man. Fults knew Clyde as well as anybody, and he believed the story was true.

Clyde Barrow went into prison an experienced thief, but there was nothing to indicate that he had a talent for violence. Once inside, however, Clyde found out that violence was a fact of life at Eastham. When it came from the guards, there wasn't much you could do about it, but when it came from another inmate, you had to make a choice—you could submit, or you could reply in kind—and that choice would probably determine your reputation in the prison population. It might also determine whether you survived. Clyde made his choice, and it taught him something important about himself—he could kill without hesitation in order to protect himself.

Soon after Clyde got to Eastham Camp 1, he became the victim of a building tender called "Big Ed."[8] Ed, at over six feet tall and 200 pounds, had a weakness for young, small "schoolboy" types. Another inmate said Ed bought the "rights" to Barrow from the guards for three packs of cigarettes—prison's universal currency. After that, Ed knew that he could do with Clyde as he pleased. Beatings and sodomy were his recreations of choice. Clyde couldn't see any way out until another building tender, named Aubrey, approached him. Aubrey was a lifer who had nothing to lose. He hated Ed for his own reasons, and he had a plan.

When Clyde Barrow entered the prison system, he really did have more in common with the young students Emma Parker thought he resembled than the violent, brutal men he would meet. If he was to live, however, that had to change. In Ralph Fults' words, Eastham changed Clyde "from a schoolboy to a rattlesnake,"[9] and dealing with Big Ed was a large part of that change.

Aubrey's plan was simple. One evening a few days later, Clyde waited until the other inmates had finished and then went alone into the toilet area at the rear of the barracks. Big Ed, unable to resist such an opportunity, followed, just as Clyde and Aubrey knew he would. It all happened quickly. Clyde stood at a urinal, and as Ed came up behind him, Barrow simply turned around and smashed him in the head with a length of pipe he had stolen to use as a weapon. Aubrey then came over, cut himself so it would look like a fight between the two building tenders, and stuck a knife in Ed's chest. Clyde went back to his bunk and was never suspected. The guards either believed Aubrey's story or, as the rest of the inmates believed, didn't really care one way or the other. What the prisoners did to each other wasn't their concern. Clyde never told the whole story to his family. He only told them he saw a lifer kill another prisoner.[10]

In prison, there is always the challenge to keep yourself from retreating into your own world and allowing your situation to prey on your mind. Prisoners of war tell stories about how they dealt with the hours, days and years of captivity and brutality by inventing games in their head, or planning houses or solving math problems—anything to keep their minds active. Clyde kept his mind on his family and Bonnie back home. He planned his revenge on the system, the raid on the farm that he and Fults had talked about, and the rest of the time he had to watch his back from the likes of Big Ed and the guards. This was plenty to keep his mind sharp. The larger challenge was physical. The inmates would get up in the morning and run the two miles or so to the fields, work the crops or clear brush in the woods for the next ten to twelve hours, and then run the same two miles back to the barracks.[11] Add to this the occasional beating by a guard or sessions on the pickle barrel, and just surviving the experience became a real victory.

Bonnie had written Clyde for the first few months he was inside, but then the letters slowed down and finally ended. For some reason, she began again just before Christmas, 1930. Clyde was glad to hear from her and answered her letter right away. He tried to encourage her that he wouldn't be in jail forever. He knew all about his mother's efforts to get the fourteen years reduced back to the original two, and he hoped she would wait for him.[12]

Clyde survived the next year, 1931, but there was no word on his sentence. Although communication between Clyde and Bonnie had again decreased substantially as 1930 turned into 1931,

Clyde always wrote to his mother, trying to put the best possible light on his miserable circumstances. One of his letters, dated December 3, 1931, and mailed from Camp No. 1, Route 16, Weldon, Texas, illustrates his outlook:

Dear Mother—

Will drop you a few lines to let you know I haven't forgotten you.

Say, what is wrong? I haven't had a letter from you in over a week. I have been worried about you all. This leaves me OK, except a little cold. Well, how is everything in big Dallas by now? It is raining down here and has been for three days. How is little Marie and L. C. and have you got your station fixed up yet? I sure wish I was there to help you. After you get everything going okay, Papa should build him a little place and handle used auto parts. You can buy them for a song. Well how is Elvin and ———? (Jack Barrow's wife's name).[13] I sure would like to see you all. Have you heard anything from Blanche or not?

Be sure and make her bring you down here and another thing, it isn't long until Xmas, so remind them all of that old cake and chicken. Well, mother, I don't know any news. So will close for this time, hoping to hear from you real soon. Your loving son,

[signed] Clyde Barrow[14]

Clyde's mention of Blanche in his letter was really a veiled reference asking how Buck was doing. He could hardly mention his fugitive older brother by name, since these letters were screened by the prison authorities. Ironically, while Clyde's escape was short and violent, Buck simply drove away and was free for almost twenty-two months. During this period of time, Buck and Blanche had gotten married in Oklahoma and were trying to make a life for themselves.

The Barrow family felt that Blanche's influence on Buck was extremely good. To them, Buck seemed to be trying to live up to the good intentions stated in his letters from prison: "to lead a worthwhile life in the future and to be a man that the people will respect and that my relatives will honor." Despite this, the fact that he was still an escaped convict hung over everyone's head like a dark cloud. Mr. Caldwell, Blanche's father, tried to convince Buck to go back to prison to finish paying his debt to society, and Blanche took up the same theme. Whenever Buck and Blanche went back through Dallas to visit, his mother added her voice and tried to talk Buck into peacefully going back to the Ferguson farm, finishing his sentence, and then living an upstanding life afterward.

That was certainly what the Barrow family thought in late 1931. The problem was, as in so many incidents involving Buck and Clyde, there were things that the family didn't know. Buck had indeed settled down with Blanche in Oklahoma, but he had not given up his criminal career. He had just gotten more careful. Over fifty years later, Blanche told author John Neal Phillips that Buck committed a number of robberies in 1930 and 1931. She knew all about it and even went with him for many of them. A teenager from west Dallas asked to go along on some of the jobs with Buck and Blanche, but they thought he was too young. They also didn't trust him. His name was Raymond Hamilton.[15]

Hamilton was born in Oklahoma on May 21, 1913, and like the Barrow boys had moved to west Dallas in the early 1920s. His mother and father divorced, and his mother remarried to a man named Steve Davis. Davis knew the Barrow boys and was involved with them in poultry rustling, among other things, in the 1920s. Raymond was the same age as Clyde's younger brother L. C. and, in spite of Marie Barrow's statements to the contrary, probably knew the Barrow boys growing up in west Dallas.[16] Considering Buck and Blanche's attitude toward him during 1930–31, Raymond probably didn't work with the Barrows until Clyde got out of prison in 1932.

When the Barrows moved to Eagle Ford Road and set up their service station, there was a good well on the property. Henry Barrow used to make a little extra money by selling water from the well at 25 cents a barrel. Marie remembers Raymond's mother buying water from her father, and this was

how she first met the Hamilton family. Marie Barrow was about the same age as Raymond Hamilton's younger sister Audrey, and the two girls ran around together as teenagers in the early 1930s. While Marie considered Audrey Hamilton one of her best friends, she had a different opinion about Audrey's brother. Over sixty years later, Marie's comment to one of her friends was very brief: "Ray Hamilton was a punk."[17]

Shortly after Clyde wrote his letter on December 3, 1931, family pressures on Buck finally paid off. Buck said he would surrender to the prison authorities at Huntsville, as long as he could spend Christmas on the outside. His family agreed with this condition, and he spent the holiday with his relatives. On December 27, 1931, Buck, Blanche, Cumie, Artie, Artie's husband, and Marie drove down to the main building in Huntsville for Buck's reintroduction to prison life. It wasn't the happiest of occasions, but everyone knew that it was necessary for Buck and Blanche to have any kind of a real future together. They went to Warden Waid and told him that Buck wanted to finish up his term. Buck asked that he be kept at The Walls because the bullet wounds that put Buck in the prison hospital back in early 1930 were still bothering him.

Marie Barrow thought Warden Waid was impressed by Buck's voluntary return to prison, because he agreed to the family's requests. Her mother thought that Waid was a nice man, and he told them that it was "a mighty fine thing to do." Buck was even allowed to take up where he left off, with no time added to his sentence for his escape. One of the things that enabled Buck to go back to the penal farm was the knowledge that Blanche would be taken care of while he was in prison. It was arranged that Blanche would live part of the time with the Barrow family and part of the time with Artie in Denison, Texas, where she would work at Artie's beauty salon.

When Buck Barrow returned to Huntsville on December 27, 1931, Clyde was still at Eastham Camp 1 near Weldon Texas. It may have taken a while, but the word got to him that his brother was back. On January 27, 1932, Clyde was admitted to the main infirmary at Huntsville with two toes missing from his left foot. This wasn't an accident, and it wasn't just coincidence.

Some authors say that he had another inmate cut off the toes to get out of the back-breaking labor. Others say he did it himself. Certainly, self-mutilation was the most reliable method used by the prisoners as a means of escaping the situation on the farms. Severed toes and fingers, and even full amputations, were common events. For those not quite up to chopping off their own body parts, an alternative method was injecting dirty water or kerosene into the legs to induce a disabling infection. As crude as this may sound, there was a certain amount of skill required to do it right. A botched job might result in the guards just putting on a dirty bandage and sending you back out to the field the next day, even less able to keep up the

work because of your injury.[18] It's easy to imagine what life on the Texas State Prison Farms must have been like in the early 1930s if personally removing one of your own appendages or giving yourself a life-threatening infection—in the days before antibiotics—were considered attractive options.

Although the incident with Clyde's toes fit the common pattern, his motivation seems to have been a little different. Getting out of the brutal work schedule was certainly welcome, but Clyde told Fults that he did it to get back to Huntsville so he could be with Buck. Whichever story is true, Clyde must have kicked himself more than once about his timing. Six days after he arrived at the hospital, his mother's work paid off and he received a conditional pardon. On February 2, 1932, he went home on crutches.[19]

CHAPTER 12
The Ex-Con

Things had changed in west Dallas for the Barrow family while Clyde was gone.

Sometime before Clyde went to jail, his parents, with some financial assistance from their older children, finally got out of the campground in west Dallas. Nell Barrow bought a lot at 1620 Eagle Ford Road in west Dallas for her parents, and when Henry Barrow moved from the campground, he moved his house along with his family. The moving of this house is another of the notable memories from Marie Barrow's childhood. She was allowed to ride inside the house as it was moved and thought it was a grand adventure. It was only a few blocks, but to a little girl, every foot of the trip was an exciting experience.

In his letter of December 3, 1931, Clyde had asked his mother how things were going with the service station. Clyde knew that his father had bigger plans for the lot on Eagle Ford Road than just a place to live. Henry believed if he could put in a gas station, it would provide an income for himself and Cumie in their senior years. The Barrow business, called the Star Service Station, started out in the same house Henry had built on the campground. The service station part of the building was added onto the living quarters after it was moved to the

Two views of the Star Service Station, operated by Henry Barrow at 1620 Eagle Ford Road in west Dallas.

—Courtesy Marie Barrow Scoma and author Phillip W. Steele

40

Eagle Ford Road site. What the family called the "oil room" was added onto Henry and Cumie's bedroom. This was where the business for the service station was conducted, and these were the changes Clyde asked about in his letter.[1] When Clyde arrived home, they were still working on the station.

Henry also added kitchen facilities after the house was moved. Even so, life on Eagle Ford Road still had a lot in common with the primitive existence on the campground. One thing Marie Barrow remembered was the cold. Their little house had no insulation. Newspapers were often nailed to the walls in order to keep the cold winds from blowing through. Marie remembered her mother heating irons on the stove and wrapping them in clothes to be put under the covers for heat. There was no indoor running water and, of course, no indoor plumbing. Water was brought in from the pump, and way out in the back yard was the outhouse. Marie remembered it as a "two holer" complete with Sears and Roebuck catalog. Cumie did the washing outside with a tub and washboard.

The family's circumstances weren't the only thing that had changed in the last two years. The Clyde who came home on crutches was not the same person who was arrested two years before. Clyde's prison experience had left him both physically and psychologically scarred. The two missing toes would heal, but the psychological damage was permanent. Clyde absolutely refused to discuss his experiences with any of his family members. All he ever said about it was that the Eastham prison farm was "a burning hell."[2] Marie said that Clyde's attitude toward life changed. He began to tell his mother that everyone had just one time to die and that "we all go when our time comes." This new Clyde made the rest of his family uneasy.

At times, Clyde tried to pick up his life where he left off. For a while he considered putting up an automobile garage on the empty lot next to the service station. Clyde's illegal activities would eventually provide the money for his father to buy the lot, but the economic facts of life couldn't be ignored. In early 1932, honest, hard-working men were in breadlines. Where did that leave ex-cons? In the fall of 1929, just before Clyde and Buck

pulled the Denton job, the unemployment rate was about 5 percent. When Clyde came home from prison, it was over 20 percent. Times were hard. That doesn't excuse Clyde's later actions, but that's the way things were. America's economy was on its knees.

About the only thing that went well for Clyde in the early weeks after his release was that Bonnie Parker was glad to see him. At that time, Bonnie was living with her mother and was seeing other men. The second day Clyde was back, he went over to the Parker house to find out how things stood. Bonnie was overjoyed to see him again and might have jumped into his arms if he hadn't been hobbling around on his crutches. Her current boyfriend, who was there at the time, got the message and left.

Bonnie again became a regular fixture around the Barrow home. She helped Clyde until he was free of his crutches, and then he assisted his father around the service station where he could. As he got stronger, he tried to keep a job, but the police kept showing up and talking to his boss. There's no evidence that Clyde ever caused any trouble or stole from any of his employers, but with so many men fighting for work, employers didn't need the aggravation of the police hassling them about ex-cons. It was much easier to just get someone else. In frustration, Clyde finally agreed to try a job in Massachusetts, arranged by his family. They all hoped his reputation wouldn't follow him to New England. For Clyde, however, his reputation wasn't the problem—it was what he had to leave back in Texas.

Clyde left Dallas in early March 1932, to try and rebuild his life. This trip was the first time that Clyde had been that far away from his family. His sister Nell had arranged for the job, and the family had hopes that it would work out. He wrote a letter home that sounded upbeat, but, as it turned out, Clyde lasted about two weeks before he headed back to Texas.[3]

Dear Mother—
Just a few lines to let you know that I haven't forgotten you.
I got here Monday night and I sure was tired

out, but I like it up here and I guess I will go to work Monday. Well, how is everyone at home? I sure wish I could see you. I am lonesome already, but Jim is sure a good fellow and I am going to write to Nell over at ———— [Jack Barrow's wife's name]. I guess she will get it there. Have you seen Buck yet? Tell him hello for me. I am going to send him a box, soon as I work awhile. Well Mother, I don't know anything much right now, but will write more when I hear from you, so answer real soon and let me know how everything is in Dallas. Tell everyone hello for me and send my mail to:

FRAMINGHAM, MASS.
General Delivery.
Send it to Jack Stuwart—JACK STUWART, that is my name here.[4]

Cumie received this letter in late March of 1932 but for some reason it was dated April 30, 1932.[5]

Clyde's return from Massachusetts made his family uneasy concerning his frame of mind. They knew that this trip had been a last resort. Like Bonnie, Clyde was unable to be away from his family in general and his mother in particular, yet trying to maintain a job around west Dallas seemed to be an almost impossible proposition with the cops constantly keeping tabs on him. The family wondered what his next move would be, and it wasn't long in coming.

Most likely, the main reason Clyde couldn't stick it out in Massachusetts was Bonnie. One of the first things he did after returning home was to reunite with her. Clyde also had a surprise visitor when he got back to Dallas. All the family knew was that a friend of his from the prison farm had come around looking

for him. He told Henry that he and Clyde had "pulled chain" together at Eastham. The fellow was Ralph Fults, and of course, there was nothing said about Ralph and Clyde's real project—the raid on Eastham Camp 1.

Ralph Fults had been released from prison on August 25, 1931, with a pardon from Governor Ross Sterling, and he decided to go home to McKinney, Texas. He hadn't been back in a long time, so, having spent most of his time in the school for boys or state prison, he felt a little out of place. There weren't any jobs to be had, so he supported himself from his winnings in poker games and waited for Clyde to get out.

Fults watched the newspapers for lists of pardons and paroles issued, but January 1932 rolled around with still no word on Clyde. One day, on his way home, he passed by the McKinney jail and heard a familiar voice yell his name out one of the windows. It was an old friend from Eastham, and he had a cellmate who said he knew Clyde. Ralph went to the window and was introduced to an eighteen-year-old kid named Raymond Hamilton.[6]

Hamilton had been caught the previous September driving a stolen car with four stolen tires in the back. He got a suspended sentence in Dallas

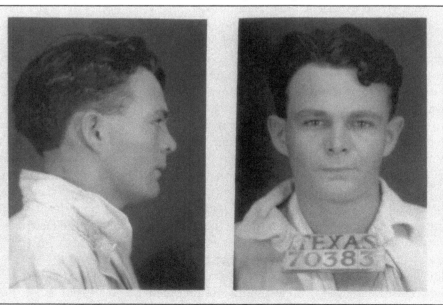

Ralph Fults' mug shot. Texas State Prison.
—Courtesy the Texas Ranger Hall of Fame and Museum, Waco, Texas

for the tires, but the car was stolen in McKinney, and there he was put in jail.[7] By January, Ray was ready for his freedom, and after a short conversation about their mutual friend, Clyde Barrow, Fults agreed to help him. Ralph slipped a couple of hacksaw blades in the spine of a magazine that was then passed to Hamilton. Deputy Sheriff Jimmy Beldon noticed that Hamilton suddenly began talking a lot, but he didn't think anything of it. The inmate was just trying to cover the noise of those blades working on the bars of his cell.[8] About daylight on January 27, 1932, the sawing was finished and Ray Hamilton was gone. His escape was the main topic of conversation at the cafe where Ralph Fults had breakfast. In a related piece of good news, Clyde Barrow's name was listed in the paper for February release.[9] By late March, Clyde had returned from New England to find Ralph Fults waiting for him. It was time to start planning the Eastham raid they had talked about so often.

The raid was going to take some financing and some extra manpower. They addressed the money problem first. The place Clyde had in mind was the Simms Oil Refinery, not far down the road from his father's service station. Clyde had some inside information about the payroll and planned to take it, but they needed a third man, so Raymond Hamilton was recruited as the junior member of the team. He agreed reluctantly—stealing cars was more his game.[10]

On the evening of March 25, 1932, Clyde, Fults, and Hamilton cut through the fence, took four employees hostage, and cracked the safe. It turned out that their information was faulty—the safe was empty. All they could do was tie up the hostages and leave.[11] After several more small burglaries, Clyde and Fults decided that, in order to raise the kind of money they needed for the raid, they would have to go after bigger game. They began to look for a bank.

For some reason, the boys decided to leave Texas and head north in search of a suitable victim. They made it as far as Minnesota, where they found a nice little bank in Okabena, just northeast of Worthington, but they finally decided to pass it up. There was still too much snow and ice on the roads for them to be confident of a clean getaway. Clyde filed the little bank away in his memory for future reference, however. The trio decided to turn back and take a closer look at some banks they had seen on the way north. It was a long drive, and they finally had to stop and sleep in the car because none of the three could stay awake. The car kept winding up in corn fields.[12]

According to several different people, somewhere on their return trip from Minnesota these three small-time crooks happened onto one of the biggest scores any of them would ever make, but there are also problems with some of the testimony. All three of them were seen with substantial amounts of money soon after their return to Texas, but exactly where they got it is unclear. Ralph Fults said that they hit a bank and got away with $33,000, but the details he gives for the robbery raise as many questions as they answer[13] [for a discussion of Fults' story, see Appendix Four].

Wherever the robbery was, Fults said that they wound up hiding out in East St. Louis, Illinois. None of them had ever had anything like that amount of money before, and they each had their own ideas how to use it. One thing was certain, however. Raymond Hamilton, the teenage car thief and escape artist who was reluctant to go on the road trip, had found his calling. After they counted the money, Ray said, "Let's take another bank right away."[14] Throughout his criminal career, Clyde Barrow hit mostly small places—filling stations and stores—and became famous for shooting policemen, but from then on, Raymond Hamilton was an enthusiastic convert to the bank robbery business.

CHAPTER 13
Mud, Mules, and the Lake Dallas Gang

According to Ralph Fults, the reason behind the Simms Oil robbery and the road trip that ended with the big score somewhere in the Midwest went beyond just the need for money. He and Clyde were building a war chest to finance a raid on the prison farm at Eastham. As soon as they divided up the take from the bank, they went shopping for additional weapons. They connected with an underworld arms dealer and bought several guns and some bulletproof vests. The vests promised protection from handgun and shotgun rounds but proved to be about as effective as khaki shirts. The weapons were also a disappointment and included Clyde's first (and probably last) experience with the famous but finicky Thompson sub-machine guns. Neither he nor Fults liked them, and Clyde soon graduated to bigger things.

Ray Hamilton had kept his money in his pocket. He finally told Fults and Clyde that he had no interest in raiding some prison to release a bunch of guys he didn't know. He was not quite nineteen years old, and his $11,000 share of the bank job was surely more money than he had ever seen in his life, so Ray left Clyde and Ralph to their plans and set out on his own for Michigan, where his father worked. Clyde felt that Hamilton had run out on them and said that he "hoped the little rat choked on that wad of money."[1] Nevertheless, they went their separate ways.[2]

Clyde and Fults went back to north Texas and began to assemble the additional men needed for the Eastham raid. Clyde had a favorite hideout near Lake Dallas, in the Denton area, and both he and Fults knew some local people who might be interested. Eventually, they managed to get five other guys together. Two of them, Jack and "Fuzz," were friends of Clyde and Buck. A guy named Johnny had been at Gatesville with Ralph, but the other two were new. One was a friend of Jack's named "Red," and the last man was Ted Rogers. Ted was a cool customer and looked a lot like Ray Hamilton. That fact would come back to haunt them both.[3]

Another bank job was planned—two, in fact. The seven guys decided to imitate the Dalton gang and rob both banks in Denton, Texas, at the same time. This was probably a little ambitious, but they would never know for sure. Just before the robbery, Ralph spotted a car parked nearby, pointed away from the curb for a quick getaway. One of the gang recognized the two men inside as Texas Rangers and wisely canceled the operation. The Rangers being there seemed more than just bad luck, and Barrow and Fults began to suspect a leak in the group.[4]

There would be one more recruiting trip before the raid on Eastham. Clyde and Fults decided to go to Amarillo to look for two brothers they knew who might be interested, and "Red," one of the new men, asked to go along. He seemed to want to impress them with how tough he was, so Clyde and

Ralph took him, but the trip turned out to be a waste of time and a little dangerous besides.

In Amarillo, the two brothers weren't around, and on the way back the three had a series of mishaps. In Electra, Texas, they were stopped and wound up kidnapping James T. Taylor, the chief of police, J. C. Harris, who ran the water department, and A. F. McCormick, an oil and gas agent, to make their getaway. "Red," the tough guy, ran away at the first sign of trouble.[5] The three hostages were released unharmed, but when their car ran out of gas, Clyde and Ralph had to do it all over again. This time the victim was a rural mail carrier named Owens. He spent several anxious hours with Barrow and Fults as they drove north—once running through a chain at a toll bridge over the Red River as they crossed into Oklahoma and attracting some gunfire. Sometime later, they stopped and let the frightened mailman out, but this time it was Clyde and Ralph's turn to be surprised. What were they going to do with his car? the mailman asked. They told him they would just leave it somewhere and he could get it back. Well, Owens said, if it was all the same to them, he'd appreciate it if they would just set it on fire. If it were destroyed, he explained, the government would have to buy him a new one. It must have been hard for them to keep a straight face, but the two desperadoes promised to burn up the car the first chance they got—and they did.[6]

When Clyde and Ralph got back to Lake Dallas, the remaining six members of the gang decided to go ahead with the raid using the manpower they had, but there were a few more things to do first. Someone needed to go to Eastham and make the final arrangements, and for the first time Clyde decided to use his girlfriend. During the prison's Sunday visiting hours, Bonnie would go in and pass the plan to Clyde's friend Aubrey, the building tender, so that the men on the inside would be ready. The rest would steal weapons and ammunition from a hardware store in Celina so they could supply the escaping inmates. The day after the trip to Eastham, Clyde and Fults would go to the Tyler area and steal a couple of cars to be positioned for the getaway. It sounded like a good plan to everyone.[7]

On April 17, Bonnie Parker mixed with the visitors at the prison, posing as Aubrey's cousin, and passed the message. Everything went smoothly, and by that evening they were back in Dallas. The next evening, Clyde and Ralph left Dallas for Tyler to find the getaway cars, and since Bonnie was already involved, they decided that she could come along. Car theft was, after all, a skill that Clyde and Ralph had long since mastered. The time it took them to steal an automobile—from start to finish—was measured in seconds rather than minutes. On the way to Tyler, they stopped in the smaller town of Kaufman so that Ralph could buy some ammunition at a hardware store.[8]

The city of Tyler proved to be perfect for a couple of car thieves, and everything went as planned. Rather than their favorite Ford roadster or sedan, Clyde and Ralph went for the bigger models, since they didn't know how many escaped prisoners they might have to carry away after the break. They settled on a Buick and a Chrysler, and headed back the way they had come.[9] But Clyde and Ralph were about to make a crucial mistake.

Ralph had been impressed with that hardware store in Kaufman. (Other sources say Mabank; see note 10 below.) They had a good selection of guns and ammunition, so he and Clyde decided to check it out on the return trip. The other boys were supposed to get the guns from the store in Celina, but something might go wrong. It wouldn't hurt to have some extra—just in case.

It was around midnight by the time they pulled up behind the hardware store and went to work on the rear door.[10] No problem there. Breaking and entering was a way of life for them. Unfortunately, the town night watchman had seen the two large cars roll through the town square at an hour when everybody who had any business there was home in bed, and he came around the corner with his gun drawn. Clyde snapped off a shot, the watchman fired back, and what should have been a nice quiet drive back to Dallas turned into a daylong nightmare for the two burglars and the girl who just wanted to be with her boyfriend.[11]

The exchange of a couple of shots was enough for the watchman, and he retreated, but then someone began ringing a bell and Clyde and Ralph knew it was time to go. They tried to leave town on the main highway but found it blocked. They back-tracked and finally got out of town to the east on a little dirt road. Unfortunately, the area had recently had some rain, and now another thundershower came along. The dirt turned to mud, and soon both cars were stuck. What had been a bad situation was rapidly getting worse.

With no other alternative, the three of them started across the fields on foot. Before long, they came to a farmhouse, woke up the owner, a Mr. Rogers, and demanded his car. The owner was sorry—he had no car, but, since they were holding a gun on him, they were welcome to his two mules. It was a stunning reversal of fortunes. An hour earlier, they were planning a raid on the state prison, and now they were reduced to stealing mules. Clyde got on one of the animals, with Bonnie behind him, and Ralph mounted the other. It was Ralph's bad luck to pick the mule that was known for its pitching, and in a second, he was face down in the mud. A few choice words later, Ralph was back on and they rode off in the rain.[12]

The little town of Kemp, Texas, is a few miles south of the larger city of Kaufman, and it was just before dawn on Tuesday, April 19, when the soaked, mule-riding fugitives arrived. They saw a car at the home of a Dr. Scarsdale and got in, leaving the livestock behind. It seemed like things were finally starting to break their way, but only a mile or so out of town, the car ran out of gas and they were on foot again.[13] The sun was coming up, and search parties were beginning to form. They knew that the mules would soon be found, so all they could do was get off the road and hide in the underbrush.

The search was on. The city marshal in Kemp and the chief of police in Mabank rounded up the local men and started beating the bushes for the fugitives. One posse member even remembered the officers stopping strangers and checking the seat of their pants for mule hair. This went on all day with no results.[14] Late in the afternoon, Clyde, Bonnie, and Ralph decided to try to get to a small store on the other side of the main road and steal a car. By now, though, everybody in the country was on the

lookout for them, and they were seen crossing the road. One phone call and the posse converged on the area.

They were cornered a short time later in the bottomland near Cedar Creek, and shots were fired from both sides. Barrow and Fults fired over the heads of the posse, hoping they would keep their distance, but the posse was shooting to kill. This was all becoming a lot more intense than Bonnie had bargained for. A few more shots and Ralph was hit in the left arm. Clyde now made a decision. He told Ralph and Bonnie that he was going to run for it. If he made it, he'd get help and come back for them. If not—well, he had already decided he wasn't going back to prison. This time, Clyde's combination of good instincts and good luck worked for him. He broke through the line of officers on a dead run. He went directly between two men who were both looking down to reload and neither one saw him.

Once Clyde was clear, Ralph told Bonnie to give herself up. She had no record and would probably be all right. Ralph told her to make up any kind of story she wanted. Bonnie loaded Ralph's gun for him, climbed out of the ditch, and was promptly captured. Ralph tried to slip away in the twilight but was caught a few minutes later. He and Bonnie spent the night in a little jail in Kemp that was about the size of a large outhouse.[15] Clyde stole a truck in Kemp, and later a car in nearby Peeltown, and finally made it back to Dallas.[16]

Clyde first made contact with his brother L. C. and his sister-in-law Blanche and asked them to go to Kaufman and see how Bonnie and Ralph were doing. His next stop was at the Lake Dallas hide-out to pick up the other members of the gang and make plans to get Bonnie and Ralph out, but when he got there, he found only Ted Rogers and Johnny. Jack and Fuzz were gone somewhere, and they still hadn't done the Celina hardware store job. Clyde didn't have time to wait around, so he, Ted, and Johnny hit the hardware store that night (April 20), in a somewhat messy affair.[17]

The three gang members took the new weapons back to Lake Dallas and tried them out, and as luck would have it, the shots were heard and reported to

Denton County sheriff G. C. Cockrell. Late in the afternoon of April 21, Cockrell's posse arrived at the hideout. Clyde, Ted, and Johnny saw them coming, slipped out the back into the woods, and got away, but Jack and Fuzz, finally returning to the gang's headquarters, drove right into the middle of it all and were captured.[18] Clyde's Ford V-8 was parked in front and was soon identified as the car from Peeltown, Texas. Mabank officers were contacted, and they came up and promptly identified Jack as the third man who had gotten away, even though none of them had gotten a good look at Clyde, much less Jack, who wasn't even there.[19]

The Lake Dallas gang was history. Three members were in jail, one had left for parts unknown,[20] and the remaining three, Clyde, Ted Rogers, and Johnny, had lost everything except what they carried with them in their escape. Clyde's promise to help Ralph and Bonnie was simply overcome by events. Before he could do anything, Ralph was moved. Clyde was further advised by his family that Bonnie would probably get out as soon as the grand jury met, so any attempt to break her out would just make things worse. Even so, Clyde had to do something. He had given away most of the money from the Midwest bank job, so he, Ted, and Johnny were just about broke. Clyde, however, did remember that a fellow named Bucher he used to run around with lived in Hillsboro—and, more importantly, his parents ran a store.

CHAPTER 14
Suicide Sal

Ralph and Bonnie caused a lot of excitement when they were taken to Kemp to spend the night, and most of the townsfolk turned out to see the desperadoes. One of the local ladies was scandalized that they were going to put "that little girl" in the same cell with Ralph to spend the night. The sheriff assured her that the two had already spent the previous night and most of the day together in the woods. In any case, Ralph was in no condition to be a danger to a young girl or anybody else. His wounded arm was killing him. When a doctor was called, it turned out to be the same man whose car they had stolen, and he refused to treat Ralph. It wasn't until the next morning, after they were moved to Kaufman, that anything was done. As they had promised, L. C. and Blanche went to Kaufman to check on the prisoners, and once in Kaufman, Bonnie called her mother.[1]

Emma Parker tells her version of the story of Bonnie's capture in *Fugitives*. Mrs. Parker's version contains many errors which have been passed down by several authors, including giving the date of Bonnie's arrival at the Kaufman jail as March 22, 1932—a month too early.[2]

This little escapade was Bonnie's first brush with the law and her first glimpse of what life might be like with Clyde Barrow. It's hard to know what Bonnie really thought, because she gave two different impressions of her feelings about the whole situation, depending on her audience. To her mother, she was sorry about the whole thing and felt that Clyde had abandoned her. By the time she got out of Kaufman two months later, she was telling her

Kemp, Texas, Jail where Bonnie Parker and Ralph Fults were held overnight following their capture on April 19, 1932—as it looks today.

—From the author's collection

mother that she was through with Clyde for good.[3] To Clyde's family, who visited her regularly and brought her clothes and other things, she showed no sign of such feelings.[4]

On April 24, the police chief of Electra, Texas, and Mr. Owens, the mail carrier, went to Kaufman and identified Ralph as one of the men involved in that kidnapping. He was moved from Kaufman a few days later and taken to Wichita Falls for trial.[5] Mr. Owens, understandably, made no mention of his request to the kidnappers that they burn up his government car.

Mrs. Parker says that Bonnie was treated well by the jailer and his wife, Mr. and Mrs. Adams, and that she was advised to let Bonnie sit out the time until the grand jury met, to teach her a lesson. For that reason, plus the stark reality that she didn't have the money, Mrs. Parker didn't make Bonnie's bail. Bonnie Thornton (she gave her married name to the newspapers) sat in the Kaufman jail from April 20 until June 17, 1932.[6]

Probably to pass the time, Bonnie began composing a poem while at Kaufman. She may well have dabbled in writing verse before, but this is the first long, involved poem we know about, and she called it "Suicide Sal." In the poem, Sal, the heroine, is "done wrong" by her lover, Jack. Many people assume that Sal's revenge in the poem reflects Bonnie's anger at being left behind by Clyde at Kaufman. If that is so, it's hard to explain why she kept the poem long after she and Clyde got back together.

Reading the poem, Emma Parker was shocked at Bonnie's obvious knowledge of criminal vocabulary.[7] This poem was probably started out of boredom and revised and polished over the next year just for fun. Bonnie's second and last major attempt at poetry would be much more poignant and, unfortunately, more prophetic, but that was two years away.

The Story of Suicide Sal
by Bonnie Parker

We each of us have a good "alibi"
For being down here in the "joint;"

But few of them really are justified
If you get right down to the point.

You've heard of a woman's glory
Being spent on a "downright cur,"
Still you can't always judge the story
As true, being told by her.

As long as I've stayed on this "island,"
And heard "confidence tales" from each "gal,"
Only one seemed interesting and truthful—
The story of "Suicide Sal."

Now "Sal" was a gal of rare beauty,
Though her features were coarse and tough;
She never once faltered from duty
To play on the "up and up."

"Sal" told me this tale on the evening
Before she was turned out "free,"
And I'll do my best to relate it
Just as she told it to me:

I was born on a ranch in Wyoming;
Not treated like Helen of Troy;
I was taught that "rods are rulers"
And "ranked" as a greasy cowboy.

Then I left my old home for the city
To play in its mad dizzy whirl,
Not knowing how little pity
It holds for a country girl.

There I fell for "the line" of a "henchman,"
A "professional killer" from "Chi;"
I couldn't help loving him madly;
For him even now I would die.

One year we were desperately happy;
Our "ill gotten gains" we spent free;
I was taught the ways of the "underworld;"
Jack was just like a "god" to me.

I got on the "F.B.A." payroll
To get the "inside lay" of the "job;"
The bank was "turning big money!"
It looked like a "cinch" for the "mob."

Eighty grand without even a "rumble"—
Jack was last with the "loot" in the door,

When the "teller" dead-aimed a revolver
From where they forced him to the floor.

I knew I had only a moment—
He would surely get Jack as he ran;
So I staged a "big fade out" beside him
And knocked the forty-five out of his hand.

They "rapped me down big" at the station,
And informed me that I'd get the blame
For the "dramatic stunt" pulled on the "teller"
Looked to them too much like a "game."

The "police" called it a "frame-up,"
Said it was an "inside job,"
But I steadily denied any knowledge
Or dealings with "underworld mobs,"

The "gang" hired a couple of lawyers,
The best "fixers" in any man's town,
But it takes more than lawyers and money
When Uncle Sam starts "shaking you down."

I was charged as a "scion of gangland"
And tried for my wages of sin;
The "dirty dozen" found me guilty—
From five to fifty years in the pen.

I took the "rap" like good people,
And never one "squawk" did I make.
Jack "dropped himself" on the promise
That we make a "sensational break."

Well, to shorten a sad lengthy story,
Five years have gone over my head
Without even so much as a letter—
At first I thought he was dead.

But not long ago I discovered
From a gal in the joint named Lyle,
That Jack and his "moll" had "got over"
And were living in true "gangster style."

If he had returned to me sometime,
Though he hadn't a cent to give,
I'd forget all this hell that he's caused me,
And love him as long as I live.

But there's no chance of his ever coming,
For he and his moll have no fears

But that I will die in prison,
Or "flatten" this fifty years.

Tomorrow I'll be on the "outside"
And I'll "drop myself" on it today:
I'll "bump 'em" if they give me the "hot squat"
On this island out here in the bay.

The iron doors swung wide next morning
For a gruesome woman of waste,
Who at last had a chance to "fix it."
Murder showed in her cynical face.

Not long ago I read in the paper
That a gal on the East Side got "hot,"
And when the smoke finally retreated,
Two of gangdom were found "on the spot."

It related the colorful story
Of a "jilted gangster gal."
Two days later, a "sub-gun" ended
The story of "Suicide Sal."[8]

It's hard not to see Bonnie's recent past and present circumstances as part of the inspiration for this, her first major work of literature. The poem's style owes a lot to the romance and detective magazines Bonnie loved to read, and the cryptic gangster slang and dialogue could have come out of an Edward G. Robinson movie. The poem, whatever its motivation, obviously meant a lot to Bonnie, because she kept it with her and revised it several times during the next ten months. After the police found it in Joplin, Missouri, in April 1933, it was printed over and over again by the news media. Thanks to the help of the very people who were chasing her, Bonnie Parker became the only depression-era gun moll who was also a published poet.

While Bonnie was passing the time in the Kaufman jail doing creative writing, Clyde and what was left of his gang were trying to make some money. The store in Hillsboro seemed like as good a prospect as any, so near the end of April, they went there to case the job. As with many stores at that time, J. N. Bucher sold a lot of things. The group looked the place over, and Johnny bought a knife, but Mrs. Bucher remembered

$250.00 REWARD

FRANK ALBERT CLAUSE

Frank Albert Clause—Description as follows: Age 21 to 22, weight 125 to 135, height 5 ft. 9½ inches, hair blond, eyes hazel, complexion light, build slender. Tatoo, left arm, Heart-Love, right arm, Kewpie.

F. P. Class

| 22 | 9 | 18 |
| 4 | 1 M | |

CLYDE CHAMPION BARROW

Clyde Champion Barrow—Description as follows: Age 22 to 23, height 5 ft. 6 inches, weight 125 pounds, eyes brown, hair dark and wavy, complexion, medium fair, build medium, said to walk with a limp, brown mole point of right shoulder. Tattoo, Heart-Dagger, Letters E. B. W. left front arm, Shield and Letters, U. S. N. and Girls Head right arm.

F. P. Class

| 29 | MO | 9 |
| 26 | U | 00 | 4 |

I hold Felony Warrants for the Parties whose Photographs appear above—

These parties are wanted for the brutal murder of J. N. Bucher on night of April 30th, 1932, and the robbery of his place. Articles taken were as follows: $35.00 to $40.00 in money taken, 71-100 carat ladies' ring in white mounting, three 51-100 carat ladies' ring in white mounting, five 59-100 carat ladies' rings in white mounting, one 51-100 carat ladies' ring in white mounting, five ladies' rings in white mounting, ranging from 25 to 15 points, one old model 45 caliber Colts pistol, blue barrel.

Our information is that these parties range from Fort Worth, Dallas, Waco, San Antonio, Houston, into the oil fields of East Texas. We hope to see these parties arrested in the near future, and receive the $250.00 reward offered by the Governor of Texas for the parties who committed this crime. Take no chances on them as they are desperate men. Barrow is out of Penitentiary on furlough at present.

J. W. FREELAND, Sheriff Hill County, Hillsboro, Tex

Wanted poster for Clyde Barrow and Frank Clause, issued by the sheriff of Hill County, Texas, shortly after the killing of J. N. Bucher at Hillsboro, Texas, April 30, 1932. Frank Clause was Barrow's partner in a string of home burglaries during 1928–29 but was not involved in the Bucher killing.

—From the author's collection

Clyde as a friend of her son.[9] Clyde felt that this complicated the issue but agreed to go ahead with the robbery if he could stay out of sight. He would drive the getaway car while Ted and Johnny did the inside work.

On Saturday night, April 30, the three went back to Bucher's store. The plan was to get there late so nobody else would be around, get Mr. Bucher to open up on some pretext, make a purchase with a large bill so he would have to open the safe for change, grab the goods, and run.

Everything went as planned—up to a point. About 10:00 P.M., they got Mr. Bucher to open up and bought a 25 cent guitar string with a $10 bill. Mr. Bucher called his wife to open the safe, and then things started to go wrong. As soon as the safe was open, Ted pulled out a pistol and demanded the money, but Mr. Bucher had a pistol in the safe and pulled it also. Ted was faster and shot the old man in the chest. Johnny grabbed Mrs. Bucher, who was trying to pick up her husband's gun, and Ted cleaned out the safe—$40 in cash, and jewelry worth about $1,500. When they got to the car, they told Clyde what had happened. According to Ted Rogers, Clyde said, "Damn! Now we're in for it."[10] Those words would turn out to be a massive understatement.

The killing of Mr. Bucher set off a manhunt around Hillsboro, but the Lake Dallas boys had already split up. Ted went his own way and was picked up on another charge within a month or so. The authorities never connected him with the Bucher killing. By the end of 1932, he was in Huntsville with Jack and Ralph. Jack introduced them to an old friend of his who was finishing up his sentence—Buck Barrow. It was there in Huntsville that Ted told them what really happened at Hillsboro.[11]

In order to identify the killers of Mr. Bucher, the police in Hillsboro asked for help from the Dallas Sheriff's Office, which sent down some mug shots for Mrs. Bucher to view. Clyde Barrow was well known in Dallas and, of course, his picture was there, along with his old partner, Frank Clause. Mrs. Bucher picked him out, probably because he had been there with the others the first time. The fact that the man present at the shooting that night was described as being five inches taller than Barrow—before Clyde's mug shot was shown to Mrs. Bucher—was just a detail. The second man was another matter.

Ted Rogers was not well known, but Raymond Hamilton was. He was an escaped prisoner and a wanted man even then. Rogers and Hamilton looked so much alike that it was the better-known Hamilton's mug shot that was picked as the second man. Before he was through, Raymond Hamilton would richly deserve the punishment he got, but he was almost certainly in Michigan at the time Bucher was killed. Even so, he was eventually tried, convicted, and given a life sentence for Bucher's murder.[12]

With Bonnie in jail and most of his friends either locked up or scattered, Clyde kept a very low profile. He was now a wanted man also. Unfortunately, there is very little real evidence to show his movements during the months of May, June, and July 1932. He knew the amount of heat that was on because of the Hillsboro shooting. Being a burglar and a car thief was one thing, but a murder charge put Clyde in a different league. Clyde was identified, along with Frank Clause, in a couple of robberies at Lufkin, Texas, in early May, and his family seemed to believe the reports, but no one knew for sure. Mistaken identification by eyewitnesses was a fact of life—then as now—and it would happen over and over again during Bonnie and Clyde's last two years.

Clyde's family continued to visit Bonnie in Kaufman and Buck in Huntsville during this time. Marie Barrow remembers being used to try on dresses for Bonnie. She was just fourteen, but she and Bonnie wore the same sizes in almost everything. Marie says that Clyde moved around a lot during May and June, keeping away from Dallas and staying with friends and relatives.[13]

On June 17, 1932, the grand jury met in Kaufman. Bonnie claimed she was kidnapped and didn't know either of the two men with her. The jury let her go, and she went back to Dallas with her mother. Mrs. Parker recalled that when the subject of Clyde came up Bonnie said, "I'm through with him. I'm never going to have anything more to do with him." Just what her mother wanted to hear.[14]

CHAPTER 15
A Bad Night in Oklahoma

Little is known about Clyde Barrow's whereabouts during May and June 1932. By the first of July, however, leads begin to surface. By most accounts, Clyde had gotten back together with Raymond Hamilton by this time. The date of Hamilton's arrival back in Texas from Michigan, however, is open to question. Hamilton's biographer gives two different time frames. First he says Ray arrived back in Dallas "several days after the Bucher murder."[1] Then he reports that, at Ray's trial for the Bucher murder, a witness, J. W. Ringo, swore that Ray was in Michigan during April and May.[2] Marie Barrow remembered late June as the time Clyde and Ray got back together.[3]

As stated earlier, Marie Barrow believed that she was the main connection between the Barrow and Hamilton families up until this point, due to her friendship with Ray's younger sister Audrey. Marie thought that Clyde and Ray teamed up for the first time in late June 1932.[4] She didn't know about Ray being in on the Simms Oil job or the Midwest bank robbery. Also, even though she and Blanche were good friends, Marie didn't seem to know that Ray had tried to get in with Buck and Blanche when they were robbing payrolls in 1930–31. Blanche said they wouldn't take him along, because he was too young (Ray was just seventeen in the summer of 1930) and because Buck didn't like him or trust him.[5]

Although Buck and Blanche wouldn't work with Ray, Clyde worked with him during three periods, but their relationship was a stormy one. The first time ended when Ray refused to go along with the Eastham raid; the second time ended with the killing of one police officer, the kidnaping of another, and a near capture southwest of Houston; and the last time began when Clyde broke Ray out of Eastham and ended with Clyde claiming that Ray was stealing from the gang. For now, though (July 1932), both Clyde and Ray were wanted for murder, and each one needed a partner.

During July, two Texas robberies were attributed to Barrow and Hamilton but are still disputed by some sources. One concerned an ice company at Palestine, and the other was a bank in Willis. Hamilton's biographer says that Clyde and Ray did them both,[6] but the Barrow family didn't think so.[7] Neither Ray's biographer nor the Barrows offer any solid evidence, but the Home Ice Company robbery may be one of the earliest examples of someone trying to put the blame on Clyde and Raymond to cover their own tracks. On July 16, 1932, Roy Evans, the bookkeeper of the Home Ice Company in Palestine, claimed he was abducted and beaten, and the payroll stolen. Five days after the robbery, Evans admitted that he had made up the story of the robbery to hide the fact that he was embezzling funds.[8] As for the Willis bank job, if the pair did that, they were in disguise. On July 27, 1932, two men walked into the First State Bank of Willis and walked out with $3,575.50. The two men were described as "about 30 years old, heavily whiskered, and dressed in overalls and khaki shirts."[9]

Probably the strongest argument for Clyde and Ray teaming up in late June is the fact that Bonnie left home at exactly that time, telling her mother that she had job as a waitress in Wichita Falls. Of course, Bonnie said nothing about Clyde in her letters home, but Mrs. Parker said she found out later that Bonnie, Clyde, and Ray had been living in a rented place in Wichita Falls all during July.[10] On July 29, two men robbed the Interurban train station in Grand Prairie. They missed a $700 haul by an hour or so and got only a few dollars. This job is credited to Hamilton,[11] but Ray's biographer and the Barrow family say that Clyde was with him.[12] Whether Barrow and Hamilton did any of these jobs, it is certain that by August, they were back in action.

On August 1, 1932, Clyde dropped Bonnie off at the Star Service Station on Eagle Ford Road and told her to listen to the radio to hear if they made their getaway. He and Ray were going to rob the Neuhoff Brothers Packing Company. To help in the job, they had picked up another fellow, named Ross Dyer.[13] Clyde and Ray would go inside and Dyer would drive the car. They hoped for a fair amount of money since it was payday at the packing plant.

It was 4:00 P.M. and Elsie Wullschleger was counting out the payroll in the plant's office when the two young men came in. When she spoke to them, they pulled pistols and walked past her to the rear of the office, where Joe and Henry Nuehoff were working. "This is a holdup," one of them said. The other took out a grocery bag and the $440 payroll disappeared inside. An old safe stood in the corner, and one of the bandits found a box inside, but it contained only some change used to buy stamps. Clyde and Ray backed out the door, went through the loading dock, and entered the waiting car. Before long they picked Bonnie up at the Barrows' station and went to lie low at a place they used near Grand Prairie.[14]

Four days later, Clyde dropped Bonnie off at the Barrow station again. She wanted to visit her mother but took a taxi from the Barrows' home so her family wouldn't know she was back with Clyde. Barrow, Ray Hamilton, and Ross Dyer planned to go north into Oklahoma, but Clyde told his mother he would meet her the next morning at a relative's house. The boys were driving a car they had stolen in Corsicana, Texas. A fourth name, Everett Milligan, is mentioned in later news coverage, but this would turn out to be an alias used by Dyer.[15]

Late on that Friday evening, the three of them were passing through Stringtown, Oklahoma, just north of Atoka, when they came upon a dance held at an outdoor pavilion. Music was provided by a group of teenagers including Ralph "Duke" Ellis, who remembers the car parking behind the stage near the band. He saw three men and said they took turns—one coming on the dance floor and two staying in the car.[16] There are several versions of why they decided to stop and exactly how the trouble started, but it is certain that something about the group attracted the attention of Sheriff C. G. Maxwell.

Around 11:00 P.M., Sheriff Maxwell and his undersheriff, Eugene C. Moore, approached the car where Clyde Barrow and Raymond Hamilton were sitting. One of the men in the car (probably Hamilton) was taking a pull on a bottle of whiskey. "You four can consider yourselves under arrest," Maxwell said, thinking they were just a bunch of bootleggers.[17] He didn't know that these young men were wanted for murder and a great many other things and would never come quietly. Clyde and Ray both picked up their pistols and started shooting, and both officers fell as the car started and pulled away. Maxwell was hit several times but emptied his pistol at them. Moore never even drew his gun. He died there behind the bandstand. He was thirty-one years old and left a wife and three small children.[18] Clyde and Ray pulled out of their parking place and headed for the highway. Ross Dyer, who was on the dance floor at the time, was left on his own.

The outbreak of gunfire pretty much closed down the dance for the evening. Duke Ellis says that there were other county and local lawmen present and that more gunfire was exchanged between Clyde and Raymond and other officers after Moore and Maxwell were shot. In the middle of all this, people were running in all directions. At least one bystander was hit in the shoulder, and another man hurt himself when he tried to jump a ditch and wound up straddling a barbed-wire fence. Ellis himself took cover in an old garage. After the shooting stopped, he emerged with his shirt covered in motor oil. One of his friends saw him and thought it was blood. They ripped off Ellis' shirt, looking for the gunshot wounds, before they discovered their mistake.[19]

Clyde and Ray ran, but they didn't get far. Trying to drive onto the highway, they hit a culvert and turned over. They managed to crawl through the culvert and stole a car belonging to Cleve Brady, which they drove away to the east, along a country road that is today Highway 43. When Brady's car lost a wheel, they appeared at John Redden's house, saying they were in an accident and needed to get someone to the doctor. Redden's son volunteered but soon found a gun in his ribs, and the group again headed east. Finally, in Clayton, Oklahoma, they took Frank Smith's car and disappeared.[20]

Clyde and Raymond drove all night, bypassing Dallas and abandoning the car in the small town of Grandview, south of the city. They picked up another car, and by 7:00 or 8:00 in the morning they were back at Clyde's cousin's house, where he had told his mother he would meet her.

Cumie Barrow arrived at her nephew's house the next morning and found Clyde and Raymond waiting for her. When she asked about Ross Dyer, Clyde said, "We lost him." Clyde then asked his mother if she had seen the morning paper. She had. They discussed the Oklahoma shooting, but all Clyde would say was that he had never killed anyone. His mother found out the whole story later.[21]

Meanwhile, some witnesses at Stringtown remembered a stranger who hitched a ride to the bus station and bought a ticket for McKinney, Texas. The police in Atoka called ahead, and the Texas authorities arrested him as he got off the bus. The Oklahoma newspaper identified him as Everett Milligan, and he was taken back to Atoka, then transferred to the state prison at McAllister for safekeeping.[22] Milligan's true identity was soon discovered. His record at the state prison shows that he was checked in on August 7, 1932, as Ross Dyer, alias Clifford Milligan.[23] The Barrow family believed that Ross Dyer hopped a boxcar out of Oklahoma and returned to Texas, where he was picked up and gave police the names of Clyde and Raymond in exchange for his freedom, but this doesn't seem to be the case.[24] On August 12, 1932, Ross Dyer was transferred back to Atoka, Oklahoma, and charged with murder (case #4496). Clyde Barrow and Raymond Hamilton were also charged the same day, their case number (4497) coming immediately after Dyer's. At this point, Ross Dyer's record ends. Apparently he was never brought to trial and eventually was released. Clyde and Raymond's charges were not dropped until March 5, 1937, after they were both long dead.[25]

Clyde Barrow and Raymond Hamilton would forever protest their innocence in the killing of J. N. Bucher, the crime that first branded them both as killers, and technically they were right. Neither one of them actually pulled the trigger. Now, however, they had a killing they could truly call their own—they had irrevocably broken into the "bigtime."[26] Eugene Moore was the first of nine lawmen to die at the hands of that collection of outlaws that would become known as the Barrow gang.

Chapter 16

On the Run

Clyde and Ray had gone back to Clyde's cousin's house because he had told his mother he would meet her there, but with all the attention they were sure to receive as soon as the police in Oklahoma identified them, they couldn't stay. Clyde's first priority was to pick up Bonnie from her mother's house, but he didn't dare go himself. After talking with his mother for a while, Clyde and Ray left to plan their next move.[1]

Cumie went back to the Barrow service station and told the rest of the family what had happened. All the Barrows could do at that point was worry and wonder what would happen next. They knew it was too late for Clyde to ever live on the right side of the law. Marie remembered that this realization hit her and her brother L. C. especially hard. Clyde was the only one of their siblings they had really grown up with; he was the only one they knew as "big brother." Now Clyde could never return home to live as he had in the past. Any contact with him would have to be quick and quiet. This sad state of affairs was confirmed when Clyde and Ray were identified as the shooters at Stringtown.[2] The chase was on.

The Barrow family followed the turn of events closely. It pained them that Clyde would be forever beyond the law, but they also felt extremely bad for those who were injured due to the things Clyde had done. His parents were hit hard when they heard about Eugene Moore.[3] Like many lawmen Clyde would face in the coming months, Moore was not a trained or experienced professional. He had been undersheriff for a year and was just trying to make an honest dollar in hard times. He had grown up in Calera, Oklahoma, moved to Stringtown, married a local girl, and started a family. Moore was probably at the dance that night to make a little overtime, and now his wife was a widow and his three children fatherless—all because of Clyde.[4]

Bonnie's mother, Emma, said that she and Bonnie read about the Oklahoma shooting in the morning paper of August 6. Whatever she might have suspected, Emma Parker didn't find out the truth until later. At the time, neither of them knew that Clyde was involved, and Bonnie had planned to take an early bus back to Wichita Falls the next morning.[5] This could well have been part of a plan she and Clyde agreed on before his trip to Oklahoma—"You visit with your momma, and I'll meet you back in Wichita Falls in a couple of days," he might have said. He and Bonnie had been staying there for the last month or so, after all. But everything had changed now. About 8:00 P.M., Emma and Bonnie were sitting on the front porch in the cool of the evening when a car pulled up in front of 2430 Douglas, driven by a man Emma didn't recognize.[6] Bonnie knew him, though. She went down and talked to him for a minute and then told her mother that she had a free ride to Wichita Falls. She gave Emma the money she had saved for bus fare and left.[7]

For the next few days, Bonnie and Clyde hid out. According to his biographer, Hamilton separated from Bonnie and Clyde but kept in touch through his older brother Floyd.[8] Whatever the truth, Marie Barrow believes it was Bonnie who decided their next move. They all knew they had to put some distance between themselves and north central Texas and Oklahoma, so Bonnie suggested a trip to visit an aunt she hadn't seen in a while. This was Emma Parker's sister, Millie Stamps, who lived in Carlsbad, New Mexico, about 400 miles from the Dallas area and even farther from Oklahoma. It was the best idea anybody had come up with, so a few days later, Clyde, Bonnie, and Raymond headed west.

This time, Bonnie and Clyde didn't make any real mistakes. The trip to New Mexico should have been a smart move, but the timing was wrong. Just a few days before, it had been discovered that a large car theft ring was operating in that part of the state. Naturally, New Mexico law officers were now on the lookout for suspicious vehicles—and stolen cars were the only kind Clyde ever drove.[9]

Bonnie's mother said her sister told her what happened. She said that the three kids arrived at Millie's farm outside Carlsbad on Saturday the 13th of August and spent the night. Bonnie's aunt had a huge garden, large enough to supply her family's needs and even stock a nearby vegetable stand that was regularly patronized by many of the local residents. The next morning, someone suggested that they should make a batch of homemade ice cream. Clyde and Ray were willing to crank the freezer, but they had no ice, so Ray offered to drive into Carlsbad and buy some. As Ray drove through town, Deputy Sheriff Joe Johns noticed the car, which matched the description of one reported stolen. When Ray came back by, Johns followed him out to Millie's farm.[10]

This, at least, is the story Emma Parker heard from her sister and the one Johns told the newspapers. The Barrow family believed otherwise. Marie said the family initially thought that the run-in between Clyde and Deputy Joe Johns was indeed an accidental meeting due to the lawman noticing the stolen car. Later, she says, they learned that the

contact between the three kids and the deputy sheriff was instigated by Bonnie's aunt. Emma Parker said her sister had no idea Clyde or Ray were wanted for anything,[11] but Marie said the Barrow family eventually found out that Aunt Millie saw Bonnie handwashing some bloodstained clothing (or caught a glimpse of some of Clyde's guns) and grew scared. The Barrows don't say how they got that information, and Millie—at least through her sister Emma—denied it, so the question remains unresolved. Whatever the cause, a few minutes after Ray got back from town that Sunday morning, Eddy County Deputy Sheriff Joe Johns was knocking on Aunt Millie's front door.

Bonnie answered the door and saw a police officer standing there. "Whose Ford is this?" he asked. The little waitress was by now a veteran and didn't give her surprise away. "Oh, the car belongs to one of the boys. They're dressing—I'll send them out in a minute," she said. This sounded perfectly normal but was a prearranged signal to Clyde and Ray that the law was there.[12] While he was waiting, Johns decided to take a closer look at the car, but it was locked.

This was an unusual situation for Clyde and Ray. Normally, Clyde was never more than arm's length from a firearm of some kind, but in order not to alarm Bonnie's aunt, all their artillery was now locked in the trunk of the car the deputy was examining. Finally they found a shotgun in a closet, went out the back door, and got the drop on Johns. The paper said that Johns actually went for his gun until Clyde fired a charge of bird shot over his head, knocking off his hat.[13]

The visit with Aunt Millie had lasted just one day. By shooting the hat off a deputy sheriff in Bonnie's aunt's front yard, the trio had already worn out their welcome. Once again they had to go, but this time they decided to take the lawman with them. They quickly gathered up their things and drove off with Deputy Johns toward Texas. By that night, they were about 500 miles away in San Antonio. The time they took to get there was reported variously as between eight[14] and thirteen hours.[15] By then, the alarm had been out for several hours and several leads had surfaced. By coincidence, two truck drivers discovered the decapitated body of a man about this same time. It was easy to turn "His hat was shot off" into "His head was shot off," so for a while this body was thought to be Johns. Actually, Clyde drove around San Antonio, unsuccessfully looking for a new car to steal, and then released Deputy Johns outside of town. He phoned his office to say he was all right, just tired and a long way from home.[16]

Bonnie, Clyde, and Raymond surfaced late Monday afternoon, the 15th, when they stole a Ford V-8 sedan in Victoria, Texas, southeast of San Antonio. This must have been noticed quickly and their probable route guessed, because, for the first time, the police actually got ahead of them. The Colorado River runs just west of Wharton, Texas, and a couple of local deputies decided to stake out the highway bridge and watch for the stolen cars. The one on the west end of the bridge would make the identification and signal the one on the east end with a flashlight.

It was well after dark when the outlaws approached Wharton on their way to Houston. The first lawman saw them coming, but when he flashed the signal to his partner, he inadvertently signaled Clyde too. As soon as he saw the light blink on, Clyde, with Bonnie beside him, spun the wheel and downshifted, doing a 180-degree turn in the middle of the road and driving back past an astonished Raymond Hamilton, who was following in the second car. Ray tried the same thing but was much closer to the bridge by the time he got turned around, so he received the bulk of the officers' attention. They opened up on Ray's sedan, but he was uninjured. The two cars quickly disappeared back west down the highway and vanished into the Texas night.[17]

After the marathon trip from New Mexico, two days without sleep, and a near-death experience at Wharton, Ray Hamilton decided he'd had enough of the glamorous outlaw life for a while. As for Bonnie and Clyde, for all the law knew, they might as well have fallen off the edge of the earth.

In four months, Clyde had gone from a little-known local hood to the most wanted outlaw in Texas. Before April 1932, Bonnie Parker had no police record at all. Now her name and Clyde's were forever linked.

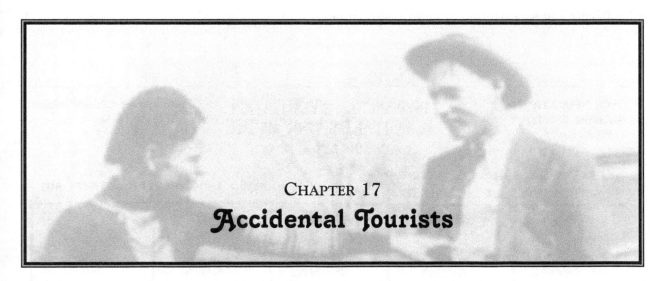

CHAPTER 17
Accidental Tourists

In the late summer and fall of 1932, Bonnie and Clyde hit the bigtime, at least in the Southwest. In April, they were virtually unknown to the general public. Now they were suspected of almost every bank, gas station, or grocery store holdup, and of taking every car that was stolen in Texas and several surrounding states. In the newspapers, Clyde's driving skills reached heroic proportions, so that the pair could be credited with two robberies several hundred miles apart on the same day. Other thieves began to copy their modus operandi, such as it was, in hopes of being misidentified as the famous pair and escaping blame themselves. Such was the price of fame. The two lovers also began to acquire a glamorous allure. Their families, however, knew the truth.

After their misadventures in New Mexico and the ambush at Wharton, Texas, the three kids headed back toward Dallas. They came to rest at an abandoned farmhouse near Grand Prairie and stayed there for almost two weeks. Clyde and Bonnie visited their families in west Dallas frequently from this hideout.[1]

While Bonnie and Clyde recuperated at Grand Prairie, Raymond decided to go back to Michigan. Hamilton felt it was time to go to a "cooler" climate, in terms of both weather and police pursuit. Clyde and Bonnie knew they needed to get away too, so they agreed to drive Ray to Bay City, leaving about the first of September.[2]

Until now, Bonnie and Clyde had been the concern of two or three southwestern states, but this trip would bring them to the attention of the U.S. government agency that would later become the FBI. None of the offenses Clyde was accused of at this point, including the two murders, were federal crimes. It was up to individual states to catch him—if they could. Still with so many serious charges already against him, the federal charge came almost as an anticlimax.

Bonnie and Clyde delivered Raymond to his father in Bay City, Michigan, probably by the second week of September, and then set out on their own. Later that same month, a stolen Ford was found abandoned near Jackson, Michigan, 100 miles south of Bay City. The Ford came from Pawhuska, Oklahoma, and a check with the Pawhuska police found that another stolen Ford, from Illinois, was abandoned there. Federal agents discovered in the Illinois Ford an empty medicine bottle and eventually traced it to Clyde Barrow's aunt. Further investigation implicated Bonnie and Clyde as well as Clyde's brother L. C. in the theft of the Illinois Ford. Eight months later, on May 20, 1933, they were finally charged with interstate transportation of a stolen car—a federal offense.[3]

Exactly where Bonnie and Clyde spent the next month or so is not known, but the family said that they kept in touch via a series of unsigned letters as they traveled through the Midwest, living off the

59

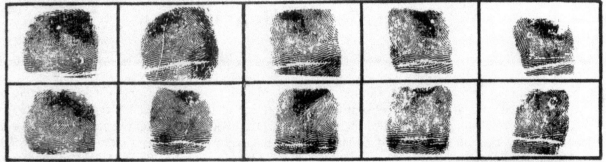

IDENTIFICATION ORDER NO. 1211
October 24, 1933

DIVISION OF INVESTIGATION
U. S. DEPARTMENT OF JUSTICE
WASHINGTON, D. C.

Fingerprint Classification
13 29 W MO 9
26 U 00 9

WANTED
CLYDE CHAMPION BARROW, aliases CLYDE BARROW, ELVIN WILLIAMS, ELDIN WILLIAMS, JACK HALE, ROY BAILEY.

NATIONAL MOTOR VEHICLE THEFT ACT

DESCRIPTION
Age, 23 years
Height, 5 feet, 7 inches, bare feet
Weight, 150 pounds
Build, medium; Hair, dark brown, wavy, reported dyed black; Eyes, hazel; Complexion, light; Marks, shield and anchor with U.S.N., on right forearm outer; Girl's bust, left inner forearm; Residence, West Dallas, Texas.

RELATIVES:
Mrs. Cumie F. Barrow, mother,
  Rural Route 6, Dallas, Texas
I. C. Barrow, brother,
  Rural Route 6, Dallas, Texas
Mrs. Ortis Wilber, sister,
  Denison, Texas
Mrs. Clyde Barrow, aliases
  Bonnie Barrow, Bonnie Parker,
  Mrs. Roy Harding, wife,
  probably accompanying Barrow
Mrs. Emma Parker, mother of Mrs.
  Clyde Barrow, Dallas, Texas.

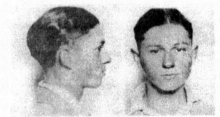

le lyde Barrow

CRIMINAL RECORD
As Clyde Champion Barrow, No. 6048, arrested police department, Dallas,Texas, December 3, 1926; charge, auto theft; indictment dismissed.
  As Clyde Champion Barrow, No. 4316, arrested police department, Fort Worth, Texas, February 22, 1928; charge, investigation; dismissed.
  As Clyde Barrow, No. 6048, arrested police department, Dallas, Texas, October 13, 1929; charge attempted burglary and safe burglary; indictment quashed.
  As Clyde Barrow, alias Elvin Williams, No. 414, arrested police department,Waco, Texas, March 2, 1930; charge, burglary; sentence, 14 years Texas State Penitentiary; escaped County Jail, Waco, Texas, March 11, 1930.
  As Clyde Barrow, No. 765, arrested police department Middletown, Ohio, March 18, 1930; charge, fugitive.
  As Clyde Barrow, No. 63527, received Texas State Penitentiary, Huntsville, Texas, April 21, 1930, from McLennan County; charge, burglary, theft over and from the person; sentence 14 years (7-2's, cum.); paroled February 2, 1932.

  This man is very dangerous and extreme caution must be exercised by arresting officers as he is wanted in connection with assault and murder of officers.

  Complaint was filed at Dallas, Texas, on May 20, 1933, charging Clyde Champion Barrow and Mrs. Roy Harding, nee Bonnie Parker, with transporting Ford Coupe, Motor No. A-1878100, property of Dr. E. L. Damron of Effingham, Illinois, from Dallas, Texas, to Pawhuska, Oklahoma, on or about September 16, 1932.
  Law enforcement agencies kindly transmit any additional information or criminal record to nearest office, Division of Investigation, U. S. Department of Justice.
  If apprehended, please notify the Director, Division of Investigation, U. S. Department of Justice, Washington, D. C., or the Special Agent in Charge of the office of the Division of Investigation listed on the back hereof, which is nearest your city.
                    (over)   Issued by: J. EDGAR HOOVER, DIRECTOR.

Wanted poster, Clyde Barrow, October 24, 1933. Issued by the Department of Investigation, forerunner to the FBI, for Barrow's only federal crime—interstate transportation of a stolen car.

—Courtesy of Sandy Jones–The John Dillinger Historical Society proceeds of grocery store and gas station robberies.[4] By the first of October, according to the Barrow family, Bonnie and Clyde were in the Kansas City area.[5] The three Texas desperadoes had separated and managed to lie low for over a month, but the calm period was about over. On October 8, 1932, a young man walked into the First State Bank at Cedar Hill, Texas, and robbed it of $1,400. Ray Hamilton was back in Texas and back in business.[6] Three days later, there was a killing in Sherman, Texas. The law said Clyde Barrow did it, but the question is still open to this day.

At 6:30 Tuesday afternoon, October 11, a young man walked into Little's Grocery at the corner of Vaden Street and Wells Avenue in Sherman, Texas. He was about 5'6", 130 pounds, clean-shaven and light-complexioned. He wore a gray felt hat, tan lumber jacket, and dark pants. He looked to be twenty to twenty-five years old. Mr. Little, the owner of the store, had left only minutes before with most of the day's receipts, and two other employees were closing for the day. The young man picked up a loaf of bread as he approached Homer Glaze, who was at the cash register. To the bread he added a half-dozen eggs, and then he asked Howard Hall, who was behind the meat counter, for a dime's worth of lunch meat. He gave Glaze a dollar bill, but as soon as the till was opened, he pulled a pistol.

As the robber was taking about $60 from the register, Hall came out from behind the meat counter and said, "Young man, you can't do that!" The thief said he would show Hall what he could do and ordered Hall and Glaze toward the door that opened out onto Wells Avenue. He seemed to take his anger out on Hall, pushing and kicking him all the way. Finally, at the door, he hit Hall in the head, knocking his glasses out into the street. At this point, the butcher made a grab for the gun and the bandit started shooting. Hall went down on the sidewalk with two bullet wounds. A third shot missed. The bandit then put a fourth shot into Hall as he lay on the ground. Homer Glaze ran out of the store to help his friend and the shooter turned on him. Glaze would have been left bleeding on the sidewalk too, except that, instead of a fifth shot, the pistol snapped. The young man then

turned and ran past Mrs. L. C. Butler, who had seen the whole thing, and down Wells for a block finally turning onto Hazelwood. Two boys saw two men get into a large black sedan and drive away. Howard Hall was taken across the street to St. Vincent's Sanitarium, where he died an hour later. He was fifty-seven years old and left a widow, one son, one brother, and two sisters.

By October 13, thanks to mug shots sent up from Dallas, Clyde Barrow had been identified as the killer of Howard Hall.[7] In addition to Homer Glaze's identification, Walter Enloe, a Grayson County deputy sheriff, claimed that Clyde had entered the county jail earlier on the day of the shooting to visit his brother, L. C., who was a prisoner there.[8]

Clyde Barrow is generally associated with twelve murders during his two years on the run (the killing of Big Ed when he was in prison would make thirteen, and there was a fourteenth, which will be discussed later). He can be shown to have been a shooter, or at least present and therefore an accessory, in ten of them. Of these ten, there is a real possibility that he could have actually fired the fatal shot in seven cases. An eleventh killing, the shooting of Alma, Arkansas, City Marshal Henry Humphrey, will later be shown to actually have been the work of Clyde's brother Buck, with Clyde not present. The only murder attributed to Clyde Barrow in which his participation remains in any serious doubt today is the killing of Howard Hall, just described. How does the evidence stack up?

Clyde is placed at the scene of the crime as Hall's killer only by Homer Glaze's identification of him from a Dallas mug shot. Glaze got a very good look at the killer and gave a detailed description to police before seeing any photos. In spite of that, any policeman or attorney will tell you how reliable eyewitness testimony and identification involving high-stress situations really is. The accurate identification of a face seen over the barrel of a gun as you fear for your life is not as easy as it sounds.

Clyde Barrow, Raymond Hamilton, W. D. Jones, Ted Rogers, and many other criminals of similar age and description were routinely misidentified, mistaken for each other, and their pictures mislabeled in newspapers and magazines. In the killing of J. N. Bucher, Clyde was identified even though he wasn't inside the store but outside in the car. Ted Rogers, who later admitted shooting Bucher, was identified as Raymond Hamilton, who was later convicted of the crime. Clyde was identified by several eyewitnesses in northwest Arkansas as a party to the killing of a lawman and the rape and assault of a housewife, although the bulk of the evidence indicates that he was not present in either case.

The only other identification comes from Deputy Sheriff Walter Enloe. He said that Barrow walked into the county jail at noon on the day of the shooting and asked to visit L. C. Barrow, who was a prisoner there. Enloe said he recognized Barrow from wanted posters. This would, at least, put Barrow in Sherman and not in Kansas, as he later claimed to his family.[9]

Clyde Barrow's involvement in the killing of Howard Hall rests entirely on these two eyewitness reports—one that puts him in the area on the same day, and another that puts him at the scene. Over the years, a version of the event that features a blond woman waiting in a car at the curb for the killer—indicating that Bonnie was involved as well—has been put forward, but it has no support in primary sources.[10]

Homer Glaze's identification stands on its own, but Enloe's claim has at least one weak point. Enloe says that the man he saw in the county jail at noon on October 11 asked to visit L. C. Barrow, Clyde's younger brother, who was held there pending the resolution of a charge of car theft. L. C. Barrow was, indeed, in jail at Sherman on a car theft charge in 1932—he eventually "beat the rap," as Enloe also says. The problem is that on L. C.'s arrest record, now in the hands of the

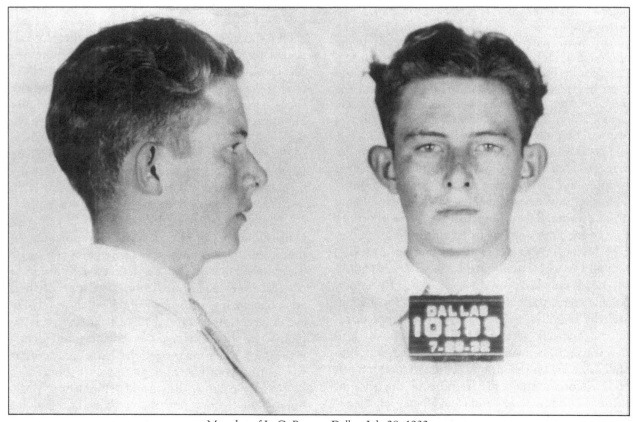

Mug shot of L. C. Barrow. Dallas, July 28, 1932.
—From the collections of the Texas/Dallas History and Archives Division, Dallas Public Library

Barrow family, there is an entry that says, "Dallas, Texas," dated July 1932, and the next entry says, "Sherman, Texas," and is dated early December 1932—two months after Hall's murder. It's possible that the December date indicates a trial or hearing and that L. C. may have been moved from Dallas to Sherman as early as October. It's also possible that the December date is correct and Enloe saw somebody else in the jail that day. The truth may never be known.[11]

Several things about the robbery and shooting also seem to go against Clyde's temperament and way of operating. Clyde preferred to hit stores around noontime when business tended to be slow. The Sherman robber seems to have known to wait until closing in order to get the full day's receipts, indicating a degree of local knowledge. He missed by a just few minutes. Also, Clyde didn't tend to lose his cool or abuse innocent bystanders during his jobs. If he was in danger, Clyde would not have hesitated to shoot, as he proved on many occasions, but contrary to later versions, Hall, the butcher, never threatened the young robber with a meat cleaver or anything else. According to reports at the time, Hall was on the receiving end of all the abuse. In all Clyde's robberies and kidnappings, non-threatening individuals were treated very well. Finally, in all the accounts we have of Clyde contacting anyone who was in jail, he always used other people as messengers instead of going in himself. Of course, nobody is perfectly consistent, and Clyde could have had a bad day and acted out of character. With circumstantial evidence on one side and the departure from Clyde's normal style on the other, there remains enough doubt for the question of who really killed Howard Hall to remain open.

Whether Bonnie and Clyde were involved in the Sherman shooting or not, they were definitely back in Texas and visiting their family within a week or so of the event. They were, of course, questioned by their family about the Sherman killing, but Clyde insisted they had been in Kansas at the time. Clyde would have probably given the same answer, whether it was the truth or not. The killing of a defenseless old man wasn't anything to

be proud of. Shortly after Halloween, they left Texas for Missouri with two new partners, Frank Hardy and Hollis Hale.[12]

Bonnie and Clyde spent most of November 1932 in southwestern Missouri, which was to become one of their favorite areas of operation outside of Texas. Toward the end of the month, they moved into a tourist camp near Carthage and began to plan a bank job.[13] The target Clyde had picked was the Farmers and Miner's Bank in Oronogo, a small town just north of Joplin. Clyde was determined to do this one right, so they took their time. Bonnie was sent in about a week before to examine the inside layout, and Clyde drove over the nearby roads, planning the escape.[14]

About 8:00 A.M. Wednesday morning, November 30, they stole a Chevrolet sedan from Hugo Weidler's home on Lyon Street in Carthage, Missouri, and headed west. Bonnie was set up about a mile west of Oronogo on a country road with the getaway car, a Ford V-8, while Clyde and his two new partners took the Chevy into town.

When Clyde and Frank Hardy entered the bank at about 11:30, there were only two people inside. R. A. "Doc" Norton was the cashier, and his only customer was a Frisco train dispatcher named Farrar.[15] It should have been a cinch. Clyde and Frank entered the bank, produced a pistol and a sawed-off shotgun, and demanded the money. Unfortunately for them, Doc Norton had been down this road before, and he was prepared. Instead of giving up in fright, he dropped down behind the counter, which had been fitted with a steel plate for just such an occasion, and opened fire with a handgun.[16] Clyde blew a couple of holes in the wooden teller's cage with the shotgun but made no dent in the steel plate. To the immense relief of Mr. Farrar, who was in the crossfire, Norton's gun jammed after the third shot and he gave up, but for Clyde and his partners, things continued to go wrong. Hardy broke the glass in the teller's door, cutting his hand in the process, and grabbed what cash he could find—about $100.[17]

Outside, reaction to the gunfire was swift. Jack Watson, a miner working on a derrick across the street, began yelling, "They're robbing the bank!"

Site of the Farmer's and Miner's Bank, Oronogo, Missouri, robbed by Clyde Barrow, Frank Hardy, and Hollis Hale, November 30, 1932—as it looks today. The bank occupied the front of the building, with the entrance being the small white door just above the trunk of the white car. In 1932, the rear of the building was occupied by the local post office and the postmaster's living quarters.

—From the author's collection

Hearing Watson's shouts, Berly Wetsel, owner of a garage, and Carl Capp, his mechanic, picked up hunting rifles and started toward the scene. Seeing this, Hollis Hale, in the getaway car, began honking the horn. As the armed men came out of the bank, Wetsel, Capp, and several other men retreated to the garage and took cover behind a Phillips Petroleum truck. As luck would have it, the route to Bonnie and the real getaway car ran right by Wetsel's garage, so a brief but lively firefight broke out as the Chevrolet went by. Thanks to an amazing display of marksmanship by all concerned, no one on either side was hit. The robbers drove on to meet Bonnie, changed cars, and went back to the tourist court outside Carthage.[18]

Whether it was the disappointing take of the robbery or the experience of dodging bullets, Hollis Hale and Frank Hardy decided they'd had enough, but they didn't bother to tell this to Clyde. They left the tourist court on some excuse and simply kept going. Bonnie and Clyde were on their own with only a few dollars between them. They later told their family that Clyde tried another bank job on his own only to find out that there was no money, since the bank had failed only a few days before. Clyde told this story as a joke on himself, and there is no independent confirmation, so it may or may not have happened. In the end, the couple gave up on southwest Missouri and returned to Texas early in December.[19]

CHAPTER 18

"Deacon" Jones

Back in the Dallas area, Bonnie and Clyde managed to keep out of sight and catch up with their family. A week or so later, word came through the grapevine that Ralph Fults, their partner who was captured with Bonnie at Kemp, Texas, back in April, had been moved to the McKinney, Texas, jail. By the time the news reached Barrow, Fults had been convicted of car theft in connection with his and Clyde's adventures in and around Electra, Texas, in April. By coincidence, Ted Rogers, one of Clyde's partners in the Bucher robbery, was also at McKinney, on an unrelated charge. Both were awaiting transportation back to Huntsville.

On December 19, someone called to Fults, "Your cousin is here to see you." The "cousin" was Bonnie Parker. She and Clyde had come to break him out. Due to the way the keys were held, however, no escape was possible until the next morning. Unfortunately, by morning Fults and Rogers were on their way back to prison. Bonnie and Clyde had missed their chance by a day.[1] In a few days, however, they would have a new partner.

On Christmas Eve, Bonnie and Clyde were working their way toward the Barrows' station on Eagle Ford Road when they spotted Henry Barrow's old truck. L. C. Barrow was driving, and with him was a friend of his, William Daniel Jones. People called him W. D. or "Dub" or "Deacon." His family and the Barrows had been friends ever since they were all living at the campground. W. D's

older brother was one of Clyde's closest friends—before Clyde went to prison. Jones claimed to be sixteen years old on this occasion.[2] When he was captured in November of the following year, he gave his birthdate as May 12, 1916, and gave the same date on his 1950 Social Security application.[3] Some feel that Jones may have understated his age to receive more lenient treatment as a juvenile when he was arrested in November 1933. The Barrow family remember him as being about the same age as L. C. Barrow, who was nineteen in December 1932. Indeed, in the pictures of Jones, taken when he was on the run with Bonnie and Clyde, he looks older than sixteen. In all the police descriptions of Jones as an unknown accomplice, he is said to be twenty to twenty-five years old. Even so, all documentary evidence indicates a 1916 birthdate.

L. C. and W. D. had picked up two girls and a bottle of moonshine earlier in the evening. By the time Clyde met them, they had taken the girls home and almost finished off the whiskey. Jones stayed with Clyde while L. C. left to bring his mother and his sister Marie to the meeting. After the family visit was over, Clyde said he wanted Jones to go with them. He said they had driven a long way and needed someone to keep watch while they slept.[4] Looking back on it years later, Jones would claim that this was the biggest mistake of his life, but at the time he went willingly. He had known Clyde and L. C. Barrow most of his life and had asked to go with them before. Ralph Fults remembered Jones hanging around the Barrow station back in March and April 1932 and said Jones would sometimes steal license plates for Clyde.[5]

With Jones in the car, Clyde drove south to Temple, Texas, and they all checked into a motel. Later that morning, Christmas Day, Jones put on two new tires Clyde had with him,[6] and they went off in search of a store to rob. According to Jones' various statements over the years, he either waited outside while Clyde went in and robbed a grocery store (the story he told *Playboy* in 1968), or he went in with Clyde but lost his nerve and walked out of the store before Clyde could hold it up, earning himself a severe tongue-lashing (the story he told the Dallas County sheriff in 1933). Whichever story is true, "Deacon" Jones' first day as a part of the Barrow gang was not going well, and it was about to get a lot worse.

The three of them continued to drive around Temple in Clyde's Ford V-8 coupe, looking for a score. About 2:30 P.M., they went by a Ford roadster parked in front of 606 South Thirteenth Street. Clyde told W. D. to get out and steal the car. He tried. Even if he was just sixteen years old, this probably wasn't the first car he had boosted, but for some reason he couldn't get it started. Clyde got out to help, and Bonnie took the coupe and parked a short distance away. The newspaper says that Clyde and Jones were actually pushing the car along the street when they were spotted.

Inside the house, Doyle Johnson's in-laws had come over for their granddaughter's first Christmas. Johnson's car was parked outside his house on Thirteenth Street, but he was inside taking a nap. Henry Krauser, his father-in-law, was the one who looked out the window and saw the car thieves. He ran out, followed by his son Clarence and Johnson's wife, Tillie. Seeing the people come out of the house, Clyde and W. D. jumped into the car and tried, once again, to start it. As the Krauser men closed in on the car, however, they got back out and warned them off at gunpoint.

House at 606 South Thirteenth Street, Temple, Texas, as it looks today. On Christmas Day, 1932, this was the home of Doyle Johnson, his wife Tillie, and their infant daughter. This picture was taken from the approximate spot where Johnson was killed by Clyde Barrow and W. D. Jones as he tried to stop them from stealing his car.

—From the author's collection

Clyde was back in the driver's seat, trying again to start the car, when Doyle Johnson, awakened by all the shouting, came out of the house and ran down to the curb. Johnson jumped on the running board, reached in, and grabbed the fellow who was trying to steal his car. Barrow responded by pushing a .38 caliber pistol into the man's side and pulling the trigger. By a great stroke of good luck, Johnson managed to divert the pistol at the last moment so that the bullet went through the left front fender, bounced under the car, and was later found on the ground.

Unfortunately, Johnson's luck lasted only a few more seconds. That was when W. D. Jones fired from across the car. The bullet went through Johnson's neck from right to left, striking the spinal cord. He fell off the side of the car, which had final-ly started, and Clyde and Jones drove away. After all that trouble and bloodshed, they simply drove around the block far enough to get out of sight and abandoned Johnson's car. Doyle Johnson died shortly after the shooting and was buried on December 27. He was survived by his wife of five years, Tillie Krauser Johnson, and their infant daughter. He was twenty-seven years old.[7]

W. D. Jones had been with Bonnie and Clyde less than twenty-four hours and he and Clyde had just killed a man for his car, which they kept for less than five minutes. Bonnie, who had gone unnoticed as she sat in the Ford coupe, followed and picked up the boys at Avenue F and Seventeenth Street. In the words of W. D. Jones thirty-six years later, they "lit a shuck out of town."[8]

CHAPTER 19
"Don't Shoot ... Think of My Babies!"

Doyle Johnson is the only unarmed civilian definitely known to have been killed during any of the Barrows' shootings.[1] Although the Barrow family said that Clyde was furious with Jones for the killing,[2] the fact remains that Clyde had tried his best to shoot Johnson also. The firsthand report clearly says that both men in the car fired at Johnson.[3] W. D. just happened to be the one who hit him. Clyde probably left the impression with his family that there wouldn't have been any shooting if that Jones kid hadn't lost his head, but it just isn't so.

The good news for the outlaws was that they got away clean. On the outskirts of town, Clyde had stopped and sent Jones up a telephone pole to cut the wires.[4] They weren't identified at the time, and for almost a year the police had no idea they were involved. After the Johnson shooting, the three of them went back to the Dallas area, Jones went home and Bonnie and Clyde hid out near Grand Prairie.[5] Their next public appearance would be the result of helping a friend and just plain bad luck.

The friend in need was Raymond Hamilton. Bonnie and Clyde hadn't seen him since they dropped him off in Michigan in September, but they had followed his story. Ray was back in Texas by early October and had hit the bank at Cedar Hill alone on the 8th. After that, he teamed up with Gene O'Dare to rob the Carmen State Bank in LaGrange on November 9 and went back to

Cedar Hill with a partner named Les on November 25. Flush with funds for the moment, Les went back to west Dallas, and Ray and Gene went back to Bay City, Michigan. Hamilton and O'Dare immediately began using their new wealth to impress some of the local young ladies and attracted the attention of the police as well. Tipped off that the two suspects would be at the local roller rink on the evening of December 6, the officers waited until each one was safely established on wheels and then made their move. They caught Ray on the main floor and Gene in the men's room.[6]

Hamilton and O'Dare were back in the Dallas jail by December 14. O'Dare was wanted for bank robbery, but Ray Hamilton was the star prisoner. Ray had been in touch with Clyde through Floyd Hamilton, his older brother, but there wasn't much anybody could do while Ray was in the Dallas jail. Just after Christmas, though, Ray was moved to Hillsboro to answer charges of murder in the Bucher case. The Hillsboro jail was nothing like the one in Dallas, so Clyde and Floyd Hamilton began trying to get some hacksaw blades inside to Ray.[7] About the same time, two other west Dallas boys, Les Stewart, who had been with Raymond Hamilton at Cedar Hill, and Odell Chambless, who happened to be Gene O'Dare's brother-in-law, went into business for themselves and almost got Clyde Barrow killed.

Stewart and Chambless robbed the bank in

Grapevine, Texas, on December 29 and got away with almost $3,000. During the getaway, their car slid off the road, so they split up and continued on foot. Les was arrested a few hours later, but Odell made his way back to west Dallas, where he went to one of Raymond Hamilton's sisters for assistance. Shortly after that, he left town.

Stewart hadn't been as lucky as Chambless, so he tried to cut his losses by telling the authorities everything they wanted to know, including his and Odell's connections with the Hamilton family. Just after New Year's, the Tarrant County District Attorney's Office contacted the new sheriff of Dallas County, R. A. "Smoot" Schmid, and told him what they had discovered. They agreed on a joint operation centered around one of Ray Hamilton's married sisters, Lillian McBride. She lived in west Dallas, on County Avenue, just a few blocks east and around the corner from Henry Barrow's Star Service Station. On the evening of January 6, 1933, everything came together.

Earlier in the day, a Dallas County deputy, Ed Castor, had come by and asked Mrs. McBride a few questions, which made her suspicious. About 11:00 P.M. several more men returned. Since they hoped to catch Chambless for the Grapevine bank job, most of the officers were from Tarrant County. Assistant District Attorney W. T. Evans and Special Ranger J. F. Van Noy were there, along with Fort Worth Deputies Dusty Rhodes and Malcolm Davis. Representing Dallas County was Deputy Sheriff Fred Bradberry

Instead of finding Lillian McBride at home, they found her younger sister, Maggie Fairris, and her children. The lawmen decided to wait anyway. Evans and Davis went around to the back porch while Bradberry, Van Noy, and Rhodes settled down in the front room and began to question Mrs. Fairris. They could tell she was nervous. After a while, she got up and put the kids to bed, and then Deputy Bradberry told her to put out the lights. That was fine, she said, but could she just leave on a small red light—for the children? The deputy agreed. He didn't realize that the little red light was not a child's night-light. It was a signal. Unknown to the lawmen, the Grapevine bank robbery and

Clyde Barrow's plan to help Ray Hamilton break out of the Hillsboro jail were about to come together at Lillian McBride's house, and somebody was going to die.

Just after sundown that same day, Clyde Barrow had knocked on Lillian McBride's door. He wanted to find out if the hacksaw blades, hidden in a small radio, had been delivered to Ray Hamilton. This was the plan he, Raymond and Floyd Hamilton, and Lillian had worked out. Ray had sawed himself out of the jail in McKinney a year before, and he thought he could do it again. Like the lawmen, Clyde also found Maggie Fairris the only one at home, and she was quick to tell him about the visit by police earlier in the day.[8] Clyde said he would try again after midnight, but if the law returned, she should leave a red light on in the window. So far, the plan was working.

Maggie Fairris was indeed worried, just as Deputy Bradberry observed, but she had managed to turn on the red light, so maybe Clyde would get the message and stay away. Just after midnight, a Ford coupe drove slowly down the deserted street and almost stopped, but then went on around the corner. Bradberry's instincts told him this was not a random car, and he insisted that the red light be turned out. Sure enough, in a couple of minutes, the car came back and stopped in front of the house. A small man in a hat and overcoat got out and walked to the front porch. Bradberry told Maggie to open the door, since he thought they had a two-bit thief named Odell Chambless. Maggie Fairris, however, knew exactly who it was, and she guessed what was coming. Knowing the position she was in, her nerve finally broke. As she opened the door, she cried, "Don't shoot . . . Think of my babies!"

Clyde had been caught in a bad position. His instincts, which usually told him when the law was present, had failed him, but his reflexes didn't. He opened his overcoat, swung up a 16-gauge shotgun, and fired from a distance of ten feet—not at Maggie in the doorway, but through the front window at the lawmen. The window sash and most of the glass blew into the room and all the officers hit the floor. Clyde backed off the porch as he tried to pry out the empty shell that had jammed in the shotgun's breech.[9]

Meanwhile, the blast that put the officers in the house on the floor jarred the officers on the back porch into action. Evans and Malcolm Davis raced from the back of the house to the front. Unfortunately for Davis, he won, running up just as Clyde cleared the jam in his shotgun. "Get back!" Clyde shouted as the officers came around the side of the house. Davis kept coming, and Clyde fired. From a few feet away, he couldn't miss, and Davis took the load of buckshot in the chest. Evans hit the ground in time to avoid a second shot in his direction.

In a few seconds, the quiet neighborhood had erupted in chaos. To make matters worse, W. D. Jones, who had just rejoined them, began shooting toward the house from the back seat of the Ford parked at the curb. Men were running, women were screaming, people on both sides were firing into the dark, and Malcolm Davis was dying. The confusion was such that, a couple of minutes later, one of the officers fired on a group of men he thought were more of the outlaws. In fact, they were lifting the mortally wounded Davis into a car to rush him to the hospital. Mercifully, no one was hit.

Bonnie had sense enough to stop Jones, saying he was more likely to hit Clyde or somebody in one of the houses. She later told the family that she knew Clyde was either already dead or trying to get away, so she drove the Ford away and turned west on Eagle Ford Road. After he shot Davis, Clyde ran down the side of the McBride house and headed for the main road. Bonnie saw him running between houses and stopped for him. He took the wheel and began cranking a large siren he used to clear traffic during getaways. As he drove west, he passed his younger sister, Marie, going home on her bicycle. She was coming from the house of her best friend, Audrey Hamilton, another of Ray's sisters.

By daylight, Bonnie, Clyde, and Jones had left Texas for Oklahoma. Before long, they were back in southwest Missouri, where they disappeared for about three weeks. Clyde and W. D. Jones had now killed two men in less than two weeks—one over a car they kept for about five minutes, and the other because Clyde walked into someone else's troubles. Even the plan that sent Clyde to the McBride house fell apart. Two days after the shooting, Raymond was discovered sawing away in his cell at Hillsboro and was sent back to Dallas.[10]

Police reenactment of the killing of Deputy Malcolm Davis at the home of Lillian McBride, 507 County Avenue, January 6, 1933.

—From the collections of the Texas/Dallas History and Archives Division, Dallas Public Library

Lillian McBride's house in west Dallas, as it looks today.

—Courtesy Marie Barrow Scoma and author Phillip W. Steele

CHAPTER 20
The Midnight Ride of Tom Persell

In April 1932 Harry D. Durst began his term as mayor of the city of Springfield, Missouri, and one of the first things he did was appoint some new men to the Springfield police force. One of the first new recruits was a twenty-four-year-old adding machine salesman named Tom Persell. Within ninety days of his appointment, he had chased down and captured two car thieves. By January 1933, Persell was assigned to motorcycle duty.

Just before 6:00 P.M. on January 26, 1933, Officer Persell noticed three people in a Ford V-8 sedan involved in what he suspected was "car spotting" near the Shrine mosque in downtown Springfield. By that he meant they acted like car thieves looking for a victim. One car had already been reported stolen that day. Convinced they were up to no good, the officer followed them. They were headed north, and just as they started over the Benton Street viaduct, Persell motioned for them to pull over. He might have chosen this spot to make it difficult for his suspects to try and escape, but Clyde Barrow was not about to let himself be trapped in the middle of an elevated bridge over a railroad track, so he just kept on going. He didn't speed up to make a getaway, but he insisted on clearing the bridge before stopping. At the north end of the bridge, Clyde turned right onto Pine Street, past the Pitts M.E. Church on the corner, and stopped in the middle of the block.

Persell had dealt with car thieves before, but Clyde Barrow had been involved in four murders and was wanted for three of them plus numerous other crimes. He couldn't allow any law officer to get the "drop" on him. Persell parked his motorcycle and approached the car only to find himself looking down the barrel of a pistol and a sawed-off shotgun. Clyde simply said, "Get in or I'll blow you up." W. D. Jones got out of the car, disarmed Persell, and forced him into the front seat between him and Clyde. Bonnie sat in the back. The abduction was witnessed by several people, but the car pulled away before anyone could intervene—which was fortunate, since Clyde would not have hesitated to shoot if he was threatened.

Picking up a local policeman for a nice ride was obviously not in Clyde's plans, so he just had to improvise. They headed north out of the city, filling up with gasoline at a local station along the way, and drove around the countryside for about seven hours. Persell later gave a pretty good account of their route even though he was under a blanket on the floor part of the time. They simply made a large half-circle north and west of Springfield. With all that time on their hands, the bandits and the policeman had several long conversations. For instance, Persell told them that the reason he had been alert for car thieves was because a tan Ford V-8 had been reported stolen that afternoon by a Mr. Kerr. Yes, they had done that, Clyde told him, but they decided the color was too conspicuous so they left it out in the country.[1] They even told him where to find it, and it was recovered the same day Persell returned.

About five hours into the evening ride, a crisis developed. It seemed that the generator on their Ford had failed, and now the battery had finally run down as well. By this time, they were on the outskirts of the town of Oronogo, a few miles west of Carthage. According to Officer Persell, a short discussion was held on how to solve their car troubles.

Oronogo was familiar territory for Clyde. Back in November, he and Bonnie and two partners had spent a month in the area, hiding out around Carthage and working the whole area. They had, in fact, spent considerable time exploring the Oronogo area prior to robbing the bank less than sixty days before. Clyde remembered that a Chrysler automobile was always parked on the street in front of a certain house. It was decided that W. D. Jones would take Persell with him and steal the battery out of the Chrysler. They walked into town and found the right house, but the car wasn't there.

Roy Ferguson, the car's owner, remembered that cold January night in 1933 very well. "I guess putting that Chrysler up probably saved my life," he said. In his early nineties, Roy may have been the oldest person in Oronogo, Missouri, when he was interviewed by the author (October 2000). His mind was still sharp, and he remembered hearing the policeman tell about Clyde and Jones discussing his car. "That car always stayed parked close to my bedroom window, and I was a light sleeper," he said. "Those old batteries were in the floorboard of the car in those days, so I know I would have heard them trying to

get it out. I would have probably gone out there to see what was going on and got killed." For some reason, Roy had made arrangements to have the car put up in a garage the day before. W. D. and Officer Persell had to settle for the battery out of Wayne Watson's car, which was parked across the street.[2]

When the two men rejoined Bonnie and Clyde and got their car running again, Jones complimented Persell on his assistance in the felony.

Clyde Barrow, 1933.
—Courtesy Sandy Jones–The John Dillinger Historical Society

Persell even shared the job of lugging the heavy battery back. The idea of the officer being so much help in a robbery probably appealed to their sense of humor. The group drove south to Joplin, cruised around for a while, and then headed northwest out of town.

By now, it was about 12:30 in the morning, and they were near a place called Poundstone's Corner. Clyde stopped the car, opened the door, and simply said, "Go on in." Persell got out of the car, but then he turned to Clyde and asked for his sidearm back! "You've got all the guns you need," he said. Persell had recently bought the revolver for half a month's salary and fitted it with custom Staghorn grips, and he hated to lose it. Clyde admired the policeman's nerve, but not enough to give back the pistol. (Three months later, Officer Persell's distinctive weapon would appear on the hood of a car in some of the most famous pictures ever taken of Bonnie

and Clyde.) The three outlaws then drove off west toward Carl Junction, leaving Tom Persell several miles from the nearest phone. The officer walked the distance in about an hour and a half and called his chief in Springfield to send a car for him.

By the next morning, twenty-five-year-old Tom Persell was safely back in Springfield with his pregnant twenty-three-year-old wife, Hazel, and three-year-old daughter—a little tired, but with a great story to tell.[3] As always, a search was mounted, but no trace of the Barrows was found. Bonnie and Clyde would be out of sight for over two months. In fact, the next member of the Barrow gang to make a public appearance was older brother Buck.

Clyde Barrow the "desperado" with the tool of his trade—a .45 automatic in his belt under his left arm, a Browning automatic rifle in his hands, and another BAR and a "Whippit Gun" (automatic shotgun) leaning against his favorite car, a Ford V-8. Note the second .45 automatic on the hood and Clyde's coat covering the license plate. 1933.

—Courtesy Marie Barrow Scoma and author Phillip W. Steele

Clyde Barrow the "gentleman" and his faithful Ford V-8. Clyde disliked getting his hands dirty and liked to dress the part of a well-to-do young businessman. He was once mistaken for a bank examiner during one of his robberies. Note the hat covering the license plate. 1933.

—Courtesy Marie Barrow Scoma and author Phillip W. Steele

CHAPTER 21

Joplin

During the first year of Clyde Barrow and Bonnie Parker's outlaw career, Clyde's older brother was cooling his heels in the Texas State Prison at Huntsville, following their exploits as best he could. It was family pressure that put Buck Barrow back behind the walls at Huntsville, in December 1931, but his mother and his wife were working to see that he didn't stay there any longer than necessary. As soon as Buck was back inside, Cumie and Blanche went to work, just like they had for Clyde. It took over a year, but on March 22, 1933, Governor Miriam "Ma" Ferguson granted him a full pardon.[1]

Blanche has been credited by the family with the maneuver that may have finally gotten her husband released. According to their stories, Blanche made her way down to Austin to speak with Governor "Ma" Ferguson, bringing along three children, and apparently pregnant with a fourth. These "children" of hers must have touched Ma's motherly heart, because the governor got to work on Buck's case. The three children were said to be products of a previous marriage, with the one she was "carrying" being Buck's.

Evidently, Governor Ferguson didn't bother to check out the story. First, Blanche had no children from a previous marriage. Second, Buck had already been in jail for over a year, so any child with which she was "pregnant" could not have been his. Marie Barrow said Blanche borrowed three children from

someone and padded herself to look pregnant in order to impress "Ma" Ferguson with her dire straits. Whether it happened exactly that way or not, Buck was released shortly thereafter.[2]

Buck immediately returned to his family in west Dallas, and naturally, Blanche and the Barrow family were overjoyed to have him back home. Not only was Buck no longer in prison, but the fact that he was pardoned meant that no crime from his past could come back to haunt him. He had been given a new lease on life. He now had a good, supportive wife and the knowledge that his old life could be put behind him. His release was a bright spot in a very dark time for the Barrow family, but their joy was to be short-lived. Immediately upon getting home, Buck began talking about going to see Clyde.

Beginning with *Fugitives* in 1934, the reason given for Buck's desire to visit Clyde was to try and convince Clyde to give himself up. The family said that Buck felt a sense of guilt for his own part in bringing Clyde to his present condition.[3] Marie Barrow even claimed that trying to get Clyde to surrender was part of the deal to get Buck's pardon,[4] but there is no confirmation of this from other sources. On the other hand, Ralph Fults knew Buck for the last ten months Barrow was in prison, talked with him often about his exploits with Clyde, and never heard him express any guilt feelings.[5] Blanche also said, in an interview late in her life, that Buck didn't feel particularly guilty about Clyde's situation.[6] There may actually be some truth in both views. Buck could have had mixed feelings and given whatever impression his audience expected—prison buddy or family member. Regardless, everybody Buck talked to told him the same thing. They said that getting Clyde to give himself up was impossible and, if Buck was found with him, he would go down too.[7] Unfortunately, they were right.

There's no way of knowing whether Buck actually believed there was a chance to convince Clyde to surrender (Clyde was wanted for murder, kidnapping, and uncounted numbers of car thefts and robberies at this point)[8] or if he was just using that as an excuse to get back together with his brother. He insisted that he had to see Clyde and began to make arrangements. It was agreed that they would meet somewhere near Fort Smith, Arkansas.[9] The main thing Buck and Blanche needed was some transportation. In the past, Buck would have just gone out and stolen a car, but he was not a criminal anymore, so he had to do it the old-fashioned way. He went to see an old friend, Carl Beaty, and made a deal for a 1929 Marmon. Beaty later told police he took two Ford coupes in trade, and $100 cash. Where Buck, seven days out of prison, got two Ford coupes was not explained.[10] Some sources say Buck's sister Nell loaned him the cash.[11]

Blanche, of course, went with Buck to meet Clyde. She must have been a little apprehensive, but she wasn't the terrified little wife, crying for two days straight before they left, as she is pictured in *Fugitives* and most other works afterward.[12] Besides, Blanche had a new companion to keep her company—a little white dog named "Snowball." Buck wasn't an escaped convict now and shouldn't have needed to make fast getaways anymore, but Blanche was training the dog to run to the car on command, just in case.[13]

Buck made the deal for the Marmon on March 29 and he, Blanche, and Snowball left Dallas late that day or early the next. They met Clyde, Bonnie, and the ever-present W. D. Jones outside Fort Smith and drove north to Joplin, Missouri, where they began looking for a place to stay. On March 31, two women went to Smith's Garage in south Joplin and talked to Mr. and Mrs. Ellis Smith about a furnished house for rent at 2314 Virginia Avenue. The ladies must have liked it, because they gave the Smiths a month's rent in advance to hold it for them. The next day, however, the women returned and asked for the money back. They had decided not to take it. One of the two women—the redhead—was later identified from photos as Bonnie Parker.[14]

On April 1, a man and two women called on Paul Freeman about a property he had for rent in the new Freeman Grove subdivision. One of the ladies gave their names as Mr. and Mrs. W. L. Callahan, from Minnesota, and Mrs. Callahan's sister. She said Mr. Callahan was a civil engineer. They wanted to rent the apartment over the garage of Mr. Freeman's house at 3347 Oak Ridge Drive. From the way Mr. Freeman reported it to the newspaper, Blanche did most of the talking. With his limited education, Buck probably would not have been very convincing as a civil engineer, so the less he said, the better.[15] The main house faced west on the corner of Thirty-fourth Street and Oak Ridge Drive, but the apartment and driveway faced south on Thirty-fourth Street.

The apartment in Freeman's Grove had a lot to recommend it as a hideout. It was made of stone, it was two short blocks from a main highway, and it was close to the Oklahoma, Kansas, and Arkansas state lines. It only had one drawback—no back door. There were spaces for two cars underneath the apartment, but one of them was taken by the tenant in the main house, a salesman named Harold Hill. At the time, Buck and Clyde had three cars between them, and since two of them were stolen, they didn't want to leave them out on the street. Buck went to Mr. Hill and rented his half of the garage. An alley behind the apartment provided access to a garage for the house next door, and eventually, Buck went to Sam Langford and rented that garage also. His Marmon was kept there.[16]

The five of them settled in for what would be one of the longest periods of peace and comfort in Bonnie and Clyde's two years on the run. It lasted almost two weeks. The neighbors noticed they kept their curtains closed all the time and the lights on late at night but said they were generally quiet and caused no trouble. They would call a local grocery for food but would always meet the delivery boy at the door. Occasionally they would go to the grocery themselves, and the owner, Clyde Snodgrass, remembered them as nice, ordinary people.[17]

From what the family heard later, Buck really did try to get Clyde to consider giving himself up. If there was anybody Clyde might have listened to, it was probably his big brother. Buck's main argument seems to have been the experience of Clyde's one-time partner, Raymond Hamilton. Since being captured in Michigan five months before, Ray was being shuttled around from court to court, seemingly put on nonstop trial for the crimes that he and Clyde had been accused of committing during 1932. Hamilton was eventually given the following sentences: twenty-five years for the Neuhoff Packing Company robbery; thirty years for the Cedar Hill bank holdups; ten years for a couple of car thefts; ninety-nine years for the LaGrange bank job; and, finally, ninety-nine years for the Bucher murder, the only charge of which he was innocent. In addition, a three-year suspended sentence was reinstated.

Hamilton's sentences totaled 266 years, but Buck emphasized to Clyde that Raymond had not received any death sentences. Buck also pointed out that Hamilton had not been extradited to Oklahoma to face charges concerning the murder of Eugene Moore and the shooting of Sheriff Maxwell. Buck did agree that almost four lifetimes in prison was pretty bad, but he argued that it was still not as bad as death by either the electric chair or a police bullet. Besides, there was always the chance that something could be worked out. Clyde had only served two years of what could have been a fourteen-year sentence, and Buck served less than half his original term even though he escaped once.

Clyde listened to Buck's reasoning and responded that there would still be no chance of anything but the electric chair for him. It was true that Raymond Hamilton had evaded the ultimate sentence, but Clyde knew that he had additional capital charges against him above and beyond what Raymond had faced, plus one the law hadn't even charged him with yet (Clyde and W. D. still had not been connected with the Doyle Johnson murder). There was the Howard Hall killing in Sherman, the Malcolm Davis shooting in west Dallas, and Eugene Moore in Stringtown, Oklahoma. Clyde said he wasn't even in Texas when Hall was shot, but he was definitely there when Davis was killed in Dallas and when Moore was killed in Oklahoma.

According to the family, the two brothers debated this issue every day, and Clyde resisted any notion of surrender or leaving the country. He was also starting to get restless. Joplin in 1933 was known as very "outlaw friendly," but they had been there for almost two weeks. To remain that long in any one place was pushing their luck. Clyde felt that it was time Buck and Blanche packed up and returned to Texas while he, Bonnie, and W. D. got back out on the road.[18]

Despite Clyde's misgivings, their visit had seemingly been a quiet one. The five of them didn't have much to do with their neighbors or go out of their way to make anyone's acquaintance due to their status as fugitives from the law, but the people Clyde and Buck did deal with in that neighborhood were treated with consideration. There was a little girl named Beth who made friends with Bonnie. Beth visited their apartment a few times and even had supper with them one day.[19] There was also a law enforcement officer, Mack Parker, who lived in that neighborhood and had a sideline of providing securing services for the area. For a dollar a month, he would make frequent patrols of the area, watching for any suspicious activity. This patrolman called on Clyde and his group at the apartment. The Barrow brothers agreed to accept his services and paid the fee. You could never tell what desperadoes might be around.[20]

Clyde and Bonnie always had to practice caution. Either Bonnie or Blanche would meet the delivery people with their groceries and clean laundry at the door of the apartment. The two girls would assume the whole burden of the grocery bags and the laundry bundles themselves and would not let the delivery people carry them upstairs. One of the laundry delivery boys later recalled that Blanche was upset about something when she met him at the door of their apartment. At that time the delivery boy attributed no significance to Blanche's emotional state and felt it wasn't his business.[21]

Much information regarding the brothers' time in Joplin came from other family members, but, once again, there were things that the family didn't know. During the time Clyde and Buck were in Joplin (March 31–April 13), there were several robberies in the area. Buck may have been trying to talk Clyde into surrendering, but he seems to have been helping Clyde and W. D. raise money as well. Clyde and Buck were tentatively identified in connection with robberies of a tourist camp, a grocery store, and of the Neosho Milling Company. Harry Bacon, who with his wife was held captive while the milling company safe was robbed, was particularly impressed with Clyde's "whippit gun," hung under his right arm, secured by a zipper, and covered by his coat.[22]

Several things finally led to the outlaws' discovery. The people in the neighborhood became suspicious of the out-of-state cars seen at the apartment and notified Sergeant G. B. Kahler of the Missouri State Highway Patrol.[23] Clyde also accidently fired a BAR in the garage, which must have startled the neighborhood.[24] Before Sergeant Kahler could follow up on the car report, he received a call from a man who was concerned about the people living in the Thirty-fourth Street apartment. Somewhat melodramatically, he said they seemed like "frightened animals."[25] More importantly, one of the cars there matched the description of the car seen at the Neosho Milling Company robbery.[26] Sergeant Kahler contacted the Joplin City Police, but they had heard nothing about it.

Kahler made some inquires of his own, and a picture came together of people with something to hide.[27] His best guess was a bootlegging operation. He told Joplin City Chief of Detectives Ed Portley that he wanted to raid the place, and Portley agreed to assign two of his men, Tom DeGraff and

Harry McGinnis, to assist. Kahler brought W. E. Grammar, one of his state patrolmen, along. There just remained one detail—a jurisdictional problem. The city of Joplin had grown to the extent that some of the south suburbs were over the county line. The Freeman Grove subdivision was one of these. Thirty-second Street formed the southern limit of Jasper County, which contained Joplin proper. The house on Thirty-fourth Street was two blocks south of the line, so the search warrant would have to be issued in Newton County. Because of this, they had to enlist a Newton County official, Wes Harryman, constable of Shoal Creek Township, to serve the warrant. By the time they were ready, it was almost 4:00 P.M. on Thursday, April 13.

The family reported that it was on that same morning that Buck finally gave up on trying to talk Clyde into surrendering and agreed to go back to Texas, but he said he wanted another day in which to pack and to get their car ready for the return trip. Clyde, meanwhile, had already begun to make his own plans to leave Joplin. Among other things, he told W. D. Jones to take their Ford coupe (the one used in the Neosho robbery) and replace it. On April 12, Earl Stanton of Miami, Oklahoma, lost a perfectly good Ford roadster, and now it sat in the Joplin apartment garage.[28]

Just before 4:00 P.M., Clyde decided he would take W. D. Jones out "scouting" in their new roadster. Maybe he thought they would stay a few days longer, or maybe they needed some money for the trip. The family's story, from 1934 on, was that shortly after Clyde and W. D left the apartment, Clyde had a premonition that something was going to happen and went back.[29] Maybe so, but the more likely explanation is that they had a low tire and the car was handling badly.[30] Whatever the reason, Clyde and W. D. pulled back into the garage just as Sergeant Kahler's two-car liquor raid turned west off Main Street onto Thirty-fourth— two blocks away. What happened next happened quickly. Both sides were caught by surprise.

Kahler and Grammar were leading in a state police car. They pulled up to the curb facing west, just past the double driveway, and saw a man trying to pull one of the garage doors closed.[31] At this moment, the second car, driven by Tom DeGraff, came up, saw the same thing, and turned into the drive and up to the door. DeGraff later testified that he told Harryman, who was seated next to him in the front seat, "Get in there as quickly as you can, before they close that door."[32]

Clyde and W. D. had just gotten out and discovered the low tire and were closing the door when the police car pulled up and blocked the driveway. When an officer jumped out of the car with his gun drawn, their response was automatic. One of them blasted him with a shotgun. Harryman got off one shot in return and fell in the garage door. He was hit with ten buckshot in the right shoulder and neck, cutting two arteries, and bled to death almost immediately. Just as Harryman went down, Harry McGinnis jumped out of the left rear door and ran to the garage door. He fired three times through a pane of glass before the sawed-off shotgun got him too. He was hit in the left side and the face, and his right arm was almost severed at the elbow.[33] All this happened in the time it took Tom DeGraff to stop the car, set the brake, and slide out the left-hand door. He fired two shots and ran to the other side of the police car in time for McGinnis to fall in front of him. He fired two more shots, picked up McGinnis' pistol, and ran down the east side to the rear of the building.[34]

As soon as Officer DeGraff disappeared down the side of the building, Clyde turned his attention to the other two officers. Grammar, in the passenger's seat of the state police car, had jumped out as the shooting started and run down the west side of the building, where he met DeGraff in the back alley. W. D. Jones had been hit in the stomach (probably from one of McGinnis' bullets) and was on the way upstairs, so, for the moment, it was just Clyde and Officer Kahler trading shots.

Upstairs, Buck was taking a nap, Blanche was playing solitaire, and Bonnie was cooking red beans and cornbread. When the shooting started, there was a frozen moment when they wondered if Clyde had fired another shot by accident, and then they knew. What followed was a mad scramble. Buck, after telling the women to run for the car, headed down to the garage, passing Jones on the

stairs.[35] He picked up a shotgun and joined Clyde at the garage door.

Kahler had kept Clyde occupied with pistol fire from behind the state police car, but just as Buck arrived, the officer fired his fifth round and ran west toward the main house to reload. Clyde stepped out of the garage and fired a load of buckshot at him. Kahler, ducking to avoid the shot, tripped and fell as the buckshot hit the corner of the house. Clyde thought he had knocked the sergeant down and immediately began looking for the other two officers. Buck came out of the garage at this point, and Kahler heard Clyde ask him, "Where'd that other fellow go?" With Clyde's attention diverted, Kahler took aim and fired his last round, which forced Clyde and Buck back in the garage. Kahler testified that he thought he hit one of the men.[36]

Sergeant Kahler had just fired the last shot from the police in the fight, but he didn't know it at the time. He began to reload and prepare for the next round. Meanwhile, there was a tense moment behind the apartment as DeGraff ran toward Officer Grammar in the alley. Hearing someone behind him, Grammar turned and almost shot the Joplin policeman.[37] DeGraff then said, "For God's sake, call the station." Grammar went to the main house and called for help, and DeGraff began reloading.[38]

A few moments after Kahler's last shot, the women went down to the garage, followed by Jones, who was bleeding on the floor.[39] Clyde and Jones pulled back the other garage door, where a Ford B-400 V-8 sedan was parked, and told the women to pile inside. Buck stood with a shotgun and watched for the policemen to come back.[40] Jones, with Clyde and even Blanche helping, tried to push the police car blocking the driveway, but they couldn't release the parking brake. They all went back inside the garage, and it was then that Blanche realized Snowball's training hadn't worked. Instead of running to the car, the little dog ran outside and down the street. To the astonishment of everybody on both sides, Blanche calmly walked out of the garage and into the street, calling for her dog.[41]

Clyde decided they would have to push the police car with the Ford. Just then, Buck saw officer McGinnis lying on the driveway. Before getting in the car, Buck moved the wounded man so he wouldn't get run over as they drove away.[42] It was a fine gesture, but the officer would die of his wounds anyway later that evening. With the way clear, Clyde rammed the police car, which rolled across the street and into a tree. They picked up Blanche—Snowball was long gone—and headed east to Main Street and then southwest toward Oklahoma. They were last seen when they took a curve too fast and almost went into a creek at a place called Reding's Mill bridge.[43]

Contrary to the scene painted by most authors of this incident, the "Barrow gang," as they called them, didn't make their getaway in a hail of gunfire. The later testimony of all the officers present reveals that the policemen fired exactly fourteen shots in the gun battle (Harryman one, McGinnis three, DeGraff four, Kahler six, Grammar none), with Kahler firing the final shot before the getaway car was even out of the garage.[44] This is why Blanche could stroll down the street looking for her dog and Buck could move the wounded officer out of the way without being shot. The gunfight was already over, although it had certainly been deadly enough while it lasted. The Barrows probably fired at least as many rounds as the police, making thirty-plus shots fired in all. Minutes after the Barrows escaped, other police and medical units arrived. Harryman was dead at the scene. McGinnis was taken to Saint John's Hospital, where he died later that night.[45]

When the Barrows fled, they left almost everything they had.

As the police searched the area, they found all sorts of things. They found seven weapons, including a BAR, a guitar, a money bag from a Springfield bank, five diamonds stolen from the Neosho Milling Company, and some of Bonnie's poetry—the latest version of "Suicide Sal." The jackpot was in Blanche's purse and her camera.[46]

Blanche loved to take pictures and almost always had a camera with her. In the apartment was one of her cameras that Bonnie and Clyde had

Bonnie and Clyde—late March 1933. Picture from film recovered at Joplin. Bonnie mimics stickup with one of Clyde's whippit guns. Note stump of cigar in Clyde's left hand. Minutes later, as a joke, Bonnie will borrow the stogie and pose for the famous photo that marked her as a cigar-smoking "gun moll."

—Courtesy the Bob Fischer/Renay Stanard collection

borrowed while Buck was still in prison. Just before they came to Joplin, Clyde, Bonnie, and W. D. Jones took turns photographing themselves posed with their weapons beside the 1932 Ford V-8 B-400 two-door sedan they had just stolen. The film was still in the camera. Police rushed the film to the photo department of the Joplin *Globe,* which developed the soon-to-be famous set of images. They were even able to trace the car due to the license plate (1933 Texas 587-956), which could be read in several shots. It belonged to a Marshall, Texas, insurance salesman named Bob Roseborough. Clyde had stolen the car from Roseborough's front yard just before Buck was released from prison. It was found several weeks later near Vinita, Oklahoma.[47]

Even worse for Buck Barrow were the contents of Blanche's purse, which included their marriage license, Buck's pardon from prison, and the papers to the Marmon. As soon as these were found, Buck became the focus of the investigation. In the newspaper coverage, Buck was made out to be the leader of the "gang," with Clyde only mentioned in passing. For several days, they weren't even sure there had been a third man. From that moment on, Buck's life as a free man was over.

According to the Barrow family, Clyde drove from Joplin to Amarillo, Texas, before stopping for medicine to treat Jones' wound. To the rest of the world, they had simply disappeared. They would not be sighted again for two weeks.

Bonnie, the hard-smoking, hard-shooting gun moll. Of all her pictures, this one, taken as a joke, did more to create her image in the mind of the public and the law than any other. What bothered Bonnie most was not that she was shown holding a gun but that people actually believed she smoked cigars, which she felt would have been vulgar and unladylike. She smoked cigarettes.

—Courtesy the Bob Fischer/Renay Stanard collection

William Daniel Jones. This picture was taken in late March 1933. The car is a 1932 Ford B-400 Clyde had just stolen in Marshall, Texas. The pistol hanging upside down from the hood ornament was taken from motorcycle patrolman Tom Persell in Springfield, Missouri, two months earlier. This picture was one of a group found by police at Joplin, Missouri, April 13, 1933.

—Courtesy Marie Barrow Scoma and
author Phillip W. Steele

Buck and Blanche in happier times.
—Courtesy Marie Barrow Scoma
and author Phillip W. Steele

WANTED FOR MURDER
JOPLIN, MISSOURI

F.P.C. 29 - MO. 9
26 U 00 6

CLYDE CHAMPION BARROW, age 24, 5'7", 130#, hair dark brown and wavy, eyes hazel, light complexion, home West Dallas, Texas. This man killed Detective Harry McGinnis and Constable J.W. Harryman in this city, April 13, 1933.

BONNIE PARKER   CLYDE BARROW   CLYDE BARROW

This man is dangerous and is known to have committed the following murders: Howard Hall, Sherman, Texas; J.N. Bucher, Hillsboro, Texas; a deputy sheriff at Atoka, Okla; deputy sheriff at West Dallas, Texas; also a man at Belden, Texas.

The above photos are kodaks taken by Barrow and his companions in various poses, and we believe they are better for identification than regular police pictures.

Wire or write any information to the

Police Department,
Joplin, Missouri.

Wanted poster issued by the Joplin, Missouri, Police Department after the April 13, 1933, shootout that killed two police officers.

—Courtesy the Texas Ranger Hall of Fame and Museum, Waco, Texas

Below Left: Dewayne L. Tuttle, current owner of the property at 3347 Oak Ridge Drive. Mr. Tuttle is standing in about the spot where Officer Wes Harriman fell.

Below Right: Garage apartment at 3347 Oak Ridge Drive, Joplin, Missouri, as it looks today. This was the scene of the shootout that left two police officers dead on April 13, 1933. Bonnie and Clyde, Buck and Blanche, and W. D. Jones were living upstairs when they were surprised by police investigating what they thought was a bootleg whiskey operation.

—From the author's collection

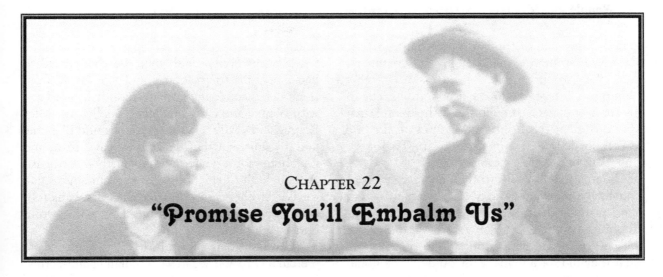

CHAPTER 22
"Promise You'll Embalm Us"

Two weeks after the shootout in Joplin, the Barrows surfaced. The nice new Ford B-400 they drove away from Joplin was long gone, and the beat-up Ford sedan they now had was on its last legs. That's why they were cruising the streets of Ruston, a quiet university town in northwest Louisiana. It was 1:20 P.M. on Thursday, April 27, 1933, when they spotted a Chevrolet parked in front of a boardinghouse on North Trenton Street. The fact that Clyde would consider stealing something other than his standard Ford V-8 shows how desperate their car situation was.[1] W. D. Jones was sent out to steal the Chevy, found the keys in the ignition, and started to drive off. Unfortunately, the owner, H. D. Darby, saw the whole thing, ran out of the boardinghouse, and chased Jones to the corner. Sophia Stone saw the whole thing too and offered Darby the use of her car. He jumped in, and the two of them started after the thief. Had they known that the young man they were chasing was probably armed, was the veteran of two full-fledged gunfights with police, and had participated in four murders in the past five months, they might have had second thoughts.

A few miles north of Ruston, Darby spotted his car as it entered the town of Dubach and turned west toward Homer. They followed through the even smaller town of Hico and then decided to give up the chase. For the two of them, however, the fun was just beginning. As they turned around

and started back, they were flagged down, near Foster's Store in Hico, by a car with four people in it. The driver asked Darby if he had seen a black Chevy go by. Darby replied that he had, then got out and walked over to the other car. The man asked him, "Why are you following that car?" to which Darby replied "Because it's my car!" At that point, things got a little ugly.

The stolen Chevrolet had been part of Clyde's plan to rob a bank in Ruston that day. Now, because of this fellow, everything was fouled up. W. D. had outrun Darby and Miss Stone, all right, but he had outrun Clyde too. Now Clyde had lost both Jones and the new car on the back roads of rural Louisiana. No car, no W. D., no bank robbery. For one of the very few times in dealing with unarmed civilians, Clyde lost his temper. He jumped out of the car and knocked Darby down with a gun butt. Seeing how things were going, Bonnie ran to the car and dragged Miss Stone out, tapping her lightly on the head with a pistol also. With Buck and Blanche, there were now six of them, squeezed into the rickety Ford, when they drove off toward Bernice, Louisiana.

Clyde was steamed. He kept yelling that he was going to kill them—and Buck would taunt him, "What are you waiting for?" Lucky for Darby and Stone, the moment passed and cooler heads prevailed, but the victims' fear of death was only slightly reduced. If Clyde didn't shoot them, the ruined suspension of the Ford, the country roads, and Clyde's almost suicidal driving convinced them they would probably die in a car wreck. Things were constantly flying around the inside of the car as it plowed through the potholes and ruts. Miss Stone, in the front seat, wound up holding several loaded BAR clips in her lap. They kept falling out of the glove compartment.[2]

Bonnie liked to talk to the people they occasionally took for rides, and now she wanted to find out all about their guests. Before long, she was chatting with the two prisoners like old friends. In the course of the conversation, she asked them what they did for a living. Miss Stone was a home demonstration agent, but Darby had a more serious trade that, for some bizarre reason, struck Bonnie funny. He was a mortician. Bonnie laughed and said, "I know we'll get it sooner or later, and you'd probably enjoy embalming us. Promise you will."[3] On that happy note, they drove across the state line into southern Arkansas.

Later, on a country road outside of Waldo, Arkansas, Clyde stopped the car and told them to get out. At first the Ford drove away, but then it stopped and backed up. Too scared to run, Darby and Stone just stood there. "You're probably farther from home than you planned on going. Call the sheriff. He'll give you a ride home," Clyde said. Out the window sailed a $5 bill, and the Ford drove away. The two got a ride into Waldo and then on to Magnolia, where they finally contacted the sheriff. Darby's brother-in-law came and drove them back to Ruston.

At this point, what the law and the newspapers knew as "the Barrow gang" split up. In Waldo, Buck and Blanche stole themselves a car and took off for Oklahoma to see some of Blanche's relatives. Bonnie and Clyde spent another day trying to find W. D. Jones—without success—and then headed back to Texas. Jones was nowhere near Magnolia, anyway. Darby's car was found the next day near McGee, Arkansas, over 100 miles to the east.[4]

The whereabouts of the gang members for the next month and a half is open to question, but there are enough clues available to give us a good idea. The Barrow family says that Jones went back

to Dallas to try and hook up with Bonnie and Clyde again. They claim that everybody tried to persuade him to go home and stay away from them.[5] He kept trying anyway and finally got back with Bonnie and Clyde in early June. By early May, Bonnie and Clyde had rejoined Buck and Blanche, and it seems that they decided to leave Texas and Oklahoma for a while, roaming farther northeast. Although the evidence is largely circumstantial, the two brothers probably tried their first bank robbery together, not in Texas, but in a small town in northern Indiana.

On Thursday, May 11, 1933, two men were seen in a Ford V-8 sedan with Indiana plates, cruising the streets of Lucerne, Indiana, just north of Logansport.[6] Later that evening, the two men broke into the Lucerne State Bank and were hiding on top of the vault when the first two employees came to work Friday morning. Everett Gregg and Lawson Selders arrived about 7:30 A.M. and began to prepare the bank for the day's business. Some minutes later, Gregg went into the vault and left Selders alone out front. With the men now separated, one of the bandits yelled, "Put 'em up," and threatened the bookkeeper with a pistol. Instead of freezing, Selders ran for the vault while the bandit fired at him but missed. Just about this time, Ed Frushour walked past the bank and, hearing the shot, looked in the front window. The robbers yelled at Frushour to come inside, but he turned and ran, and they fired four shots through the window, almost hitting a passing mail carrier. The bandits' plans had fallen apart.

Like many small-town banks, the vault at Lucerne contained firearms for just such an occasion, so by now, Cashier Gregg had a rifle trained on the entrance to the vault. The two bandits must have suspected this, because they made no attempt to enter, but, probably out of frustration, they did fire seven shots at the outside of the vault and nine more into the back wall and windows of the bank.

As soon as the shooting started, two women drove a Ford V-8 sedan up to the rear door of the bank. They had been seen in town, waiting in the car, for the last hour, and now the two would-be bank robbers joined them and the group headed

out of town, firing as they went. As the car rounded a corner, Ura Witters tried to wreck them by
throwing a large chunk of wood into the street.
The driver had to swerve through someone's lawn
to avoid the log but straightened out and left town,
pursued by two civilians. The two men followed
the bandits as far west as Winamac but then lost
the trail. During this fiasco, about forty shots were
fired, two women bystanders were slightly wounded, and two pigs were killed when the bandits
drove through a herd of swine while making their
getaway. No money was taken from the bank.[7]

There were probably hundreds of bank robberies in the Midwest that hot summer of 1933,
and there was no shortage of criminals, famous and
unknown, to pin them on. The main thing about
the Lucerne robbery that points to Clyde and Buck
Barrow is the very unusual detail of the local man
trying to stop them by throwing a log into the
street. A year later, in *Fugitives*, Clyde's sister Nell
tells exactly the same story but combines it with
details of the next robbery done by the brothers a
week after Lucerne.[8] It's easy to understand how
she could have gotten this confused, since the two
robberies were almost carbon copies of each other.

Sometime during the night of May 18, 1933, a
car containing two men and two women stopped
behind the First State Bank of Okabena, Minnesota.
The two men got out and the women drove to the
outskirts of town to wait. The men broke into the
bank through a window and were waiting when
R. M. Jones, the assistant cashier, arrived the next
morning. Several other people came in during the
robbery and were put on the floor. The two men
took a little over $1,400 and left through the rear
door, where the women were waiting. One of the
men in the bank had managed to trip the alarm, so
the owner of the adjoining hardware store was
alerted and was able to get off three shots at the
robbers as they ran to the car. One of the men fired
back with what was described as a machine gun.

The local paper provided details of a getaway down
the main street, with the desperadoes spraying bullets in all directions. It also stated that there were
two women in the getaway car and that one of
them was firing as they left town.[9]

Fugitives, Cumie Barrow, and several other
sources all say that Clyde and Buck did the
Okabena job. Clyde's mother even gives the
take—$1,600, with $700 of that in silver dollars,
close to the newspaper's figure.[10] However, two
brothers, Floyd and Anthony Strain, and
Anthony's common-law wife, Mildred, were arrested and convicted of the Okabena robbery. All
three protested their innocence, and in view of the
evidence, they were probably right.[11]

After the Okabena robbery, the four current
members of "the Barrow gang" drove south to
Texas and contacted their families to arrange a
meeting. In the account in *Fugitives*, Clyde's sister
Nell is the narrator and describes a meeting near
Commerce, Texas, three days after Mother's Day,
which would put it on May 17, 1933.[12] Given the
details of the Okabena job, that date can't be correct. Most likely, the family meeting took place
May 22 or later, and details of both the Lucerne
and Okabena robberies were combined into the
story by the *Fugitives* author. At this meeting,
Bonnie and Clyde told the family their version of
all the things that had happened since Buck got
out of prison. Even given the problems with
Fortune's account in many places, it is interesting
reading.[13]

The four fugitives left the family meeting
together, and there are stories of them traveling as
far as Florida. Whatever the truth, by the first of
June they had separated again, with Bonnie and
Clyde returning to the Dallas area and Buck and
Blanche probably going to southeastern Oklahoma,
where Blanche's father lived. Before they parted,
they agreed on a rendevous at a place in western
Oklahoma the second weekend in June.

CHAPTER 23
Crash and Burn

The sun had set on the Texas Panhandle the evening of June 10, 1933, and the breeze coming in the window of Clyde Barrow's stolen 1933 Ford V-8 coupe was beginning to cool down a little. Just as Clyde was becoming a hunted man, Ford had introduced a new sixty-five-horsepower V-8 engine for its 1932 models. The two-door coupe was sportier and had enough room for him and Bonnie. If there were more people traveling with him, the four-door sedan was the better choice, but with the steel body and the V-8 engine that would push them up to seventy-five miles an hour, either model was equal to the best he was likely to be up against from the other side of the law. Bonnie was Clyde's love, but his car was his life—even before his guns. By now Clyde was carrying a small arsenal with him at all times, but he knew one thing: He might shoot some of them, but if he couldn't run, he was dead—as simple as that.

Clyde's love of fast cars might have begun as teenage "macho," as it does with a lot of guys, but now it was all business. In Clyde's world of 1933 law enforcement, a fast car and driving skills could make all the difference. The places he operated and his choice of hideouts show that Clyde was acutely aware of jurisdictional lines. If he had to jump and run, he was almost always just a short distance from a county or state line, and with few radio cars to coordinate the pursuit between authorities, this gave Clyde precious minutes of extra time.

Unfortunately for the law, Clyde Barrow with a few minutes' head start almost anywhere in the Southwest or Midwest was as good as gone. He had practically unlimited confidence in his ability to outdrive them all—and with good reason. In twenty-five months on the run, involving escapes from at least fifteen shootings or gunfights, five kidnappings, and uncounted numbers of robberies, he was never run down by police pursuit.

The outlaw couple had left Dallas the day before, spending the night of June 9 in a tourist court near Vernon, Texas. W. D. Jones, whom they hadn't seen in over a month, had contacted them just before they left Dallas and wanted to go back on the road with them. Jones had a case of hero worship where Clyde Barrow was concerned. He was reasonably dependable, had no qualms about shooting at the least provocation,[1] and didn't mind doing the dirty, greasy work on the cars that Clyde avoided. He was almost the perfect sidekick. According to Clyde's mother, everybody—including Clyde—told him to stay home and try to go straight, believing that nobody knew about his involvement with them during four murders.[2] Regardless, he was still determined to go. As Clyde drove north out of Wellington, Texas, Jones was asleep in the coupe's back seat.

Clyde had been out of prison for sixteen months and was a wanted man for thirteen of those. Except for her two months in the Kaufman jail, Bonnie had been with him for most of that time. Because of Clyde's criminal activities, at least six people had already died, but so far, neither Clyde nor Bonnie nor any of their family had been seriously hurt. That was about to change.

About seven miles north of Wellington, where the highway crosses the Salt Fork of the Red River, there was an area of construction involving a new road branching off the main Wellington-Shamrock highway. Clyde missed the signs and drove straight off a twelve-foot drop into a ravine.[3] The coupe rolled over a couple of times, and Clyde was thrown clear. As he ran back to the car, the now wide-awake W. D. Jones was freeing himself, but Bonnie was pinned in the right front seat. To make matters even worse, sulfuric acid began to leak from the battery onto Bonnie's right leg. It quickly turned into a nightmare—Clyde frantic to get Bonnie out of the car, and Bonnie screaming at them to do something or shoot her so she wouldn't burn.[4]

Sam Pritchard and his son-in-law Alonzo Cartwright saved them, and according to a recent interview with Gladys Pritchard Cartwright, the Pritchards' daughter and an eyewitness, here's what happened:

Gladys and Alonzo Cartwright were visiting Gladys' parents, whose house overlooked the accident site, and when Clyde crashed, the two men ran to help. Along with Clyde and Jones, they were able to free Bonnie, but not before the battery acid had covered most of her right leg. Bonnie was carried to the Pritchard house, where Gladys and her mother immediately saw that she was badly burned. All they could do was apply wet baking soda (which mercifully neutralized some of the acid) and Cloverine Salve, a standard country home remedy. The worst burns covered her right knee and were easily second-degree in severity. Mrs. Pritchard wanted to call a doctor right away, but both Clyde and Bonnie refused.

While the ladies tended Bonnie, Clyde went back to the car to salvage their weapons. The guns Clyde was carrying plus their suspicious behavior convinced Alonzo that these were dangerous people, so, in the confusion, he

Bonnie and Clyde—late March 1933. The car is a 1932 Ford B-400 stolen in mid-March in Marshall, Texas. The picture is one of a group found in the Joplin, Missouri, apartment after the April 13, 1933, shootout.

—Courtesy Sandy Jones–The John Dillinger Historical Society

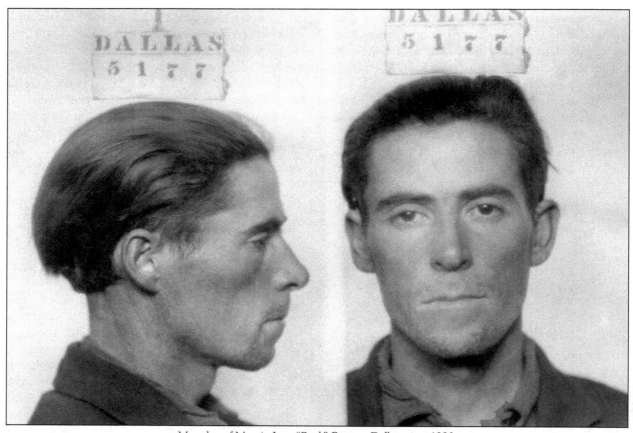

Mug shot of Marvin Ivan "Buck" Barrow, Dallas, circa 1930.
—From the collections of the Texas/Dallas History and Archives Division, Dallas Public Library

went to his father-in-law's car, pushed it quietly down the driveway, and went for the law. Before long, though, Alonzo was missed, and Clyde correctly guessed where he had gone. At that point, the relations between the Pritchards and the outlaws became a little strained. On the other hand, Alonzo's escape served as a warning. So when Sheriff George Corry and Wellington City Marshal Paul Hardy arrived a few minutes later, Clyde was ready.

Due to the placement of the Pritchard house, when the two officers drove up, they went in the back door and then proceeded through the front of the house. Bonnie had gotten out of bed and limped to the front yard with Clyde and Jones where the three of them disarmed the two lawmen as soon as they stepped out the front door. W. D. Jones then walked around the house to make sure the two officers had come alone, but saw movement

in the kitchen. He fired a shotgun blast through the window at what he thought was another policeman, but hit Gladys Cartwright, who had gone back inside and was trying to lock the back door. She was hit in the right hand by six pellets, and her four-month-old son, on her hip, was cut by flying metal.[5]

Things were getting out of hand, and Clyde decided, in spite of Bonnie's injury, that it was time to go. They were supposed to meet Buck and Blanche in Oklahoma in a few hours anyway. The lawmen were handcuffed together, put in the back seat of their own police car, and Bonnie lay across their laps. Just before they drove off into the night, W. D. Jones took a .45 automatic and shot out the tires on the Cartwrights' car. Seventy years later, Gladys still keeps some of those recovered .45 slugs as souvenirs.

The two outlaws, two lawmen, and one small,

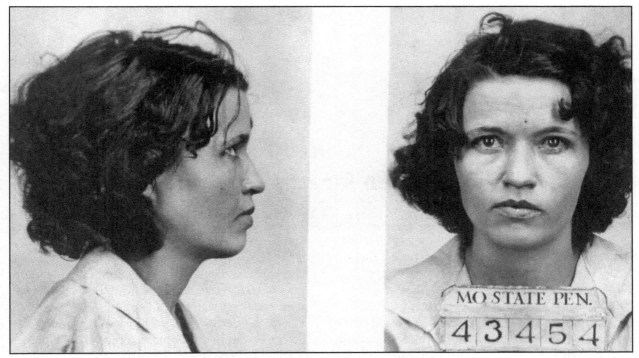

Mug shot of Blanche Caldwell Barrow, Missouri State Prison, fall 1933.
—From the collections of the Texas/Dallas History and Archives Division, Dallas Public Library

burned woman left the Pritchard house about 11:30 P.M. Around 3:00 A.M., they arrived at one end of a bridge near Erick, Oklahoma. Clyde stopped and honked the horn, and was answered by a honk from the other side. Soon Buck Barrow joined them. Clyde explained what had happened, took the policemen out of the car, and sent Jones and Bonnie across in the police car to meet Blanche on the other side. Buck looked at the two policemen and said, "What will we do with them? Kill them?"

"No," Clyde said. "I'm used to them now. I kinda like them."

The officers were tied to a tree with barbed wire. The Barrows then disappeared. It took Corry and Hardy about thirty minutes to free themselves, find a farmer's house, and call officers at nearby Sayre, Oklahoma. The Barrows' trail led toward Pampa in the Texas Panhandle but was lost when

they hit the main road. They must have stolen another car soon after they left Erick, because Corry's Chevy was found a short distance away, and Buck's Ford convertible coupe couldn't carry all five of them any distance—especially with Bonnie burned so badly.[6]

By daylight on Sunday, June 11, the Barrows had disappeared into the Texas-Oklahoma Panhandle area. For the next three days, they hid out and worked their way north into Kansas. By then, Bonnie was in a bad way. She had gone untreated for more than three days with at least second-degree burns over much of her right leg. She simply couldn't survive much longer in the back seat of a car. They had to find a place for her to recover. On Wednesday the 14th, Clyde stole a Ford V-8 sedan in Hutchinson, Kansas, and the group drove through the evening toward Arkansas.[7]

CHAPTER 24
"Worse than Pretty Boy Floyd"

In the early hours of Thursday morning, June 15, 1933, two carloads of worn-out people pulled into a tourist camp at the corner of North Eleventh Street[1] and Waldron Road, located on the northern edge of Fort Smith, Arkansas. It was about a mile from the county line and the bridge over the Arkansas River that led into Van Buren. From there, Crawford County stretched north into a part of the Ozarks called the Boston Mountains, some of the wildest country between the Mississippi and the Rockies. The Twin Cities Tourist Camp (later called the Dennis Motel) was a fairly modern establishment, as these places went. The cabins were almost new, and they featured indoor plumbing, showers, mattresses on the beds, hot plates, and enclosed garages for the cars. The Barrows rented two cabins, for $1 a day each.[2]

Clyde's first priority was treatment for Bonnie. As a cover story, he told Mr. and Mrs. Sid Dennis, the owners, that his "wife" had been burned when a camp stove exploded, and Dr. Walter Eberle was called to see her.[3] His opinion was that she should be in a hospital, but, of course, Clyde couldn't allow that. If she couldn't go to the hospital, the doctor said, at least they should have a nurse come every day to check on her and change the dressings. Even this was a risk, but Clyde knew that Bonnie's life was at stake, so the arrangements were made. Fortunately, the Dennises' daughter, Hazel, had worked in a hospital and had some

experience with burn victims. She helped out where she could and took Bonnie ice cream and lemonade to help her cope with the 100-degree heat that was plaguing the area.[4]

As the Barrows settled in to wait, Blanche was almost certainly the primary caregiver for Bonnie. No doubt Clyde was very worried about her condition, but the statement by the family that "He never left her bedside, day or night, for a week"[5] is not true. Mrs. Dennis said that Clyde would "come out every morning, all dressed up, and drive into town. All of them acted real nice and were very clean."[6] This is confirmed by several townspeople who later recalled Clyde shopping at a drugstore and buying groceries.

According to Clyde's mother, it was during this time that he and Buck tried to make contact with the Floyd family near Sallisaw, Oklahoma, only about twenty-five miles away.[7] The Barrows were now well known to law enforcement agencies in the Southwest, and since Joplin, they were becoming known in Missouri and the Midwest, but they hadn't quite become household names to the general public. By the end of the summer, that would change, but at the time, the undisputed champion of Southwest outlaws was still Charles Arthur Floyd.

Born in Bartow County, Georgia, on February 3, 1904, young Charlie moved with his family to Sequoyah County, Oklahoma, when he was seven years old. He grew up around Akin, just north of

Sallisaw, a well-liked, fun-loving—if wild—young man. In 1925, Charley went to St. Louis with a fellow he met during the wheat harvest, leaving his wife, Ruby, and their infant son, Dempsey, in Oklahoma. Once in Missouri, the two men began robbing grocery stores. On September 11, Floyd and two other men hit the Kroger headquarters payroll in St. Louis, and got over $11,000. Two days later, Charley returned to Sallisaw with a roll of cash and a brand new Studebaker.

Floyd's new wealth didn't go unnoticed, and within days he was picked up by Oklahoma authorities. The police description from St. Louis labeled the fellow who carried the gun in the Kroger robbery as "a pretty boy with apple cheeks," which fit Charley to a T, and his famous nickname was born. "Pretty Boy" was a rather unfortunate title to take with you to prison, but that was where Charley was going. On December 18, 1925, he entered the Missouri State Penitentiary at Jefferson City, sentenced to five years. "Pretty Boy" actually did three years and three months, being released March 7, 1929.[8] From then on, there is no evidence that he was ever on the right side of the law.

By the time Clyde and Buck went looking for him in June 1933, Floyd had been out of prison and operating for four years. He was the scourge of small-town banks in Oklahoma and the Ozarks, and his name appeared almost daily in newspapers connected with the latest robbery, car theft, or abduction. In spite of this, he came and went in the area around Sallisaw and the Cookson Hills of eastern Oklahoma with relative ease, so Clyde's idea of making contact with Floyd's family—and possibly even meeting Floyd himself—was reasonable. Clyde is said to have met with Floyd's brother E. W. and set up a way for Charley to contact him,[9] but what he really wanted was for the Floyd family to help him find a better place to stay than some tourist camp while Bonnie recovered. In this, he was disappointed.

Although Clyde looked up to Floyd as the best in the business, the feeling was not mutual. Floyd considered Bonnie and Clyde trigger-happy punks and not true professionals. He had told his family and the people in the Cookson Hills not to help

them and to get word to the law if they stayed around more than a day or two.[10] It is possible that Clyde and Floyd met later, but there is no evidence they ever worked together.[11]

Even if Floyd had wanted to help them, Clyde and Buck would have missed him on this trip. Floyd had, indeed, been in and around eastern Oklahoma in May and early June. He had even gone to church in Sallisaw with his mother on Mother's Day. Floyd had last been seen about 100 miles west near the town of Cromwell, where he and Adam Richetti stole a car late on the evening of June 8.[12] The Barrows missed him by a week. About the time Clyde and Buck went looking for him, Floyd and Richetti were in Bolivar, Missouri. On June 16, they kidnapped the county sheriff and drove to Kansas City. They released Sheriff Killingsworth late in the evening and disappeared, but they had stepped out of the frying pan and into the fire.[13]

As the Barrows turned in for the evening and Floyd and Richetti arrived in Kansas City, late on Friday, June 16, another group of people arrived at Fort Smith, Arkansas. The car that drove by the entrance to the Twin City Tourist Camp and on to the county jail contained two federal agents, an Oklahoma police chief, and an escaped bank robber. Federal Agents Joe Lackey and Frank Smith, and McAlester, Oklahoma, Police Chief Ott Reed, none of whom had any jurisdiction there, had literally snatched Frank "Jelly" Nash off the street in Hot Springs, Arkansas, earlier that day. Nash had a long history of bank robbery and was currently wanted for his October 19, 1930, escape from the federal prison at Leavenworth, Kansas. At Fort Smith, the lawmen transferred to the Missouri Pacific train, and they arrived in Kansas City at 7:00 A.M. Saturday morning. A few minutes later, Ott Reed, Frank Nash, a federal agent, and two Kansas City police officers were dead, and Pretty Boy Floyd was a prime suspect in what became known as the Union Station Massacre.[14]

While the shooting in Kansas City took over the headlines, the situation at the Twin City Tourist Camp was becoming grim. By Sunday the 18th, Bonnie's condition was still very serious, and

Clyde knew something had to be done. He decided to go to Dallas and bring back some help. Bonnie needed to see some of her family, and Clyde needed to do something. Whatever else he was, Clyde was a man of action, and being behind the wheel in a dash to Dallas—even though it was very dangerous—was probably more comfortable to him than sitting helpless at Bonnie's bedside.

According to the Barrow family, Clyde left Fort Smith around noon and arrived in Dallas about 8:00 P.M. Both Clyde and Bonnie's mothers wanted to go back with him immediately, but Clyde wouldn't take them. Not only was he afraid the mothers were being watched by the law, but he knew how dangerous it was for them to be with him. He didn't want to put either mother in the position of being arrested—or shot—on his account.[15] Billie Jean Parker Mace, Bonnie's younger sister, was the one Clyde had come for. She got back from a movie about 11:00 P.M., and the two of them left soon afterward.[16] About midnight, on their way out of town, Clyde was spotted by Ted Hinton, a local deputy sheriff who knew Clyde. He chased them for a while, but Clyde disappeared into the night. The deputy was a little confused because the woman with Clyde didn't look like Bonnie.[17] (The next time Hinton and Clyde met, things would be very different.) Clyde and Billie Jean got back to Fort Smith a few hours later. This was about midmorning Monday the 19th.[18] Maybe it was just coincidence, but two and a half days later, a small-town bank, thirteen miles away, was robbed.

In 1933, Alma, Arkansas, was a town of about 800 people and sat at the intersection of U.S. 64 running between Fort Smith and Little Rock, and U.S. 71 running north to Fayetteville. Henry D. Humphrey, a fifty-one-year-old farmer and handyman at the local high school, had been elected city marshal on May 1. The marshal's job paid $15 a month, and its primary duty was as a night watchman. In this capacity, Humphrey chased a fellow down an alley about 1:50 A.M. on Thursday morning, June 22, only to find himself facing a man with a rifle. He had been suckered.

The man and his partner took Henry's pistol and flashlight, bound him with baling wire, and went to the rear window of the Commercial Bank building on the west side of Alma's main street.[19] They spread the bars with an automobile jack, got in the window, and opened the front door from the inside. All Marshal Humphrey could do was lie on the floor and watch them work. An hour and fifteen minutes later, the two robbers winched a 4,000-pound safe containing $3,600 out the front door into a stolen truck parked in the middle of the main street, and they drove south out of town toward the small community of Kibler.[20] Marshal Humphrey then freed himself and called the county sheriff.

Later that day, in the aftermath of the robbery, a salesman convinced the mayor and town council to order Marshal Humphrey a steel bullet-proof vest, saying that it could be delivered in about a week. While it's doubtful he would have worn it in the sweltering heat of the summer, that question turned out to be academic. He would be dead before it arrived.[21]

By the time Clyde and Billie Jean returned to the tourist camp, Bonnie had begun to rally. Having her sister there helped her spirits, and it began to look as though she would recover. While Bonnie's health was improving, however, the gang's financial situation was becoming dire. Bonnie's care and medicine, their rent, and their food all took cash, and they were down to their last few dollars. After some discussion, it was decided that Buck and W. D. Jones would try to raise some cash while Clyde stayed with the girls. Buck also wanted to find a Ford sedan to replace his roadster, if he could. They agreed to operate far enough away from the motel so that any police response would not endanger Clyde and the women.

Buck and W. D. left the Twin City Tourist Camp about noon on Friday the 23rd, and headed north toward Fayetteville.[22] W. D. Jones was now a six-month veteran of robberies, car thefts, and gunfights, and Buck Barrow had been staging robberies for at least ten years. You would think that with so much experience, the simple task of sticking up a grocery store and getting away should have been easy. Instead, except for the very real bullets and blood, the next few hours could have been written for Laurel and Hardy.

Buck and W. D. began casing the stores in Fayetteville late in the afternoon. Far from behaving like professionals, they were so obvious that they attracted the attention of the owner of Bates Brothers Market, who took down their description and license number. About 5:30 P.M., Buck parked a block away, and W. D. walked across to Brown's Grocery at 111 West Lafayette. When W. D. entered the store, Mrs. Robert L. Brown was behind the counter, and the only other person in the store was the bag boy, Ewell Trammell. W. D. produced a pistol and told them both to be quiet. He then went to the cash register, but he couldn't open it. Mrs. Brown opened it for him but immediately put both hands back in her apron pockets. Jones got $20 out of the cash drawer and missed the two diamond rings on Mrs. Brown's fingers. On the way out, he frisked the bag boy and got another thirty-five cents.

With Buck parked all of a block away, Jones then decided to steal the Model A delivery truck parked outside. Mrs. Brown said, "The keys are in it," but neglected to add that the battery was dead. W. D. ran for the truck, knocking down seven-year-old Wanda Audit, who was just coming in. Jones finally had to start the truck by pushing it down the hill and popping the clutch. He drove a couple of blocks, to the bottom of the hill, across one block and then back up the hill, to where Buck waited in the Ford sedan. They were last seen driving south on U.S. 71.[23]

Thanks to Mr. Bates' information plus Mrs. Brown's call, the Fayetteville police had a good start. By 6:00 P.M., they were on the phone to communities along the getaway route, asking for help. One of the most obvious places to watch was Alma, since it was at the intersection of the two major highways in the region. They reached Marshal Humphrey at the AHC Garage, run by his son Vernon, gave him the license number and

Building that housed Brown's Grocery in Fayetteville, Arkansas, which was robbed by Buck Barrow or W. D. Jones, June 23, 1933.

—From the author's collection

description of the car, and asked him to watch the road for the two men. Fresh from his experience at the bank thirty-six hours before, this may have sounded like the same fellows. Who knows? Maybe the chance for a little payback crossed his mind.

A town the size of Alma was lucky to have a marshal. A deputy was out of the question. If Humphrey was going to have any help, it would probably have to come from his son, but Vernon couldn't leave the service station unattended. He had a night mechanic, Weber Wilson, who was supposed to come in at 6:00 P.M., but he was late that day. Ansel M. "Red" Salyers offered to go instead. He worked for the Mississippi Valley Power Company but was also what we today would call a reserve deputy sheriff. About 6:20 P.M., Humphrey and Salyers left the AHC heading north up U.S. 71 in Salyers' maroon Ford sedan.[24] Humphrey had lost his service revolver to the bank robbers but had borrowed another .38 pistol from his brother-in-law. Salyers had a Winchester .30-30 he had taken from a customer in trade for his electric bill.[25] About two and a half miles north of town, on U.S. 71, Salyers topped a hill and met a blue Chevrolet driven by the late-to-work mechanic, Weber Wilson. He and Humphrey waved and continued down the hill toward what was locally known as "Kaundart Curve," named after the family who lived there. Before they got to the bottom, they met a black Ford sedan that was traveling very fast.[26]

The distance from the Brown Grocery Store in Fayetteville to the site north of Alma is just over fifty miles. Highway 71, from Fayetteville to Alma, was considered, until a few years ago, one of the ten most dangerous highways in America. In 1933, it was a two-lane blacktop road over some of the worst mountains in the Ozarks. Today, with an interstate highway, the trip takes at least forty minutes. Buck made it in about fifty minutes, averaging almost sixty miles per hour. It must have been quite a ride.

Even though the trip to Fayetteville had only netted $20, had alerted the police in two counties, and had failed to secure a replacement car for Buck's roadster, the outlaws' luck seemed to be improving. They had just passed, undetected, the only lawmen for several miles in any direction and were only twenty minutes or so from the tourist camp. Their good luck lasted a few seconds more—until Buck topped the hill and crashed into the rear end of Weber Wilson's blue Chevy.

Salyers and Humphrey knew exactly what had happened. They didn't know that the black Ford was the car they had come out to find—yet—but they knew it was going too fast. It was 102 degrees that day, so, with all the windows down, they heard the crash as well. At the bottom of the hill, they turned around and drove back to the site of the accident, which was about fifty yards past the crest of the hill, facing south.[27] As they approached the rear of the wrecked Ford, Humphrey finally saw the license plate the Fayetteville police had called in (1933 Indiana 225-646) and told Salyers, who stopped, facing east, blocking the road behind the car.

At this point, several things happened more or less simultaneously. Buck and W. D. Jones began to recover from the shock of the crash and saw Wilson crawl out of his overturned car, pick up a large rock, and start toward them, furious at the men who had rear-ended him, and they saw the red car stop and block the road behind them. Of course, neither of them could afford to be questioned by the law or even delayed for long, so the response was automatic. They came out shooting.

Wilson was lucky. He saw the guns, dropped the rock, and, showing good sense, ran the other way. Humphrey had just come out the right door of Salyers' car—the side nearest the wrecked Ford—when Buck opened the fight with a load of number-four buckshot from a sawed-off .12 gauge shotgun. It caught Humphrey full in the chest and blew him into the ditch by the side of the road.[28] Salyers was somewhat shielded by the car body as he got out with his rifle. This probably saved him, because W. D. Jones came out firing a Browning automatic rifle (BAR).[29] Salyers did what he could, but with his seven-shot deer rifle, he was severely overmatched.

Several shots were exchanged, and then Buck's shotgun jammed and Jones stopped to load a fresh magazine in the automatic rifle. Salyers knew they would kill him if he stayed where he was, so he ran for a house about seventy-five yards away. Even though Salyers was motivated, long before he could make it to shelter, W. D. was firing again. Fortunately, he managed to hit everything but the deputy. Jones put rounds into the house, the barn, and even into a strawberry field several hundred yards away, but he missed the lawman. Salyers got behind the rock chimney and reloaded while Buck and W. D. ran to Salyers' car—the only one left that would run.

As one of the men got in and started the car, the other one went to check on Marshal Humphrey, who was lying in the ditch beside the road. "I ought to kill you" the outlaw said.

"I think you already have," Humphrey replied and watched as the man took his brother-in-law's pistol—the second gun he had lost in two days—and ran to Salyers' car. Just as they started to drive away, Salyers got in a couple more shots from the house. One of them knocked off the horn button and took off two of W. D. Jones' fingertips. As they drove away, Buck and W. D. also fired at a passing motorist.[30]

When Buck and W. D. left the gunfight site, they were headed back the way they had come—north toward Fayetteville. This was to cause confusion for later authors, but not at the time. Deputy Salyers saw them drive off to the north, but only for a few hundred yards. At that point, he watched them turn west onto a small lane. About a mile later, they turned back south on Rudy Road, where they were seen by a local family named Farris, and a couple of miles later reached U.S. 64.[31] At this point, they were about twelve miles from the motel.

Back at the gunfight site, Deputy Salyers went to a nearby phone and called the county sheriff's office in Van Buren while others attended to Marshal Humphrey. B. C. Ames, the motorist who was fired on by the outlaws, stopped and volunteered to take Marshal Humphrey to the hospital. From Alma, he would take U.S. 64 west, just like the shooters, and would only be a few minutes behind them. At Van Buren, Humphrey was transferred to an ambulance and taken to Saint John's Hospital in Fort Smith. Meanwhile, Salyers searched the wrecked Ford.[32]

About three miles east of Van Buren, Buck and

W. D. decided, for some reason, to dump Salyers' maroon Ford. At the intersection of U.S. 64 and what is now Shibley Road, they pulled across the highway and stopped the first car coming the other way, containing Mark Lofton and his wife. With much shouting and swearing, the Loftons were taken out of their car, robbed, and put into Salyers' car. They both jumped out the other side and ran away. The whole thing was witnessed by Mrs. Jim Brewer from her store across the road.[33]

Buck and W. D. were now only five miles from the tourist camp, but they had to cross the Arkansas River, and the only way across, for at least twenty-five miles in any direction, was the bridge at Van Buren. Unfortunately for them, the bridge was now guarded.[34] Buck couldn't just run past the lawmen and risk pursuit, because Clyde and the women were only a mile away on the other side. Having no room to maneuver, Buck and W. D. turned north on Highway 59. This road climbs immediately to a bluff called Mt. Vista, overlooking the river. It was on Skyline Drive, a lane on top of this bluff, that the Loftons' car— with a flat tire—was found a few hours later.[35]

The police didn't know who the outlaws were, but they knew that they had driven toward Van Buren and stolen the Loftons' car. When the car was discovered on Mt. Vista later in the evening, the lawmen were sure the men were on foot in that wooded area. Every man who could be rounded up was deputized and searched the area all night, from Mt. Vista west to the Oklahoma line near the town of Dora, but Buck and W. D. had vanished. In fact, they were probably back at the tourist camp before the Loftons' car was even found. Unnoticed, they simply went back down the hill into downtown Van Buren and, just after dark, walked across the unguarded Frisco railroad trestle which ran alongside the guarded automobile bridge. They then walked another mile, to the rear of the Twin City Tourist Camp, and slipped inside.[36] It must have been almost 10:00 P.M. by the time Buck and W. D. got back and began to tell Clyde their story.

Buck's day as leader of the gang's operations had been a disaster. Instead of the cash they desperately needed, they got just $20. Instead of getting another sedan to replace Buck's roadster, they wrecked the sedan they had and lost two other cars during their escape. Instead of keeping a low profile so Bonnie could continue to recuperate in peace, they had caused a car wreck, shot a police officer, and created a manhunt that would eventually include all the lawmen in three counties.

As much as he hated moving Bonnie, Clyde knew that staying where they were wasn't an option. Having only the Ford roadster made matters worse. There was no way all six of them could fit into that car, so Clyde left Buck and W. D. at the tourist camp and took the women out first. This was done very quickly—Clyde was seen leaving with the women at 10:40 P.M.[37] After a hair-raising trip into the eastern Oklahoma woods, Clyde left the women and went back for Buck and W. D.[38]

By first light on Saturday morning, June 24, the Barrows were gone, but none of this was known to the lawmen who had spent the night thrashing through the brush. By this time, Crawford County Sheriff Albert Maxey had returned from Joplin, Missouri, and taken over the search his deputies had organized. Since they had found nothing in the area north and west of Van Buren, Maxey began to shift the search area more to the east. Then came the incident that would confuse the issue of the Barrows' escape and paint them, in the minds of many, as even more depraved than the killers they certainly were.

About 11:00 A.M., a call came in to the Crawford County Sheriff's Office from Winslow, a small community about twenty-seven miles, as the crow flies, northeast of Van Buren. Twenty-six-year-old Clara Rogers was in her kitchen making grape jelly when two men came in and demanded the keys to her car. When she refused, they beat her with a chain, stabbed her in the hip, and sexually assaulted her. Even so, through Mrs. Rogers' efforts or by an accident on the part of the thieves, the car was disabled and the two men fled on foot.[39] Since the lawmen had just spent all night looking for two men on foot who badly needed a car (and had no idea that these two men were now resting in the woods of eastern Oklahoma), this seemed to explain where they had gone. All search

efforts were immediately shifted to the area around Winslow, with Washington County officers now being added to the posse as well.

The assault on Mrs. Rogers fit so well into the scheme of things that nobody seems to have asked how two men on foot could have moved—in the dark—more than twenty-five miles through some of the worst mountain terrain in the central United States in just over twelve hours. When it was discovered on Saturday night that the rest of the gang had been staying in the Twin City Tourist Camp, less than two miles from the fugitives' last known position, and in the opposite direction, this should have raised some questions also. Without the assault on Mrs. Rogers as a lead, however, there was no place else to go, so the posse continued searching the area around Winslow for four more days, and the Barrows would add rape to the list of crimes for which they were wanted. Somebody certainly assaulted Clara Rogers in her home that Saturday morning, but it was almost as certainly not the Barrows.

On Monday the 26th, Sheriff Maxey made a statement that summed up the opinion of many of the lawmen who had been involved in pursuing the Barrows since the Joplin killings in April. He described the brothers as killers and said they were "far worse than Pretty Boy Floyd because they go crazy and don't use their heads."[40] While they certainly weren't crazy, Maxey's comment about lack of headwork during Buck and W. D. Jones' adventure couldn't be denied.

While the Crawford and Washington county officers searched the mountains, Sebastian County Sheriff John Williams was doing the detective work. He had discovered that a group of people, with a badly burned woman, had been staying at the Twin City Tourist Camp for the past several days. By Saturday night, he had been in touch with Sheriff Corey in Wellington, Texas, and strongly suspected the Barrows. By Sunday evening, he had pictures. The gunfight witnesses—including the rapidly failing Marshal Humphrey—recognized Buck, but opinion about Clyde's presence was divided. He was identified by several merchants and the people at the tourist camp, however. W. D.

Jones was still unidentified. On Monday morning, June 26, Henry Humphrey died at Saint John's Hospital. He was the fifth lawman killed by the Barrows.

While lawmen from three counties searched for them in Arkansas, the Barrows were in Oklahoma trying to solve several problems of their own. In order to keep the group together, they had to have another car. Bonnie needed continuing care and medicine. Also, since Clyde had decided it was too dangerous for her to stay, they had to find some way to get Billie home. The answer to all these concerns came together in the town of Enid. On Monday, June 26, Clyde followed the vehicle of Dr. Julian Fields to a parking lot near a hospital. Dr. Fields left his bag in the back seat and went inside, but when he came back, Clyde had taken the car.[41] Later that evening, they put Billie on the Dallas Interurban train at Sherman, Texas, and drove back north.[42] Doctor Fields' car was found outside Enid the next day, but the medical bag was missing.[43]

Alma, Arkansas, town marshal Henry D. Humphrey and family. This picture was taken about 1913, twenty years before Humphrey was shot and killed by Marvin I. "Buck" Barrow. Pictured with Humphrey are, left to right, his son Vernon, daughter Viola, wife Alice, and youngest daughter Velma.

—From the author's collection. Picture provided to the author by Bonnie Cook, Fort Smith, Arkansas

Back in northwest Arkansas, the search was winding down, but there was still one more "Keystone Cops" episode left. On Tuesday afternoon, June 27, a funeral home in Fort Smith received a strange request for an ambulance. The man refused to identify himself but asked that it be sent to a point about twelve miles north of Van Buren. "We'll flag you down on the highway. We've got plenty of money to pay you," he said. The call was immediately reported to Sheriff John B. Williams.

When the ambulance left for the meeting, it contained four armed deputies and was preceded and followed by more in unmarked cars. By the time it got through Van Buren, it had picked up another carload of Crawford County officers. This heavily armed convoy drove north on Highway 59 as far as Natural Dam, seeing only a few campers, and then turned back. Meanwhile, a merchant and his helper left Van Buren, driving north for Siloam Springs with a load of overalls. As luck would have it, they were hauling them in a black ambulance.

The overalls ambulance, heading north, and the decoy ambulance, heading south, met just north of Van Buren. As the black ambulance shot by them at high speed, the lawmen jumped to the obvious conclusion, wheeled around, and gave chase. The merchant, seeing the unmarked cars full of armed men behind him, decided that he and his overalls were in danger of being hijacked, so he put his foot down and ran for all he was worth. The chase lasted for ten miles before the merchant was finally forced to stop. After some tense moments, identities were checked and everything was cleared up, but given the level of adrenaline and suspicion, and the presence of several newly acquired automatic weapons, the wonder is that nobody was killed.[44]

On Wednesday, June 28, after a funeral that overflowed the First Baptist Church at Alma, Marshal Humphrey was laid to rest. The manhunt had been called off, and everybody was becoming resigned to the fact that the Barrow gang had escaped again. In fact, by now they were several hundred miles away. After a couple of nights in the Oklahoma woods and the trip to Sherman, Texas, to put Billie on the train, the gang had driven north and settled into another tourist camp, in Great Bend, Kansas.[45] It would

WANTED for Murder and Rape

I hold two felony warrants, each for Clyde and Melvin Barrow, who on June 23rd shot and killed Marshal Henry Humphrey while he was trying to arrest them on a robbery charge and on the next day, June 24th, they went to the home of Mrs Frank Rogers, tried to take her auto, and raped her.

Reading from left to right will describe them as follows:

No. 1: Bonnie Parker (alias Mrs. Clyde Barrow). I understand that she is burned very bad. The best that I can find out the burns are on her right thigh and right arm. Has tattoo 8 inches above right knee.

No. 2: Clyde Barrow, description as follows: Age 24 years, height 5 feet 7 inches barefoot, weigfht 125 lbs., hair dark brown wavy, complexion light, eyes hazel. He has slit in upper lip. Nose crooked, probably broken. Limps in left foot. His finger prints classification is as follows:

29 -- M O 9
26 U O O 9

No. 3: Do not know his hame but can give you his description. Height 5 feet 7 inches. Age, about 28 years, weight about 130 or 135, hair, dark, medium dark complexion, square shoulders but drooped forward sharply.

No. 4: Blanch Caldwell (Mrs. Melvin Barrow). Do not know anything about her description.

No. 5: Melvin Barrow. Description as follows: Age 31 years, height, 5 feet 5 inches barefeet, weight 110 pounds, hair chestnut, eyes maroon, complexion ruddy. Finger print classification is as follows:

9 U 11 9
1 R 11 11

I will pay personally $250.00 each for the Barrow Brothers delivered to me any where in the United States. To receive the reward there does not have to be a conviction, just the delivery to me and I will pay the reward.

There were six in the party when they were here, three men and three women. Search all tourist parks as that is where they stay. And inquire of your doctors if they have been called to treat a woman that has been burned in a car wreck.

If you locate these men, arrest, wire me collect and will come for them and will pay you $250.00 each for them. Do not want you to wait for a conviction but will pay the reward for their arrest and delivery to me.

These men are very dangerous and use all precaution when you locate them. These boys home is West Dallas, Texas.

Albert Maxey, Sheriff
Van Buren, Crawford County, Arkansas

Wanted poster issued by Crawford County (Arkansas) Sheriff Albert Maxey following the killing of Henry D. Humphrey, town marshal, Alma, Arkansas. Late June 1933.

—From the author's collection

be just over two weeks before they surfaced again, but when they did, it would make the little shootout at Alma look like a church social.

CHAPTER 25
Platte City

During the episode in northwest Arkansas, the Barrows had managed to stay one step ahead of the law. By the time the manhunt started, they were already on the move. They spent a few uncomfortable nights in the woods but were never in any serious danger. They managed to get Billie safely back home and now had settled down in a motel in Kansas.

The plan was essentially the same: lie low and let Bonnie heal while financing themselves with small hit-and-run robberies staged far enough away to avoid police pressure in the area around Great Bend. As it turned out, the plan worked much better in Kansas than it did in Arkansas. Once they were set up in Great Bend and got a few dollars ahead, Clyde was ready to address one last problem left over from the Arkansas disaster. During the wreck, shooting, and escape, they had lost much of their firepower. Most of their guns and ammunition were either lost or abandoned.

On Friday evening, July 7, Clyde and Buck entered the campus of Phillips University in Enid, Oklahoma, and pulled up to the rear entrance of the Headquarters Battery, First Battalion, 189th Field Artillery. They removed a pane of glass and got into the building, which contained the unit's armory. To Clyde Barrow, who lived by his firearms, it must have seemed like Christmas in July. Officials later admitted to the loss of thirty-five Colt .45 automatic pistols, eighty magazines, and several pairs of field glasses.[1] What the authorities did not admit was that they had also lost several Browning automatic rifles and a large quantity of ammunition.[2] Clyde cut down the barrel of one of the BARs and cut the stock back as much as he could. His hope was to make a compact automatic rifle he could use in tight places—like the front seat of a Ford V-8.[3] W. D. Jones said he also had an extended magazine made that would hold almost three times the normal amount of ammunition. The cut-down rifle, which Clyde called his "scatter gun," was later recovered by police, but the extended magazine was not, and some researchers doubt that it really existed.[4]

Two weeks of relative peace and quiet allowed Bonnie to recover enough to travel, even though she still had to be carried to the car. Damaged ligaments had caused her burned leg to draw up so that it was impossible for her to walk normally. As always, too long in one place made Clyde nervous, so by July 10, they left Great Bend and moved to north central Iowa.[5]

On July 11, some citizen of Storm Lake, Iowa, lost a set of license plates (1933 Iowa 11-2399). About July 17, a Mr. Shaffer of Spencer, Iowa, lost a 1929 Chevrolet sedan. Just before 11:00 A.M. the next day, Mr. Shaffer's Chevrolet, now wearing the Storm Lake plates and driven by Buck Barrow, rolled into the Continental Oil service station at Twelfth Street and Second Avenue in Fort Dodge, Iowa. Harold Anderson, the attendant, watched as one of the three men in the car jumped out and pulled a gun on him. Anderson empted his pockets and the safe, and was then "invited" to get in the car. He reported that the men didn't say much— just that they had a couple more stops to make.

Next stop was the Standard Oil station at Fifteenth Street and Eighth Avenue, where Harry Stark saw a gun and heard the words, "No monkey business or I'll kill you." After giving up all his money, Stark joined Anderson in the back seat. As they pulled out, Stark kicked a back door open but only managed to get it smashed by some metal shelves as they went by. One of the gang pulled him back in, and they drove a block north to Leon Chevalier's Texaco station. Leon and his brother Justin were standing in the driveway when the gunmen arrived, and, for the third time in ten minutes, the Barrow brothers gathered up what petty cash they could. Three was pushing even Clyde Barrow's luck, so they took the keys to Justin Chevalier's car—just in case he decided to fol- low—let out their two hostages, and said goodbye. As they drove off, Justin asked if they wouldn't mind throwing his keys out after a few blocks, to save him the trouble of having a new set made. To his amazement, they did just that. The Chevy was found later that day on a side road a few miles north of Fort Dodge.[6] By evening, the gang had driven 250 miles south and were at a service sta- tion about six miles south of Platte City, Missouri, at the intersection of Highways 71 and 59.[7]

Delbert Crabtree was working at the service station when Clyde pulled in and stopped past the gas pumps. Clyde told Crabtree that he had his wife and mother-in-law with him and wanted to see the two cabins across the street.[8] Crabtree told him the cabins belonged to the Red Crown Tavern, a restaurant with a ballroom next door to the cab- ins. Neal Houser, the manager, checked them in as Blanche paid in advance with small change. There was something not quite right about the group, so Houser and his nephew, William Searles, kept an eye on them. Others noticed them too. Kermit Crawford and his sister operated the filling station where Clyde first stopped. It was called Slim's Castle and included a small grocery store. From

there, Crawford could look directly across the street at the two cabins connected by a garage, and he watched the people going back and forth between the two rooms. Crawford never dreamed that they were killers. He had never even heard of the Barrow gang. He actually thought they were school kids shacking up for the weekend.[9]

The next day, when Buck, Blanche, and W. D. Jones ate lunch at the Red Crown Tavern, their waitress was Kermit Crawford's fiancee, Mildred Anderson. She thought they were nice, quiet folks. In later years, Blanche remembered having lunch at the Red Crown. She also remembered that, as they paid their bill—again with small change—she and Buck noticed Sheriff Holt Coffee watching them.

Later, Blanche went into Platte City to buy medical supplies for Bonnie. Alerts on the Barrows and on any unknown persons buying medical sup- plies had been issued by several states, dating all the way back to the shooting in Joplin in April, so the druggist immediately called Sheriff Coffee.[10] The people at the Red Crown had already come to Coffee with their doubts about the people in the cabins, and now, with the druggist's call, Sheriff Coffee went to work. Before long, he was sure he was dealing with the Barrows, or someone like them. Most of the general public around Platte City had never heard of them. Before the night was over, that would change.

Once Sheriff Coffee was convinced of the seri- ousness of the situation, he called in Captain William Baxter of the Missouri Highway Patrol. Baxter, in turn, called in some extra men from Kansas City and an armored car. The men began arriving at the Red Crown early that evening, but they planned to wait until after closing to make their move.

Everything was quiet in the cabins until about 10:30. Then a young man came out, walked over to Slim's Castle, and ordered five sandwiches and five sodas. Kermit Crawford waited on him but noticed that he seemed nervous and kept looking toward the Red Crown. Slim's Castle and the tav- ern closed at 11:00, but Crawford, his sister, and his fiancée, Miss Anderson, stayed around, knowing something was about to happen. Several people were also watching from the Red Crown.[11]

Bonnie and Clyde had been on the run for fifteen months and had been in several gunfights and other tight places, but this was different. The other shooting scrapes had been spur-of-the-moment affairs that caught the police surprised and outgunned. The worst that had happened to any of them was a few flesh wounds. Now, for the first time, the law was ahead of them. The police suspected who they were, had time to make a plan, and had them trapped and outnumbered by at least five to one. It should have been the end of the line for the Barrow gang. The police thought they were ready for anything, but they were about to get a lesson in firepower.

About 11:30 P.M., Sheriff Coffee and his men moved in. They drove the armored car up so that it blocked both garage doors and parked a truck in front of the Red Crown to block access to Highway 71. Sheriff Coffee—either very brave or very foolish—took a steel shield, walked up to the right-hand cabin, and knocked on the door. This happened to be Buck and Blanche's room. Bonnie, Clyde, and W. D. Jones were across the garage.

According to Blanche Barrow, when Sheriff Coffee knocked, she was washing out some of Bonnie's clothes. When she asked who it was, Coffee said, "I need to talk to the boys." Blanche was enough of a veteran by now to know exactly what was happening. Even though she was surprised and scared, she played for time and also gave the predetermined signal for the law loudly enough to be heard in the other cabin: "Just a minute. Let us get dressed."

Coffee seemed to relax a little, not knowing that inside the cabins there was a flurry of activity. In the left-hand cabin, Clyde told W. D. Jones to go start the car and grabbed his "scatter gun" BAR. As Coffee waited on Blanche's doorstep, his back was almost turned to Clyde, so when Barrow raised his BAR and fired a burst from the other cabin, Coffee never saw it coming. It blew out the glass in the inside door and the garage door. Coffee was hit in the neck, his shield went flying, and he staggered back toward the Red Crown.[12] At this point,

in the words of Kermit Crawford, who was watching from his driveway across the street, "All hell broke loose."[13]

The police were surprised but quickly recovered. As Coffee retreated, they opened fire and began raking both cabins. Clyde, thinking he might be surrounded, began firing blindly out every window—just in case. Next, he looked out the front again and took on the armored car. This wasn't a real military-type armored car, but just a regular automobile with some reinforcement. Whatever the police considered to be "armor" on this car meant nothing to Clyde's BAR. A burst of 30-06 full-metal-jacket military rounds went completely through the car, wounding the driver, George Highfill, in both knees. It also hit the horn button, causing it to sound, and hit one of the headlights so that it now shone straight up. That was enough for Highfill, who backed the car out of the way toward the Red Crown.[14]

Clyde may have won the first skirmish, but the war wasn't over. By now, the gunfight was in full swing. Across the street, Crawford and the two ladies retreated inside Slim's Castle after several bullets went whistling by their ears, the lawmen were firing from several directions, and Buck had opened up with another BAR from the right-hand cabin. One source said that Buck actually fired more than either Clyde or W. D.[15] During all this, Bonnie was trying to get to the car, parked in the garage attached to the left cabin, while W. D. Jones was starting it and firing as well. Bonnie and Clyde's cabin was connected to the garage with the car, but Buck and Blanche's cabin was not. They had to come out their front door and run for it.[16]

Just as Clyde was opening the garage door, Buck and Blanche made their break. Buck was firing a BAR to cover them, but before he got to the car, he was hit. Just in front of the garage, a .45 slug caught him in the left temple, fracturing his skull and exiting from his forehead. He went over backward, his BAR continuing to fire into the air. Blanche began screaming and trying to get Buck to his feet. Buck was not killed outright, nor even completely unconscious, but he couldn't get up. Clyde got the door open, and he and Blanche managed to drag Buck inside the car. As they came out of the garage, a bullet shattered one of the windows, and slivers of glass went into Blanche's eyes, but then the shooting stopped. Clyde came out of the driveway, finding just enough room to slide by the parked truck. They hit the highway and disappeared into the night. One of the state troopers wanted to chase him, but nobody else would go.[17]

After the Barrows escaped, everybody went to the cabins to see what was left behind. There were several articles of clothing, empty soda bottles and the remains of sandwiches, and quite a few weapons. Henry Humphrey's brother-in-law's .38 revolver, taken from him at Alma, was found along with the medical bag stolen from Dr. Fields' car at Enid, Oklahoma.[18]

For the first time, the police had the initiative, knew who they were dealing with, and had time to develop a plan of attack. In spite of all this, the Barrows escaped again. A myth of invincibility was beginning to form around them, but they knew better. This time, they got away, but not unhurt. Buck had a hideous head wound that would eventually kill him, and the glass in Blanche's eyes would later cost her part of her sight. Out of necessity, Clyde had become a pretty fair amateur doctor when dealing with cuts and bruises and flesh wounds, but this was completely out of his league. In the end, it made no difference. Both brothers were now convinced they would get a quick trip to the electric chair if caught, so going to a hospital only postponed the inevitable. In spite of Blanche's pleadings, Buck, in his conscious moments, agreed with Clyde. There was nothing to do but keep driving.[19]

CHAPTER 26
"Take Blanche and Run for It . . . I'm Done For"[1]

All Clyde could do for his brother and sister-in-law was wash Blanche's eyes out with water from a creek and pour hydrogen peroxide into the hole in Buck's skull. The sheer ferocity of the Barrows' firepower had left the officers at the Red Crown Tavern in a sort of shock following the gunfight, so that Clyde was able to drive away. This seemed to happen in all of the Barrows' shootouts. There would be a violent encounter, but no followup or chase by police until it was too late. In this case, and several others, the Barrows might have been caught easily if the police had been able to mount an effective pursuit. Not far from the Red Crown, Clyde pulled onto a side road. They had to change a tire and take stock of their injuries. It was here that Clyde first got a good look at his brother's wound.[2]

By morning, they were back in Iowa. Late that afternoon, July 20, they had found a place to lie low for a while. Just north of Dexter, Iowa, there had once been a park called Dexfield. It had opened in 1915, and, for a few years, was famous throughout the state. Open every Sunday, it was not unusual for several thousand people to come from as far away as Des Moines. It had a concrete swimming pool, a dance floor, a large amusement park, and even a small zoo. It was all abandoned now, the area around it grown up in underbrush. Other than serving as a local "lover's lane" for young people, the place was largely unused. Clyde

was able to pull off the road and back into a small clearing out of sight. They set up camp and tried to make Buck as comfortable as possible.[3]

The next morning, Friday the 21st, Clyde began running the errands required to provide for the rest of his group, but first he made a stop for himself. One thing people noticed about Clyde, even as a teenager with almost no money, was that he liked to keep clean and dress well. This day, he drove into Dexter and went into a clothing store. In the back, he found John Love working in the shoe shop. Clyde seemed at ease as he asked for some white shirts and a new pair of shoes. When Love came back with the things, Clyde suddenly seemed nervous, paid his bill, and left in a hurry. John Love's deputy sheriff badge was just visible inside his shirt pocket.

There was no such distraction at Blohm's Meat Market. Wilma Blohm just remembers a nice, polite young man ordering five dinners to go—complete with china and silverware—and a block of ice. While this was being prepared, Clyde went across to Pohle's Pharmacy and bought medical supplies. He returned to town on Saturday and Sunday and did the same thing—five dinners, a block of ice, and a trip to the pharmacy. By now, both the Blohms and the druggist knew something was strange about the young man, but neither said anything.[4]

By Sunday the 23rd, Buck was in a bad way. His brain had begun to swell from the trauma, and

The interior of Pohle's Drug Store as it looked when Clyde Barrow was a customer. The lady on the right is Lilian Pohle, who waited on him.
—Courtesy Robert Weesner

Dexfield Park in its heyday, circa 1920.
—Courtesy Robert Weesner

In July 1933, this building was the E. B. Pohle Drug Store in Dexter, Iowa, where Clyde Barrow bought medical supplies while the gang was hiding out at Dexfield Park. This picture was taken from across the street, from the approximate location of Blohm's Meat Market, where Wilma Blohm sold Barrow take-out dinners and ice, and loaned him china and silverware, which he returned.

—From the author's collection

tissue was coming out of the wound. Blanche was also in constant pain from the glass in her eye. On top of all that, Clyde was getting nervous about their car. They had managed to cover the Platte City bullet holes with mud, but it was only a matter of time before the car was spotted. Just after noon, Clyde and Jones drove north to the town of Perry in search of a replacement.

About 2:00 on Sunday afternoon, members of his family heard Ed Stoner's Ford V-8 sedan start and drive away from his house on Sixth Street. They assumed that a relative, Bob Stoner, had borrowed it, but when Bob came in the house an hour later, they realized the car had been stolen. By then, it was parked at the Barrows' campsite at Dexfield.[5]

That same Sunday afternoon, Henry Nye went for a walk near the old Dexfield property. The Ford parked in the woods didn't bother him—there had been campers there before—but the bloodstained shirt he found sure did. He called John Love, the deputy sheriff/shoemaker, who told him he had already had a couple of other calls about the folks at the park. Love went over to see for himself and then called his boss, Sheriff Clint Knee.[6]

Sheriff Knee didn't take long to make the connection. The shootout in Platte City was too fresh. At least in the law enforcement community, the

Barrow gang was on everybody's mind. While he couldn't be sure who the people were, Knee drove to Dexter and begin questioning townspeople while, at the same time, calling for reinforcements.

The presence of desperate outlaws just outside of town became the worst-kept secret in Dexter, Iowa. A young man who worked at Blohm's Market finished his day planning to join the crowd out at Dexfield and watch the desperadoes get captured the next morning. Just before closing time, he looked up, and there stood Clyde Barrow. Very un-outlawlike, Clyde was just returning Wilma Blohm's silverware and china, as he had promised her he would. He set the dishes down, bought some wieners and other things, and exited, leaving a very nervous clerk behind.[7]

Sheriff Knee's call for reinforcements yielded a few real lawmen, but the predominant result was a crowd of spectators. A couple of state officers, "Rags" Riley and Bill Arthur, showed up, and Dr. H. W. Keller, a dentist and National Guard officer, brought some Des Moines men, but the majority of the posse that would confront the Barrows would be local citizens. As the night wore on, the crowd grew in size and moved out to Dexfield Park. Word got around, and folks came out to see the show. Some brought their dates, and a number brought some very illegal "adult beverages." The manhunt was turning into a party.[8] Fortunately, the crowd was kept far enough away that they didn't alert the guests of honor.

In the campsite, there was activity late into the night—loading weapons, repacking ammunition, and running engines—suggesting that the group intended to leave the area. After all, they finally had a new car in good condition. They had been nursing the shot-up Platte City car for almost a week, but the Stoner Ford V-8 from Perry, now with new Texas plates, opened up the possibility of traveling in relative comfort and safety. The Barrow family says that the brothers had promised each other that if one was mortally wounded or killed, the other would take him home to the family in Dallas. The family contends that Buck's condition had gotten so bad that Clyde decided it was time to go home.[9] There might be some truth in this, but, in fact, Buck's head wound looked worse than it was—for the moment, at least. Buck was conscious and lucid but very weak. He would later succumb to infection because of the wound, but there was very little actual brain damage, even though the wound itself looked awful. Clyde's intentions, whatever they were, didn't matter in the end. The Barrows were about to be overcome by events.

As the sun came up on Monday, July 24, the posse that was going to confront whoever was camped out at Dexfield was divided into three squads. Sheriff Knee, the two state men Riley and Arthur, Dr. Keller, and two others would be the "point." They would move in for the actual arrest. Two other groups, one from Redfield, and the other from Dexter, would guard the exits from the park. The rest of the audience, those who had lasted through the night, were further back, waiting for

the show to start. At first light, Sheriff Knee and his men made their move, but if they hoped to catch the outlaws asleep, they were disappointed.[10]

It was just after 5:00 A.M., and at the campsite everybody was awake. Blanche was getting Buck a glass of water, Bonnie and Clyde were sitting on a seat cushion they had pulled out from the Platte City car, and W. D. was roasting the last of the hot dogs from the night before. It was either Bonnie or Clyde who happened to look up and see the figures moving through the underbrush. In that instant, whatever plans Clyde may have had were changed.

Surprise and extreme stress have all kinds of effects on people. Most people—even law enforcement officers—are so seldom put suddenly into true life-or-death situations that it's almost impossible to prepare for them. This was an area where Clyde Barrow had a natural advantage. When confronted with a sudden threat, some people will run, some will become hysterical, and some will simply freeze. Clyde seemed, from his earliest brushes with danger, to be the kind of person who could continue to think and function in the middle of fear and

Some members of the posse at Dexfield Park, Monday morning, July 24, 1933.

—Courtesy Rick Mattix

chaos. Since he also had several opportunities to experience and live through truly frightening gunfights, he was almost always better prepared to deal with the situation than was his opposition. This, along with the awesome firepower he carried, gave him a few seconds' head start, and a few seconds could mean the difference between life and death.

In an instant Clyde saw it all. He yelled to everyone to run for the car, picked up the nearest BAR, and emptied a magazine over the lawmen's heads.[11] Nobody in his right mind stands up as a military machine gun fires at him, so the six lawmen were immediately on the ground or behind cover. People up to 100 yards away were surprised to find leaves, branches, and entire limbs falling around them as the .30 caliber bullets cut through the trees. "Rags" Riley went down, stunned by a glancing blow to the head. He was the only lawman wounded.[12]

Clyde got his few seconds, but that was all. These Iowa men were shocked—as lawmen always were—at the firepower, but they didn't run and they didn't freeze. Within a few seconds, they were all returning fire. W. D. Jones was hit with buckshot and knocked down twice before he made it to the car—small but painful flesh wounds. Bonnie limped along, helping Buck and Blanche into the back seat as Clyde covered the group as best he could. W. D. couldn't get the Ford started, so Clyde shoved him over and took his place.[13]

As soon as the engine caught, Clyde was backing the Stoner car away from the lawmen. He then turned and started out of the park but was met by gunfire from another part of the posse. As he backed away again, he was hit in the shoulder and lost control of the car. It ran over a stump and hung up on the bumper. W. D. made a quick try to pry it loose, but they were stuck fast. Clyde got everybody out and headed back for the other car, but it was no use. The posse shot out all the windows and tires and ruined the engine. The only thing left was to try and hide.

As the Barrows headed for the woods, the posse continued to fire. W. D. was stunned again by a glancing shot, Bonnie took shotgun pellets to the midsection, and Buck was hit again, but they got a few minutes' relief as they disappeared into the underbrush and out of sight. Sheriff Knee and his men had not given up, but tracking desperate killers through thick brush was a dangerous business, so the pursuit slowed down. Clyde moved everybody as fast as he could, but Buck was on his last legs. The group made it to the top of a rise overlooking the South Racoon River, where Buck finally collapsed. He asked Clyde to take Blanche and run for it— "I'm done for," he said—but Blanche wasn't having any of it. She had stood by Buck when he was an escaped convict, when he was in prison, and all through his disastrous reunion with Clyde. This was her third pitched gun battle—although there is no evidence she ever fired a gun—in four months. She was not about to leave him now.[14]

Clyde told them all to hide as best they could, and he would find a car and come back for them. With that, he took a BAR and a pistol and headed down the hill toward a bridge where the road crossed the river. W. D. took Bonnie and crawled into some bushes while Buck and Blanche hid near an old baseball diamond.[15]

Off in the direction Clyde had gone, there was a flurry of gunshots, and Bonnie was sure Clyde had been killed, but a few minutes later he returned. He had run into some posse members, lost the BAR, and turned back. Now they were separated from Buck and Blanche and had only Clyde's .45, which was empty. They were all wounded and in a generally sorry state, but Clyde knew their only chance was to keep moving. The only way to go was across the Racoon River, so down the bank they went, then into the water, blood trailing behind them. They paddled across with Bonnie on W. D.'s back and hid in a corn field.[16]

It wasn't yet 6:00 A.M., but Iowa farm families were early risers, so young Marvelle Fellers was already at work around the barn, along with his father, Valley Fellers, and his uncle, Walt, when his dog began to bark and run toward the corn field. The young man followed and saw a small, bloody, wet, and bedraggled man holding a pistol. "Call this dog off, or I'll kill him," he said. Marvelle grabbed his dog, and the man called to the other two men to come down where he could watch them. Clyde

The South Racoon River viewed from the bridge where Clyde Barrow had a short firefight with officers during his first attempt to find a getaway car after they were chased into the brush by the posse. Clyde retreated back up the hillside and found Bonnie and W. D. Jones, and the three of them came down to the river again and swam across just out of sight around the bend. The old Dexfield Park was on top of the ridge to the right.

—From the author's collection

then whistled and W. D. approached the barn, half carrying Bonnie. Clyde told the men that he didn't want to hurt anybody, but they had to have a car because "the laws are shooting the devil out of us." Of the three cars on the farm, only one would run, so Clyde watched as Marvelle backed a 1929 Plymouth out of the garage and the other two men lifted Bonnie inside. As they were about to leave, Clyde ask Valley Fellers, "You ain't going to shoot us in the back while we're driving off, are you?" Mr. Fellers replied that he only had one shotgun shell, and it was in the house. With that, what was left of the Barrow gang drove out of sight.[17]

Bonnie, Clyde, and W. D. Jones had made it across the river, but Buck and Blanche weren't going anywhere. As the posse closed in, they hid behind a large log. Buck managed to get his pistol up but was shot again as he tried to shield Blanche.[18] At that point, she stood up and begged the lawmen to stop. "You've already killed him," she said.[19] A few more tense moments and they

were prisoners. Blanche had come through the shootout with hardly a scratch, but with the glass in her eye, she could barely see. Buck, on the other hand, now had three new bullet holes to go with his five-day-old head wound. He was in and out of consciousness, so the lawmen decided to take them to the nearest medical help available.

Doctors Keith Chapler and Robert Osborn were in the middle of a tonsillectomy in their office in Dexter when they were descended upon by a group of bloody, agitated people, most of whom were heavily armed. After the confusion died down and the situation was explained, the poor tonsillectomy patient was forgotten and the doctors began to examine the two prisoners. Blanche's main injury was the crushed glass that had been in both eyes for the last five days. She had developed what the doctors called "traumatic conjunctivitis." Part of the time, she was calm and cooperative, but other times, they found her aggressive and slightly hysterical. During one trip to the restroom, Blanche tried to run out a side entrance but was stopped by the nurse.

Buck's condition was much more serious. The old head wound was the most obvious problem. Dr. Chapler and Dr. Osborn both examined it and asked Buck about it. He told them that they had just poured hydrogen peroxide into the hole in his forehead and let it run out the one in his temple—three or four times a day. All he had for the pain was aspirin. His skull was badly fractured, and brain tissue was seeping out of the two openings, but the wound was amazingly clean, and Buck said it wasn't bothering him all that much. What was hurting him at the moment were the three new bullet wounds, two in his hip, and, especially, the

Dexter posse members gathered around the fallen Marvin Ivan "Buck" Barrow. The figure in the white undershirt, kneeling with his back to the camera, is often mistaken for the wounded outlaw, but he is, in fact, a member of the posse from Dexter named Virgil Musselman. Buck Barrow's upper body and right leg can be seen on the ground just in front of Musselman.
—Courtesy Robert Weesner

Buck Barrow, head bandaged, just above the corner of the open car door, is helped into a car after being captured at Dexfield Park. He and Blanche were taken to Dexter, Iowa, for first aid medical treatment. Buck was then taken to a hospital in Perry, Iowa, and Blanche remained in custody. July 24, 1933.
—Courtesy Rick Mattix

one in his back. The doctors found that a .45 slug had entered his back, bounced off a rib, and was lodged in his chest cavity. They could give only first aid, but promised to follow Buck to the hospital and do what they could.

Getting Buck and Blanche out of Dexter and up to the hospital in Perry was now the problem. Word had gotten out by now that it was the famous Barrow gang in the shootout, and the streets of Dexter had filled up for blocks around the doctor's office with curious folks who wanted a look at the desperadoes. Also, the gang's reputation was such that everyone believed there was a real possibility that the escaped members might come back. The lawmen used this fear to disperse the crowd. A policeman was sent out with a bullhorn to announce that they had just received a phone call that Bonnie and Clyde were on the way back to Dexter to rescue Buck and Blanche. It was a lie, of course, but it was something the crowd seemed ready to believe. In the words of Dr. Chapler, "In five or six minutes ... you could have shot a cannonball down Main Street and never touched a soul."[20]

By midday, Buck was in Perry, Iowa. He was taken to King's Daughters Hospital, where Chapler and Osborn were able to remove the bullet from his chest. The two bullets in his hip could not be located easily, but they presented little danger compared to the other two wounds. The doctors agreed that he would probably develop meningitis from the head wound or pneumonia from the chest wound. Either way, there was little hope for his recovery.[21] Blanche was taken first to the county seat of Adel, and then to Des Moines. Late Tuesday evening, July 25, she was moved to

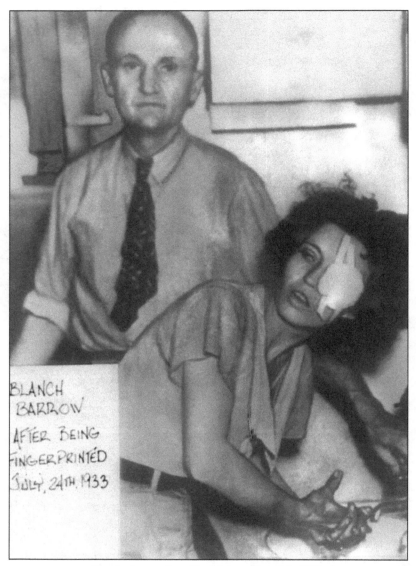

Blanche in custody at Des Moines, Iowa. July 1933.
—Courtesy Marie Barrow Scoma and author Phillip W. Steele

Platte City, Missouri. She never saw her husband again.

While all this was going on, the free members of the gang had troubles of their own. The only way to go from the Fellers farm was north to the town of Panora. From there, they drove generally eastward for a while. Before long, though, the blue '29 Plymouth, which had seemed like their salvation, had a flat.[22] The two wounded men managed

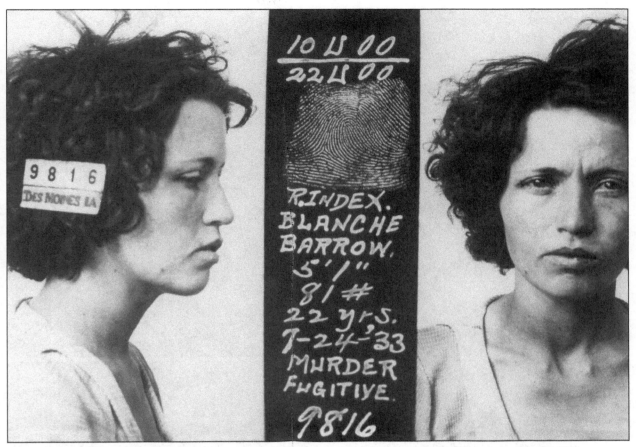

Blanche Barrow, identification card from Des Moines, Iowa, following the shootout near Dexter, Iowa, July 24, 1933.

—Courtesy Rick Mattix

King's Daughters Hospital, Perry, Iowa. Buck Barrow was taken here for surgery to remove a bullet from his chest after the Dexfield shootout. His mother and brother, L. C., arrived two days later, but Buck developed pneumonia and possibly meningitis from his wounds and died here on July 29, 1933.

—Courtesy Rick Mattix

to change the tire, but the old Plymouth didn't seem like it would last for the long haul. Shortly after the flat, they lost control and sideswiped a telephone pole. By now, they were near the town of Polk City, north of Des Moines, so they robbed a gas station and stole a Chevrolet.[23] Then, as they had done so many times before, they simply disappeared. Over the following several days, they would be reported in many places in the Midwest, but they had gone to ground. It would be four months before another lawman got a clear shot at Bonnie and Clyde.

One of the cars abandoned by the Barrow gang at Dexter, Iowa, July 24, 1933. This car was stolen in Perry, Iowa, from Edward Stoner on July 23, 1933, and recovered the next day, after the gunfight. The Ford V-8 was later put on display at a gas station in Dexter, Iowa, and finally cut up during a scrap-metal drive during World War II.

—Courtesy the Texas Ranger Hall of Fame and Museum, Waco, Texas

CHAPTER 27

"He Was a Good Boy When He Was Little"

News of the Dexter shootout and the capture and wounding of Buck Barrow reached the Barrow family in Dallas late on Monday, July 24. At 1:00 A.M. Tuesday morning, Cumie Barrow and her son L. C. left for Iowa. With them went Bonnie's mother, Emma Parker, and her sister, Billie Mace. A friend of Blanche's, May Turner, went also, but Blanche had been moved before she got there. The group from Texas arrived just before noon on Wednesday the 26th. By then, Buck was in and out of consciousness and running a fever of 104. All Cumie could do was sit by him and hold his hand. A reporter for the Perry paper was so impressed by Cumie's sorrow that he wrote a short column about her. When the reporter asked about Buck, Cumie just said, "He was a good boy when he was little."[1] Four months before, Buck had walked out of prison a free man and gone home to his wife with a pardon from the state of Texas. Now it had come to this.

During the first couple of days that Buck was in King's Daughters Hospital—before the high fever and coma set in—he talked freely to everyone and had a lot of visitors. Among the various lawmen who wanted to question him was Crawford County (Arkansas) Sheriff Albert Maxey. As soon as word came of Buck's capture, Maxey and Deputy Salyers, who had survived the gunfight that killed Marshal Henry Humphrey, started for Iowa. Buck had been identified by several witness-

es, and they wanted to talk to him. On Tuesday afternoon, they got in to see him. "Do you remember me, Buck?" Salyers asked.

"I sure do," Buck said. "It was a good thing you got out of the way, or you might have got yours."[2]

Buck talked at some length to Sheriff Maxey and freely confessed that he had been the one who shot Marshal Humphrey.[3] He also answered other questions that cleared up several things about the Crawford County incident. For instance, nobody knew how Buck and his partner got back together with the rest of the gang at the motel, or even who the partner was. Most folks assumed it was Clyde, but Buck was very firm in saying that Clyde was not at the shooting. He had stayed at the motel with Bonnie. Buck told Maxey about walking across the railroad bridge to get back to the motel and that, while the police were combing the brush north of Van Buren on Friday night, the gang was moving to Oklahoma. Contrary to the statement made later in the book *Fugitives*, Buck also denied any involvement in the attack on Mrs. Rogers and stated that the entire Barrow group was in eastern Oklahoma at the time.[4]

The one thing Buck would not talk about was the identity of his partner at the Alma shooting. Other than saying that Clyde was not involved, he had no comment. W. D. had used the alias "Jack Sherman," and that name was circulating, but his real identity was still unknown to authorities.[5]

Thirty miles away, the authorities were leaning on Blanche for the same information. Buck had used a silent approach, but Blanche decided on a different strategy. She lied.

While Buck was moved to the hospital in Perry, Blanche ended up in custody in Des Moines. There she was interrogated Monday evening and on through Tuesday. Blanche said that even J. Edgar Hoover flew in to question her. She had a patch over one eye, and she said that Hoover threatened to "gouge out" her other eye if she didn't talk.[6] Blanche talked, all right, and they thought she had given them what they wanted—the name of the third man. Nobody believed the "Jack Sherman" alias for long, but Blanche gave them another name—Hubert Bleigh. Something about Blanche's "cooperation" must have impressed the lawmen, because they immediately began to look for this man.

Hubert Newton Bleigh, alias Herbert Blythe, age twenty-six, was certainly not the man the law was seeking—W. D. Jones was still at large and unidentified—but he wasn't a fictitious character like "Jack Sherman" either. He was probably some small-time crook whom Blanche remembered from the gang's earlier dealings. Whoever he was, he was alive and well two days later when Oklahoma authorities found him reading a newspaper in an oil field grocery store near Seminole and arrested him.[7] He claimed that he had been in Oklahoma visiting his brother for the last three weeks. Of course, nobody expected him to admit that he was Clyde Barrow's partner in any case. There was also a matter of some stolen goods found in his car. Blythe spent Friday in Oklahoma City with federal officers. In Kansas City, his picture was identified by Platte City witnesses. On Saturday, July 29, Marvin Ivan "Buck" Barrow died in Perry, Iowa, and Herbert Blythe was "positively" identified as Buck's accomplice in the Alma shooting by the two living witnesses, Deputy Salyers and Weber Wilson, who had been driven to Oklahoma City to see him.[8] Federal officers turned him over to Sheriff Albert Maxey, and by Saturday evening, Blythe was sitting in the Crawford County Jail at Van Buren.[9] To no one's surprise, Blythe told anyone who would listen that they had the wrong man. He swore he was not involved in any of the Barrows' shootings. He was telling the truth, but nobody believed him.

The case against Blythe seemed solid. By August 1, the *Fort Smith Times Record* was reporting that Crawford County prosecuting attorney Finis F. Batchelor was ready to file first-degree murder charges. The promise of a big trial and the prospect of justice served was not to be, however. As the days went by, the eyewitnesses became less positive. By August 11, Sheriff Maxey and Prosecuting Attorney Batchelor had given up. Several of the eyewitnesses now said that Blythe resembled one of the men, but no one was prepared to testify against him in a murder trial. Blythe had always denied any part in the Alma shooting, but he was not away free and clear. There was still that matter of the stolen goods found in his car. On August 11, when Blythe was released in Van Buren, U.S. Marshal Cooper Hudspeth took charge of him and transported him to Muskogee, Oklahoma, for arraignment on robbery charges. But that was better than being linked to Bonnie and Clyde.[10]

Meanwhile, the clues to the whereabouts of Bonnie and Clyde were few and far between. The car they stole in Polk City, Iowa, was recovered three days later in Broken Bow, Nebraska, but, other than that, the trail was cold.[11] What we know about their movements during August comes almost exclusively from the testimony of W. D. Jones and the memory of Clyde's sister, Marie, and the two versions don't always coincide.

Both agree that the three of them spent most of August moving around, holding up service stations and grocery stores, and healing from their wounds. Jones later said that they broke into an armory in Illinois for weapons and ammunition. There is no confirmation for this, but since they left Dexter with one empty pistol between the three of them, weapons would be one of Clyde's top priorities.[12] Around the first of September, W. D. Jones left the gang for good, but there are conflicting accounts about how it happened.

On two different occasions, W. D. Jones said

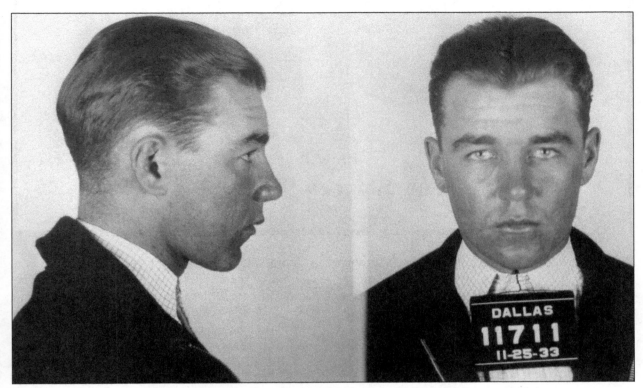

Mug shot of William Daniel Jones. Taken in Dallas, November 25, 1933, three months after he left Bonnie and Clyde.
—From the collections of the Texas/Dallas History and Archives Division, Dallas Public Library

that when he left Bonnie and Clyde for the last time, he had to run away from them. He said he got away after putting gas in one of their stolen cars near Clarksdale, Mississippi, and then hitchhiked, or "hoboed," back to the Houston, Texas, area, where his mother lived.[13]

Marie Barrow remembers it differently. She said that Jones agreed to stay with Bonnie and Clyde until they had recovered enough to go it alone. Meanwhile, they coached Jones on what he should say if he was ever arrested. The story was similar to the one Bonnie had used when she was arrested at Kaufman, Texas, the year before. Jones was to say that he was Clyde's prisoner, that he was tied to trees at night to keep him from escaping. He would also claim he was unconscious when any shooting or killing was going on. Marie said that just after the first of September, Bonnie and Clyde took Jones back to west Dallas themselves.[14] Whether Jones escaped or was taken home by his

heroes, and whether he made up his story himself or was coached by Clyde, in less than three months, Jones would have a chance to tell his story to police.

In fact, W. D. Jones actually told his story a third time. A little over a year after he was arrested and gave his statement to Dallas authorities, he, along with several others, was tried for harboring Bonnie and Clyde. In his testimony at the trial, Jones ended his account of his time with the Barrow gang by saying that sometime after the August 20, 1933, robbery of the armory in Illinois, he returned to Dallas with Bonnie and Clyde, contradicting his earlier testimony in Dallas.[15] Whatever the truth of the events surrounding William Daniel "Deacon" Jones' final separation from the Barrow gang, one thing is certain. The young man had enjoyed about all the glamorous outlaw life he could stand. He considered himself lucky to be alive and was happy to go back to picking cotton.[16]

CHAPTER 28

The Sowers Ambush

If you were to give the time from March through October 1933 a name, it might be "Gangster Summer." The list of people active during this time reads like a who's who of depression-era outlaws. Rarely in American history have so many infamous characters been in the news at the same time. Reputations and careers—on both sides of the law—were made during this time. One man, the director of a small investigative arm of the Justice Department, took advantage of government reorganization under new president Franklin D. Roosevelt and public interest in the crime wave that seemed to be sweeping the country to lay the foundation of a personal empire that would last for forty years. The agency that would become J. Edgar Hoover's FBI would play only a small part in the Bonnie and Clyde story, however. Its fame was gained by going after other famous criminals, and, in the summer of 1933, there were a lot to choose from.

Headlines featured the Barrows' three major shootouts, along with Pretty Boy Floyd, Vern Miller, "Jelly" Nash, and the Union Station Massacre in Kansas City. The Barker brothers and Alvin Karpis in Minnesota, and George "Machine Gun" Kelly and his wife Kathryn in Oklahoma got into the kidnapping business, and Harvey Bailey, Wilbur Underhill (the Tri-State Terror), and nine others broke out of the Kansas State Prison—all before Labor Day. Unnoticed amid all this activity, on May 22, 1933, an unknown thirty-year-old from

Mooresville, Indiana, was released from prison after nine years. While Bonnie and Clyde would be known by their first names, this fellow's last name would be his trademark. John Dillinger's career only lasted a year, but among all the other bad men of the depression, he would become the superstar.

All this activity made for booming newspaper sales, but when Bonnie and Clyde got back to Dallas in early September, they would have been happy to never read their names in the headlines again. The past four months had made them famous—and almost destroyed them in the process. Every member of the Barrow gang of 1933 had been killed, wounded, or captured. They wanted nothing more than to reconnect with their families and keep their heads down.

The family in Dallas, who hadn't seen them since early June, immediately noticed the changes in Bonnie and Clyde. First were the obvious physical changes. Both were thin from hard living and scarred from several gunshot wounds. Emma Parker, who hadn't seen her daughter since before the Wellington wreck, was shocked. Never very large to begin with, Bonnie was even thinner and looked older than her twenty-three years. Bonnie's right leg looked awful from the burns and was drawn up underneath her so that she couldn't walk normally.[1] Marie Barrow said that the family noticed psychological changes as well. The pair both seemed, more than ever, fatalistic about their future. Buck's death affected Clyde deeply, and he and Bonnie had no illusions as to what awaited them. They seemed to feel that they would rather face it in Texas, where they were near the only people they loved and trusted.[2]

At this point, Bonnie and Clyde were living completely in their car or in abandoned farmhouses. Their families helped them as much as they could with food and blankets, and Clyde supported them with low-profile, nickel-and-dime robberies. Faced with this sort of situation, it helps if you are a little creative, and they were. One of their favorite tricks was to drive into a town late at night and park in somebody's driveway. The police always assumed the car belonged there, so they could sleep almost all night. The only time it didn't work was when an irate wife saw them and accused her husband of having his drinking buddies sneak by to pick him up. They heard her yelling and didn't wait around to hear the end of the argument.[3]

Bonnie and Clyde had been away almost four months, so now that they were back in the area, they stayed close to home. Emma Parker said that they came by either her house or the Barrow filling station almost every night during September and October. Why the Dallas Sheriff's Department didn't just stake out the two places and catch them was a source of amazement to both families, but "the kids," as the families called them, came and went pretty much at will.[4] When they weren't coming by to visit, the family was meeting them out in the country somewhere.

Marie Barrow remembered some humorous incidents that took their minds off the cloud that hung over them all, at least for a while, and in one of them, Clyde's ego got the best of him. It seems that Clyde's brother L. C. had come by a motorcycle from some source, and, at one of their country meetings, Clyde decided to demonstrate his driving skills. As it happened, his mastery of the Ford V-8 didn't translate to the two-wheeler. Clyde got on the motorcycle and drove down the country road and out of sight. He said he would be right back, but the minutes passed with no sign of him. Just as they were preparing to organize a search party, they heard a gunshot and hurried off in that direction. Instead of a posse, they found Clyde in a field beside

the road—pinned under the motorcycle. It had gotten away from him, and he had to use the only signaling device he had, his ever-present pistol. Luckily, nothing was bruised but Clyde's pride.[5]

Along with the happiness that came from being back home that autumn, there was also sorrow. Bonnie loved babies, and, since she had none of her own, her favorites were her little nephews, Buddy and Jackie, Billie Jean Mace's children. On October 11, 1933, two-year-old Jackie became ill and died two days later. Bonnie took the news very hard. On Sunday the 15th, Mrs. Parker met Bonnie again and told her that four-year-old Buddy was now sick as well. By the next day, he was in the hospital, and by Tuesday night he was dead also. When Mrs. Parker came to tell Bonnie the news on Wednesday evening, Bonnie told her that she had already seen Buddy dead in a dream.[6]

The deaths of the two little children came at a time when Clyde was looking ahead to his own end. Buck had been in the ground a little over two months, but there was still no headstone. These were hard times, and the Barrows, like most of their neighbors, were forced to be practical. By now, everybody accepted the fact that Clyde would never surrender and that even if he did, the electric chair was waiting for him. It was agreed that both brothers would be buried side by side and one stone used for both. Clyde even picked the color and his inscription: "Gone But Not Forgotten."[7]

October turned into November, and things remained calm. Of course, Bonnie and Clyde sightings still occurred almost every day, and the newspapers linked Clyde with a series of robberies all over the area. Sometimes, Clyde really was involved—they had to eat, after all—but most of these were cases of a well-known name being put to a face seen only over the barrel of a gun. The family meetings continued every few days, and everybody kept their fingers crossed.

The family meeting was a thing Clyde Barrow had perfected over the last year and a half. There were literally dozens of places in the countryside outside Dallas where he and Bonnie could meet with family and friends in relative safety. The secret to keeping the meetings safe was short notice and unpredictability. Clyde would leave word at his father's Star Service Station, and his mother would pass the message to the rest of the Barrow and Parker families by using code words in phone calls. No one knew exactly where the meeting would be until the last minute. In this way, the risk was kept to a minium. On November 21, 1933, a meeting was held on a strip of newly graded road near the tiny town of Sowers. If you drive by it today, on your way to Dallas/Fort Worth Airport, you see a Ramada Inn, a McDonald's, and a Red Lobster because Sowers is near the intersection of Texas State Highway 183 and Esters Road, just west of Irving, but in the winter of 1933, it was out in the boondocks. The property along the road was owned by Charlie Stovall, who ran a dairy farm.[8]

Bonnie and Clyde had been out of town and drove in from Oklahoma. They spent most of the day visiting, because it was a special occasion—Cumie Barrow's fifty-ninth birthday. The only thing wrong with the birthday party was that Clyde didn't have a present for his mother. Cumie, whose best present was waking up in the morning to find that Clyde was still alive, didn't care about that, but Clyde insisted that he would bring one the next day. For some reason—maybe out of convenience, or maybe due to carelessness—he decided they could meet at the same place the next evening. Clyde had several favorite meeting places, but he never used the same one twice in a row. Tomorrow he would, and would live to regret it.[9]

Sometime after 6:00 P.M. the next evening, November 22, a car drove by the Stovall farm from the east. It slowed down and finally turned around and parked, facing back toward Dallas. The car was driven by Joe Bill Francis and contained the same people who had been there the day before, Joe Bill's soon-to-be-wife, Marie Barrow, L. C. Barrow, Cumie Barrow, Emma Parker, and Billie Jean Mace. About 6:45, a black Ford V-8 coupe approached from the north on Esters Road and stopped at the intersection. Clyde later told his family that he asked Bonnie, "How do you feel about it, honey? It seems phony tonight."[10] It didn't feel right, but he could see Joe Bill's car just down the road, so he decided to chance it.

As he approached the parked car, the bad feeling increased. Clyde caught a glimpse of something out of place and decided to keep going.[11] Just as he passed his family's car and shifted to second gear, four lawmen opened fire from a ditch about twenty-five yards away. Everybody in the parked car hit the floor—they were almost in the line of fire—and Clyde floored the gas pedal, even as glass shattered around him and pieces of the steering wheel came off in his hand. Dallas County Sheriff Smoot Schmid and deputies Ted Hinton, Ed Caster, and Bob Alcorn had been waiting for an hour or so for Bonnie and Clyde to come by. Schmid and Hinton had .45 caliber Thompson submachine guns, and Caster had a .351 rifle—all of which did nothing against the steel Ford body except break glass and make a great deal of noise. In fact, Sheriff Schmid, in all the excitement, jammed his Thompson and didn't even get a shot off.[12] The only one who did any good was Bob Alcorn. He had decided to match Clyde's firepower and had acquired a .30 caliber Browning automatic rifle. It shot completely through the car, and one round wounded both Bonnie and Clyde in the legs.[13]

As soon as he could, Joe Bill started his car and drove away from the firefight. Everybody else was on the floor except fifteen-year-old Marie. She just had to watch out the back window to see what happened. In a few seconds, she triumphantly announced to her mother that Clyde had made it over the hill and escaped.[14] In Clyde's Ford V-8 coupe, there were a few seconds of noise and flying glass as the car shook from the impact of bullets, windows broke, and a tire blew out, but Clyde was already on the move when the shooting started and after a few seconds was out of range. He and Bonnie returned fire from one or two pistols but really didn't know where the lawmen were and feared that they might hit some of their family instead.[15] Their main goal was to get out of sight.

Sheriff Schmid and his posse just stood in the road and watched them go. They had parked so far away that pursuit was impossible. At least, for all their trouble, they had managed to wound both Bonnie and Clyde. Unfortunately, they had created a "friendly fire" incident as well. One of Bob

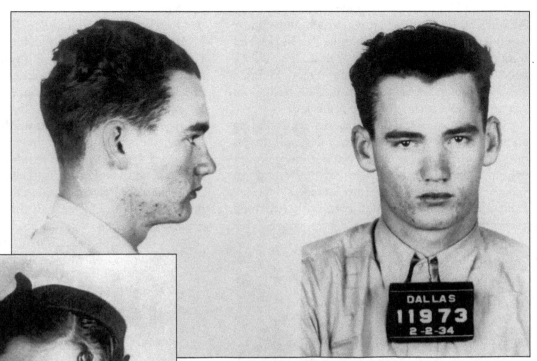

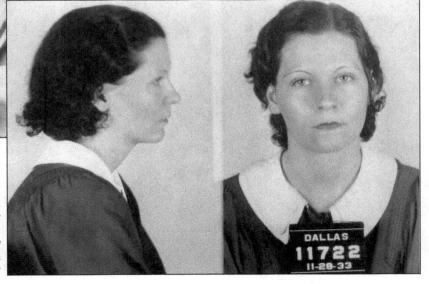

Joe Bill Francis mug shot. Taken at the Dallas (Texas) Sheriff's Department, February 2, 1934. Joe Bill married Marie Barrow a week before Bonnie and Clyde were killed.

—Courtesy the Texas Ranger Hall of Fame and Museum, Waco, Texas

Marie Barrow about the time of her marriage to Joe Bill Francis. May 1934.

—Courtesy Marie Barrow Scoma and author Phillip W. Steele

Mug shot of Billie Jean Parker Mace. Taken in Dallas, November 28, 1933, six days after the Sowers ambush.

—From the collections of the Texas/ Dallas History and Archives Division, Dallas Public Library

Alcorn's 30-06 rounds had gone high and slightly wounded Mrs. Stovall, the dairyman's wife, several hundred yards away. All this was not going to look good in the morning papers, but Smoot Schmid was a politician first and foremost, and he had an ace in the hole sitting in a cell at his jail.

Meanwhile, Clyde's first priority was securing another car. He was running on a flat, and, for all he knew, there was a whole posse a few minutes behind him. About four miles from the ambush site, they passed near the Army Air Corps' Hensley Field and stopped an older Ford with two men

Bonnie Parker. Taken during a family meeting near Dallas. November 1933.
—From the collections of the Texas/Dallas History and Archives Division, Dallas Public Library

inside. Thomas James and Paul Reich, both of Fort Worth, were on their way home from a Masonic Lodge reunion. They were in no mood to be hijacked, so they didn't get out of the car as Clyde ordered. Under the circumstances, Clyde was a little cranky himself, so rather than argue the issue, he just put his .16 gauge sawed-off shotgun up against the window, aimed over the men's heads, and fired. It blew out two windows, put a hole in the roof, and took one man's hat off. The men inside immediately reconsidered, and within seconds, Bonnie and Clyde had the car all to themselves—not that it was any prize. This older four-cylinder model was not Clyde's style, but it would have to do.[16] After fumbling around to find the ignition switch, he and Bonnie disappeared in the darkness.

At one point in their escape along country roads, Clyde had to get out and open a gate. He stepped out of the car and promptly fell down in the mud. Bonnie tried to help him and fell down also. Later they found blood on the floor and finally discovered that they had been shot through the knees. In all the excitement, they simply hadn't noticed. Floyd Hamilton later said that they found an underworld doctor in Oklahoma to treat them. Six days later, they were back in Dallas.[17]

The next day, Dallas newsboys were calling, "Read all about it! Sheriff escapes from Clyde Barrow."[18] In spite of his failure to capture the famous outlaws, however, Sheriff Schmid managed to avoid much of the criticism by redirecting the interest of the news media. He had a bullet-riddled, blood-soaked car to put on display, and a public relations secret weapon as well. A few days before the ambush, W. D. Jones had been picked up in Houston and brought to Dallas.[19] Jones underwent intensive interrogation and on November 18 dictated a twenty-eight-page statement covering his time with Bonnie and Clyde. Up until now, Sheriff Schmid had kept Jones under wraps and flatly denied press reports about a Barrow gang member being held, but with the ambush a failure, it was time to show "Deacon" Jones to the public.[20]

Looking back from the vantage point of the twenty-first century, Jones' statement is an intriguing document—an interesting mixture of fact and fiction. Much of it simply tells the story as it was. Jones was smart enough to lie as little as possible. His objective seemed to be just what Clyde suggested—he didn't deny being with them, he just played down his role as much as possible. While much of the account was truthful, his portrayal of the gunfights and the killings were a little too self-serving. Even the police didn't believe for a second that he was Bonnie and Clyde's prisoner, or that he was unconscious during all the shooting, but W. D. knew how to play the part of the victim pretty well. The clean-cut, scared-looking young man the police showed the press bore little resemblance to the cigar-chomping, tough-looking gangster in the pictures that came out of Joplin. In fact, W. D. Jones had been involved in scores of robberies, six gunfights or shootings, and at least one murder, all before he was eighteen years old.

There were several surprises for the police in Jones' statement, but one had immediate impact on one of Bonnie and Clyde's former partners. Frank Hardy had been with Bonnie and Clyde briefly about a year before, in Missouri, but left them for good soon after the bank job in Oronogo at the end of November 1932. A few weeks later, on Christmas Day, Clyde and W. D Jones killed Doyle Johnson in Temple, Texas, but they were not identified or connected with the murder. It was poor Frank Hardy who was eventually arrested for it. Hardy had just been tried, but the result was a

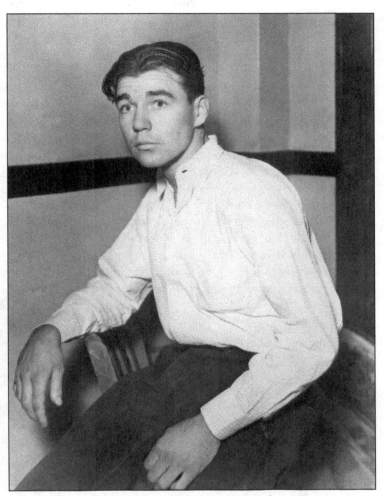

W. D. Jones in the Dallas jail. Early December 1933.
—From the collections of the Texas/Dallas History and Archives Division, Dallas Public Library

hung jury. He was waiting for his second trial to begin when W. D. Jones was caught. Fortunately for Hardy, when Jones told his story, all of that changed. It seemed that the law was willing to believe Jones' story and lay the Johnson killing on Clyde instead. They were almost right. Clyde was there, for sure, and tried his best to shoot Johnson, but it was actually W. D.'s bullet that killed him. Frank Hardy didn't care who they blamed as long as it wasn't him.[21]

W.D. also served Sheriff Schmid in another capacity. One of the big questions asked after the Sowers ambush was "Who tipped off the law?" Neither the press nor the Barrow family believed that the ambush was just a lucky break for the sheriff. Both sides knew someone had talked. For the benefit of the public, who didn't know the real situation, the Dallas Sheriff's Office said that they "acted on a tip received from a prisoner in the county jail."[22] As soon as Jones' capture became known, it was obvious who they meant. On the other hand, Ted Hinton, forty-five years after Clyde was dead and buried, identified Stovall, the dairy farmer, as the source of the information.[23]

The Barrow family, however, didn't believe either story. They knew that W. D. was not the informer. He simply couldn't have known, and Stovall's name didn't come up until later. That left, in their minds, a very short list. The issue was still alive as recently as a few years ago, according to a conversation between Ted Hinton's son and Marie Barrow. Hinton's son stood by his father's statement that Stovall was the informant, but, in Marie's mind, it came down to Joe Bill Francis (her ex-husband) or Billie Mace. The question can't be resolved either way, but Mr. Stovall's daughter was recently interviewed and expressed serious doubts that her father had provided any information on Bonnie and Clyde.[24]

As December 1933 began, nothing really had changed. The newspapers had another headline; the law was no closer to Bonnie and Clyde than they had been since July; and the famous outlaw couple had gained a little more media attention, a few more scars, and were right back where they had been before.

Members of the Sowers Ambush posse with captured items. From left to right: Sheriff R. A. "Smoot" Schmid, Deputy Ed Castor, Deputy Ted Hinton, and Deputy Robert Alcorn. November 23, 1933.

—From the collections of the Texas/Dallas History and Archives Division, Dallas Public Library

CHAPTER 29
The Eastham Raid

When Clyde got back to Dallas at the beginning of December, he was angry. As Bonnie would later say in her most famous poem, he had "been shot at before,"[1] but this last ambush was different. In Clyde's way of thinking, as rough as the game was, there were still some basic rules. Clyde accepted the fact that he and even Bonnie were fair game, but, to him, the sheriff placing his mother and Mrs. Parker in the line of fire was unforgivable. In Clyde's mind, they had broken the rules, and he wanted to make them pay. For the first time since he and the trusty at Eastham Prison Farm had killed his tormentor, "Big Ed," Clyde Barrow was considering premeditated, cold-blooded murder. In the presence of his family and others, he threatened the lives of Sheriff Schmid and Deputies Bob Alcorn and Ted Hinton. Clyde is even said to have found out where Schmid and Alcorn lived and staked out their homes with the idea of killing them if he got the chance. His family considered this to be revenge and tried to talk him out of it.[2]

Singling out revenge as a wrong motivation for murder may seem odd, since Clyde already was linked to nine killings. But right or wrong, Clyde looked upon his fight with the law almost like combat, and so far, he felt that all his killings had come in the heat of battle. The way he looked at it, lawmen had to take their chances just like he did. Clyde took no joy in killing—after the first couple of shootings, he told his sister that he felt sick

about it afterward—but was also firm in his belief that "it was him or me."[3] To Clyde's mother and father and others in his family, who had to read in the paper about the men he killed and the wives and children they left behind, that was about the only thread they had to cling to.

As bad as the other killings were (especially of unarmed civilians like Doyle Johnson and possibly Howard Hall), to Clyde's family, what he was planning now was worse. Clyde was already being called a "Mad Dog Killer" by the police and the news media. That wasn't the son and brother they knew, and they told people so. They didn't want it to finally become true. Fortunately, when Clyde's initial efforts failed, he was talked out of the idea.[4] Before long, something else came along to capture his interest.

Raymond Hamilton had been in custody and out of circulation for a year (except for a couple of hours when he broke out of the Hill County Jail on March 23, 1933).[5] He had been moved around from trial to trial until he had accumulated about four lifetimes' worth of jail time.[6] On August 8, 1933, Ray was finally taken to Huntsville and then to Eastham Farm. Although he wouldn't help Clyde and Ralph Fults to free convicts from Eastham a year and a half before, now the plan for a raid on the prison farm began to look pretty good to him. During a visit, Ray showed his brother Floyd a ring he had made. When the time came for the escape, he said, whoever brought the ring with him would be Ray's messenger.[7] On January 12, 1934, a man knocked on Floyd Hamilton's door in west Dallas and showed him Ray's ring, but the man himself didn't inspire much confidence.

When he arrived at Floyd Hamilton's door, James Mullins looked all of his forty-eight hard years. Mullins was a career criminal (he had already served jail time before Clyde Barrow was born), a drug addict, and a suspected stool pigeon, so he was not chosen for his reliability but simply because he was getting released. Ray had promised him $1,000 to carry the message and help in the escape. He was to find Floyd Hamilton, and Floyd would do the rest. Floyd had the contacts, all right, and before long they were parked on a country road near Irving, explaining Ray's plan to a skeptical Clyde Barrow.[8]

Raymond's scheme was a far cry from the mass escape envisioned by Clyde and Ralph Fults back in April 1932. Mullins and Floyd Hamilton were to get some guns and ammunition and hide them under a bridge near the Eastham Farm buildings. A trusty was set up to bring the guns inside and get them to Ray.[9] The break would be made early in the morning as the prisoners were marched out to work. Clyde's part was to help Floyd and Mullins with the guns, cover the escape, and have a getaway car ready.

This, at least, is the story generally told, but several things about it suggest that Clyde Barrow may have been involved earlier in the planning. All the major players were friends of Clyde's from the time he spent in Eastham. Ray, on the other hand, had only been at Eastham for five months and was not well liked. It's hard to believe that Ray could have gained the trust and participation of these veteran cons without at least some word from Clyde or Ralph Fults on Ray's behalf. Both Fults and another convict, Jack Hammett, told author John Neal Phillips that communication was relatively easy from inside either the main prison at Huntsville or the farms. Both said that they knew about the break before it happened. Fults was at the Walls unit at Huntsville and was told to get out to Eastham to be part of the break, but he was

unable to manage it. He sent word that Hilton Bybee should go in his place.[10] All this suggests greater involvement on Barrow's part in the planning stages. Messages may have been going back and forth between Clyde on the outside and Fults and Hamilton on the inside since Bonnie and Clyde's return to the Dallas area in September.[11]

Even so, Clyde had serious misgivings. He was sure the plan would work. He and Fults had worked it out from the inside almost three years before. What worried him was the human element. Raymond Hamilton was not the most discreet or humble guy in the world. He had a reputation as a smart aleck, and as soon as he got to Huntsville, he began bragging that Clyde Barrow would come and break him out. The only good news was that nobody in the prison administration took him seriously.[12] The other weak link, James Mullins—alias Jimmy LaMont—was so unstable that, under normal circumstances, Clyde wouldn't have come within a mile of him.[13] In the end, partly because of urging from Bonnie, Clyde decided to go along with the plan anyway. Raymond was his old partner, after all. Clyde may actually have been glad to take any opportunity to shake up the folks at Eastham. He hated the place with a passion.

Mullins bought some .45 ammunition, and Floyd Hamilton and Clyde each contributed a pistol.[14] These were sealed up in a piece of old inner tube. Before daylight Sunday morning, January 14, 1934, the four of them stopped a mile or so from Eastham Farm. What came next was the dangerous part. The guns were to be placed under a bridge within 200 yards of the main building, and Clyde wasn't going to try that on the word of a dope addict. He had already told Mullins that he would have to plant the guns himself. Mullins finally convinced Floyd Hamilton to go with him and the two of them started off into the night.[15] Sometime later, they came back, shaking, but successful.

Floyd Hamilton had left his car in a garage in Corsicana, Texas, so Bonnie and Clyde took him back to get it. Floyd and his wife were to visit Raymond that Sunday afternoon and set the final details. During the visit, Floyd confirmed that the guns were placed where they had agreed, and Ray

Eastham Prison, as it is today.

confirmed that the convict squads were working in the place they expected. In the summer, they would have been in the fields, but now, in the middle of the winter, they were cutting wood and clearing brush. The break would happen at the large brush piles near the road. Floyd met the others later Sunday evening and told them everything was set. Hamilton then drove back to Dallas to wait, but Bonnie and Clyde kept Mullins with them. He wasn't going to be allowed out of their sight until the break was over. They drove the roads around Eastham and, during the night, took turns sleeping in the car. About 6:30 or 7:00 in the morning on Tuesday, January 16, the three of them stopped their car on Calhoun's Ferry Road near the edge of some woods. It was time.[16]

The original plan seems to have been for Raymond Hamilton to escape with Ralph Fults and two other prisoners. As mentioned before, Ralph was unavoidably detained at the Huntsville Unit and asked that Hilton Bybee be included in his place. He and Fults had been together in a failed escape attempt in Wichita Falls. Bybee was from Cottle County, Texas, and was in the army when he first got in trouble. After he left the service, he and his brother Otis robbed a fellow of $104 and then, just for fun, Hilton shot him between the shoulder blades as he ran away. Hilton managed to avoid the death penalty, but, due to other crimes, he was now serving two concurrent life terms plus twenty-five years.[17]

The other two were old friends of Clyde's and were already in place at Eastham. One of them was twenty-one-year-old Henry Methvin from Louisiana. Methvin was serving ten years for assault with the intent to murder and theft of a 1929 Ford worth about $350.[18] Henry was called "Scar Neck" because of an old ax wound and was known at Eastham as a real "Tush Hog," which, in the convicts' language, meant a hard case, or tough guy.[19] The other member of the original escape party was an inmate who, in many ways, was the opposite of Raymond Hamilton. His name was Joseph Conger Palmer.

Joe Palmer was a veteran con. He was currently serving his fourth stretch in prison (three in Texas, one in Oklahoma) during the last twelve years and had already escaped from Eastham once before. In September 1933, Palmer stole a guard's horse and rode away, Old West style. He stayed at large for one day and was recaptured. For this, he officially received thirty lashes.[20] Given the culture at Eastham, he surely received some unofficial attention from the guards as well.

Where Ray Hamilton was twenty years old and

Convicts in the field at Eastham Prison Farm Camp One, near the site of the escape, with mounted guard in the background. The prisoners in stripes are escapees or parole violators. This picture was taken by Hugh Kennedy about two months after Clyde Barrow's Eastham Raid.

—Courtesy the Hugh Kennedy/Pat McConal collection

before and expected to do the same that day. He had no idea that a break was planned, but he would wind up in the middle of it. The trustee had brought in the two .45s and given them to Hamilton the day before. Joe Palmer faked an asthma attack, which allowed him to stay in bed on Monday and hide the guns in his mattress. Ray picked up one during the night, and now there remained only one little detail to arrange.[23]

Hugh Kennedy was the lead man of Plow Squad One, assigned to Guard Olin Bozeman. This squad contained all the escape plan members except Ray Hamilton. He was in Squad Two, guarded by Mr. Bishop. For the plan to work, Hamilton had to jump squads somehow. As the prisoners were lining up, Ray moved

in the best of health, Joe Palmer was eleven years older and a sick man. Joe suffered from asthma, had a bleeding ulcer, and may have had tuberculosis as well.[21] Where Ray was known as a braggart and prone to bend the facts to suit his purpose, Joe talked very little. Ray was not respected or trusted by most of his peers, but Joe Palmer was admired, at least as a man of "nerve and ability," even by Lee Simmons, the manager of the prison system.[22] Hamilton liked to brag about what a bad man he was and about his outlaw friends. Palmer endured a lot at the hands of the guards because he often fell behind in the field work. He kept his temper, but he never forgot. If you made an enemy of Ray Hamilton, you would have to watch your back. Joe Palmer was more likely to bide his time, then look you in the eye, and kill you. Raymond Hamilton was a somewhat obnoxious but gifted bank robber, car thief, and escape artist, but Joe Palmer was a truly dangerous man.

Tuesday morning, January 16, 1934, started out like most other mornings for Hugh Kennedy, one of the other prisoners at Eastham. He had stacked wood the day

Hugh Kennedy with the plow squad mules at Eastham Prison Farm. This picture, like most of Kennedy's photos, was taken with a small hidden camera and smuggled out to be developed.

—Courtesy the Hugh Kennedy/Pat McConal collection

over to Squad One, but the convicts were always counted before they left for work, and Squad One now had one too many. "I've got a bad count," someone yelled, just as Kennedy felt something shove him from behind. It was Ray Hamilton solving the count problem by knifing one of Squad One's members in the back. As the man fell against Kennedy, Ray stuck him again for good measure, pushed him out of the way, and fell in behind Kennedy. Now the count was good and they could go to work.[24]

As the squads marched out to the woods, Guard Bozeman noticed Hamilton in his group and knew it was wrong but decided to wait until they got to the work area to straighten things out. As they marched, Hugh Kennedy noticed something else strange. His guard, Olin Bozeman, was mounted, but there was also another mounted officer ahead of them. This wasn't unusual in itself, but the other guard was Major Crowson, the high rider.[25] The prison system general manager, Lee Simmons, had instituted the use of a "High Rider" or "Backfield Man" at the Huntsville farms. This was a guard, selected for his marksmanship, who had no squad to oversee, but stayed on the edges of the work area and watched for escapes. The prisoners didn't always know where he was, but they knew that his only job was to kill them with his rifle if they ran.[26]

As Plow Squad One neared their work area, Bozeman called Crowson over. "Tell the captain to come and get Raymond Hamilton and put him back in the squad he belongs in," Bozeman said.

"All right," said Crowson. "You better look out. That means something." Crowson and Bozeman were now side by side on their horses. Crowson had violated his assignment as high rider by coming in among the squads, and it was about to cost him his life.

As the two guards talked, Hugh Kennedy saw Joe Palmer walk toward them.

He heard Palmer say "All right," and then watched as Joe pulled out a .45 and shot Major Crowson in the stomach from point-blank range.[27] Joe then turned on Bozeman, but the other guard leaned over his horse and away from Palmer so that only his gun was hit. Ray Hamilton then ran to the other side of the horse and shot Bozeman in the hip. By now, the horses were spooked and ran away, taking the two guards with them.[28] Joe Palmer later told Lee Simmons that the plan had been to get the drop on the guards. Henry Methvin was to collect their guns when they put their

Chow time in the field at Eastham. Taken by Hugh Kennedy with a hidden camera.
—Courtesy the Hugh Kennedy/Pat McConal collection

hands up and nobody was supposed to get hurt, but that wasn't the approach Hugh Kennedy saw.[29]

As the horses carried the wounded guards away, Hamilton, Palmer, Methvin, and Bybee ran for the road. Hamilton called to Hugh Kennedy to follow him, but the lead man made his best decision of the morning and stayed where he was. "I'm not following you anywhere," Kennedy yelled as Hamilton ran for the woods.[30] As they ran toward the car, Joe Palmer yelled, "Give us something else!" and Clyde Barrow and James Mullins, who were about 200 yards away near a creek, began firing Browning automatic rifles through the tree-tops. At this point, whatever order remained was lost. A few guards reacted and fired a shot or two, and Guard Bullard of Squad Six stood his ground and held the prisoners around him with his shotgun. Two other guards, however, lost their nerve and ran. Unguarded prisoners dove for cover or just milled around; Crowson and Bozeman, both wounded, rode back toward Eastham; tree limbs fell all around the rest of the prisoners and guards as Clyde kept up his covering fire; and Bonnie honked the horn to guide the men through the ground fog that covered part of the area. Only one other convict, J. B. French, actually ran away, but he went in a different direction. He wasn't part of the escaping group, so he had no plan and no outside help. He just acted on the spur of the moment and was recaptured the next day.[31]

Excited and out of breath, the four escapees ran up to the car only to face a new problem. A 1934 Ford V-8 will carry four adults in relative comfort—five or six if they are small and don't mind a lot of bodily contact. Seven grown people plus a couple of automatic rifles and whatever else Clyde had brought with him was quite a challenge. Mullins announced that only Hamilton and

Bridge on Calhoun Ferry Road. During the Eastham escape, Bonnie Parker was parked near here with the getaway car.

—Courtesy the Hugh Kennedy/Pat McConal collection

Palmer could get in. The rest would just have to go back. With two guards shot and the whole Texas Prison System about to come down on their heads? Not a chance! Their life expectancy would have been measured in seconds.

Clyde simply told Mullins to shut up. It was his car, and he wasn't leaving anybody.[32] Somehow, he got everybody shoe horned into the Ford. Brew Hubbard was moving a cow on the Calhoun road that morning and saw the men run up and get into the car. He wasn't armed, so they left him alone, and he watched as the car drove away with Joe Palmer sitting in the "turtle back" and holding a pistol.[33]

Once the shooting stopped, many of the prisoners began drifting back toward the main building at Eastham, where they just sat around for the rest of the day. According to Hugh Kennedy, there was no supper served, several men were beaten by enraged guards just because they were nearby, and one prisoner, who had been missing most of the day, was found and shot to death.[34] Crowson and Bozeman were taken to Huntsville's Memorial Hospital in the same car. Bozeman recovered, but Crowson developed pneumonia and died on January 27. In his last statement to his boss, Lee Simmons, Crowson said, "Joe Palmer shot me in cold blood. He didn't give me a dog's chance. I

Major Joseph Crowson, the high rider mortally wounded by Joe Palmer during the escape.

—Courtesy Marc Crowson

Crowson's gravesite at Lovelady, Texas.

—Courtesy the Hugh Kennedy/Pat McConal collection

hope you catch him and put him in the electric chair."[35] That was exactly what Simmons had in mind.

The overloaded Ford traveled as fast as it could away from Eastham Farm, but a few miles west of Weldon, they had to stop and resuscitate Joe Palmer. Riding in the trunk or "turtle" of the Ford, Joe had been overcome by exhaust fumes and passed out, so they moved him up into the already overcrowded front seat.[36] As they continued northwest, Clyde worked his way around several roadblocks, sometimes leaving the roads altogether and going cross country. After about 125 miles, they stopped at a filling station in Hillsboro, only to find out that the news had gotten there ahead of them. "Did you hear about Raymond Hamilton escaping from prison?" the gas station attendant asked.

"No, really?" Clyde said, acting as innocent as he could.

"Oh, yeah," said the attendant and then went on to tell how the radio was saying that Clyde and Bonnie had walked right into the dining room at Eastham and taken Ray out.[37] It was all the escapees could do to keep a straight face. Not even Clyde Barrow could outrun the rumors.

Marie Barrow said that a phone call to the Barrow house in Dallas set up the next meeting. The call asked that L. C. Barrow and Floyd Hamilton meet the group near Rhome, Texas, a few miles northwest of Fort Worth, with something for the convicts to wear. The meeting was short but vital. Although the group had made it almost 200 miles from Eastham without incident, they had thrown the white prison uniforms in a creek.[38] After that, some of the boys were showing a lot of skin, and January in north Texas can be pretty cold.

After the stop at Rhome, the group went into hiding for a few days. During this time, Bonnie and Clyde drove back to Dallas to see their family. The date was January 18, 1934. We know this because after the ambush at Sowers, Clyde's mother began marking the dates of "the kids'" visits on the wall of her house. It would be almost a month before they came back.[39]

CHAPTER 30
The Professionals: The Gang

The Eastham Prison Farm break marked the beginning of a new phase of Clyde Barrow's criminal career. Up until then, it had been mostly Clyde and Bonnie with the occasional unknown partners. What the press had called "the Bloody Barrow Gang" in the summer of 1933 was not planned. Clyde's brother and sister-in-law were just visiting in Joplin, and set to go home the next day. Then there was the shootout and two policemen were killed, and everything changed. The first "Barrow gang" was an accident. The only plan was to stay alive, but this new gang was different.

The Clyde Barrow who helped stage the Eastham raid was, in some ways, different from the one who endured the long, hot, deadly summer of 1933. He had been shot at and wounded several times. He had killed men, and, in turn, seen people he loved killed and wounded. In the end, he and Bonnie barely escaped with their lives.

If Barrow was more fatalistic, he was also more experienced. He knew himself and his capabilities. He knew the territory. He wasn't just a Texas bandit anymore. He had a year and a half's experience in driving and hiding out all over the central United States. He trusted his instincts. Eighteen months of survival had given him a feeling for situations, and he could tell when things weren't right. He trusted his nerve. He knew he would not flinch or freeze up in a crisis. He knew that most men—especially lawmen—had a hard time shooting without warning. They hesitated that one extra second when they had a living, breathing human being in their sights. Clyde knew he wouldn't. He always wanted to get in the first shot for the shock value it provided.

Finally, Clyde knew that he was a natural leader. Men would and did follow him. Had Clyde been born ten years later and entered the United States military at the beginning of World War II instead of the Texas State Prison at the beginning of the depression, we might know his name as a decorated combat soldier instead of an outlaw. At any rate, the Clyde Barrow of late January 1934 was older, wiser, more competent, more resigned to his fate, and more dangerous. He was also the leader of a new Barrow gang. For the authorities, this was not good news.

This new gang was not made up of family members or devoted underlings. They were all experienced criminals and, at least in theory, independent contractors. They were, of course, indebted to Clyde for breaking them out, but each had his own agenda, and, like many other outlaw gangs, they stuck together only as long as it suited their purpose. This was strictly business. While the gang was together, though, Clyde was the leader. Clyde was always the leader. Even when Clyde and Buck were together and the newspapers were proclaiming the older brother as the leader of the "Bloody Barrows," it wasn't true. The few times that Buck went out on his own inevitably turned into disasters.

One week after they escaped from Eastham Prison Farm, the new, professional Barrow gang went into action. The first order of business was to raise some money. They had expenses, but they also had debts. Jimmy Mullins had been promised $1,000 for his part in the escape, so they began looking for a quick score—a big one.[1]

Lloyd Haraldson probably considered himself a lucky man. At the depth of the Great Depression, when hundreds of small-town banks had failed, he still had his job as cashier of the First National Bank of Rembrandt, Iowa, a small farming community just north of Storm Lake. Not that things had been easy. The bank had been operating under a conservatorship since March 1933, by order of the comptroller of the currency. While not the best situation, First National was still afloat, and there were encouraging rumors that the operation might be put back in local hands soon.[2] All this may have been on Haraldson's mind as he reopened the bank after lunch on Tuesday afternoon, January 23. Whatever he was thinking about, he didn't notice the four men parked nearby in the tan Ford V-8 sedan with Kansas plates.

At 1:15 P.M., just after the time lock had released, two men entered the bank and one of them asked for change for a large bill. The next thing the cashier heard was "Keep quiet and stick 'em up." Haraldson and the only customer, J. F. McGrew, were covered by one man with a gun while the other gathered up the money. Both McGrew and Haraldson were impressed with the coolness with which the bandits worked. During the robbery, people walked past on the sidewalk, and several actually looked in and saw the rob-

bery in progress. The bandits never wavered. They just got the money and went out the back door, which opened into an alley where the tan Ford with the two other men was waiting. They were last seen driving eastward out of town. Sheriff E. A. Thompson was notified immediately and put the eastern part of the county on alert, but the bandits were gone without a trace. The bank would only say they got "over $3,000."[3]

The Buena Vista County sheriff had no leads as to the identity of the robbers, but the two men in the bank were almost certainly Hilton Bybee and

Clyde Barrow and Bonnie Parker. Taken during a family meeting near Dallas. November 1933.

—From the collections of the Texas/Dallas History and Archives Division, Dallas Public Library

Raymond Hamilton.[4] The two men in the car were Clyde Barrow and Henry Methvin. What the sheriff didn't know was that there was a fifth man. Joe Palmer was willing, but his body betrayed him. He was so weak that he was curled up on the floor of the back seat. Nobody saw him, and he slept through the whole thing, but Clyde insisted that the loot (which Palmer said was $3,800) be split six ways. That way, Bonnie, who was probably outside of town with a second car, and Palmer both got a share. Not surprisingly, Joe Palmer considered Clyde a real standup guy.[5] Before long, Joe would have an even better reason to value Clyde's friendship.

The best thing to do after a bank job was to put a lot of distance between you and the sheriff who was looking for you, and that's what the gang did. Hilton Bybee went his own way after the Rembrandt robbery,[6] and by the next day, the rest of them were in Oklahoma, where they stole another car to set up for the next job.[7] All of these men were veteran car thieves, but one of them really excelled

at it, so whenever a car was needed, Ray Hamilton got the job. Joe Palmer, certainly no friend of Ray's at the time, nevertheless admitted that "Raymond stole all the cars; best car thief I ever saw. He was fast."[8] The plan was the same: a fairly common car for the job and initial getaway, and then another, unreported car to throw off pursuit.

Forty-six hours after the Rembrandt, Iowa, robbery (and 550 miles away), three men entered the Central National Bank at Poteau, Oklahoma, just southwest of Fort Smith, Arkansas, while one or two others waited outside in a car. The cashier and a male customer were forced to lie on the floor while, in a small act of gallantry, Miss May Vasser was allowed to sit in a chair. She later described the men as "somewhat nicely dressed" but very rough-spoken. The leader, dressed in a suit, gray overcoat, and kid gloves, cleaned out the cash drawers and the safe.[9] Two more local men came into the bank while the robbery was in progress—one was even armed to investigate what he thought were suspi-

Hilton Bybee mug shot. Texas State Prison.
——Courtesy the Texas Ranger Hall of Fame and Museum, Waco, Texas

cious goings-on—but they were quietly captured and put on the floor also. It was all over in a few minutes, and the robbers left with $1,500. Officers were notified, calls were made to surrounding towns, and a posse was in pursuit within ten minutes, but it made no difference. Again, they disappeared without a trace. Their getaway car, a blue Plymouth sedan, was found abandoned near Page, Oklahoma, a week later.[10]

There's no hard evidence about what the gang did for the next few days, but based on what was to happen later, it probably went something like this: After the Poteau job, the gang drove south to Houston, where Joe Palmer

HENRY METHVIN.
Age 20 (1931).Ht 5-9½ Wt 170. Hair Lt.Brown
Eyes blue. Complex Fair. Marks and Scars:
1 dim horizontal cut scar left middle
finger 1st joint 2 dagger pierced and
lettered "love" right forearm inner.

Henry Methvin mug shot. Texas State Prison.
—Courtesy the Texas Ranger Hall of Fame and Museum, Waco, Texas

had an appointment with a lawyer. Now that Joe had some money from the two bank jobs, he wanted to settle an old score. At Eastham, Joe had been victimized by several guards, but there was one building tender in particular whom he hated, and now Joe wanted him on the outside where he could get at him. Joe paid a lawyer to arrange for a furlough for this man. Once he was released, Joe, Henry Methvin, and Clyde would do the rest.[11]

After setting Joe's plan in motion in Houston, the gang began to work its way north again, but all was not well among its members. Palmer was still sick. Probably because of his ulcer and other afflictions, he was very prone to motion sickness. Since the gang was almost always on the road, Joe was always miserable. To add to Palmer's woes, Raymond Hamilton was really starting to get on his nerves. Palmer had never liked Hamilton when they were in prison. For one thing, Joe was convinced Hamilton was an informant.[12] Since they had escaped, things had only gotten worse. Finally, Joe

got tired of Ray's complaining and called the twenty-year-old kid a "punk, blabbermouth braggart" in front of everybody. Raymond did nothing, because even a carsick Joe Palmer was not a man to trifle with, but he didn't forget the insult. Sometime later, when Joe was asleep on the floorboard of the car, Hamilton drew a pistol. Palmer later said that he was convinced that Hamilton intended to kill him while he slept.[13] Clyde seemed to think so too, because, even though he was driving, he reached into the back seat and slapped Ray across the face. This saved Joe Palmer's life, but Clyde also ran the car in the ditch and broke a wheel.

Palmer knew that something had to be done. He had to get away from Ray Hamilton, and, besides that, he was too sick to ride in the floorboard of that Ford any longer, so he decided to lie low for a while. On or about January 30, 1934, Clyde, driving a new car to replace the wrecked one, let Joe out in front of the Conner Hotel in Joplin, Missouri. They promised to keep in touch

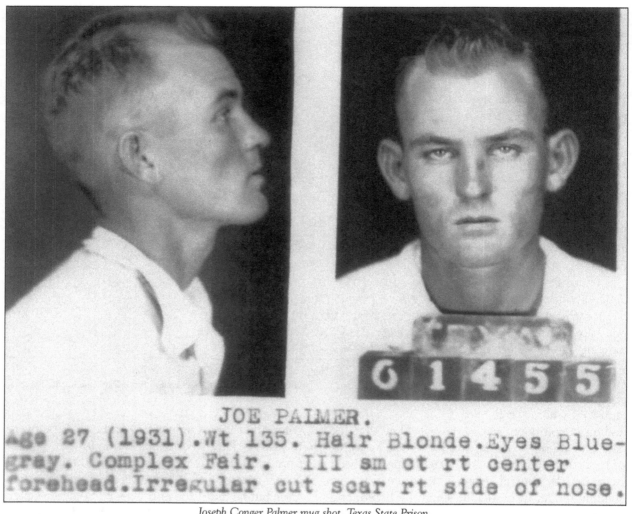

JOE PALMER.
Age 27 (1931).Wt 135. Hair Blonde.Eyes Blue-gray. Complex Fair. III sm ct rt center forehead.Irregular cut scar rt side of nose.

Joseph Conger Palmer mug shot. Texas State Prison.

—Courtesy the Texas Ranger Hall of Fame and Museum, Waco, Texas

and come back for Joe in four to six weeks.[14] The rest of the gang then headed further north.

On January 31, they stole a pair of license plates issued to Gross Hildreth in Rockwell City, Iowa.[15] Later that evening, in the nearby small town of Knierim, F. W. Kahley noticed a car with three men and one woman drive by his combination filling station and lunchroom. The car returned and one of the men got out and ordered four steak dinners. The car left again but came back in a few minutes to pick up the dinners. All this made Kahley suspicious. He later said he thought the men were part of the Dillinger gang.

Mr. Kahley was concerned enough that, the next morning, he went to the State Savings Bank in town and told the cashier, Albert Arenson, to be on the alert. "There are some bad men around town," Kahley said. One hour later, Clyde Barrow and Henry Methvin walked through the bank's front door and robbed the place. After getting the money—between the bank and a customer, they only got about $300—they pushed cashier Arenson and three patrons into the vault but couldn't get it to lock. The thieves gave up and ran to their car, followed by Arenson. The cashier managed to wing one shot at them with a revolver kept in the bank, but, as in the other two jobs, the thieves drove out of town and vanished without a trace.[16] Clyde was identified a week later by cashier Arenson and one of the customers from photographs provided by authorities.[17] The gang had hit three banks in eight days, traveling at least 2,000 miles in the process and netting about $5,600.

For almost two weeks, the gang was out of sight, and then, on February 12, on their way back home, they stole a car in Springfield, Missouri. That afternoon, while running from local lawmen just west of Reed Springs, Missouri, they stopped Joe Gunn and asked directions to Highway 13. Rather than wait, one of the men pulled a pistol and forced Gunn into the car to show the way. Before they got to the highway, the road was blocked by officers and a lively little gunfight took place. The Chevrolet escaped, and Gunn was set free, but later he would testify that Henry Methvin was one of the men in the car.[18] The next day, Ray Hamilton was dropped off near Wichita Falls, Texas, while Bonnie, Clyde, and Methvin went back to the Dallas area.

Bonnie and Clyde met some family members on February 13[19] and again on the 18th. This second time, Raymond Hamilton was there as well, and he brought along his new girlfriend. While in Wichita Falls, Ray had made contact with Mary O'Dare, the wife of his former partner Gene O'Dare. Ray and Gene had robbed a bank or two back in late 1932 and been arrested in Bay City, Michigan. Since Gene was safely locked away in prison,[20] Mary decided she would take up with Raymond and go on the road with the gang—just like Bonnie.

Unfortunately, Mary O'Dare wasn't like Bonnie at all. Raymond's brother, Floyd, referred to Mary as a prostitute and a gold digger with enough makeup on her face to "grow a crop." Later in life, when asked about Mary O'Dare, Floyd Hamilton would just shake his

head and say "My brother sure could pick 'em."[21] Clyde, Bonnie, and Henry Methvin all disliked Mary immediately, and the situation only worsened with time. They called her "the washerwoman" and other, less complimentary names. In spite of the personal feelings, however, the meeting on February 18 was important. The gang was about to go back into business. The next score, though, wouldn't be for money. It would be for artillery.

At 4:00 A.M. Tuesday morning, February 20, Patrolman Jack Roach made his rounds in Ranger, Texas, near Eastland. On Rusk Street, he found the front door of the National Guard Armory broken open. Clyde and Raymond had gone through the storerooms with a professional eye for armament. One rack held seven Browning automatic rifles. Two were old and one was broken. Only the four new ones were taken. Thirteen Colt .45s were taken, but the standard-issue Springfield rifles were left. Of course, a lot of extra magazines and ammunition disappeared too. The gang wouldn't lack for firepower for a while.

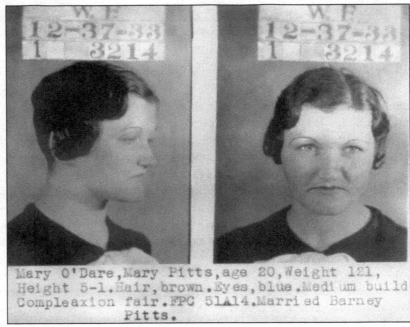

Mary O'Dare, Mary Pitts, age 20, Weight 121, Height 5-1. Hair, brown. Eyes, blue. Medium build Compleaxion fair. FPC 51A14. Married Barney Pitts.

Mary O'Dare. Called "the washerwoman," she was intensely disliked by Bonnie and Clyde. Mary was the wife of Gene O'Dare, one of Raymond Hamilton's bank-robbing partners who was in prison. After the Eastham break, she became Hamilton's girlfriend and traveled with the gang for about three weeks—from mid-February till early March 1934.
—Courtesy the Texas Ranger Hall of Fame and Museum, Waco, Texas

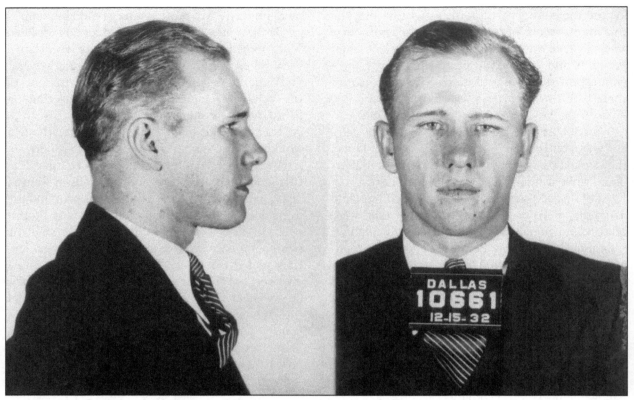

Mug shot of Raymond Elzie Hamilton taken after he was captured in Bay City, Michigan, and returned to Texas. Dallas, December 15, 1932.
—From the collections of the Texas/Dallas History and Archives Division, Dallas Public Library

When it was suggested that the Clyde Barrow gang might have done the break-in, the local police, and even the Texas Rangers, discounted the possibility. Eventually, some local labor activists were arrested for the crime, but no indictments were ever returned.[22] The Barrow gang's part became known a couple of months later when some of the guns turned up in Dallas and were linked to them. For the moment, the gang took what they could use and left the rest with Floyd Hamilton for safekeeping.[23] On February 26, there was another meeting of the gang and family members near Rockwall, Texas.[24] What was not mentioned to the family was that Clyde and Raymond had picked their next victim.

Ollie Worley worked for the WPA, one of the government programs established by President Roosevelt to combat the 25 percent unemployment rate prevailing in the country when he had taken office almost a year before. It wasn't glamorous

work, but at least Ollie had a $27 paycheck to cash. That's why he was standing at the teller's window of the R. P. Henry and Sons Bank in Lancaster, Texas, just before noon on Tuesday, February 27. Mr. Henry, the cashier, had just handed Ollie two tens, two ones, and a five-dollar bill when two men entered the bank and walked behind the counter. They were dressed quite well, and Ollie figured they were bank examiners. When one of them grabbed Ollie's $27 and the other produced what Worley later called "the biggest gun I had ever seen," he knew he was wrong.

That morning, Clyde, Raymond, and Henry Methvin had left Bonnie and Mary O'Dare out in the country with a Ford V-8 sedan and taken a Chevy into Lancaster. Henry waited in the car by the bank's side entrance while Clyde and Ray went in the front door. They were low-key and all business. "Okay, everybody on the floor," Clyde said as

"Partners in Crime." A very rare shot of three members of the 1934 Barrow gang together. Left to right: Clyde Barrow, Henry Methvin, and Raymond Hamilton. Taken soon after the Eastham jailbreak. Probably mid-February 1934.

—Courtesy the Texas Ranger Hall of Fame and Museum, Waco, Texas

"bank examiners" were leaving through the side door when something happened that Ollie Worley remembered for the rest of his life. The man who had taken his earnings turned around and said to him, "You worked like hell for this, didn't you?"

"Yes, sir," Worley replied. "Digging ditches."

Clyde Barrow handed back the bills and said, "We don't want your money. Just the bank's." Worley stood there in amazement as the robbers calmly got into the Chevy and drove away. Ollie still had his money, but the bank lost almost $4,200.[25] The men drove back to where Bonnie and Mary waited, ditched the Chevy, and drove away toward Oklahoma in a Ford V-8, formerly the property of the Earle Johnson Motor Company of Temple, Texas.[26] A professional job and a clean getaway—everyone should have been happy, but it didn't work out that way.

On the way to Oklahoma, Raymond wanted to divide up the money. Clyde agreed, but then the question came up of how many shares to make. Ray wanted to give Mary a share, but Clyde said no. Later Clyde saw, in the rearview mirror, Ray giving Mary some money anyway. Clyde pulled over and searched Ray and found that he had been holding out almost $600 from the take. The idea of stealing from a grocery store owner or a gas station attendant, or killing a man for his car, didn't seem to bother Clyde, his generosity to the WPA worker notwithstanding, but the idea that one of his partners would steal from him was too much.[27]

Like so many episodes in the lives of these elusive bandits, this one has another version. Floyd

Raymond took out a sack and began picking up the money. Everybody complied except an elderly gentleman who couldn't hear well and didn't understand what was going on. Worley finally had to pull the old man down to the floor over his objections.

All the cash drawers were emptied, and then it was back to the vault with Mr. Henry to open the safe—it was over in a couple of minutes. The two

Hamilton, Ray's brother, later claimed that it was all just a misunderstanding. He says that Ray was just trying to make it up to his girlfriend by giving her some money out of the common "expense bag" because Clyde was too stingy to give her a cut of the proceeds.[28] Whatever the truth, things went from bad to worse. Never on the best of terms, Clyde's relationship with Raymond Hamilton had hit a new low. Their association had one week left.

The gang proceeded through Oklahoma and further north and east until they stopped for a few days in Terre Haute, Indiana. They did some shopping and tried to relax, but the quarrel erupted again. Clyde and Bonnie complained that nineteen-year-old Mary didn't understand how it was on the road. They had learned to keep a low profile—get food to go, sleep in the car or in tourist courts—but Mary wanted to eat in restaurants and stay in nice hotels. Once, Bonnie and Clyde had a fight over something. Mary sympathized with Bonnie and then suggested to Bonnie that she give Clyde knockout drops, steal his money, and go home. As mad as she was at Clyde, Bonnie couldn't believe Mary would suggest such a thing.[29] Ray didn't like Henry Methvin and what he called his hair-trigger mentality, but, when Ray was not around, Mary would "come on" to Henry anyway. All these incidents worked to pull the gang apart. Clyde, Bonnie, and Henry all agreed—none of them liked Raymond, and none of them trusted Mary. They wouldn't let her out of their sight for fear that she might set them up. The whole thing was a disaster waiting to happen.

A large part of the tension probably came from the fact that Raymond felt that he shouldn't have to take orders anymore. According to the newspapers, he was a bigtime desperado in his own right. At Terre Haute, it all came to an end. On March 6, finally tired of all the bickering, Raymond stole a

Clyde Barrow and Raymond Hamilton, February 1934.
—Courtesy the Texas Ranger Hall of Fame and Museum, Waco, Texas

car for himself and Mary and told Clyde Barrow goodbye, to everyone's great relief.[30] Ray and Mary left for Beaumont, Texas,[31] and Clyde, Bonnie, and Henry headed for Louisiana for a quick visit with the Methvin family. Raymond Hamilton and Clyde Barrow never saw each other again.

CHAPTER 31
The Professionals: The Law

The Eastham break and the formation of the new Barrow gang that followed it may have marked a new chapter in the career of Bonnie and Clyde, but it also marked a change in the way Texas authorities planned to deal with them. One of the reasons the Barrows had been able to survive and elude capture for so long was that they learned to exploit the weakness of the law enforcement system of the early 1930s. With little or no communications in patrol cars, and poor coordination between many jurisdictions, the police were almost always too late to mount an effective pursuit. Add to that the fact that Bonnie and Clyde could show up anywhere in the southwestern or midwestern United States on a given day, and you have an almost insurmountable problem. A couple of times, through luck and some good police work, the law was able to close in on them, but the pair still got away, and the cycle started all over again. In addition to skill, they seemed to have a lot of plain good fortune.

At the time of the Eastham break, the only law enforcement agency that had anyone dedicated full-time to the capture of Bonnie and Clyde was the Dallas County Sheriff's Department. Sheriff "Smoot" Schmid, who had come close with his ambush at Sowers in November, had one deputy working more or less exclusively on Barrow.[1] Outside of the Dallas area, though, the attention focused on Bonnie and Clyde was hit-or-miss. After Eastham, this changed.

Lee Simmons had been general manager of the Texas Prison System for almost four years when the Eastham raid happened. There had been escapes before, and guards had been killed before—one just a few months earlier—but Simmons saw the Eastham raid in a different light, as an assault on the prison system itself and a personal embarrassment. Because of this, and because of the death of Major Crowson, Simmons was determined to make an example out of the people responsible.[2] Simmons managed to get a new position created: the "Special Escape Investigator for the Texas Prison System." Regardless of the title, whoever got the job would only have one assignment—to hunt down Clyde Barrow.

Miriam A. "Ma" Ferguson was elected governor of Texas in 1932, after her husband, Jim Ferguson, had been impeached from the same office some years before.[3] She had already agreed to the creation of the new position, but Simmons needed her word on two more things. About the first of February 1934, Simmons met with Governor Ferguson and her husband in Austin to settle these questions. First, the man he had in mind for the position was not on good terms—personally or politically—with the governor. He was a former Texas Ranger, and like many people in law enforcement, he thought Governor Ferguson was much too soft on criminals—she was the one who had pardoned Buck Barrow after Blanche showed up with her fake pregnancy and borrowed children. If Simmons picked this man, who was a political enemy, would she still give her support? Mrs. Ferguson said she held nothing against the ex-Ranger, and if he was Simmons' choice it was all right with her. Secondly, Simmons said that, in order to get the cooperation of some of Barrow's associates, he might have to "put somebody on the ground," meaning promise clemency from the state. Governor Ferguson agreed to honor the offer Simmons was prepared to make, and the prison manager left to hire his man to track down Clyde Barrow.[4]

Francis Augustus "Frank" Hamer was almost fifty years old when Lee Simmons met with him early in February 1934. Hamer was a former captain of the Texas Rangers, and had an unequaled reputation in the Southwest for professionalism and toughness. In fact, the Hamer name was something of a legend in the Rangers. In all, four Hamer brothers served with distinction. Besides Frank, there were Dennis Estill, Harrison Lester, and Flavious Letheridge Hamer. They were all known as tough lawmen and dead shots. The brothers said that Harrison was the best detective but when it came to getting their man, Frank had no peer.[5]

As respected as he was among the Rangers, however, Frank Hamer was not without his detractors. He was once reprimanded by a judge for what

Hamer brothers. This picture of a group of Texas Rangers, probably taken in the late 1920s, shows three of the four Hamer brothers who served as Rangers. First row, far right, is Francis Augustus "Frank" Hamer. Top row, far right, is Harrison Lester Hamer, and, next to him and just over Frank's right shoulder is Flavious Letherage Hamer, the youngest of the four brothers. Not pictured is Dennis Estill Hamer.

—Courtesy Harrison Hamer, grandson of Harrison Lester Hamer

he said was an unconstitutional search. The press later asked Hamer if the judge's remarks would affect the way he did his job. "No," he said. Hamer had a well-deserved reputation for doings things his own way—and for getting results, even if he did occasionally stretch the letter of the law.[6] Also, as already mentioned, there was no love lost between Hamer and either former governor Jim Ferguson or his wife Miriam, the present governor. When Mrs. Ferguson was elected in 1932, Hamer left the Rangers rather than work under her.[7] It was because of these hard feelings that Simmons felt that he needed the governor's assurance before he offered Hamer the job.[8]

When Simmons met with Hamer, he told him that his assignment would be known only to himself and the governor. Simmons pulled no punches. There was a slight chance that Barrow might be captured if he could somehow be separated from his guns and his Ford V-8, but that was a long shot. Simmons had no real expectation of taking Barrow alive. He told Hamer to do what he thought best, but in Simmons' view, he should "put them on the spot and shoot everyone in sight."[9] Simmons promised his full support, however long it took, and on that basis, Frank Hamer accepted the job.

At the time, Hamer was making pretty good money working for an oil company in Houston, but he took a cut in pay for the chance to track Barrow. Part of it was the challenge, of course. He was later quoted as saying that not even John Dillinger could match Barrow for "cleverness, desperation, and reckless bravado,"[10] but Hamer was not a glory seeker. He seldom spoke to the press and was happy to be left alone. He took the job because he truly believed that killers should be brought to justice— one way or another. Hamer had been a lawman for twenty-eight years, preferring to work alone or with one or two trusted men. He was said to have been in over fifty gunfights and survived enough bullet wounds to kill a squad of soldiers. A lawman like Frank Hamer was the worst nightmare of a wanted

man like Barrow. And on February 10, 1934, Hamer began the hunt.[11]

Hamer's first move was to go to Dallas and check in with the law enforcement agency most experienced with Clyde Barrow, the Dallas County Sheriff's Department. Sheriff Schmid introduced Hamer to Deputy Bob Alcorn, his Clyde Barrow "specialist," and suggested that the two join forces. By early March, Hamer and Alcorn were in Bienville Parish, Louisiana, where the local sheriff was asked to make contact with members of Henry Methvin's family.[12] Before long, a meeting was set up.

Present at the meeting that sealed the fate of Bonnie and Clyde were Frank Hamer and Bob Alcorn from Texas; Lester Kendale, a special agent of the Department of Justice; Henderson Jordan, sheriff of Bienville Parish; and John Joyner, a friend acting on behalf of Henry Methvin's parents. The message, relayed by Joyner, was simple. Henry Methvin, the escaped convict who was at the moment traveling with Bonnie and Clyde, was willing to convince the couple to accompany him back to Louisiana, where he would set them up for the lawmen. In return, he was to be given a full pardon from the state of Texas. The whole deal was to be set down in writing and signed by the governor of Texas before the Methvins would move ahead with the plan. Hamer and the others agreed to the conditions, and each side began preparations.[13]

After the fact, there were those who believed that Henry Methvin himself was not involved in the ambush plot, but that is probably just wishful thinking.[14] Henry later testified, under oath, that he was involved, and, in any case, it's almost impossible to see how anything could have been done without his active participation.[15] At the time of the first meeting (early March), a pardon from Texas would have left Henry a free man. His earlier conviction and escape would have been erased. Before the ambush could be set up, however, the situation would change drastically, and Henry would have troubles that even a Texas pardon wouldn't solve.

CHAPTER 32
Easter Sunday

Soon after Raymond Hamilton and Mary O'Dare left the gang in early March, Clyde, Bonnie and Henry Methvin swung down by Henry's home in Louisiana. A few days later, they picked up Joe Palmer in southwest Missouri and returned to Texas. Their whereabouts for most of the rest of March are unknown except for a few meetings with their family. On March 10, they met near Lancaster, Texas—in a cemetery, which matched their somber mood. Clyde tried once again to convince Bonnie to surrender to police rather than face the end he knew was coming for him. He believed that if she would write a letter offering to give herself up, she could avoid the death penalty. Bonnie again refused.[1]

Looking back on it, Clyde's plan, melodramatic though it may sound, probably had a good chance of succeeding. Even though she had been traveling with Clyde for almost two years and had been with him in all but two of the murders for which he was wanted, Bonnie was not implicated as an active participant in any of them. The headlines usually read "Clyde Barrow" or "The Barrow Gang." Bonnie was usually mentioned as "female companion" or something similar. By this time, Bonnie's name was beginning to be used in news reports along with Clyde's, but the permanent arrangement of the two names as "Bonnie and Clyde" occurred in the years after their death.[2]

With a good lawyer, Bonnie might very well

have pleaded guilty, thrown herself on the mercy of the court, and gotten a reasonable sentence. Blanche had gotten a maximum of ten years for being with them at Platte City and would serve only six. Even Raymond Hamilton, who was convicted of murder, had so far avoided the death penalty. In spite of all that had happened, in March 1934 there was still a good chance for Bonnie to salvage something of her life, if she would only take it. Everybody tried to convince her. All she had to do was walk away, but she had decided to die with Clyde.

Within a few weeks, the situation would change, and Bonnie's chance would be gone.

Sometime in March 1934, there were two incidents that indicate that Clyde Barrow had finally crossed that line which his family feared. No one denied that Clyde would kill when he was cornered, but now, since the Sowers ambush, he seemed to be dealing in revenge as well.

The first plot involved Clyde's recently departed partner, Raymond Hamilton. After the breakup, Clyde, Bonnie, and Henry Methvin speculated among themselves about killing Mary O'Dare after Ray got caught—they were sure the police would get Ray soon.[3] This seems to have been just idle talk, but soon after Joe Palmer rejoined the gang, Clyde began using him as a messenger, sending him out to try and set up a meeting with Raymond. The first two times, Joe thought he wanted Ray for a bank job, but the third time, Joe found out the truth.

Clyde was no longer interested in what happened to Mary O'Dare. He wanted the meeting so he could kill Raymond Hamilton. Joe was never able to set up the meetings, so this plot didn't succeed.[4] The next one did. It was, in fact, the successful completion of the plan Joe Palmer began in Houston in late January.

Wade Hampton McNabb had been convicted of robbery with firearms and sent to Eastham in August 1932, six months after Clyde Barrow was released. On February 24, 1934, McNabb was granted a sixty-day furlough by Governor Ferguson to visit his sick father at Greenville, Texas. By the end of March, he had finished about half of the time. On Thursday, March 29, McNabb was riding with his sister, Cleo Kirkland, and brother-in-law in Gladewater, Texas. "He must have seen somebody he knew, or somebody called him," Mrs. Kirkland said, "for he jumped out and rushed into a domino parlor. Then he ran out and went into another. That's the last we saw of him."[5] A few days later, the *Houston Press,* home of famous reporter and prison-reform crusader Harry McCormick, received a note in the mail, detailing the abuse of prisoners at Eastham Farm. It was written on white wrapping paper and included a detailed map that the caption said would lead to "the carcass of one of the prison system's chief rats."[6]

The *Press* sent one of its reporters, Dick Vaughn, to check out the claim. Thinking the map showed a place in Louisiana, Vaughn went to Shreveport and checked in with the sheriff. Vaughn and a Louisiana deputy then followed the map to a spot

that turned out to be just on the Texas side of the state line, about ten miles north of Waskom. There they found the body of Wade McNabb. He was face down, with his head in his hat. He had been hit with a blunt instrument and shot several times in the head. McNabb had been dead four or five days.[7] The police were never able to prove, to their satisfaction, who had killed Wade McNabb, and

Bonnie Parker and Henry Methvin. February or March 1934.
—Courtesy Sandy Jones—The John Dillinger Historical Society

Clyde Barrow and Joe Palmer—March or April 1934.
—Courtesy Sandy Jones—The John Dillinger Historical Society

persuaded Clyde to take him to Houston, where Joe paid a lawyer to arrange a furlough for McNabb.[9] On March 29, so Fults' story continues, it was Clyde Barrow, Joe Palmer, and Henry Methvin (presumably with Bonnie along as well) who kidnapped McNabb off the street in Gladewater and took him into the woods north of Waskom. There he was beaten, and then Joe Palmer killed him and afterward mailed the note to the Houston newspaper.[10] Nothing we know about the movements and whereabouts of the people involved would challenge Fults' versions of events. Even though he didn't know McNabb, it seems as though Clyde Barrow was now involved in a cold-blooded murder.

When Clyde Barrow and Raymond Hamilton split up, on less than friendly terms, neither stayed away from Texas for long. While Clyde was swinging through Louisiana and Missouri and returning Joe Palmer to his gang, Ray and Mary were relaxing in Beaumont, Texas. As soon as they arrived, Ray sent Mary to Dallas to contact his brother. In response to Ray's request, Floyd Hamilton and a friend named "Baldy" Whatley drove to Beaumont with some of the guns from the Ranger armory. With Mary along, Ray ran through his money pretty quickly, so he was anxious to resume the bank-robbing business as soon as possible.[11]

By the middle of March, Ray was back in Dallas and was ready to compete with Clyde for newspaper headlines. On March 19, Raymond, along with his brother Floyd and a friend of Floyd's named John Basden, robbed the Grand Prairie

we only have the word of Ralph Fults that any of the Barrow gang was involved, but Fults has proven very reliable in everything else he told biographer John Neal Phillips, and his version of events makes good sense.

As mentioned earlier, Joe Palmer was not much of a talker, but he never forgot a friend or forgave an enemy. At Eastham, Joe was said to have been the victim of several severe beatings at the hands of McNabb.[8] As related earlier, Fults said that Palmer

State Bank of $1,543.74.[12] Twelve days later, Raymond alone, with Mary waiting in the car, robbed the State National Bank at West, Texas, of $1,867.74.[13] The robbery went smoothly, but the getaway did not.

Mary was behind the wheel when they left town, so that Ray could watch for pursuit. A few miles away, near the town of Leroy, they got stuck on the muddy road and had to be pulled out by a team of mules. A few miles farther east, Mary lost control and they ran into an embankment. Ray hit the windshield, which cut his face and broke his nose, and Mary was knocked unconscious. Just as Mary was coming around, Mrs. Cam Gunter happened by and stopped to help. Mary and Raymond commandeered her car and forced her along as a hostage. A few hours later, they were in a rented room in Houston.

The next morning—April 1, Easter Sunday—Ray stole a new Ford sedan, and Mrs. Gunter was released with her car and some money for her trouble. Mary liked the new Ford because it had yellow wheels.[14] Ray and Mary drove north toward Dallas, not knowing they were headed into a hornet's nest. That same Easter Sunday morning, about five miles north of Grapevine, Texas, Clyde Barrow, Bonnie Parker, Henry Methvin, and Joe Palmer parked on a dirt road just off Texas State Highway 114. As luck would have it, their car was a virtual twin of the one Ray Hamilton had just stolen in Houston—right down to the yellow wheels.

There was actually a fifth passenger in the Barrow car that morning. His name was "Sonny Boy," and he was a white rabbit. Bonnie had picked him up somewhere along the way and now wanted to give the "Easter bunny" to her mother. That was fine with Clyde, who was not fond of the rabbit as a traveling companion.[15] They had arrived about 10:30 that morning, and Clyde sent Joe Palmer hitchhiking into Dallas to tell the family where to meet them. Palmer found nobody at home at the Parker house, and only Clyde's father Henry minding the Star Service Station. He delivered the message and then decided to wait there a while.[16] Back at the car, the other three were enjoying a quiet Sunday afternoon.

Meanwhile, near Grapevine, three Texas Highway motorcycle patrolmen, Polk Ivy, H. D. Murphy, and E. B. Wheeler, were on their way north on Highway 114 and decided to stop for a little target practice. About 3:30 P.M., they started out again. Officer Ivy, with a pair of highway test scales in his sidecar, was in the lead, with Officers Murphy and Wheeler following. Ivy went by the side road without seeing anything, but Officer Wheeler noticed the black sedan parked there and motioned to Murphy, who was riding beside him, to follow him as he turned to investigate. Wheeler, twenty-six, was a four-year veteran, and Murphy, twenty-four, was on his first day of motorcycle duty.[17]

Clyde was asleep in the back seat. Bonnie had been playing with the rabbit and had just gotten back in the front seat. Henry Methvin paced back and forth beside the car. As the motorcycles turned into the lane, Henry moved back to the car and picked up a BAR while Bonnie shook Clyde and said, "It's the law." Clyde was instantly awake and laid his hand on his shotgun. The officers drove up calmly, and Clyde could see that they didn't suspect anything. On at least five other occasions, Clyde had been confronted by an unsuspecting police officer or civilian. In every case, he had captured them, taken them for a long ride, and released them unharmed. This seemed like a perfect setup to take a couple more hostages. "Let's take them," Clyde whispered to Methvin, knowing they had the drop on both officers. Unfortunately for Clyde, and tragically for the two policemen, Henry had never been in this situation before. It didn't help matters that Henry was generally known to be a little unstable and trigger-happy under the best conditions, or that Henry and Bonnie had been nipping at a bottle of bootleg whiskey. Clyde watched helplessly as he saw Henry nod and then swing the barrel of the BAR up and fire.[18]

Henry Methvin's first volley from the BAR caught E. B. Wheeler completely by surprise, and he fell dead, with his cycle falling on top of him. Murphy carried a sawed-off shotgun on his cycle but kept it unloaded for fear of an accidental discharge. As he fumbled in his pocket for shells, he too was shot, either by Methvin or by Clyde. Both men then ran to the officers, and Methvin rolled Murphy over and shot him several more times as he lay in the road. The men then ran back to the car and drove away. Not far from the scene, Bonnie and Clyde met a car driven by Clyde's brother L. C. with his sister Marie also along. They had finally gotten the word from Joe Palmer and were headed to the meeting place. "Get out of here!" Clyde yelled. "Henry just killed two cops." [19]

Patrolman Ivy couldn't hear the gunshots over the noise of his motorcycle, but he noticed that the other two patrolmen weren't behind him anymore and turned around to investigate. Pointed to the scene by witnesses, he found Wheeler dead and Murphy mortally wounded. [20]

This shooting was witnessed by two groups. First was a husband and wife out for a Sunday drive. Mr. and Mrs. Fred Giggal had been following the three motorcycles on Highway 114 when they saw two of them turn up a side road and head toward a black sedan parked there. Moments later, they heard a flurry of shots and circled back to see what had happened. They arrived back at the entrance to the lane just in time to see "the taller of the two men" fire several shots into a body on the ground. [21] (Henry Methvin was at least a head taller than Clyde Barrow.) This is essentially the story Clyde later told to his family. Not long after the shooting, Henry Methvin told Emma Park that he killed both policemen at Grapevine. [22] As bad as this real story would have been, the story that got all the play in the newspapers was worse, especially for Bonnie.

Unfortunately, it wasn't the Giggals' story that caught on with the public and, more importantly, with law enforcement. There was another witness, and his version made for much better headlines. William Schieffer lived several hundred yards away but within sight of the shooting site. In his account, he said that a man and a woman did the shooting and that it was the woman

Clyde Barrow, left, and Henry Methvin. Taken in February 1934, probably just before or after the Lancaster, Texas, bank job.

—Courtesy Marie Barrow Scoma and author Phillip W. Steele

who shot Officer Murphy again while he was on the ground. Unlike other times when the police declined to speculate on who the killers might be, this time, Clyde Barrow was immediately listed as the most likely suspect. That meant that the woman had to be Bonnie Parker. In addition, the police reported finding a cigar with the imprint of "small teeth" at the scene. By now, of course, everybody believed that was Bonnie's trademark, so the case—at least in the newspapers—seemed to be open-and-shut. For the first time, Bonnie was seen as a killer, actually pulling the trigger—just like Clyde.[23] Whatever chance she had for clemency had just been drastically reduced, but as the fugitives drove out of the state, the ones left behind had their problems as well.

About the time of the shooting in Grapevine, Mrs. Parker and some other family members returned home and got the message to meet "the kids." They headed toward Grapevine unaware of what had happened. They drove around for several hours and then gave up. They didn't know what all the police were doing out there until they got back home and were told by Henry Barrow.[24] About the same time, Raymond Hamilton let Mary O'Dare out less than a block from his brother Floyd's house, which was itself not far from the Barrow gas station. Floyd, who had heard the news of the shooting on the radio, was shocked when Mary told him where Ray wanted to meet. It was within a mile of the Grapevine shooting site. When Mary told him how pretty the yellow wheels on their car were, Floyd almost choked. The description of Clyde's car had been broadcast, but Ray had no radio in his car, so he had no idea. Fortunately for Raymond, his brother was able to intercept him before the police did. They exchanged the yellow wheels for black ones from Floyd's car, and Ray and Mary left for New Orleans.[25] Joe Palmer, left on his own by all this, fled Dallas, presumably for a prearranged meeting place—probably in the Joplin, Missouri, area.[26]

The way Clyde was portrayed in the media as an indiscriminant killer, you would think that he was filling up graveyards on a regular basis. In fact, it had been twelve days short of a year since anyone had died from Clyde Barrow's gun, but that made no difference now. Clyde was involved in the murder of two policemen—on Easter Sunday, of all days. However badly the Texas authorities had wanted him before, the Grapevine killings raised their resolve to a new level. The family said that Clyde swore at Henry for two days after the shooting. Clyde didn't mourn the dead policemen—he just didn't need the increased "heat" it brought down on their heads. In Clyde's mind, it wasn't wrong to shoot Murphy and Wheeler—it was just stupid.[27]

L. G. Phares, Officers Murphy and Wheeler's boss at the Texas Highway Patrol, offered $1,000 for the bodies of the Grapevine killers—not their capture, just the bodies.[28] When Phares learned about Frank Hamer and Bob Alcorn's efforts, he also asked to have a representative on their team. As it happened, Hamer knew a friend and ex-Ranger whom he trusted—and who needed the work. B. M. "Manny" Gault was given a post on the Highway Patrol and joined the group. Bob Alcorn went to his boss, Dallas County Sheriff Schmid, and asked for a partner as well. The natural choice was Ted Hinton, who had been one of the ambush group at Sowers and who knew Clyde and Bonnie by sight.[29]

Throughout the rest of April, the four-man special force kept busy following leads. There was always the chance that they would catch up with Clyde on the road somewhere, but the smart money was on the plan, already in motion, to trap him near his hideout in northwest Louisiana. By the first of May, things were falling into place in Bienville Parish. The written agreement, signed by Governor Ferguson, had been delivered to Sheriff Jordan for safekeeping, and all that remained was for Henry Methvin to lure Bonnie and Clyde into position. That was easy to say, but everybody knew Clyde's reputation for smelling trouble. If he was spooked somehow before they were ready, they might have to start all over. Whether Bonnie and Clyde knew it or not, though, the net was closing.

CHAPTER 33
"Tell Them I Don't Smoke Cigars"

The murders at Grapevine had stirred up a storm of publicity. The killing of policemen was bad enough, but the details that came out of the witness statements made it especially gruesome. State law enforcement officials were outraged and immediately began intensive searches all over north Texas. Naturally, as soon as the search started, reports of sightings came in from several places. It's not known exactly where Bonnie, Clyde, and Henry Methvin were from April 1 through April 5, but they were reported in Texas, Oklahoma, and Arkansas.

On Wednesday afternoon, April 4, they were reported by police in Durant, Oklahoma, but disappeared.[1] Later that evening, the trio were said to have robbed a filling station in DeKalb, Texas, taking the attendant and a customer for a ride before releasing them outside of town.[2] By Thursday the 5th, they were being reported in Texarkana, Arkansas. Searches were started in all these places, and they all led nowhere. Bonnie and Clyde finally surfaced in northeast Oklahoma on Friday morning, April 6.

About 2:30 A.M., Clyde stopped on the side of a muddy road near the "Lost Trail" and "Crab Apple" mines just south of Commerce, Oklahoma, turning the car to face back east toward the main highway. As was his standard practice, Clyde, Bonnie and Henry took turns sleeping. When the sun came up, traffic on the side road began to pick

up, and one motorist, on his way into Commerce, reported the car to Constable Cal Campbell. Commerce Police Chief Percy Boyd was contacted, and the two men drove out to investigate. They assumed that it was a carload of drunks sleeping it off after a hard night, a fairly common occurrence.[3]

It was about 9:30 A.M. by the time Campbell and Boyd arrived on the scene. The dark blue Ford sedan was still there, just as the citizen had reported. Unfortunately for the lawmen, when they stopped their car, they were blocking the way to the main highway. That was all Clyde Barrow needed to see. He immediately started the car, slammed it into reverse, and started backing down the road away from the lawmen. Clyde made it about a hundred yards before the muddy road got the best of him. The back end started to weave and went into a ditch. When the suspicious sedan backed off into the mud, Campbell and Boyd got out of their car and started toward it on foot. As they got closer, Cal Campbell saw a gun in the hands of someone inside and made what turned out to be a fatal decision. Percy Boyd, walking beside Campbell, didn't expect any trouble until he saw his friend reach for his pistol. Before he could say anything, the fight was on. Boyd later told the press, "I don't believe there would have been any shooting if Cal hadn't fired first," but that was probably wishful thinking.[4]

When Cal Campbell saw the gun, he reacted

instinctively. He drew his revolver and fired. Two shotgun blasts answered from the car, and then the doors flew open and two men came out firing Browning automatic rifles. Cal Campbell fired twice more and then was hit in the chest, cutting his aorta. He groaned and fell in the muddy road, where he died. Percy Boyd got off four rounds, two of which went through the Ford's windshield, barely missing Clyde. Later, when he and Clyde were on speaking terms, Barrow told him, "You nearly got me. I heard it zip close."[5]

A few seconds after Campbell fell, Boyd was hit a glancing blow in the head by a bullet and went down also. He later told reporters, "When that bullet knocked me off my feet, I stayed down, and, believe me, I almost dug into the dirt." As soon as both lawmen were down, the shooting stopped. This time, Clyde made sure there were no misunderstandings between him and Methvin. He told Henry to go get the policemen and bring them to the car. Barrow then ran to a nearby farmhouse and "borrowed" a pickup truck and a rope. When Clyde returned, he found Henry there with only one of the lawmen, who was bleeding from a head wound. One look had told Methvin that Cal Campbell was finished, so he still lay where he had fallen. With Bonnie behind the wheel, Clyde and Henry hooked up the rope and told Boyd to get behind the bogged-down Ford and push.[6]

About that time, into all this mess drove Jack Boydson. At first it looked like a normal case of a car stuck in the mud, but then he saw a dead man lying in the road. He tried to back away, but Clyde ran up with a BAR, and Boydson joined Percy Boyd behind the stranded Ford. They pushed and Clyde pulled with the pickup, but the rope broke and the Ford was still stuck. A few more unlucky passersby were drafted, but with no more success. By this time, things were getting tense. Clyde was shouting orders and Henry was waving an automatic rifle around, and at nearby houses, people were standing on their porches, watching the drama in the middle of the road.[7] One of the men on the road, William F. Hughes, remembered Clyde saying, "Boys, one good man has already been killed, and if you don't follow orders, others are liable to be."[8]

Charley Dodson lived nearby, and when he heard the shooting, he got into his truck and started toward the mine. Clyde had almost given up on the Ford and was about to take another vehicle from a nearby house when the truck drove up to the scene. Charley may have saved some lives, because he carried a chain with him. Clyde ran over—still waving a gun and shouting—and within a minute or two, the truck was hooked up and the Ford was free. Without further delay, Percy Boyd was shoved into the back seat and the mud-covered V-8 sedan drove off to the west, leaving a bewildered and relieved crowd of helpers standing in the road.[9]

Clyde Barrow without his Ford V-8 was like a fish out of water, so there was great relief at being back on the road. As it turned out, however, the Barrow gang weren't the only ones having trouble with the mud that morning. About three miles down the way, they had to stop again. A. N. Butterfield, a local farmer, and his brother had mired up their own car, and it blocked the road. For Clyde, who always dressed well, liked clean shirts, and hated to get his hands dirty, this morning was turning into a bloody, muddy mess. He and Henry jumped out and ran up to the stalled car and shouted, "We've just killed two men and we're in a hurry. The law is after us."[10] With Clyde and Henry's help, the road was cleared and the gang drove off north toward Chetopa, a small town just over the state line into Kansas.

At first, Percy Boyd considered his prospects pretty bleak. He wasn't sure who these people were, but he had a good guess. He had seen them kill one man already, and now he counted three automatic rifles, two shotguns, and several pistols in the car. He wasn't sure which worried him more; the possibility that the outlaws might decide to just shoot him, or the possibility that they might run into more police officers and he might be killed in the resulting gunfight. But, when time went by and neither of the things he feared had happened, things relaxed a little. The outlaws bandaged his head wound, which, though not serious, had bled a lot, and he finally got up the nerve to ask Henry Methvin a question. "Is that Clyde Barrow?" When

Methvin nodded his head yes, Boyd's suspicions were confirmed.[11] Although he now knew that Barrow was the leader of the group, Boyd never did find out the name of the fellow who answered his question.[12]

After reaching the Kansas state line, Clyde turned west to the town of Bartlett, where he stopped for gas. After that, they just drove around the countryside. Boyd got the impression that Clyde didn't know the local roads very well, since he seemed to just be wandering around. Boyd did begin to develop a little respect for Clyde's choice of cars and driving ability, however. He said that the Ford was almost new, with about three thousand miles on it, and that, on good roads, Clyde would go flat out. Boyd said he saw ninety on the speedometer more than once.[13]

Back in Commerce, an all-out manhunt was organized, using men from several different law enforcement agencies in three states.[14] This time, a new twist was added. About two hours after the shooting, Andy Walker, a local pilot, took off from nearby Miami and flew over the area along the Oklahoma–Kansas line, trying to spot the car. Later, Boyd told authorities that Clyde stopped once because he heard an airplane, so Walker may have come close.[15]

By late afternoon, they were in the Fort Scott, Kansas, area, where they got stuck again but were pulled out without incident. Henry Methvin got out and bought a newspaper, and later he bought food for their dinners. The newspaper confirmed that Cal Campbell had been killed. "I'm sorry about shooting the old man," Clyde said (Campbell was sixty years old), but Boyd wasn't sure he meant it.[16]

By now, Boyd was talking freely with the outlaws. He asked Clyde about the Grapevine shootings, and Clyde lied to him with a straight face, saying that they weren't involved at all and was upset at the newspapers for saying so. When asked about the Joplin killings, Clyde, in so many words, said that it was mainly the policemen's fault for not running away. Boyd later told reporters that Clyde seemed to think quite highly of himself. "He acted like he owned the earth," Boyd said. "He was the coolest operator I ever saw."[17]

Boyd also had long conversations with Bonnie. They told each other about their families, and Bonnie asked Boyd to make her a promise. Sonny Boy, the rabbit, was still with them. If they got caught or killed while Boyd was with them, would he see that Sonny Boy got to Bonnie's mother? "Of course," Boyd told her. What else could he say to the girlfriend of the man who held his life in his hands?

Around midnight, Clyde stopped the car about nine miles south of Fort Scott. They had given Boyd a new shirt and tie and offered him a new suit, but it was too small. Now they gave him a ten-dollar bill[18] and told him to stay there until they went over a hill in the distance. Before they drove away, Boyd asked, "Bonnie, what do you want me to tell the press?"

"Tell them I don't smoke cigars," the nation's most notorious female said. She had earlier explained to Boyd that the famous picture of her with a cigar in her mouth was a joke. Of all her bad publicity, this may have bothered Bonnie the most.[19] As Percy Boyd stood by the road in the dark, Bonnie and Clyde, and the man who would betray them, drove away. Boyd walked to a nearby house and called the police. He was back home by 7:30 the next morning.

Of Bonnie and Clyde's eleven known captives, all of whom were treated well, Boyd seems to have been their favorite. Clyde would later say that the Commerce police chief showed "more real guts" than anybody he had ever met.[20] Bonnie said, "We liked him." What she liked the most was that Boyd kept his word about the cigar picture. As soon as he got back to Commerce, he told the press what Bonnie had said. Later, Bonnie joyfully told her mother, "It was in all the Oklahoma newspapers!"[21]

CHAPTER 34
The Barrow—Hamilton Newspaper Feud

After Percy Boyd was let out on the road south of Fort Scott, Kansas, Clyde, Bonnie, and Henry headed north toward Topeka and disappeared for ten days. During that time, a letter was mailed from Tulsa to "Mr. Henry Ford, Detroit, Mich." It was dated April 10 and received on the 13th. It was a short note telling Mr. Ford what a great car his Ford V-8 was. According to the text, the Ford "has got every other car skinned." The note was signed, "Clyde Champion Barrow."

Tulsa Okla
10th April

Mr. Henry Ford
Detroit Mich.
Dear Sir:

While I still have got breath in my lungs I will tell you what a dandy car you make. I have drove Fords exclusivly [sic] when I could get away with one. For sustained speed and freedom from trouble the Ford has got ever other car skinned, and even if my business hasn't [sic] been strickty [sic] legal it don't hurt anything to tell you what a fine car you got in the V-8.
                    Yours truly
                    Clyde Champion Barrow[1]

Even though they may well have been in the Tulsa area about the time this letter was mailed, and it does sound like something Clyde might enjoy doing, the handwriting doesn't match Clyde's, Bonnie's, or that of any other gang member. While the letter certainly states Clyde's feelings about the Ford V-8, the Barrow family doesn't think Clyde would ever have signed his name "Clyde Champion Barrow" when his real middle name was Chestnut.[2] Whether the letter to Henry Ford is genuine or not, Clyde's longest literary effort was still to come. Everyone agrees that it is real, and it was aimed not at the law but at his ex-partner. It would have to wait for a couple of weeks, though. Barrow had some other things to do first.

Early on Monday morning, April 16, 1934, a Pontiac drove into Stuart, Iowa, from the east and pulled into the Miller Brothers Standard Oil station. Vic Miller put in ten gallons of ethyl and one gallon of regular. A Mr. Bracewell also saw the car and wrote down the license number—1934 Iowa 13-1234—because he thought the people in the car "were a hard looking lot." There were three people in the car, two men wearing nice clothes and hats, and a young woman dressed in red.

By 9:00 A.M., the car had been seen parked in several locations around town and the two men had been seen walking around. Once, they went by the bank. Finally, the two men went into a drug store, where Varney Lovely served them both

Downtown Stuart, Iowa, as it is today. Note the white storefront with columns, second from the left. In 1934, this was the drug store where Clyde and Henry Methvin bought Coca-Colas, while Bonnie waited in the car, just before they walked down the street to the bank, seen in the background.

—From the author's collection

First National Bank of Stuart, Iowa. Robbed by Clyde Barrow and Henry Methvin on April 16, 1934.

—From the author's collection

Cokes but thought he smelled liquor on them. At 9:10 A.M., the two men walked into the First National Bank. The taller man stood near the door while the shorter man went to the window and asked for change for a $20 bill. Harold Cronkhite, the assistant cashier, counted out the change and then looked up to see the man holding a gun and heard, "This is a holdup."

Besides Mr. Cronkhite, only one other bank employee and one customer were inside. They were told to sit on the floor. About that time, Frank Eckhardt came in to make a deposit. The tall man by the door covered him with a gun and sent him to sit with the others. Eckhardt didn't bother to tell them about the money and bank book in his pocket, or that he was a vice president of the bank. By now, the shorter of the two men was behind the counter, stuffing the bills into a red-and-white-striped bag. Then he took the assistant cashier into the vault and ordered him to open the safe kept there. Mr. Cronkhite told him that the safe was on a time lock and couldn't be opened. Finally, the robbers ordered everybody inside the vault, walked out of the bank, got into the car where the woman waited, and drove east out of town.

Everything was over in a few minutes. Several people thought something was going on over at the bank, but the bandits were in and out and gone before anyone could raise an alarm. The bank later estimated the loss at less than $1,500. Mary Holmes was the first person in the bank after the robbery, followed by Glen Bufkin. The people in the vault asked who was there, not wanting to come out and find the bandits still inside. Assured by Mr. Bufkin that the outlaws had gone, the people in the vault emerged and the chase began.

In addition to its regular lawmen, Iowa was known for its vigilantes, and a group of them from Stuart were first on the robbers' trail. Phone calls were made to surrounding towns, and word came back that the car had been seen going through Dexter. Two carloads of these civilian enforcers left Stuart in hot pursuit. They were able to follow the car's trail for several miles but lost it in the countryside southeast of Dexter.[3]

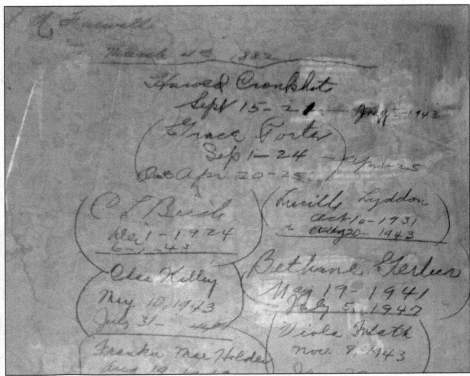

Employees' names, and the dates they worked in the bank, written on the wall inside the vault of the First National Bank of Stuart, Iowa. Note the first name at the top. Harold Cronkhite was the assistant cashier on duty the day the Barrow gang robbed the place.

—From the Author's Collection

Even though the description of the robbers and the woman who waited in the car fit Clyde Barrow, Henry Methvin, and Bonnie Parker, they were not mentioned as suspects in the initial news reports. They were only connected with the Stuart robbery when the license plate that Mr. Bracewell had seen and reported was found in Bonnie and Clyde's car after they were killed in Louisiana, four and a half weeks later.

All through the rest of Monday and into the night, Bonnie, Clyde, and Henry drove south for Texas. This time, Henry Methvin was Clyde's messenger, getting on a train at Wichita Falls and riding into Dallas to contact the Barrows for another meeting. Henry first tried Nell Barrow's beauty shop in the Sanger Hotel downtown, but it was too early and Nell wasn't there. Finally, he contacted Mrs. Parker and Mrs. Barrow and set up the meeting for later that same day in Mount Pleasant,

Texas, east of Dallas. Emma Parker said that as soon as Henry got there, he told her that he had been the one who had killed the policemen at Grapevine. He may have felt that she needed to know that the news reports about Bonnie doing the shooting were not true.

When they met later that day, Sonny Boy, the Easter bunny, was finally delivered to Bonnie's mother, and no one was more relieved than Clyde that the rabbit's outlaw days were over. He wouldn't miss the rabbit's company at all. "Keep him away from the cops," Bonnie told her mother. "He's been in two gun battles."

At this visit, the family members tried again to convince Bonnie and Clyde to do something to escape the end they all saw coming. Two years on the run had taken a toll on the young couple. You could see it on their faces and on their bodies. Never very large to begin with, they were now thin and gaunt from the constant strain, lack of rest, and poor food. Since the family realized that neither of them could ever surrender now, they begged them to leave the country. "Run for the border and try to start over. Leave Texas forever." Even this Bonnie and Clyde couldn't do. Their family was all they had left, they said. If they couldn't see them, they would rather be dead.

Clyde wouldn't run out of the country, but he did have a plan of his own. By now, they had been to Henry Methvin's parents' place in Bienville Parish, south of Arcadia, Louisiana, a few times, and Clyde thought he might buy a place near there as a hideout. Once established, the family could come visit him for a change. None of the family believed it would work, but they didn't say anything. Let Bonnie and Clyde have their fantasy. Anything was better than the hopelessness they all felt.[4]

After the meeting in Mount Pleasant, Bonnie, Clyde, and Henry drove north into the Ozarks and finally picked up Joe Palmer, who had been waiting for them for almost three weeks. With Palmer back in the gang, they headed down to Henry's home near Gibsland, Louisiana, for a few days. At this point, Clyde gave Joe two pistols, one of which had come from the armory at Ranger, Texas. They would go out in the swamps for target practice, and Joe thought Bonnie was a "fairly good shot"—at least on bottles and cans.[5]

About this time, they heard the latest news about their old partner Raymond Hamilton. It seems that the high life had drained Raymond's finances, so he had sent Mary to wait for him in Amarillo while he raised some cash. The plan was to hit a bank and then make a run for California to cool off. Ray began "riding the rails" from New Orleans and found a new partner for the job. To T. R. Brooks, of Wichita Falls, Raymond was just

another hobo like himself. How Ray convinced his new partner to take up daylight bank robbery is a mystery, but on April 25, "Teddy" Brooks was waiting in the car when Raymond came out of the First National Bank of Lewisville, Texas, with $1,000 in a bag. A chase ensued, and it turned out to be a very bad day for Ray and Teddy. At Howe, Texas, just south of Sherman, they ran into a roadblock. "Don't shoot, boys," Ray said. "I'm fresh out of guns, ammo, whiskey, and women." That wasn't strictly true. The police found two pistols on him. At that point, Hamilton decided that if he couldn't be free, at least he could be famous. "Do you know

Raymond Hamilton and T. R. Brooks. Captured after robbing a bank in Lewisville, Texas, April 25, 1934.

—From the collections of the Texas/Dallas History and Archives Division, Dallas Public Library

who you've got?" he asked. One of the officers said that he thought he did, and called him by name. "You're damned right—I'm Raymond Hamilton." The next day, April 26, Ray and Teddy were taken to the Dallas jail.[6] If Clyde Barrow had any respect left for Hamilton, it was finished by the fact that Ray was armed, but gave up without a fight. There was also a little matter about a letter Raymond had written just after Cal Campbell was killed.

If Clyde was angry at Raymond Hamilton before the Easter Sunday killings, Ray's action after the Commerce shooting made him furious. Even though Ray and Mary hadn't been with Bonnie and Clyde since the first of March, Ray's name was still being linked to Clyde's as a suspect in both the Grapevine and Commerce killings. Before he was captured, in an attempt to set the record straight—and avoid three murder charges—Raymond wrote a letter to his lawyer, trying to prove that he had an alibi for both incidents and stating, once and for all, that he didn't run with Clyde Barrow anymore.

Dear Mr. Basket,
I am sending you a bill for the hotel I was staying in at the time of that killing in Commerce, Oklahoma. I haven't been with Clyde and Bonnie since the Lancaster bank robbery. I'm sending you $100 and want this put before the public and proved right away. I'm sending you more money just as soon as I find out you are doing what I ask. I'm putting also my fingerprint on this bill. I'm also leaving a letter at this hotel for you. You can call for it. My fingerprint will be there when you call for it. You know I try to keep my promise. I want you to let the public and the whole world know I am not with Clyde Barrow, and don't go his speed. I'm a lone man and intend to stay that way. I wrote Mrs. M. A. Ferguson but I guess it was in vain. I was in Houston the night of April 4 and have been here (New Orleans) ever since April fifth.

Yours truly,
Raymond Hamilton

The letter was postmarked April 7 and appeared in the *Dallas Morning News* on April 9. It was written on stationery from the Lafayette Hotel, New Orleans.[7]

Raymond Hamilton's letter had been bothering Clyde Barrow for two weeks, and now that he finally knew where Ray was, he could reply with his own letter. From the handwriting, it was almost certainly dictated by Clyde and written by Bonnie. As they finished their visit in Louisiana and headed back north, they dropped it in a mailbox in Memphis, Tennessee. Postmarked April 27 and arriving at the Dallas County Jail on April 30, it is much longer and more personal than Hamilton's short note to his lawyer. Clyde's anger comes through in almost every line.

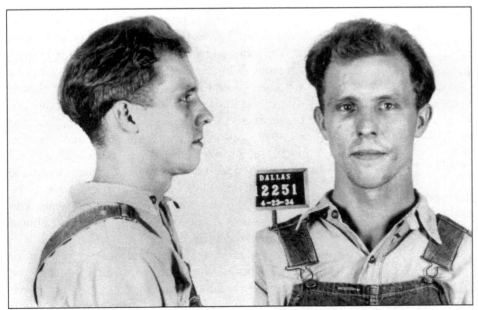

Mug shot of Floyd Garland Hamilton. Taken when he was arrested for helping his younger brother, Raymond, rob a bank at Grand Prairie, Texas. April 23, 1934.

—From the collections of the Texas/Dallas History and Archives Division, Dallas Public Library

Raymond Hamilton
505 Main Street
c/o Dallas County Jail
Dallas, Texas

Raymond:

I'm very sorry to hear of your getting captured, but due to the fact you offered no resistance, sympathy is lacking. The most I can do is hope you miss the "chair." The purpose of this letter is to remind you of all the "dirty deals" you have pulled. When I came to the farm after you I thought maybe the "joint" had changed you from a boastful punk. However I learned too soon the mistake I had made. The first thing that aroused my suspicion was your suggestion of shooting Joe Palmer in the back while he was asleep. You soon learned about how I felt about such "cat ideas." Since then I have found your reasons for wanting to do this was because Joe was on the farm with you and knew what kind of a guy you were. The next impression was when we got the road "blocked" on us in the Ozarks and you were too "yellow" to fight. You cowered on the floorboard, afraid of being shot. Now that you're in the Dallas jail, you have a tested pal, W. D. Jones. You might get a few pointers from him on how to impress the people you were an innocent, or possibly, forced companion of the ruthless Barrow gang. You might be as lucky as he was in making them believe I kept you handcuffed or tied.

When you wanted to get your Prostitute Sweetheart I thought OK. But when you were so persistent about her going to town alone that idea wasn't so "hot." I thought then and truly believe now that should she have gotten off without Bonnie she would have "spotted" us all. She hails from a "rat" family and you couldn't expect better from her.

You exposed your "hole card" when you stole the money from us on the Lancaster "job." That's what I have my rear vision mirror for, to watch suspicious people. When I demanded a "shake down" you offered such strange excuses for having the money on you I should have killed you then. I would have saved myself much bother and money looking for you. For after you writing that letter saying you didn't stoop so low as to rob filling stations I have done nothing but look for you. Should I have found you, you wouldn't have had a chance to give up. You couldn't stand the rift of the outlaw life. For one reason you were too yellow and knew you could never surrender with me and another reason you wanted to play "Big Shot," sleep in hotels and ride passenger trains. You weren't intelligent enough to know that you couldn't live like a king and stay out. I don't claim to be too smart. I know that some day they will get me but it won't be without resistance. You only carried your guns around to "show off" or else kidnap women and children.

I guess you find where your boastful long tongue has gotten you. Maybe you can talk yourself out of the "chair." Or maybe you can write a few more letters (try one to the governor) at least it will gain you some publicity.

When you started the rumor about Bonnie wanting a "cut" of the loot you sure messed your self up. I have always taken care of Bonnie and never asked any thief to help me.

I hope this will serve the purpose of letting you know that you can never expect the least of sympathy or assistance from me.

So Long—
Clyde Barrow[8]

There exists another letter that claims to be from Clyde Barrow. It was badly typed on a Western Union form, addressed to Dallas Assistant District Attorney Winter King, and included a fingerprint supposed to be Clyde's. The family never believed that it was authentic. Besides the poor typing, the grammar and spelling are awful—nothing like the relatively well-written letter that is certainly Bonnie and Clyde's work. It also tries to implicate Raymond Hamilton and Mary O'Dare in the Grapevine killings. It may have been written as a hoax, or by someone who wanted to cause Raymond some extra trouble—as if he needed any more—but it almost certainly wasn't Clyde.[9]

Bonnie, Clyde, Henry, and Joe spent a day or so in Memphis, and Bonnie insisted on buying Joe Palmer a gray suit.[10] They were headed back north to some of Clyde's favorite hunting grounds. Their vacation was over. It was time for business again.

CHAPTER 35
"The Road Gets Dimmer and Dimmer"

Nice, lazy, spring Sunday afternoons were probably a great time to steal cars. Everybody would be inside taking a nap. At least it must have seemed that way to Clyde Barrow on April 29, 1934, as he cruised the neighborhoods in Topeka, Kansas, looking for his next ride. In the driveway of Jesse and Ruth Warren's house, at 2107 Gable Street, sat an immaculate new 1934 cordoba gray Ford model 730 deluxe four-door V-8 sedan with the new accessory—an external trunk made by Potter Manufacturing, of Jackson, Michigan. The car only had 1,243 miles on it, and everything about it said "conspicuous"—not the kind of car for a young couple wanted by every police department in the mid-United States. But it was just too nice to pass up, and within seconds, Clyde was driving it away.[1]

Even though Clyde Barrow was a Texas boy through and through, he seemed to have a special fondness for the Midwest plains. Some of his first activities after he got out of prison were in this area, and he went back, time after time, over his two-year career. One of his favorite areas was western Iowa, and this was where he headed next. The area from Des Moines westward was characterized by mile after mile of fields full of corn and other grains, small towns, and—especially important for Clyde's purposes—small-town banks. He had already hit three of them in the past three months, but there were still plenty left.

Strange as it may seem, small-town bank robbery, as practiced by Clyde Barrow and his contemporaries like Raymond Hamilton and Pretty Boy Floyd, was a relatively low-risk occupation. Granted, you were very likely to end up dead or in prison eventually, but—in the early 1930s—the actual robbing of a country bank was a fairly straightforward affair. There were exceptions, of course. On November 23, 1932, Pretty Boy Floyd's old partner George Birdwell and another man were shot down by the citizens of Boley, Oklahoma, as they tried to rob a nice, easy country bank.[2] By now, though, Clyde had it down to a science. He did his homework, his technique was almost always the same, and there was never any serious opposition. Only three times was Clyde ever called upon to fire a weapon during a bank robbery or was he seriously threatened during the getaway.[3]

As far as we know, only two people were ever injured during any bank robbery in which Clyde Barrow participated. This is not to say that Clyde was a gentle man. He was just smart enough to know that it was in his best interest to get in, get the money, and get out with the least amount of fuss. Many times, Clyde was already out of sight before anybody outside the bank knew what had happened, and given a ten or fifteen minute head start, nobody could catch him.

On May 2, 1934, Bonnie and Clyde, with Henry Methvin and Joe Palmer, were driving through northwestern Iowa, getting ready for the next bank job. Normally, the countryside would have been green with the summer crops, but the last few years had not been kind to farmers in this part of the country. This year had been especially dry. There had been little snow over the winter and only about three inches of moisture since the previous fall. Rainfall for the month of April was 60 percent below normal. Farmers were resorting to hauling water for livestock because of dry wells, and the hay and other feed crops were in danger. Fifteen consecutive dust storms in the past few weeks had left topsoil piled along the side of the roads. As they approached the town of Spencer, in Clay County, the landscape looked more like the sand dunes of the Sahara Desert than the corn fields of the American Midwest.[4]

On Thursday morning, May 3, several residents of Everly, Iowa, a few miles west of Spencer, noticed a gray, sporty-looking Ford V-8, containing three men and a woman, cruising around town. Some of them noticed the Iowa license plate because of the distinctive sequence of the last four numbers—13-1234.[5] About 1:30 P.M., the car stopped across the street from the Everly branch of the Farmer's Trust and Saving Bank, and two of the men got out and went inside. Owen Goodspeed, the branch manager, was behind the teller window when one of the men asked for change for a large bill. When Goodspeed turned back to his customer, he saw a pistol and was told that this was a robbery.

Two other people in the bank, a stenographer and another customer, were seated in chairs, the teller cages were stripped of money, and Goodspeed was taken into the vault, where a safe was located. Goodspeed convinced the robbers that he couldn't open the safe, so they put the others into the vault with him. The two men then left through the side door to the gray Ford that was waiting for them, drove west out of town, and disappeared.

Again, Clyde had pulled off what seemed like a perfect operation. Speed and reliance on past experience had their drawbacks, however. Clyde and his accomplice Joe Palmer were fast and efficient, but as in several other cases, they made mistakes. The first reports of the holdup set the "take"

at about $2,000, but a later check revealed that not only had the bandits failed to get the safe open, they had missed $500 in cash, not counting silver and a Liberty Bond. The final accounting showed about $700 missing.[6]

After the Everly job, Clyde, Bonnie, and Henry were heading back to Louisiana to stay with Henry's family, and they wanted Joe to go with them. "Come on," they said. "We'll do some hunting and fishing on Black Lake—buy some swimming suits, maybe." Palmer, though, didn't like it much down in Louisiana, and suggested that they come with him to Chicago and see the World's Fair, which was in progress. Bonnie and Clyde cared as little for the World's Fair as Joe did for rural northwest Louisiana, so they agreed to part company. Clyde left Joe outside Joplin, Missouri, and drove away. In three weeks, Joe Palmer would be at Clyde Barrow's funeral.

There were many different opinions of Clyde Barrow in 1930s America. The official ones, published in the newspapers and given out by police departments, were uniformly bad. Among his family, friends, and associates in the outlaw world, the opinions varied widely—all the way from beloved son and brother to yellow coward and gun-crazy punk. Joe Palmer's was one of the most generous: "Clyde maybe was a murderer and killed folks, but he sure was good to me and the boys—and he toted fair."[7]

Sunday May 6, 1934, Bonnie and Clyde left Bienville Parish, Louisiana, for a quick trip home. They drove by the Barrow filling station in west Dallas and told the family to meet them out in the country, east of town. The Barrows and Bonnie's mother spent about two hours with them that evening. At one point in the conversation, Bonnie told her mother, "When they kill us, don't let them take me to an undertaking parlor, will you? Bring me home." Even after all that had happened, Bonnie's request still shocked Mrs. Parker. She said that Bonnie talked about it like "discussing going to the grocery store." She thought Bonnie—all of twenty-three—seemed a million years old. Bonnie also made her mother promise that, when they were killed, she wouldn't say anything "ugly" about

Clyde. At the same time, Clyde was telling his family that he was working on a deal for a place in Louisiana where they could come and visit them.[8]

It was also at this meeting that Bonnie gave her mother a copy of her latest poem.[9] It had been over a year since Bonnie had left her poem "Suicide Sal" in the apartment in Joplin, and a lot had happened since then. This new work was obviously written by someone resigned to her fate. Bonnie may have intended it as her parting statement, to be published after her death. Originally titled "The End of the Line,"[10] it has become known as "The Story of Bonnie and Clyde."

THE STORY OF BONNIE AND CLYDE
by Bonnie Parker

You've read the story of Jesse James—
Of how he lived and died;
If you're still in need
Of something to read
Here's the story of Bonnie and Clyde.

Now Bonnie and Clyde are the Barrow gang.
I'm sure you all have read
How they rob and steal
And those who squeal
Are usually found dying or dead.

There's lots of untruths to these write-ups;
They're not so ruthless as that;
Their nature is raw;
They hate the law—
The stool pigeons, spotters, and rats.

They call them cold-blooded killers;
They say they are heartless and mean;
But I say this with pride,
That I once knew Clyde
When he was honest and upright and clean.

But the laws fooled around,
Kept taking him down
And locking him up in a cell,
Till he said to me,
"I'll never be free,

So I'll meet a few of them in hell."
The road was so dimly lighted;
There were no highway signs to guide;
But they made up their minds
If all roads were blind,
They wouldn't give up till they died.

The road gets dimmer and dimmer;
Sometimes you can hardly see;
But it's fight, man to man,
And do all you can,
For they know they can never be free.

From heart-break some people have suffered;
From weariness some people have died;
But take it all in all,
Our troubles are small
Till we get like Bonnie and Clyde.

If a policeman is killed in Dallas,
And they have no clue or guide;
If they can't find a fiend,
They just wipe their slate clean
And hang it on Bonnie and Clyde.

There's two crimes committed in America
Not accredited to the Barrow mob;
They had no hand
In the kidnap demand,
Nor the Kansas City Depot job.

A newsboy once said to his buddy:
"I wish old Clyde would get jumped;
In these awful hard times
We'd make a few dimes
If five or six cops would get bumped."

The police haven't got the report yet
But Clyde called me up today;
He said, "Don't start any fights—
We aren't working nights—
We're joining the NRA."

From Irving to West Dallas viaduct
Is known as the Great Divide,
Where the women are kin,
And the men are men,

And they won't "stool" on Bonnie and Clyde.
If they try to act like citizens
And rent them a nice little flat,
About the third night
They're invited to fight
By a sub-gun's rat-tat-tat.

They don't think they're too smart or desperate,
They know that the law always wins;
They've been shot at before,
But they do not ignore
That death is the wages of sin.

Some day they'll go down together;
They'll bury them side by side;
To few it'll be grief—
To the law a relief—
But it's death for Bonnie and Clyde.[11]

After leaving the poem and a favorite photograph with Bonnie's mother and promising to return in two weeks, Bonnie and Clyde drove back to Louisiana.[12] Except for Clyde's father, none of the family saw either of "the kids" alive again.

Three days later, Clyde made a trip back to Dallas alone. He stopped at the Star Service Station on Eagle Ford Road, hoping to find his mother, but only Henry Barrow was at home. "Your momma's visiting up the road," Henry said. Clyde then asked his father to meet him down by the railroad tracks at midnight. Later that night, when the meeting took place, Clyde opened a suitcase and took out two sheets of paper, saying that he was going to "sign them for you and Momma." Henry couldn't read or write, so he had no idea what the papers were for, but he had no trouble recognizing the large stack of cash in the same suitcase. Clyde, meanwhile, was having no luck getting his pen to write. After searching for another one, he finally gave up and said he would have to bring the papers back next time. Clyde told his father goodbye and drove away.[13]

There would be no next time. Clyde Barrow had two weeks to live.

CHAPTER 36
"They Sow the Wind and Reap the Whirlwind"
Hosea 8:7

Like many other places, Bonnie and Clyde had passed through northwest Louisiana several times, but after they broke Henry Methvin out of prison in January 1934, they had a personal connection in the area around Bienville Parish, southeast of Shreveport. Clyde and Henry Methvin had arrived at Eastham Prison Farm within a few months of each other in the fall of 1930. Henry was three years younger than Clyde—just barely eighteen—when he was convicted of assault with intent to murder and car theft, and sentenced to ten years, but he was larger and better built than the little Texan.[1] In prison, Henry earned a reputation as a genuine tough guy. Henry Methvin, Joe Palmer, Ralph Fults, and Clyde Barrow endured what Clyde called the "burning hell" of Eastham together for many months. Henry was more than just another convict, so when he invited Bonnie and Clyde to hide out in the country near his family, they accepted.[2] Once they made a couple of visits, they got to like the place.

They may have made a quick stop at Henry's parents' home in the few days immediately following the Eastham escape in January, but the first real visit was probably after the split with Raymond Hamilton in early March. Several more visits followed, and by now (early May), Bienville Parish and the surrounding area had almost become their base of operations. Their presence in the area, and their connection with the Methvin family, was

becoming a very badly kept secret. The fact that the Methvins had for two months been dealing with the law to put Bonnie and Clyde "on the spot" was a much better kept one.

Henry had lots of family in Bienville and surrounding parishes, and they were the ones who protected the three outlaws when they were in the area. Before long, however, other people began to notice the young couple who frequently showed up, both with the Methvins and by themselves, at the country stores and sawmills in the area. They kept to themselves for the most part and seemed like polite, normal folks. Some people knew their identities, and more suspected, but no one bothered them. The Methvin family, responsible for Bonnie and Clyde's presence, were like many others in the area—large and poor. They were not highly thought of in some circles, either. Little has been written about them and, as a result, there is some confusion about the relationships involved.

Henry Methvin's paternal grandparents were Hamilton Terrell Methvin and Mary Barron. They had five children, but only three lived to adulthood. They were Iverson T., born in 1876; Idonia, born in 1882; and Ivy T., born in 1885. Iverson, the first born, married Sarah Mildred Elizabeth Huggins on April 30, 1899, in Red River Parish. They had nine children. Iverson T. Methvin died in 1952 at the age of seventy-six, a respected resident of Red River Parish, Louisiana.

Iverson's younger brother, Ivy T. Methvin, married Avie Stephens, and they had three children: Terrell, born in 1911; Henry, born April 4, 1912, and Cecil, born December 22, 1914. It was Ivy and Avie's middle son Henry who was Clyde Barrow's partner. Iverson Methvin was Henry's uncle and by all accounts had nothing to do with Bonnie and Clyde or any of the things that happened to them. Most accounts over the years don't seem to realize that there were two brothers— Iverson and Ivy. It was generally believed that Iverson was Henry's father and that any references to an "Ivy" Methvin was simply Iverson using a nickname.[3]

As the second week in May began, Bonnie and Clyde were making themselves at home in Bienville Parish. They met with Henry Methvin's brothers and other kinfolks at out-of-the-way places in the woods for picnics and frequented their houses for meals.[4] As for their own accommodations, they were sick and tired of living in their car, so they looked for a real house. About ten miles south of Gibsland, near Henry's parents, was a house back in the woods that belonged to a man named Otis Cole. It was locally known as the "John Cole place" for Otis' father, who had built it. The house had been empty for several years but was still very livable. One evening, Ivy Methvin went to see Otis Cole at the small store he ran. They talked about the abandoned house, and then Methvin left.[5] Some people say that Bonnie and Clyde actually made arrangements to buy the place, while others say that they just moved in.[6] Whatever the truth, Bonnie and Clyde began to be seen fairly regularly around the area, Clyde posing with Henry's father and brother Terrell as a logger. The truth, however, was becoming known to more and more people.

Henry Methvin's two brothers, who lived in the area, became important contacts in addition to Henry's parents. Both brothers had families of their own, and both provided support of one kind or another. Henry's older brother Terrell and his wife Emma met with them regularly at the picnics in the woods and had Bonnie and Clyde in their home for dinner at least once. On this occasion, the outlaws admired a small bed. Terrell and Emma had two young daughters, and their grandfather had made the girls their own little bed out of native wood. Bonnie and Clyde lay down on the bed and told everybody that it was the first time they had slept in a bed in months.

Henry's younger brother, Cecil, and his wife, Clemie, didn't have any children yet, but Clemie was expecting a baby near the end of the year. Clemie didn't go to the picnics. She had a history of miscarriages, so she stayed close to home, but she was also afraid of what might happen if the law showed up at one of the meetings. Because of this, Clemie begged her sister-in-law, Emma, not to take the little girls to the picnics, but Emma said her husband wouldn't like it if she left them.

In spite of Clemie's condition and her fear, she and Cecil also had Bonnie and Clyde over for dinner once, sometime during the third week of May. The famous outlaws, as it turned out, didn't make a very impressive entrance. When they arrived, it was evident that Bonnie had been drinking. She already had a pronounced limp, due to the burns on her right leg from the Wellington, Texas, car wreck, but now she was so drunk she couldn't walk at all. Clyde carried her into the house, but the closest he would come to an apology was to explain that he was going to "let her have all she wants" because he didn't think they had much time left. Bonnie was sober enough to appreciate a good dinner of home-cured ham and cornbread, however. She liked the cornbread so much that she took some with her.[7]

There were several stories circulating about the new young couple in the old Cole house, but one of the most interesting to the ladies was the story that Bonnie was pregnant. By this time, it was said to be common knowledge among the Methvin women and neighbor ladies that Bonnie was "expecting." Clemie Methvin was told by her sister-in-law, Emma, that she and Bonnie were due about the same time (Clemie's son, James, was born in early January 1935). Some of the older women had even offered—given Bonnie's situation as a hunted outlaw—to take the baby and raise it themselves.[8] Whether the story is true or not no one knows, but it was in circulation several weeks before Bonnie's death. Both the Barrow and Parker families say that Bonnie could not have children due to an injury and complications during the time she was with Roy Thornton. They also maintain that Clyde was sterile due to the effects of a childhood illness.[9] None of the family believe Bonnie could have been pregnant.

On May 21, 1934, Bonnie, Clyde, and Henry Methvin drove up to the Cole house. Bonnie and Clyde stayed at the house a few hours, and Henry went to see his parents, who lived nearby. When he got to Ivy and Avie's house, they told him that everything was in place. The agreement from the state of Texas, signed by the governor, was in Sheriff Jordan's possession, and the lawmen were ready. All

IDENTIFICATION ORDER NO. 1227
May 21, 1934.

DIVISION OF INVESTIGATION
U. S. DEPARTMENT OF JUSTICE
WASHINGTON, D. C.

NATIONAL MOTOR VEHICLE THEFT ACT

WANTED

MRS. ROY THORNTON, aliases BONNIE BARROW,

MRS. CLYDE BARROW, BONNIE PARKER.

DESCRIPTION

Age, 23 years (1933); Height, 5 feet, 5 inches; Weight, 100 pounds; Build, slender; Hair, auburn, bobbed; originally blonde; Eyes, blue; Complexion, fair; Scars and marks, bullet wound left foot next to little toe; bullet in left knee; burn scar on right leg from hip to knee; Peculiarities, walks with both knees slightly buckled.

RELATIVES:

Roy Thornton, husband, Texas State Penitentiary
Mrs. J. T. (Emma) Parker, mother, 1216 South Lamar St., Dallas, Texas
Mrs. Billie Parker Mace, sister, 1216 South Lamar St., Dallas, Texas
Hubert (Buster) Parker, brother, Gladewater, Texas
Nellie Gonzales, half-sister, Harwood, Gonzales County, Texas.

CRIMINAL RECORD

Arrested sheriff's office, Kaufman, Texas, June 16, 1932; charge, burglary; released.

WANTED

CLYDE CHAMPION BARROW, aliases CLYDE BARROW, ROY BAILEY, JACK HALE, ELDIN WILLIAMS, ELVIN WILLIAMS.

DESCRIPTION

Age, 23 years; Height, 5 feet, 7 inches, bare feet; Weight, 150 pounds; Build, medium; Hair, dark brown, wavy; reported dyed black; Eyes, hazel; Complexion, light, Scars and marks, shield and anchor with "U.S.N." on right forearm, outer; girl's bust, left inner forearm; bullet wound through both legs just above knees.

RELATIVES:

Henry Barrow, father, Rural Route 6, Dallas, Texas
Mrs. Cunie Barrow, mother, Rural Route 6, Dallas, Texas
L. C. Barrow, brother, County Jail, Dallas, Texas
Marie Barrow, sister, Rural Route 6, Dallas, Texas
Mrs. Artie Winkler, sister, Sanger Hotel Apartments, Dallas, Texas
Mrs. Nellie Cowan, sister, Sanger Hotel Apartments, Dallas, Texas
Mrs. Jim Muckelroy, aunt, Martinsville, Texas
Mrs. Belle Briggs, aunt, Dallas, Texas
Frank Barrow, uncle, Eureka, Navarro County, Texas
Jim Barrow, uncle, Streetman, Texas
D. Brown, cousin, Martinsville, Texas
Bertha Graham, cousin, Tyler, Texas
Claud Linthicum, cousin, San Angelo, Texas
Rommie Linthicum, cousin, San Angelo, Texas.

CRIMINAL RECORD

Criminal record and fingerprints can be obtained from Identification Order No. 1211, issued October 24, 1933.

Clyde Champion Barrow and Bonnie Parker constantly travel together and extreme caution must be exercised by arresting officers as they are wanted in connection with assault and murder of officers.

Complaint was filed at Dallas, Texas, on May 20, 1933, charging Clyde Champion Barrow and Bonnie Parker with transporting Ford Coupe, Motor No. A-1878100, property of Dr. E. L. Damron of Effingham, Illinois, from Dallas, Texas, to Pawhuska, Oklahoma, on or about September 16, 1932.

Law enforcement agencies kindly transmit any additional information or criminal record to the nearest office of the Division of Investigation, U. S. Department of Justice.

If apprehended, please notify the Director, Division of Investigation, U. S. Department of Justice, Washington, D. C., or the Special Agent in Charge of the office of the Division of Investigation listed on the back hereof which is nearest your city.

(over)

Issued by: J. EDGAR HOOVER, DIRECTOR.

Wanted poster, issued by the Division of Investigation two days before Bonnie and Clyde were killed.

—From the author's collection

they were waiting for was Henry's part in the plan. The plan itself was not complicated. It required only secrecy and a little luck to work.

One of the basic requirements of running a military unit in the field, or an outlaw gang on the run, is a rendezvous point. There is always the chance of being surprised and separated by random events, so you didn't want to be caught without one. It had happened to Clyde a year before in Ruston, Louisiana. He let W. D. Jones out to steal a car, the owner chased him, Clyde chased the owner, and W. D. ended up outrunning everybody. Clyde lost touch with him, and they had no back-up plan. Jones had to ditch the car and make his own way back to Dallas, and Bonnie and Clyde didn't see him for a month and a half. Clyde wasn't going to let that happen again. He had an understanding with Henry that if they got separated, they would meet back at Henry's parents' house in a day or so. That made Henry's part in the plan simple—get away from Bonnie and Clyde on some pretext, and let the rendevous plan kick in. Since there was really only one way to reach his parents' house, the posse could stake out a likely spot on the road and let Clyde come to them.

Henry told his parents that Clyde planned to go into Shreveport that evening and he would slip away if he could. After Henry left with Bonnie and Clyde a couple of hours later, the word was passed to John Joyner, who gave it to Sheriff Jordan, who called Sheriff Schmid in Dallas, who called the four officers in the special unit, who were already in a motel in Shreveport. They left immediately for Arcadia.[10]

In Arcadia, the county seat of Bienville Parish, the last two members were added to the posse. Frank Hamer and Manny Gault represented the Texas Prison System and the Texas State Police. Bob Alcorn and Ted Hinton represented the Dallas County Sheriff's Department, and now Sheriff Henderson Jordan and his deputy, Prentis Oakley, represented Bienville Parish, Louisiana. Besides his local knowledge, Jordan's authority and jurisdiction were needed to make the whole thing legal. Jordan was consulted about the route Clyde would have to travel, and an ambush site was selected. By 9:00 P.M., the posse was in place on top of a small embankment on the east side of Ringgold Road just south of Mount Lebanon. They had a good view back up to the north, the way Clyde would have to come, and good cover on their side of the road.[11] There were still a lot of "ifs," but the site was good and they were ready.

That same Monday evening, Bonnie and Clyde and Henry Methvin drove to Shreveport, just as Henry had told his parents, and before long, Henry got the chance he was looking for. Clyde stopped in front of a place called the Majestic Cafe and sent Henry in for some sandwiches. While Henry waited at the counter, a police car came into view, cruising down the street. Rather than risk identifi-

Aerial view of the ambush site. Bienville Parish, Louisiana. May 23, 1934.
—Courtesy the Texas Ranger Hall of Fame and Museum, Waco, Texas

cation, Clyde and Bonnie drove out of sight. Moments later, Henry got up, left the sandwiches on the counter, and walked away.[12] The plan was in motion. All Henry had to do was hide and wait.

When the sun came up on Tuesday morning, the posse was ready. They had endured the mosquitoes, ticks, and chiggers of the Louisiana countryside all night, but they were in position and anxious for it all to be over. All through the day Tuesday they waited, but nothing happened. There was a little traffic on the gravel road, but no gray Ford V-8.[13] They prepared for a second night in the brush, but if something didn't turn up pretty soon, it would mean that Clyde had gotten spooked or changed his plans. In that case, they'd be right back where they started.

Tuesday night passed with no combat, except with the swarms of insects that continued to make the men's lives miserable. Sometime before Wednesday morning, Henry's father, Ivy Methvin, arrived at the ambush site with the old log truck Clyde had bought for him, and it was set up in the southbound lane, but facing north, with the right front tire removed.[14] The hope was that this would attract Clyde's attention toward the truck and away from the posse, at the same time forcing him closer to their side of the road.[15] Between 7:30 and 8:00 A.M., a school bus came by. The driver stopped and asked if he could help—maybe take in the tire or give Ivy a lift into town. No, Methvin said, "I'm just getting ready to put it back on."[16] By 9:10 A.M., everybody was ready to admit that they had missed their chance. Just then, they heard something that made all the discomfort of the last two days fall away. Nothing else sounds quite like a Ford V-8 running flat out on a country road.[17]

Unseen since they had driven away from the Majestic Cafe on Monday night, Bonnie and Clyde reappeared at 8:00 A.M. Wednesday morning in the small town of Gibsland, about ten miles north of the Methvin place. Some of the local folks had seen them in there before, and everybody could tell they were from out of town. Bonnie had on a rust-red-colored dress with matching shoes. A local lady thought she was very pretty but too pale to have been out in the sun very much.[18] Clyde was dapper in his suit coat and blue western-style shirt. The couple stopped in front of Canfield's Cafe and went in for breakfast. As they left, they ordered two sandwiches to go. Back in the car, Clyde arranged himself for driving, as he usually did— shoes off, a sixteen-gauge sawed-off shotgun between his left side and the driver's door, and a twenty-gauge shotgun against his right leg. Bonnie took a nickel-plated .45 automatic, placed it on the seat, and covered it with a magazine, and Clyde drove out of town, on his way to find Henry Methvin.[19]

When the gray Ford came in sight of the posse, it was about half a mile away and coming fast. Ivy Methvin was standing beside his truck, and the posse was in position in the brush on the east side of the road. First in line, with a pair of field glasses, was Bob Alcorn. Since he knew Clyde by sight, his job was to make a positive identification. With all of that firepower, they didn't want to open up on some innocent person. Next was Alcorn's partner, Ted Hinton. Third was Bienville Parish Deputy Prentis Oakley, and then his boss, Sheriff Henderson Jordan. Manny Gault was fifth, and, anchoring the line, was Lee Simmons' manhunter, Frank Hamer. The most experienced of the group, Hamer was armed with a Colt Monitor machine rifle. It was Colt's effort to market a civilian version of Clyde's favorite, the Browning automatic rifle, to police departments, and it fired the same 30-06 ammunition used by the BAR. As long as Hamer was alive, Clyde Barrow would not get past him.[20]

As Clyde started up the hill, he saw Ivy Methvin and the familiar log truck blocking his lane. He had provided the money for the truck himself and ridden around on it several times in the last few weeks as he pretended to be a logger. He rolled to a stop, looked out Bonnie's window, and spoke to Henry's father. After all the waiting, the posse's plan was suddenly unfolding in front of them. The famous outlaw couple was in perfect position. All the posse had to do was not miss.

At this point, a log truck came into view in Clyde's rearview mirror. Since Methvin's truck and Clyde's Ford blocked the whole road, Clyde shifted into first to move out of the way, and, on the right side of the car, Ivy Methvin grabbed his stomach and ran toward the woods.[21] For once, Clyde Barrow's famous sixth sense for smelling trouble deserted him. For the last several years, he had sown the wind. Now the whirlwind had finally arrived.

While the gray Ford was rolling up to the disabled log truck, Bob Alcorn had whispered down the line of lawmen that it was certainly Clyde Barrow and Bonnie Parker. Now the famous outlaw couple was sitting there, maybe twenty-five feet away. Early in the stakeout, there had been some discussion about whether to shout, "Hands up," or "This is the police. You're under arrest," or something similar. The Louisiana lawmen thought they should try it, but the Texans disagreed. "Ain't no way that boy's going to give up," one of them said, and they weren't inclined to give Clyde a chance to get away again.[22] Having decided that question, however, it's unclear who was to give the command to fire, now that the time had come. As it turned out, the command was unnecessary.

The thirty-six hours spent waiting in the woods had taken their toll on everybody, and now, with the prospect of a deadly gunfight starting any second, the pressure on the lawmen became almost unbearable. In such a situation, anyone can snap, and this time it was Prentis Oakley. He later told friends that there was no challenge to Clyde, or even any command to fire. He didn't really know what happened. Oakley simply remembered being crouched down in the brush one second and on his feet firing the next.[23]

When Prentis Oakley learned that he would be involved in trying to ambush Bonnie and Clyde, he went in search of some serious firepower. He had borrowed a Remington Model 8 semi automatic rifle in .35 caliber from his friend Dr. Shehee, a local dentist, and now he emptied the five-round magazine into Clyde's window. Fortunately, when Oakley stood up, all the pressure of the last two days dropped away and his hunter's instinct took over. Since he was still looking to the right, Barrow gave Oakley a perfect profile view, and the first .35 caliber round took Clyde in the left temple, exiting two inches above his right ear, blowing off his hat,

and killing him instantly. Two more bullets hit the left front door post, one hit the windshield frame, and the last one went in the roof just above Clyde's window. None of the posse knew it, but those four bullets, as well as the 130 or so that followed, were really unnecessary.[24] Clyde Barrow was dead with the first shot.

Prentis Oakley's action took the other posse members by surprise. Some of them were far enough away in the brush that they may have even thought it was Clyde who had fired first, but it didn't matter what they thought. Once the shooting started—whoever started it—everyone else joined in. Oakley's first two shots stood out by themselves and were distinctly heard by witnesses, but the last three were swallowed up in the roar as the others opened fire.[25]

Clyde never knew what hit him,[26] but Bonnie wasn't so lucky. She had three or four more conscious seconds to scream when her lover's head exploded next to her and to understand exactly what was going to happen to her before the wave of lead and steel washed through the car.

When Oakley's first shot hit Clyde, his head snapped back and his foot came off the clutch. Since the car was in first gear, it started to move forward, and this movement only added to the confusion. It looked as though Clyde might be trying to get away. It also meant that the car slowly cruised by each of the posse members in turn, giving them all perfect shots—just like a shooting gallery. After it passed Frank Hamer, the last lawman, it ran off into the left-side ditch and stopped with the driver's door against a bank, having rolled about one hundred yards.

As the car came to rest, someone went around to the right side and put a finishing burst in the passenger window. Some of those bullets went high and into the frame just over Bonnie's window, but one hit Bonnie in the right cheek and left a gaping wound on the left side of her face.[27] A few seconds later, Ted Hinton and Bob Alcorn arrived, having almost run into the line of fire trying to catch up with the car.[28] Seeing Clyde's door wedged against an embankment, Hinton pulled the passenger door open and Bonnie fell into his arms, already dead.

Hinton had known Bonnie back when she was a waitress. He was very fond of her, always having a hard time seeing her as an outlaw, and now he had helped kill her. The sight of her lifeless body stayed with him for the rest of his life.[29]

The whole sequence—from first shot to last—had taken just over fifteen seconds. Now that it was over, silence settled over the scene. Having had seventy or eighty supersonic rifle rounds and several shotgun blasts fired in close proximity to their ears, the posse members were all practically deafened and would remain so for several hours. And, as they all approached the car, even the most hardened of them were stunned at the amount of damage they had inflicted. The left side of the car—mainly the driver's door—was riddled. When they looked inside, however, it was obvious that many of the bullets didn't get through. The Ford's door was double walled, and most of the soft lead hunting ammunition remained between the two layers of sheet metal, unless it happened to hit a place where an access panel was cut in the inner wall. Most of the bullets that penetrated the car body came from Hinton or Alcorn's BAR or Frank Hamer's Monitor rifle. On the right side, the difference was even more pronounced. For the seventy-five to one hundred holes in the left side, there were less than twenty exit holes on the right.[30]

More than enough bullets got through, in any case. Although not as mangled as later sensational stories would have you believe, the couple still made a gruesome sight. Clyde had been hit at least twenty times, including two head shots and one that severed his spinal column. Bonnie was hit twenty-six times, including three shots to the head and face.[31] Bonnie was bending forward with her head between her knees, part of a sandwich still on her lap. Clyde had fallen forward with his head through the spokes of the steering wheel. His purple-tinted sunglasses, still hooked over his ears, hung down under his chin, and his two shotguns were still on either side of him, one hit by a bullet.[32]

Along with the two dead outlaws, a great many other things were found in the Ford V-8. As Ted Hinton took pictures with a 16-millimeter movie camera, Frank Hamer and Sheriff Jordan began the inventory. First, of course, was Clyde Barrow's normal complement of weapons. They found three Browning automatic rifles, two-sawed off shotguns, nine Colt automatic pistols (in three different calibers), a Colt .45 double action, 100 BAR twenty-shot magazines, and 3,000 rounds of ammunition.[33] Besides the weapons, there were clothes, blankets, a makeup case, road maps, magazines, fifteen sets of stolen license plates, and a saxophone.[34] No mention was ever made of the suitcase containing the legal papers and the large amount of money that Henry Barrow had seen the last time Clyde visited him. No one knows what happened to it, or if it was even there, but the Barrow family has always suspected that the money made its way into the hands of some of the people involved.

Bonnie and Clyde's lives had ended—just the way Bonnie had predicted they would in her last poem. They certainly "went down together." Their career was over, but their legend was just beginning.

CHAPTER 37
A Macabre Circus

Spectators gathered near the posse's ambush position. Bienville Parish, Louisiana, May 23, 1934.
—Courtesy the Texas Ranger Hall of Fame and Museum, Waco, Texas

The ambush site was out in the country along what seemed to be a deserted road, but not long after the shooting stopped, people began to arrive. Some just happened by. Others lived nearby or had been working in the fields. Within a few minutes, a small crowd had gathered. Cleo Sneed and some friends stopped cutting wood and walked over to see what had happened. They noticed a man helping Ivy Methvin put the wheel back on his truck, and a log truck turning around, but what they saw in the shot-up gray Ford made them wish they had kept sawing timber.[1] Buddy Goldston, who was driving the log truck and had almost driven into the ambush, got a look at the scene before he turned around and drove away. Almost sixty years later, he remembered the sight. "That car was all shot up. Them people was all shot up!" he said.[2]

When the adrenaline rush of the fight wore off, the lawmen set about doing what had to be done. As soon as Sheriff Jordan and Frank Hamer searched the car, Jordan and his deputy, Oakley, left to get the coroner, Dr. J. L. Wade, to satisfy the legal requirements.[3] Hamer and Ted Hinton drove to Gibsland to find a wrecker and to report in. Hinton called Dallas County Sheriff "Smoot" Schmid, and Hamer called Lee Simmons. Each was sure their boss would want to come to Arcadia and share in the publicity bonanza that was about to explode, and they were right.[4] Manny Gault and Bob Alcorn stayed at the scene to secure the car from the crowd, which was steadily growing.

Hinton and Hamer made their calls from a Gibsland filling station, where they were overheard by a local man named Davis. He spread the word, and several carloads of people headed out to see the famous desperadoes. By the time the coroner arrived, cars and people filled the road and the souvenir hunters were in full swing. People picked up spent cartridge cases, stole glass out of the Ford's shattered windows, tramped through the brush, and even tried to dig bullets out of the surrounding trees. Others went for the bodies themselves. Taking pieces of clothing and hanks of Bonnie's hair was bad enough, but at least a couple of folks went even further. One was caught about to slice off one of Clyde's ears, and another was after his "trigger finger."[5]

The tow truck finally arrived and hooked up to the Ford V-8.[6] Everything had been left in the car—including the bodies—but an "Indian blanket" was laid over Clyde.[7] Many of the spectators followed the wrecker as it towed the car toward Arcadia. Eventually, there were almost two hundred vehicles in the procession. Word had gone ahead of them to Gibsland, and even the schoolchildren were watching the road for a glimpse of the famous outlaws. As the wrecker came in sight, somebody yelled, "Here they come," and the whole school emptied into the street. Some say that Sheriff Jordan stopped at the school in order to teach a lesson on the wages of sin, but most witnesses say that the students simply ran out and blocked the road so that the wrecker had no choice but to stop and let them have a look. Several people describe a scene of schoolchildren swarming the car and sticking their heads in the windows, only to come face to face with two bullet-riddled corpses.[8] The situation was becoming more bizarre by the minute.

After leaving Gibsland, the procession turned toward Arcadia, the county seat. There, Dr. Wade would impanel a coroner's jury and give a legal finding of the cause of death. Driving in the procession, Bob Alcorn and Ted Hinton tried unsuccessfully to rid their heads of the constant ringing caused by the gunfire. "I can't hear a damn thing!" Alcorn shouted. Hinton agreed, watching Alcorn's lips move.[9]

When the wrecker reached Arcadia, it stopped in front of Conger's Furniture Store, which faced out on the town square toward the depot. Undertaker "Boots" Bailey's funeral parlor occupied the rear of the building, and that's where Dr. Wade and his jury would preside while Bailey and his helpers began the process of embalming the bodies.

If possible, the crowds were even worse here in

The crowd gathers outside Conger's Furniture on the town square in Arcadia, Louisiana, as they wait for a chance to view the bodies of Bonnie and Clyde. May 23, 1934.

—Courtesy the Bob Fischer/Renay Stanard collection

Death car at Arcadia, Louisiana, left side, showing damage to driver's door. (Below) Right side. May 23, 1934. Note the small number of exit holes in the passenger's door, and the entry holes above the passenger's window. May 23, 1934.

—From the collections of the Texas/Dallas History and Archives Division, Dallas Public Library

Posse members at Arcadia, Louisiana, May 23, 1934. Left to right, standing: Ted Hinton, Prentis Oakley, Manny Gault. Seated: Bob Alcorn, Henderson Jordan, Frank Hamer.
—From the collections of the Texas/Dallas History and Archives Division, Dallas Public Library

town. The attendants had to push through the mass of people to carry Bonnie and Clyde inside. Even after they were on the stretchers, folks were still pulling on Bonnie's wedding ring. Everyone, though, was amazed at their size. Over the past two years, the newspapers had made Bonnie and Clyde seem nine feet tall, but in death they seemed pitifully small. Clyde had once told Ralph Fults that there was so much dying around him because people wouldn't take him seriously, even when he pulled his guns. "They think we're just school kids," he said.[10]

After the bodies were in the building, things outside kept getting crazier and more crowded. Arcadia's population, normally about 2,000[11] increased eight times. By nightfall, the population of Bienville Parish as a whole would triple.[12] In the funeral parlor, several groups struggled in the heat of the Louisiana summer to finish their own jobs. Dr. Wade hurried to finish his report so the jury could arrive at a finding of the cause of death. The physical cause was, of course, a foregone conclusion. They were shot to pieces. It was the legal finding that was important.[13] In the meantime, undertaker Bailey was having troubles of his own. It's not easy to embalm a body with so many holes in it, and pictures would later show stains around Bonnie and Clyde caused not by blood but by leaking embalming fluid. As time went by and the people outside became even more unruly, the same embalming fluid was sometimes sprayed at them as crowd control.[14]

In the late May heat, Dr. Wade and his five queasy jurymen went about their duties in the back-room funeral parlor. When the coroner finally finished his examinations and notes, he dictated two statements, which the five of them signed. In addition, he prepared a statement of identification for Bob Alcorn, the Dallas deputy sheriff who best knew Bonnie and Clyde.

We, the undersigned coroner's Jury after diligent Inquiry and thorough investigation find that Clyde Champion Barrow met his death from gun shot wounds fired by officers.

And then for Bonnie:

We the undersigned coroners Jury after diligent inquiry and thorough investigation find that Bonnie Parker came to her death from gun shot wounds fired from rifles Pistols and shot guns in the hands of officers.

Both statements were signed by the jury:

M. W. Barber
G. C. Taylor
F. W. Pentecost
B. C. Theus
J. R. Goff
[signatures]

Alcorn's statement was as follows:

R. F. Alcorn—Dallis Tex—
Being duly sworn testifies as follows: deposes and says he knows the 2 parties exami[ned] by him & that one of them is Clyde C. Barrow & the other Bonnie Parker alias also know[n] as Bonnie Thornton You [he] furthe[r] testifies that he has personally know[n] then for six or seven years. That he know[s] of his own knowledge that both were 2 [times] indited on charge of murder Case #5046&7 Criminal District Court Dallis Tex. Nov—28- 1933
R. F. Alcorn [signature]

While those in Louisiana tried to finish their work in the increasingly chaotic atmosphere of Arcadia, the news of the ambush was spreading fast. In Dallas, the phone rang at Buster Parker's house. Bonnie's mother was there visiting, and when she answered it, a reporter asked if she was alone. "No," she said. Could he speak to someone in the house? Worn out by the press, she was beginning to give him a piece of her mind until he said that Bonnie and Clyde had been killed.[15] Instead of giving him a quote he could use before his deadline, Emma Parker fainted. Marie Barrow, married to Joe Francis only three days before, heard the news on the radio at a gas station where she had stopped and immediately drove to the Star Service Station on Eagle Ford Road.[16] Each family then began to make their arrangements.

Neither of the mothers could face the prospect of dealing with the authorities in Louisiana. Henry Barrow was driven to Arcadia by his oldest son, Jack, and when he arrived, he walked into a madhouse. He had to fight his way inside the furniture store, but, in spite of everything, he seemed calm and freely talked to the people there while waiting for the officials to finish their work. Buster Parker, sent to pick up his sister's body, confused the town of Arcadia with Acadia Parish, west of Lafayette, and went to the wrong place.[17]

A local photographer, and later one from Dallas, began taking a series of photographs—everything from the undraped bodies, to more modest, if no less gruesome, shots with all the dignitaries standing in the background. The local man, King Murphy, did a brisk business. He and his wife developed the pictures themselves, washing the prints in their bathtub, and sold them to all comers—$5 for individuals; $50 for the press.[18] Denny Hayes, Dallas photojournalist, took a series of pictures of several Dallas officials with the bodies.[19]

While the embalmers were finishing up and the bodies were prepared for public viewing, newsmen from far and wide converged on the posse members. They did succeed in getting a few posed pictures, but not much information. Frank Hamer, especially, was very circumspect in what he said. Never one to talk much to reporters in the first

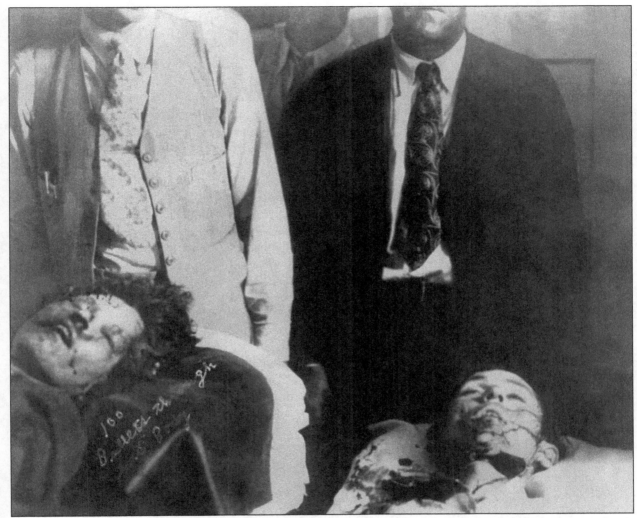

Bonnie and Clyde at the undertaker's office in the rear of Conger's Furniture Store following the ambush. Arcadia, Louisiana, May 23, 1934.
—Courtesy Sandy Jones–The John Dillinger Historical Society

place, he had to be even more careful now. He and Bob Alcorn had been involved in planning the ambush from the first meeting with Sheriff Henderson Jordan and Methvin family representative John Joyner almost three months ago, but he couldn't let that be known. Protecting his sources was a serious matter with Hamer, whether they were criminals or not.

Also, for different reasons, most of the posse members were troubled about what happened out on that road. Alcorn had known Clyde personally, and Ted Hinton was a friendy acquaintance of Bonnie. Prentis Oakley was never able to get over the fact that he fired early, with no warning, or erase from his mind the picture of Clyde's head snapping back as his bullet hit. Henderson Jordan felt that the two should have at least been given the chance to surrender. Even Frank Hamer, the consummate professional manhunter, would later say: "As they drove up that day, and I pulled down on Barrow, knowing that some of my rifle bullets were going to snuff out her life along with his . . . I hated to have to shoot her."[20] Manny Gault never made his feelings known. Also, the posse was not very communicative because all of them were still partially deaf several hours after the shooting.

Once the undertaker finished the embalming, he put the two desperadoes on public display, and the crowd filed by in a continuous line for almost six hours.[21] Through it all, Clyde's father, who had been a perfect gentleman throughout the insanity at Arcadia, was listening. He heard the name "Methvin" mentioned often enough to confirm his own suspicions.[22] Clyde had often told his family that he expected to be betrayed by a friend.

Late in the afternoon, Henry Barrow was allowed to take his son home—his second child killed by police bullets in ten months. Whatever remained of Clyde's possessions were sent home with him. This mainly consisted of the clothes he was wearing, a gold watch, and $505.32 in cash, just barely enough to cover his funeral. A diamond stick pin had disappeared.[23] It would be almost 10:00 P.M. before Buster Parker arrived for his sister, after a 300-mile detour into south Louisiana, but by the morning of May 24, 1934, America's most famous outlaw couple was back home in Dallas, where the public frenzy continued.[24]

Clyde was taken to Sparkman–Holtz–Brand Funeral Home at 2110 Ross Avenue, and the crowds arrived early. Eventually, almost 10,000 people would pass by. When the funeral home wouldn't respond to their shouts, they pounded on the doors. When everything else had failed, they began pulling up shrubbery. Henry Barrow finally consented to allow the public to view Clyde's body—as much for the beleaguered funeral home whose property was being destroyed as anything else.[25]

When the people finally began filing in, they saw Clyde laid out in a fairly plain casket and dressed in a nice gray suit, with his father and his brother L. C. standing nearby. Maybe it was because of the long wait, but, instead of some respect for the recently departed, this crowd eventually became downright rude. Finally, when a drunk staggered by and said, "I'm glad he's dead," Henry Barrow snapped. Whatever his son had done, he wasn't going to put up with this any longer. The nice, quiet, sixty-year-old gentleman physically cleared the room, and Clyde's younger brother L. C. blocked the door. That was the end of the public viewing.[26]

The public expectation that there might be a joint funeral and the couple buried together—side by side, as Bonnie's last poem had said—was quickly dispelled by both families. Clyde's funeral would

Crowd gathers at Sparkman–Holtz–Brand funeral home for Clyde Barrow's funeral, May 25, 1934.
—From the collections of the Texas/Dallas History and Archives Division, Dallas Public Library

Cumie Barrow at Clyde's grave, May 25, 1934.
—Courtesy Marie Barrow Scoma and author Phillip W. Steele

be the next day, the 25th, and he would be buried beside his brother Buck at Western Heights Cemetery. At 5:00, after a private service, the family left the funeral home for the burial. Western Heights was small, and the crowd was large, so the graveside service was a nightmare. People stole everything from flowers to dirt clods for souvenirs. A light plane flew over and dropped more flowers, and these were fought over as well. The crowd pressed in so much that some of the family couldn't get near the seating area, while others were almost pushed into the open grave. The service was mercifully short, and soon everyone was moving away.[27] Clyde's total funeral expenses were $500.[28]

One face, lost in the crowd, was that of a jug-eared man who seemed to have a stomachache. Joe Palmer had been in the lobby of the Lee Huckins Hotel in Oklahoma City when he heard the announcement that Bonnie and Clyde had been killed. With Clyde dead and Raymond Hamilton in jail, Joe was now the most wanted man in the Southwest, but he rode the bus to Dallas to pay his respects to his friend.[29]

While Clyde returned to Dallas and was buried in the family plot next to his brother Buck, Bonnie's situation was a little more complicated. Emma Parker had kept a small insurance policy on

all her children so she could afford to give her daughter the kind of attention Emma felt she deserved—hair done, nails polished, and a new silk negligee—but she wasn't able to give Bonnie her last wish. Emma wanted to bring Bonnie home, as Bonnie had requested at their last meeting, but when the police simply asked her to look out her front door at the crowds, Emma understood that it would be impossible.[30] Instead, the public was allowed to view Bonnie at McKamy-Campbell Funeral Home at 1921 Forrest Avenue. Twenty thousand people filed past. Unlike the Barrow family's experience, this crowd was quiet and respectful, and no incidents were reported.[31]

Emma Parker had immediately dismissed the notion that Bonnie would be buried next to Clyde. "Clyde had her for two years, and look what it did to her," Emma said.[32] Bonnie was to be buried in Fishtrap Cemetery, near her grandparents' home in west Dallas, but the funeral was postponed because of Bonnie's sister.

Whether for ulterior motives, as some suggest, or just from confusion, William Schieffer, the farmer who had identified Clyde and Bonnie as the ones who killed the two motorcycle policemen on Easter Sunday, had reconsidered and now said that Floyd Hamilton and Billie Jean Mace were the culprits. Floyd Hamilton, along with his brother Raymond, was already in jail on other charges, but, four days before Bonnie was killed, the Tarrant County sheriff had arrested Bonnie's sister on a charge of murder.

Both the Barrows and the Parkers knew that Billie Jean and Floyd were innocent. They were pushing the police to examine the guns found in Clyde's car and at the same time trying to delay Bonnie's service until Billie was free to attend. On Saturday morning, the 26th, preliminary ballistics tests of some of Clyde's guns indicated that they were used at Grapevine, and Billie was granted a leave to attend Bonnie's funeral.[33]

At 2:00 that afternoon, a short service was held at the funeral home. Six pallbearers, including L. C. Barrow, carried Bonnie's casket down to the hearse, and they left for the cemetery. At Fishtrap, there was a short ceremony, and among those seated at the graveside were Henry and Cumie Barrow. Bonnie Parker Thornton, twenty-three, beloved daughter and sister, popular schoolgirl and waitress, amateur poet, and the most infamous female outlaw since Belle Starr, was laid to rest beside her two little nephews, Billie's babies, who had died six months before. True to a verse in her last poem, among the carloads of flowers, one of the largest wreaths was from the newsboys of Dallas.[34] For the last two years, Bonnie and Clyde had provided these young street businessmen with a lot of headlines. The famous outlaws' deaths had sold a half-million papers in Dallas alone.[35]

In a little over two years, Clyde Barrow and Bonnie Parker had gone from an unknown twenty-three-year-old hardened, fatalistic, unemployed ex-convict and a tiny twenty-one-year-old lonely, bored, part-time waitress and abandoned housewife to the most famous and feared outlaw couple in the country. The common people of the Southwest might not know who their senator or representative was, but they knew about Bonnie and Clyde. Lawmen cursed them because they couldn't catch them, and mothers told their disobedient children, "The Barrow gang will get you if you don't watch out." Like all of us, they were people full of contradictions. They were capable of deep love for each other and their families, and extreme and seemingly senseless violence to others—sometimes all in the same day.

There is always a price for the way people

Family members and pallbearers leaving Bonnie Parker's funeral, May 26, 1934.
—From the collections of the Texas/Dallas History and Archives Division, Dallas Public Library

decide to live, and that price is often paid by the innocent as well as the guilty. The price for Bonnie and Clyde's freedom was paid by their friends and partners who died or were shot or imprisoned. It was paid by their victims who tried to arrest them, or who simply stood between them and a few dollars or their next Ford V-8. It was paid by those victims' families, who had to live on in hard times without a husband or father. It was paid by their own families, who could only watch helplessly as their children became hunted animals and, finally, bullet-riddled corpses, and as their family name became synonymous with lawlessness. This price is still being paid three generations later.[36]

Finally, the price was paid by Bonnie and Clyde themselves. Despite the cynical claims and lurid stories in the press, Bonnie and Clyde loved each other—what they endured for each other's sake proves it—but they also destroyed each other. How must it feel, at age twenty-three or twenty-five, to know beyond a shadow of a doubt that by your own actions you are doomed, and nobody can help you?

Bonnie Parker and Clyde Barrow lived their lives on their own terms, while trying to convince themselves that accepting their fate somehow made it more noble, but the price was terribly, tragically high.

(Above) Bonnie Parker's headstone at Fishtrap Cemetery, 1934. In 1945, Bonnie's remains, along with this headstone, were moved to Crown Hill Cemetery in Dallas.
—Courtesy Bob Fischer/Renay Stanard collection

(Left) The mothers. Cumie Barrow, on the left, and Emma Parker, on the right, during a break in the "Crime Does Not Pay" show, October 1934.
—Courtesy Marie Barrow Scoma and author Phillip W. Steele

CHAPTER 38
The Harboring Trial

Bonnie and Clyde were dead. Their two-year run through the back roads and newspaper headlines of the Southwest was over. After their ambush in Louisiana, law enforcement agencies in several states were able to close the books on many open cases, but the fallout wasn't quite over. The federal authorities had one more card to play.

Unlike the cases of John Dillinger, Lester "Baby Faced Nelson" Gillis, Charles "Pretty Boy" Floyd, Alvin Karpis, and others, federal agencies played a relatively minor role in the search for Clyde Barrow and Bonnie Parker. A federal agent, Lester Kendale, was present at the first meeting in Bienville Parish that set the ambush in motion, but the operation itself was carried out by Louisiana and Texas officers. The fact remained, however, that Bonnie and Clyde were wanted for a federal crime, interstate transportation of a stolen car. This allowed the United States District Court for the Northern District of Texas to step in after the state courts were finished.

A few of Bonnie and Clyde's associates had been arrested and charged with var-ious things, but everyone knew that many other people had helped them along the way. On February 22, 1935, the United States District Court in Dallas began the trial of twenty people charged with harboring Bonnie and Clyde as federal fugitives. The trial lasted four days[1] and included as defendants hardened criminals already facing life in prison, as well as teenagers, housewives, and mothers who had never spent a day in a cell. To no one's surprise, all twenty were found guilty.

What follows are the details of that trial:[2]

Cumie T. Barrow being carried into the courthouse for the harboring trial. Dallas, February 22, 1934.
—From the collections of the Texas/Dallas History and Archives Division, Dallas Public Library

Male defendants at harboring trial. Dallas, February 22, 1934.
—From the collections of the Texas/Dallas History and Archives Division, Dallas Public Library

Female defendants at harboring trial. Dallas, February 22, 1934.
—From the collections of the Texas/Dallas History and Archives Division, Dallas Public Library

John Basden was an ex-con, truck driver, and friend of Floyd Hamilton's. Needing money, he convinced Floyd to take him along when Floyd and his brother, Raymond Hamilton, robbed a bank in Grand Prairie, Texas. He also admitted going along with Floyd Hamilton and others to meet Bonnie and Clyde on two occasions. Basden was found guilty and given one year and a day in a federal penitentiary.

Mrs. Cumie T. Barrow, Clyde's mother, was shown, by the testimony of several other witnesses, to have visited her son and Bonnie Parker on many occasions and given them aid. Even though she had broken the law, most of the people felt sympathy for the sixty-one-year-old woman who had lost two sons to lawmen's guns. The judge asked her what she thought a fair sentence would be. Maybe sixty days in jail? "Well, I'm needed at home. Won't thirty days be enough?" Cumie answered. "Thirty days," the judge said.

L. C. Barrow was next. Four years younger than Clyde, L. C. had been involved from the first in helping Clyde and Bonnie. He met with them many times, did errands, provided support and intelligence, and even traveled with them a few times. He was one of the few people Clyde trusted completely. Fortunately for him, he was never with them when they encountered the law. Now twenty-one years old, L. C. was well known to Dallas police as a criminal in his own right and was accused of robbery and car theft as well as harboring. He was given one year and one day in a federal penitentiary.

Audrey Barrow was the sixteen-year-old wife of L. C. Barrow. She had no record but admitted being with L. C. once when he met with Clyde. She was given fifteen days in jail.

Blanche Caldwell Barrow, twenty-four, was Clyde's sister-in-law, the wife of his brother Buck. She and Buck were with Bonnie and Clyde for almost four months in 1933, during which time three lawmen were killed. Blanche was captured and tried by the state of Missouri as an accessory in the gunfight at Platte City. She was currently serving ten years in that state. On the federal charge, Blanche was given one year and a day.

Hilton Bybee was brought to the courtroom from the state prison at Huntsville, Texas. He was one of the prisoners involved in the Eastham Prison Farm escape in January 1934. He stayed with Bonnie and Clyde for a few days and helped them rob one bank. He was sentenced to ninety days in jail, an essentially meaningless gesture since he was already serving a life term for murder in a case unrelated to the Barrows.

Joe Chambliss was the father of Mary O'Dare, the wife of Gene O'Dare, Raymond Hamilton's partner in a bank robbery. After her husband was put in jail, Mary became Raymond's girlfriend and traveled with Bonnie and Clyde for a few weeks in early 1934. Joe, her father, was evidently involved in some of the meetings, because he was given sixty days in jail.

Alice Hamilton Davis was the mother of Raymond and Floyd Hamilton. She was involved in the harboring trial mainly because her two sons were Clyde Barrow's friends and sometime partners. She was given thirty days in jail.

Steve Davis was Alice's husband and the Hamilton boys' stepfather. Steve was known to have been involved in some petty theft, but his involvement with Bonnie and Clyde was minor. Davis received ninety days in jail.

Joe Bill Francis was twenty years old and recently married to Clyde's youngest sister, Marie. He ran around with Clyde's brother L. C. and often drove the car when the Barrow family went out in the country to see Bonnie and Clyde. Joe Bill was driving on the evening in November 1933 when his car, with several family members inside, was almost caught in the crossfire of an ambush set by the Dallas County sheriff. Francis was given sixty days in jail.

Marie Barrow Francis, Joe Bill's wife and Clyde's sister, was just sixteen years old, but she had gone to most of the family meetings and generally did whatever she could for her brother Clyde. One of the things she was perfectly suited for was shopping for Bonnie. Since they had to remain in hiding, Clyde would give the family money, and his mother and Marie would buy clothes for Bonnie. At the time, Marie had been fifteen years old and wore the same size as Bonnie in everything except shoes.[3] Because of her youth, Marie was sentenced to one hour in the custody of the United States marshal.

Floyd Hamilton was a vital contact for Clyde Barrow. Floyd's younger brother Raymond was Clyde's partner during three different periods of Barrow's career. Floyd met with them many times, providing clothes, cars, and communication to their families. Floyd also hid stolen guns for the gang. Floyd would eventually have a criminal career longer than either his brother or Clyde. For his help to the Barrow gang, Floyd was given two years in the federal penitentiary at Leavenworth, Kansas.

Mildred Hamilton, Floyd's wife, had been with him on several occasions when they saw Bonnie and Clyde, but, like Marie Barrow, she was given only one hour in the custody of the United States marshal.

William Daniel Jones had traveled with Bonnie and Clyde for about nine months. He had been with them through some of their most violent and dangerous times. Jones left them about the first of September 1933 and was picked up in Houston in the middle of November. Since then, he had been cooperating with authorities. He had given his version of his time with the outlaw couple, which minimized his role and cast him as a virtual prisoner. In fact, he had been a partner in everything they did. He also killed one man, possibly two, during that time. Jones was given two years in addition to the fifteen years he was already serving as an accessory in the killing of Malcolm Davis.

Billie Jean Parker Mace was Bonnie Parker's sister. Three years younger than Bonnie, she left her two small children and stayed with her sister for seven days when Bonnie was badly burned in a car wreck in June 1933. Billie also attended several family meetings with the rest of the Parkers and Barrows. Billie had spent several days in jail in Fort Worth under suspicion of involvement in the Grapevine killings but was released after Bonnie and Clyde were killed. For her part in nursing her sister, however, she received one year and a day in the Federal Prison for Women at Alderson, West Virginia.

Henry Methvin traveled with Bonnie and Clyde from the time he escaped, with their help, from Eastham Prison Farm, until their deaths. He had been brought from Oklahoma, where he was being held for the murder of Cal Campbell, constable of Commerce, Oklahoma. Later research would show that Henry was probably involved in at least five bank robberies and four killings with Bonnie and Clyde, but his conviction on the harboring charge only brought him fifteen months in the penitentiary. This, of course, was trivial compared to the death sentence he faced in Oklahoma.

James Mullins, alias Jimmy LaMont, was a forty-nine-year-old career criminal, informer, and drug addict who had helped set up the Eastham Prison break. He spent time with Bonnie and Clyde mainly because he was so untrustworthy that Clyde wouldn't let him out of his sight. Clyde was sure that Mullins would turn them in if he got the chance. Mullins cooperated with authorities and was given four months in jail.

Mary O'Dare traveled with Raymond Hamilton, Bonnie and Clyde, and the rest of the Barrow gang for about three weeks in February and early March 1934. She was intensely disliked and distrusted by Bonnie and Clyde. Mary and Raymond left the group about March 6, 1934. Mary eventually gave information to the police that helped capture Raymond. She was sentenced to one year and a day in the federal penitentiary.

Emma Krause Parker was Bonnie's mother. She was, of course, involved in all the family meetings during the two years her daughter was with Clyde Barrow. Many times, she pleaded with her daughter to leave Clyde and turn herself in, without success. Mrs. Parker, like Clyde's mother, received thirty days in jail

S. J. "Baldy" Whatley was an acquaintance of Floyd Hamilton and L. C. Barrow. He went along several times to meet with Bonnie and Clyde and may have gone with Clyde once on an unsuccessful robbery. Three years later, after a falling-out with L. C. Barrow, Whatley would fire into the Barrow house and wound L. C.'s mother, Cumie. For his part in harboring Bonnie and Clyde, Whatley received one year and a day.

Epilogue

THE BARROWS

Henry Barrow

In spite of the fact that he met with both of his infamous sons several times while they were wanted men, Henry Barrow was never charged with any offense connected with their activities. Other than possibly selling a little whiskey out the back door of his filling station during Prohibition, Henry was never suspected of a crime. He and Cumie continued to operate the Star Service Station for a few years after Bonnie and Clyde were killed, but a series of mishaps forced them to give it up in the late thirties. The station itself was firebombed at least once, and there was a shooting incident in which Clyde's mother was wounded by mistake. After his wife died, in the early forties, Henry Barrow continued to live in the Dallas area near his family.

Henry Barrow died in Dallas on June 19, 1957, at age eighty-three.[1]

Cumie T. Barrow

There was never any doubt that Cumie met with and helped Bonnie and Clyde as well as other members of the gang during the time they were on the run. Clyde and Buck were her sons, after all. Blanche was also family, and Bonnie might as well have been. While Cumie certainly didn't approve of the outlaws' actions, there was never any thought of just abandoning them to their fate. Like her husband, nobody really considered Cumie a criminal. She served the thirty-day sentence imposed at the harboring trial, went home, and never had any more trouble with the law. More trouble, however, from another direction, was still to come.

On the night of September 4, 1938, Cumie's two youngest children, L. C. and Marie, were involved in what the newspapers described as a "brass knuckles tavern fight" with S. J. "Baldy" Whatley, a small-time hood and acquaintance of Floyd Hamilton, Billie Jean Parker (Bonnie's sister), and others. Later that night, Whatley drove by the Star Service Station and saw several people getting out of a car. He mistook one of them—Joe Bill Francis, Marie's husband—for L. C. Barrow and fired a shotgun several times in their direction. Marie ran into the house, got a gun, and returned fire, but her mother was hit in the side of the face. Cumie recovered but lost an eye. Not long afterward, she and Henry moved out of the station.

Cumie T. Barrow died in Dallas on August 14, 1942. She was sixty-seven years old. At the time of her death, two of her seven children had been killed by police and three of the remaining five were serving time in various prisons.[2]

Elvin Wilson "Jack" Barrow

Clyde Barrow's oldest brother was the first of the Barrow children to leave the farm for the city. By the time Bonnie and Clyde became famous, Jack and his wife had four daughters and were living a normal life in Dallas. While Clyde's younger brother L. C. was active in helping the fugitives, it seems that Jack was not directly involved. He accompanied his father to Arcadia to claim Clyde's body after the ambush, but, like Henry Barrow, Jack was never charged with any crime connected with Bonnie and Clyde. Jack's only serious encounter with the law came on October 14, 1939, when he was attacked in a Dallas nightspot. In the ensuing struggle, a man named Otis Jenkins was killed.

Elvin Wilson "Jack" Barrow died of natural causes in Dallas on April 26,1947. He was fifty-two years old.[3]

Artie Adell and Nellie May Barrow

Clyde's two oldest sisters were the only Barrow children who never had a serious brush with the law. When they left home and moved to Dallas, the sisters went into the beauty parlor business. Nell was said, by the family and others, to have been involved in many of the family meetings during Bonnie and Clyde's career, but Artie was not. Neither sister was ever charged with anything connected with their two brothers' criminal activities.

By the time Clyde went to prison in 1930, Artie was already living in Denison, Texas, but Nell had stayed in the Dallas area. After Bonnie and Clyde were killed, Nell worked with author Jan Fortune and Emma Parker on the book *Fugitives.*

Artie Adell Barrow Winkler Keys died on March 3, 1981, twenty-seven days short of her eighty-second birthday. Nellie May Barrow Francis died on November 16, 1968, at age sixty-three.[4]

L. C. Barrow

Clyde and Buck Barrow's younger brother was thought by many in the law enforcement community to be certain to follow in their bloody footsteps. L. C. was nineteen years old when Bonnie and Clyde began their activities, the same age as one of their partners, Raymond Hamilton. He was involved many times in helping Bonnie and Clyde, and he would often drive the rest of the family out to the meeting sites. He also rode with Bonnie and Clyde on several occasions but was never involved in any of their robberies or shootings. L. C. was one of the very few people whom Clyde trusted to the end. L. C. freely admitted all of this, at least to family and friends. What he and the family deny to this day is his involvement in the October 27, 1934, robbery of a drug store in the Dallas area, and it's quite possible that his relationship to his famous brother had more to do with his conviction than the evidence available to the court. In any case, he received a five-year sentence, and a few months later the harboring trial added a federal sentence of one year and one day. L. C. was released in late 1938 but at the time of his mother's death in 1942 was back serving time for a parole violation.

Twenty-nine years old when his mother died, L. C. Barrow seemed headed for the life of a habitual criminal, but, in fact, he began to turn his life around. He lived quietly in the Dallas area and worked as a truck driver until he was forced to retire for health reasons. When L. C. died on September 3, 1979, at age sixty-six, he was survived by his wife, one son, three daughters, and fifteen grandchildren. His last boss had this to say about him: "I guess we'll never see a better, more loyal employee."

L. C. never talked much about his experiences with his brother Clyde, especially around the younger generation. To him, it was a tragic story, and the memory of it would often bring tears to his eyes.[5]

Lillian Marie Barrow

The Barrow family's youngest child, Marie experienced the two years of Bonnie and Clyde's exploits as a teenager. Marie was involved in most of the family meetings and remained a staunch defender of her big brother for the rest of her life. In May 1934, Marie, not quite sixteen years old, married Joe Francis, just a few days before Bonnie and Clyde were killed. At the harboring trial, Marie was sentenced to one hour in the custody of the federal marshal.

In the years following Bonnie and Clyde's death, Marie, like her brother L. C., had several run-ins with the law. At the time of her mother's

death, Marie was at the women's prison at Alderson, West Virginia, for probation violations. In the years following her mother's death, however, Marie, again like her brother L. C., avoided trouble and lived a quiet life in the Dallas area. Lillian Marie Barrow Scoma died in Mesquite, Texas, on February 3, 1999.

In the later years of her life, Marie Barrow began to discuss her experiences with researchers and friends. In addition to providing information for other authors, she collaborated with Phillip W. Steele on a book of her own, and her conversations with Jonathan Davis of Dallas form an important part of this book as well.[6]

Blanche Caldwell Barrow

In the summer of 1929, Blanche Caldwell, an eighteen-year-old farmer's daughter from Oklahoma, met a twenty-six-year-old twice-divorced petty thief and occasional poultry rustler named Marvin Ivan "Buck" Barrow. As unlikely a couple as they were, it seems that it was love at first sight. Blanche stayed with Buck through thick and thin. She married him when he was an escaped convict, waited for him when he went back to finish his sentence, and refused to leave him throughout the disastrous four months with Clyde and Bonnie in 1933 that led to Buck's death. Blanche remained loyal, refused to cooperate with authorities, and lost the sight in one eye from her injuries. When Bonnie and Clyde were killed, Blanche was serving a ten-year sentence in the Missouri State Prison, and the harboring trial added one year and a day.

In the Missouri prison, Blanche

Blanche Barrow with her father, Matthew Fountian Caldwell. Probably taken soon after Blanche's release from prison at the end of March 1939. If so, Blanche would have been twenty-nine years old, and her father sixty-nine.

—Courtesy Marie Barrow Scoma and author Phillip W. Steele

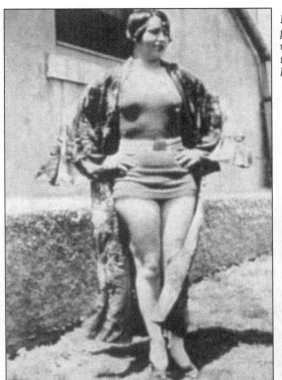

Blanche Barrow in robe and bathing suit. Taken sometime during her time in prison and mailed in a letter to her mother. On the reverse is written, "To mother with love from Blanche. See how much I have gained. I borried [sic] the bathing suit to have the picture taken, but the robe is mine. No, we don't have any bathing pool."

—Courtesy the Bob Fischer/Renay Stanard collection

Blanche Barrow. Taken on the grounds of the Missouri State Prison sometime during the five and a half years she served there, from September 1933 to March 1939.

—Courtesy the Bob Fischer/Renay Stanard collection

Blanche Barrow. All dressed up and sitting in a small tree. Date unknown.

—Courtesy the Bob Fischer/Renay Stanard collection

became friends with Sheriff Holt Coffee, who was in charge of the Platte City ambush where Buck was fatally wounded, and wrote a volume of memoirs that has only recently come to light. Blanche caused no trouble in prison, and on March 25, 1939, her sentence was commuted to time served.[7] She returned to Texas, remarried, and lived quietly in the Dallas area, where she remained in contact with the Barrow family, who always thought very highly of her. Blanche Caldwell Barrow Frasure died in Dallas, Texas, on Christmas Eve, 1988, at age seventy-seven.[8]

THE PARKERS

Emma Krause Parker

Emma Parker never gave up hope for her bright, willful, doomed middle child, even though Bonnie repeatedly told her that she would go down with Clyde when the time came. Emma constantly begged Bonnie to give herself up, but it wasn't to be. After Bonnie was killed, Emma gave her the best funeral she could afford—there would be no "side by side" burial. Shortly after Bonnie's death, Emma Parker collaborated with Nell Barrow and a writer named Jan Fortune to produce the first (and much maligned) account of Bonnie and Clyde's lives. Emma also toured for a short time, along with Henry, Cumie, and Marie Barrow and John Dillinger Sr., in a show called *Crime Does Not Pay*. This production was run by Charles Stanley and at one time also included "Pretty Boy" Floyd's wife, Ruby, and young son, Dempsey.

Emma Krause Parker died in Dallas on September 21, 1944. A year later, Bonnie and her two little nephews were moved from Fishtrap to Crown Hill Cemetery in Dallas and reburied in a single grave. Emma is buried next to them (to the right) in an unmarked grave.

Hubert Nicholas "Buster" Parker

"Buster" Parker was the oldest of Emma Parker's

children, two years older than Bonnie. It was at Buster's house that Bonnie met Clyde in January 1930.

After bringing his sister's body back from Arcadia, Louisiana, for her funeral in Dallas, Buster Parker went on with his life. He was never charged with anything connected with Clyde Barrow or his sister Bonnie. Hubert Nicholas Parker died in Irving, Texas, on March 10, 1964. He was fifty-six years old.

Billie Jean Parker Mace

The baby of the Parker children, Billie Jean Parker was married by the time she was sixteen, and, like her sister's, Billie Jean's choice in men was unfortunate. By the time Bonnie met Clyde, Billie

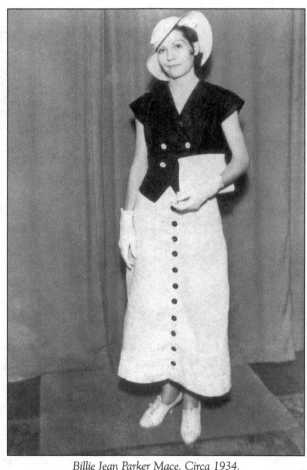

Billie Jean Parker Mace. Circa 1934.
—From the collections of the Texas/Dallas History and Archives Division, Dallas Public Library

Jean was married to Fred Mace and had a baby. They were all living in Emma Parker's house at 2430 Douglas. Two years later, Billie had two children and a husband who was in trouble with the law. Just over two weeks after Bonnie was arrested at Kaufman, Texas, in April 1932, Fred Mace was wounded while resisting arrest.[9] A year later, Billie would spend a harrowing week in Arkansas and Oklahoma with the gang. During that time, she nursed her sister after the car wreck at Wellington, and Buck Barrow killed a town marshal. In October 1933, both of Billie's children died within days of each other. In May 1934, Billie Jean was arrested for a murder that Clyde and Henry Methvin had committed. She was in the Fort Worth jail when her sister died. After Bonnie and Clyde were killed, the murder charge against Billie was dropped, but the harboring trial gave her a year and a day in prison.

After her release, Billie returned to Dallas. She later took in and raised her niece and became good friends with Blanche Barrow. Some thirty years after all their notoriety, Billie Jean and Blanche, both in their fifties, were standing in line at a local Green Stamps store when another woman, who had to leave for a moment, asked them to watch her purse. As the lady walked away, leaving her valuables in their care, Clyde Barrow's sister-in-law turned to Bonnie Parker's sister and said, "I wonder what that woman would think if she knew who we were?"

Billie Jean Parker Mace died on May 21, 1993.

THE GANG

Ralph Fults

After meeting Clyde Barrow in prison, Ralph Fults worked with him very briefly after they were both released. Ralph was arrested, along with Bonnie Parker, at Kemp, Texas, on April 19, 1932, and sent back to prison, where he remained while Bonnie and Clyde became famous. On January 10,

1935, Ralph was released from prison, but he was soon contacted by escaped convict Raymond Hamilton, whom he reluctantly joined in a series of holdups and shootouts as far east as Mississippi. On April 5, 1935, Ray Hamilton was captured, and twelve days later, Ralph was captured as well. Raymond went to the electric chair, and Ralph went back to prison in Texas. Later he was transferred to Mississippi for a bank robbery charge. In January 1944, after being granted a conditional pardon, Fults tried to enlist in the armed forces. The doctor took one look at the scars from Ralph's five gunshot wounds and one knifing and exempted him from service. He said that Fults looked like he had already been to war.

After the service turned him down, Ralph went to work in the shipyards at Pascagoula, Mississippi. There he met a young lady named Ruth, and they were married. Sometime later, he joined the Baptist Church and gave many talks to young people about his experiences and about the futility of a life of crime. After he retired, he devoted much of his time to the Buckner Home for Boys in Mesquite, Texas, where his boxing team won two state Golden Gloves titles. In the early eighties, Ralph began work with author John Neal Phillips on a book about his life. In 1992, Ralph was diagnosed with cancer. "The way I see it," he said, "I've lived sixty-odd years longer than I should have. I was given a second chance, and I've had a really great life." Ralph Fults passed away in 1993, one of the few associates of Bonnie and Clyde to die of old age.[10]

Raymond Elzie Hamilton

In April 1934, a month and a half after he and his girlfriend Mary O'Dare left the gang, Raymond Hamilton was captured. He heard about the deaths of Bonnie and Clyde while in jail awaiting execution. On July 22, 1934, Ray Hamilton was one of three convicts who succeeded in escaping from the death house at the Texas State Prison at Huntsville. Four others were either killed, wounded, or captured on the prison grounds.[11] Hamilton managed to remain at large, working with Joe

Palmer, Ralph Fults, and his brother Floyd, until the following April, when he was captured by Dallas Sheriff Deputy Bill Decker in Fort Worth. As he already under a death sentence, the law wasted little time. On May 10, 1935, Raymond Hamilton died in the electric chair at Huntsville— eleven days short of his twenty-second birthday.

Floyd Garland Hamilton

The older brother of Raymond Hamilton, Floyd Hamilton served as a support and contact person during Bonnie and Clyde's career, carrying messages and providing help with cars, guns, clothes, and whatever else was needed. Floyd was one of a small group of family and friends whose help allowed Bonnie and Clyde to stay alive as long as they did.

At the time of Bonnie and Clyde's death, Floyd was in jail because of a bank robbery he had committed with his brother Raymond and another man. At the harboring trial, Floyd Hamilton was given two years at the federal prison at Leavenworth. In 1938 Floyd teamed up with a fellow named Ted Walters and spent the summer robbing banks before being captured in August. He would pass the next twenty years in prison.

Floyd Hamilton's first stop was back at Leavenworth, but in 1940 he was transferred to Alcatraz. On "the Rock," Hamilton lived through two attempted escapes, seemingly endless days in "the hole," a full-scale riot in which a number of armed inmates (Floyd was not among them) took over part of the prison, and several years as Robert "the Bird Man" Stroud's next-door neighbor in D block, the isolation area. Floyd Hamilton was finally released on parole in 1958.

Back out in the world, Floyd, who had begun reading the Bible in prison, began speaking at various organizations about his experiences and worked to establish a halfway house for ex-convicts. He also remarried his wife, who had divorced him years before. In 1963 his sentence was commuted to time served, releasing him from parole. By 1967, he had received both a federal and Texas state pardon and had all his civil rights restored. Floyd Hamilton died in Dallas on July 24, 1984.[12]

Hollis Hale and Frank Hardy

Frank Hardy and Hollis Hale traveled with Bonnie and Clyde for about a month in late 1932. After participating with Clyde Barrow in the robbery of the Farmers and Miners Bank of Oronogo, Missouri, on November 30, 1932, they both left the outlaw couple and went back to Texas. Hollis Hale had no more contact with the Barrow gang, but Frank Hardy was not so fortunate. Less that a month after Hardy left the outlaws, Barrow and W. D. Jones killed Doyle Johnson at Temple, Texas. Unfortunately, Frank Hardy was identified as one of the shooters and charged with murder. His first trial resulted in a hung jury, and he was awaiting a second hearing when W. D. Jones was captured in November 1933. Jones' statement to police was the first time anybody suspected Clyde Barrow of the Johnson killing.[13] Frank hardy was eventually released.

Ted Rogers

Shortly after the April 30, 1932, robbery and shooting of John N. Bucher in Hillsboro, Texas, of which Clyde Barrow was accused and Ray Hamilton convicted, Ted Rogers was arrested on an unrelated charge and sent to Huntsville along with Ralph Fults. There he met Clyde's brother "Buck" Barrow, who was finishing out his sentence and told them all that he had been the one who shot Mr. Bucher. Clyde was driving the getaway car, just as he had always claimed, and Ray Hamilton was in Michigan with his father. Rogers promised to confess if Hamilton got the death penalty. Hamilton was convicted of killing Bucher but got life in prison, so Rogers kept quiet. Ted Rogers was later stabbed to death in prison by another inmate, named Pete McKenzie.[14]

William Daniel Jones

After riding with Bonnie and Clyde, off and on, for nine months in 1932–33, and participating in five killings, three kidnapings, five gunfights, and two car wrecks, seventeen-year-old W. D. "Deacon" Jones called it quits. Two months later, he was picked up in Houston and gave the Dallas authorities his version of his time with Bonnie and Clyde. Despite doing his best to picture himself as a victim, he received fifteen years as an accessory in the January 1933 killing of Malcolm Davis and another two years at the harboring trial.

When Jones was finally released, in the early fifties, he returned to Houston, married, and settled down. When the 1967 movie about Bonnie and Clyde came out, Jones told a Houston reporter a somewhat more factual story of his experience, which wound up in *Playboy* magazine. After his wife died in the late sixties, Jones developed a drug habit, and in 1971 he spent a few months in an institution that helped him "dry out." [15]

On August 20, 1974, W. D. Jones met a young lady in a bar in Houston who persuaded him to give her a ride home. When they arrived at 10616 Woody Lane, it turned out to be the home of her ex-boyfriend, with whom she began to engage in a heated argument. During the shouting match, the young lady mentioned that the man she was with used to run with Clyde Barrow and claimed he was carrying a gun (not true). When Jones, who hadn't heard that part of the conversation, got out of his car and walked toward the front door, the ex-boyfriend produced a 12 gauge and shot him three times. William Daniel Jones was pronounced dead at the scene. He was fifty-eight years old.

The man who shot him, George Arthur Jones (no relation), was tried and given fifteen years but appealed. The appeal judge eventually ordered a new trial, and George Jones was released on bond pending the proceedings. Unfortunately, before the new trial could start, someone discovered that he had a prior conviction that made him ineligible for bond. Through his attorney, Jones learned that he was to be rearrested and taken to jail. This was in August 1976. Soon after hearing the news, George Arthur Jones took the same shotgun that had killed W. D. Jones, sat down on the tailgate of his truck, put the muzzle under his chin, and ended his own life. [16]

Henry Methvin

After the ambush and death of Bonnie and Clyde, Henry Methvin remained at large, even though he was an escaped convict and his whereabouts were known by Sheriff Jordan. Because of his part in putting Bonnie and Clyde "on the spot," he was not picked up. Sheriff Jordan told him that, as long as he stayed in Bienville Parish, he would not be bothered. Henry took this good advice and lay low. He worked for his brother, Terrell, at a sawmill while he waited for the State of Texas to make good on its promise of a pardon. By August, he was getting impatient and asked the sheriff to see if anything could be done. Lee Simmons thought it was too soon but agreed to write to the governor and recommend that the pardon go forward. All this, however, was shortly overcome by events.

In late August or early September 1934, Henry Methvin fell in love. He needed money to get a marriage license and set up housekeeping, but he was unable to get an advance at work or a loan from his brother. Before long, however, Henry received word from a man in Shreveport who was interested in buying a gun that Henry had carried when he was with Bonnie and Clyde. The condition was that Henry had to bring the gun to Shreveport in person. Henry needed the money, so he went. Unfortunately for Henry, he had been set up.

Shortly after the killing of Constable Cal Campbell in Commerce, Oklahoma, on April 6, 1934, the state of Oklahoma had issued a warrant for the arrest of Clyde Barrow, Bonnie Parker, and John Doe. On September 12, 1934, the Ottawa County attorney received permission to amend the warrant to show Henry Methvin as the true name of John Doe, and the new warrant was issued the same day. Had Henry stayed in Bienville Parish, Oklahoma authorities would have had to go through Sheriff Jordan to serve the warrant. Jordan had promised Henry protection, but Shreveport police had offered no such deal. When Henry arrived in Shreveport, Oklahoma authorities took him into custody for the murder of Cal Campbell. By September 21, 1934, Henry Methvin was sitting in an Oklahoma courtroom. [17]

In Oklahoma, Henry was convicted of murder and given a death sentence. He appealed, and, largely by detailing his involvement in setting up the ambush of Bonnie and Clyde, he was able to get the sentence reduced to life in prison. In spite of the life sentence, Henry Methvin was released on parole at McAlister, Oklahoma, on March 18, 1942.[18] Henry's father died in 1946, under suspicious circumstances, and on April 19, 1948, Henry Methvin was killed as he tried to crawl under a Southern Pacific passenger train at Sulphur, Louisiana. Even though Henry's death happened in broad daylight and there were three eyewitnesses who said they saw him go under the train on his own, many of the family members still suspect foul play in the deaths of both Henry and his father, due to their involvement with Bonnie and Clyde. At Henry's funeral, spectators stole things out of the family's cars for souvenirs.[19] He was thirty-six years old.

Joseph Conger Palmer

Joe Palmer was in Oklahoma City when he heard the news about Bonnie and Clyde's death, and he attended Clyde's funeral in Dallas, in spite of being the most wanted man in the state. On June 15, 1934, Palmer was captured in St. Joseph, Missouri and taken back to Texas. Two weeks later, a Walker County, Texas, jury convicted him of the murder of Major Crowson during the Eastham Farm escape and sentenced Palmer to the electric chair. On July 22, 1934, after having been on death row for three weeks, Joe Palmer, Raymond Hamilton, and Blackie Thompson made it over the wall during the death house escape. On August 8, 1934, Joe Palmer was captured at Paducah, Kentucky, and sent back to Texas.

Joe Palmer died in the electric chair at Huntsville, Texas, just after midnight, May 10, 1935—a few minutes before his sometime partner Raymond Hamilton.[20]

Hilton Bybee

Bybee was not a part of the original group that planned the escape from Eastham Prison Farm in January 1934. He took the place of Ralph Fults, who was unable to be present, and only stayed with the group for a week. He helped rob one bank, in Rembrandt, Iowa, on January 23, 1934, and then left the group and went his own way. A week later,

he was captured at Amarillo, Texas. In early 1935, Bybee was one of the defendants at the harboring trial, where, in a meaningless gesture, the court added ninety days to the life sentence he was already serving for a 1932 murder conviction. In 1937 Bybee escaped from Eastham Prison Farm again but was later shot and killed by officers at Monticello, Arkansas.[21]

James Mullins

James Mullins, alias "Jimmie LaMont," was already a career criminal before he ever met Clyde Barrow. He was given four months at the harboring trial and afterward worked as an informer for officers in the Dallas area. No matter what, though, Mullins always seemed to wind up back behind bars. He once robbed a bank of $68 using a bottle of turpentine he claimed was nitroglycerin. During his getaway, he was captured because he literally ran into a policeman. The last record of James Mullins (this time as James Muller) is of him being sentenced to seven and a half to fifteen years for armed robbery in 1954. He was sixty-nine years old at the time.[22]

THE POSSE

Francis Augustus "Frank" Hamer

At the time of the ambush, Frank Hamer was already a legend in the Texas Rangers and remains so to this day. In February 1934, when Lee Simmons hired him as a "special escape investigator" for the prison system, Hamer's Texas Rangers days were over and he was doing industrial and freelance security work. Never one to say much to the media, he maintained that stance after Bonnie and Clyde's death and never revealed the roles of any of the others who helped set up the ambush.

Most of the things found with Bonnie and Clyde in their "death car" were passed out among the lawmen involved, on Lee Simmons' instructions, and Hamer took several of the guns, for himself. When this became known, Clyde's mother wrote him asking for the return of some of the guns which she said Clyde bought instead of stole, but the guns stayed with Hamer and his family.

Frank Hamer continued to live in Austin, Texas, and take special assignments from time to time, including getting involved in the controversial senate campaign of 1948 in which Lyndon B. Johnson was elected by a slim and very questionable margin.

Despite his portrayal in the 1967 film, Frank Hamer was never kidnapped or humiliated by Bonnie and Clyde or anyone else. The first time he ever laid eyes on the notorious couple was over his gunsight on May 23, 1934.

Francis Augustus Hamer died on July 10, 1955, at the age of seventy-one.[23]

Benjamin Maney "Manny" Gault

Manny Gault was another former Texas Ranger who had resigned in protest at the election of Miriam Ferguson as Texas governor in 1932. In April 1934, he got a call from his friend Frank Hamer. The Texas State Police had just lost two men to Clyde Barrow at Grapevine and wanted their own agent on the manhunt team. Frank Hamer insisted that he choose the man, and his choice was Manny Gault. Hamer had known Gault for a long time and trusted him to be dependable—and silent. After the ambush, Hamer said very little and Gault said even less.

By 1937, there was a new administration in office, and Manny Gault was back in the Rangers as the captain in charge of the Lubbock unit. He was still serving when he died on December 4, 1947.[24]

Robert F. "Bob" Alcorn

When the new Dallas County sheriff, "Smoot" Schmid, took office on January 1, 1933, Bob Alcorn had been a deputy for almost eight years. He had seen his share of hoodlums, especially during several run-ins with two brothers from west Dallas named Barrow. Schmid wisely kept Alcorn on the payroll, and in November, Bob Alcorn was part of Sheriff Schmid's posse that tried to ambush Bonnie and Clyde near Sowers, west of Irving.

After the failed ambush and the adverse publicity that came with it, Bob Alcorn was assigned to track Clyde Barrow full-time. In February 1934, he joined forces with Frank Hamer, and through Sheriff Jordan of Bienville Parish, Louisiana, they made contact with the Methvin family and put the final plan in motion. On Wednesday morning, May 23, 1934, Bob Alcorn was the one who identified Clyde Barrow to the rest of the posse and sealed the outlaws' fate. Alcorn was also the one who signed the official identification in the coroner's report.

In the late thirties, Alcorn left the Sheriff's Department to go into business. Later, he became a court bailiff. Robert F. Alcorn died on the thirtieth anniversary of the ambush of Bonnie and Clyde—May 23, 1964.[25]

Ted Cass Hinton

After the ambush, Ted Hinton remained in law enforcement for a few years and became a friend of the Barrow family. He also learned to fly, and during World War II, he trained pilots for the Army Air Corps. Later on, he ran a trucking company and operated a motel in Irving, Texas. In 1977, shortly after finishing a manuscript about his life, entitled "Ambush," Ted Hinton died. He was seventy-three years old and the last surviving member of the posse that killed Bonnie and Clyde.[26]

Henderson Jordan

In early 1934, Henderson Jordan was a thirty-six-year-old World War I veteran serving as sheriff of Bienville Parish, Louisiana. In late February, he was approached by Frank Hamer and Bob Alcorn and asked to help set a trap for Bonnie and Clyde. The Texas lawmen needed to contact the parents of Henry Methvin, who lived near Castor. Sheriff Jordan contacted the Methvins through their friend John Joyner, and the plan was set in motion. Three months later, Jordan was part of the posse that killed them.

Henderson Jordan was routinely reelected sheriff of Bienville Parish until he chose to retire. On June 13, 1958, at age sixty, he was killed in an automobile accident.[27]

Prentis Oakley

On Monday evening, May 21, 1934, Prentis Oakley was a twenty-nine-year-old deputy under Sheriff Henderson Jordan when the call came that the plan to ambush Bonnie and Clyde was on. Four of the lawmen were from Texas, so Jordan asked Oakley to join him on the posse to represent Bienville Parish. Oakley went by the home of a local dentist, whose hunting rifle he had often borrowed, and picked up the Remington Model 8 one more time. Both Oakley and Jordan argued that some command to surrender should be given, but on Wednesday morning, May 23, Oakley surprised everyone by opening fire before any order was given. His first shot killed Clyde Barrow. Even though Clyde Barrow had sworn never to be taken alive and had been involved, directly or indirectly, in the killing of nine lawmen, the ambush, and the fact that he had fired without any warning, haunted Oakley for the rest of his life.

Prentis Oakley was elected sheriff upon the retirement of Henderson Jordan. He died on October 15, 1957.[28]

OTHER LAWMEN

Richard Allen "Smoot" Schmid

"Smoot" Schmid had grown up in Dallas, the son of a Swiss immigrant. He was a high school football hero and later opened a bicycle shop. In 1932, he won the race for Dallas County Sheriff against six opponents, taking office on January 1, 1933. Six days later, in Schmid's new jurisdiction, Clyde Barrow killed a deputy sheriff from a neighboring county. In November, Schmid attempted to ambush Bonnie and Clyde near Sowers, Texas. The attempt was unsuccessful, but Schmid managed to ride out the bad publicity, and two of his men were part of the posse that finally killed the outlaws.

Smoot Schmid continued to serve as sheriff of Dallas County until 1946, after which he served on the State Board of Pardons and Parole. He died on July 1, 1963.[29]

Marshal Lee Simmons

After presiding over the pursuit and ambush of Bonnie and Clyde, the death house escape, and the executions of Raymond Hamilton and Joe Palmer, Lee Simmons announced his resignation as general manager of the Texas Prison System on September 2, 1935. That same year, the Osborne Association on U.S. Prisons awarded the Texas Prison System the dubious honor of being the worst in the nation.[30] When his resignation was accepted, Simmons returned to his hometown of Sherman, Texas, pursued his business interests, dabbled in politics, and in 1957 published his autobiography, *Assignment Huntsville*. Lee Simmons died later that year at the age of eighty-four.[31]

C. G. Maxwell

Against considerable odds, Sheriff C. G. "Charley" Maxwell recovered from the multiple gunshot wounds he received in the gunfight with Clyde Barrow and Raymond Hamilton at Stringtown, Oklahoma, on August 5, 1932, in which his friend and deputy Gene Moore was killed. Sheriff Maxwell was one of the witnesses at the execution of Raymond Hamilton in 1935.

James Eric "Bill" Decker

During the hunt for Bonnie and Clyde, Bill Decker was chief deputy and was essentially the intelligence officer for Sheriff R.A. "Smoot" Schmid, coordinating and evaluating the information as it came in.[32] In 1935 Decker captured Raymond Hamilton on a railroad track in Fort Worth, which led to Hamilton's date with the electric chair. Decker remained chief deputy until Sheriff Schmid was defeated in 1946. Two years later, Decker was elected Dallas County sheriff himself, retaining the post until his death. Decker gained nationwide publicity in 1963 with his office's handling of President Kennedy's assassination. After fifty-one years as a lawman, Bill Decker died on August 29, 1970.[33]

Tom Persell

After his "midnight ride" with Bonnie and Clyde, Tom Persell continued to live in Springfield, Missouri, with his family. After he left the police force, he became a postal worker. He gave a few interviews over the years but didn't talk much about the experience. In one of his few public appearances on the subject of Bonnie and Clyde, he allowed his granddaughter to take him to school with her—for show and tell.

Percy Boyd

After his encounter with Bonnie and Clyde, Boyd went back to work as the chief of police of Commerce, Oklahoma. After he retired, on May 3, 1937, Boyd went to work for the Tri-State District Mining Company and also served on the Commerce Board of Education. On August 15, 1940, Percy Boyd died of a heart attack at his home.[34]

Of all the people they kidnapped, Bonnie and Clyde liked Boyd the best. While not admirers of policemen in general, they thought that Boyd was a truly brave man. He earned Bonnie Parker's lasting respect and gratitude when, just as he had promised her, he returned home and told the waiting reporters that the famous female outlaw absolutely did not smoke cigars.

OTHERS

Ivy T. Methvin

After the ambush of Bonnie and Clyde, Ivy T. Methvin continued to live in Bienville Parish. In time, he and his wife, Avie, divorced and Ivy remarried. In 1946 he rode a bus to Shreveport to visit his son Henry, who was in the hospital. On the way back home, for some reason Ivy got off the bus at one of the earlier stops. He was later found by the side of the road, seriously injured. He was taken to a hospital but soon died. It was assumed that he had been hit by a car, but his family

believed he had been beaten to death because of his involvement with Bonnie and Clyde's death. Ivy never regained consciousness, so the cause of his death remains a mystery.[35]

Avie Stephens Methvin

Avie Methvin was considered, by some who knew her, to be the real ringleader in the plot to deliver Bonnie and Clyde in return for a pardon for her son. When Henry was arrested by Oklahoma—in spite of his Texas pardon—she made plans to free him. According to her daughter-in-law, Avie planned a bank robbery to raise some money and get Henry out of jail. Naturally, the daughter-in-law thought this was a harebrained idea. She couldn't imagine that Avie could get more than a couple of hundred dollars from those little country banks and had no idea how she planned to go about getting Henry out of jail in any case. Unfortunately, her husband, Cecil Methvin, Avie's youngest son, was enlisted in the scheme. His job was to steal a car for them to use in the holdup.

Cecil found a new car that belonged to a schoolteacher and started back to meet his mother, but he lost control of the vehicle, ran through a barbed wire fence, and hit a tree. Sheriff Jordan, who had been tipped off and was watching the whole time, arrested Cecil but was sorry he had wrecked the car, since he had wanted to catch Avie as well. The bank robbery never came off. Henry stayed in prison, and Avie was not arrested, but Cecil was sent to prison for stealing the car.[36]

John Joyner

John Joyner was a friend of Ivy and Avie Methvin and represented them at the meeting in March 1934 that set in motion the plan for the ambush of Bonnie and Clyde. He further served as a go-between several times before the actual shooting. Some witnesses say that Joyner was paid $1,000 for his part in setting up the ambush.[37] After Bonnie and Clyde were killed, Joyner continued to live in the area. When Cecil Methvin got out of prison after his mother's bank robbery scheme, John Joyner gave him and his family a place to stay and helped him find a job. Even so, Cecil's wife later remembered Joyner as being "mean."[38]

On September 24, 1942, John Joyner came home to find his wife packing a suitcase. She told him that she was leaving him for another man. In the argument that followed, a pistol was produced, and Mrs. Joyner was shot dead. When two local officers arrived, Joyner held them at gunpoint. He said the killing had been an accident but knew nobody would believe him. One officer went for the sheriff, and the other stayed at the scene. Joyner then made a phone call, went back into the bedroom, and killed himself. John Joyner was forty-three years old. In a final ironic twist, the "other man" in this fatal triangle was said to have been Henry Methvin, only recently released from prison in Oklahoma.[39]

Roy Glenn Thornton

Bonnie Parker's estranged husband was in prison at Huntsville when his wife and her lover were killed. Thornton seemed very interested in Bonnie and Clyde's relationship and asked Ralph Fults about it many times. Roy was involved in several unsuccessful escape attempts, the last one being on October 4, 1937. This time, Roy Thornton and twenty-six other inmates tried to escape from Eastham Farm. Thornton and one other prisoner were killed.[40]

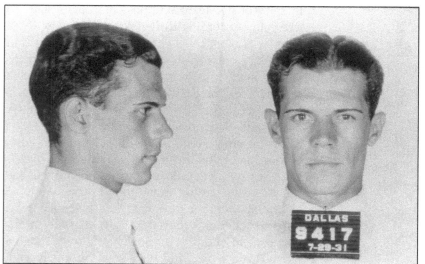

Mug shot of Roy Glenn Thornton, Bonnie Parker's estranged husband. July 23, 1931.
—From the collections of the Texas/Dallas History and Archives Division, Dallas Public Library

Even after throwing him out of her life before she ever met Clyde Barrow, Bonnie never divorced Roy Thornton. She died with his wedding ring on her finger.

Appendix One

The Ballad of Donnabell Lee

The following two pages show six verses of a poem typed by Bonnie Parker. According to her sister, Bonnie found the poem, liked it, and typed this copy. It is reproduced here, for the first time, with the permission of the owner, a private collector who purchased the original directly from the Parker family. The second page is the reverse of the typewritten page with an additional verse in Bonnie's own handwriting. Whether this verse was the start of Bonnie's effort to finish the poem or was intended as part of some other work is unknown.

Donnabell Lee—front.
—Courtesy Sandy Jones–The John Dillinger Society

```
"THE BALLAD OF DONNABELL LEE"

THIS IS THE THORN OF THE CACTUS,
   THIS IS THE RATTLER'S STING,
THIS IS THE LUST OF THE BUZZARD,
   IN THE LAND OF THE CATTLE KING:
FOR SUCH IS THE PRONG OF A SCORPION,
   SUCH IS THE FLASH OF A KNIFE,
A GRAIN OF SAND IN THE CATTLE LAND,
   IS A SNAPPED OUT HUMAN LIFE.

OLD "SIX GUN LEE" WAS THE CATTLE KING,
   WHO RULED WITH THE SEPTRE OF LEAD,
IN A HEAT-SCORCHED LAND ON THE RIO GRANDE,
   WHERE THE SUN CREMATES THE DEAD,
HIS TEMPER WAS LIKE THE DESERTS BREATH,
   THAT WITHERS THE LUNGERS FRAME,
HIS DRAW AS QUICK AS THE CACTUS PRICK,
   AND THE RUSTLERS KNEW HIS FAME,
HE HAD A DAUGHTER A DESERT FLOWER,
   WITH PETALS OF GOLDEN HEW,
WITH EYES DEMURE AND A SOUL AS PURE,
   AS THE SUNLITE ON MORNING DEW.
GENTLE WAS SHE AS THE EVENING BREEZE,
   THE PRIZE OF THE BOYS ON THE "BAR X-B",
NEVER A QUEEN HAD GREATER ESTEEM,
   FROM HER SUBJECTS THAN "DONNABELL LEE".

UP- OUT OF THE DUST OF MEXICO,
   RODE AN HUMBRE AND HIS BAND,
"MESCAL PETE" RODE THROUGH THE HEAT,
   INTO THE CATTLE LAND.
FROM STEALING THE "VIRGIN MARY"
   AT THE CHURCH IN A BORDER TOWN,
TO THE "BAR X-B" AND "DONNABELL LEE"
   HER MEN ON A CATTLE ROUND.
FOR A FAILING OF "PETE'S" WAS WOMEN,
   HE TOOK THEM AND CRUSHED THEIR HEARTS,
THEN PASSED THEM BY, OR LEFT THEM TO DIE,
   IN THE BORDER SLAVERY MARTS.
FOR WOMEN TO "PETE" WERE CATTLE,
   HE BRANDED THEM LIKE HIS STEERS,
WITH THE BURNING HISS OF A RATTLER'S KISS?
   ON LIPS TOO WHITE FOR TEARS.
AND THIS WAS THE FATE OF "DONNABELL LEE",
   THE STORY IS SHORT TO TELL,
OF HER DEATH ON THE NITE OF THE BLOODY FIGHT,
   THAT ENDED A BORDER HELL.

DOWN-OUT OF THE CATTLE COUNTRY,
   RODE THE MEN OF THE "BAR-X-B"?
THROUGH THE PALE BLUE LIGHT OF THE EVIL NITE,
   TO FIGHT WITH "SIX-GUN LEE".
TO FIGHT A BATTLE OF MEN GONE MAD,
   TO KILL WITH A BITTER SMILE,
AND CURSE THE DEAD IN A STREET GONE RED,
   WITH BLOOD FOR A QUARTER A MILE.
```

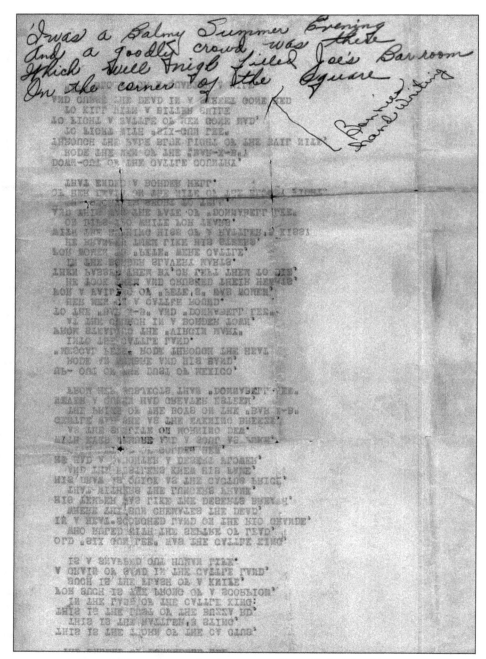

Donnabell Lee—reverse, showing a verse in Bonnie Parker's handwriting.

—Courtesy Sandy Jones–The John Dillinger Society

Appendix Two

Bonnie and Clyde Death Car History
Contributed by Sandy Jones

On a Sunday afternoon, April 29, 1934, at 2107 Gable Street, Topeka, Kansas, Ruth Warren looked out her kitchen window and noticed her new 1934 Ford Deluxe Fordor sedan was missing from the driveway. Thinking that Jess, her husband, had driven it to visit his parents, who lived just down the street, she phoned her father-in-law to inquire about the car. That was when she realized that the car had been stolen. What the Warrens didn't know until later was that they had provided the final Ford V-8 for Clyde Barrow and Bonnie Parker. Twenty-five days later, on the morning of May 24, 1934, Mrs. Warren got a call from the Associated Press in Dallas, Texas, asking for verification of the engine number, VIN 649198. Bonnie and Clyde had been ambushed and killed in it the day before, just outside Gibsland, Louisiana.

After being notified of the whereabouts of their Ford, the Warrens sent a representative to Arcadia, Louisiana, to pick up the car. When Bienville Parish Sheriff Henderson Jordan refused to release the car, another person was sent down to Arcadia but fared no better. Finally, Mrs. Warren and a friend decided to drive to Arcadia and pick the car up themselves. Upon their arrival, Mrs. Warren was interviewed by Sheriff Jordan, who

gave a little speech about how six men risked their lives trying to capture Bonnie and Clyde and added that he wasn't about to turn over the car. Mrs. Warren asked to see the car but was refused and told to contact Sheriff Jordan's attorney.

In view of the situation, Mrs. Warren hired a local Arcadia attorney, W. D. Goff, to represent her. Mr. Goff immediately filed a writ of sequestration in the federal court, but Sheriff Jordan still refused to turn over the car. The sheriff was cited and, with the help of the chief of police from Shreveport, Louisiana, the car was turned over to a U.S. marshal, who had it safely stored. Mrs. Warren was allowed to view the car, and she then returned to Topeka.

Seventy days later Mr. Goff finally called and said an agreement had been reached. They could come pick their car up at the Ford Motor Garage in Arcadia, Louisiana. The Warrens got their Ford back, on August 2, 1934, with an attached bill of $70 plus $15 for towing. Mrs. Warren actually drove the gruesome car from Arcadia to Shreveport and said the motor ran perfectly. The car still had the original keys and key ring with the suitcase key to the Potter trunk. Bonnie and Clyde had kept the car for less than a month. When Mrs. Warren parked the car on April 29, the odometer read 1,243 miles. When she picked it up in Arcadia, it read 8,855 miles. Bonnie and Clyde had

Charles Stanley, "the Crime Doctor," standing beside the death car.
—Courtesy Sandy Jones–The John Dillinger Historical Society

driven it 7,612 miles in twenty-five days, averaging 300 miles a day on 1934 roads.

After the Warrens got the car back, they began to make arrangements to exhibit it. In September 1934, more litigation followed because another person had duplicated the car and was trying to pass it off as "the Bandit Car." The Warrens ended up filing a patent on the death car. A contract to exhibit the death car finally went to Charles Stanley of Abilene, Kansas, a showman know as "the Crime Doctor." The Crime Doctor toured the car in a show called *Crime Does Not Pay,* in cooperation with the National Anti-Crime Association, until 1952. The car was then sold to Ted Toddy and his *Killers All* crime show.

In 1973 the car was sold to casino owner Pete A. Simon for $175,000. In 1979 it was transferred to Jim Brucken, owner of Movie World Cars of the Stars in Buena Park, California, and later sold to Clyde Wade of the Harrah's collection. In 1988,

after some modification, the car ran in the Great American Race. Finally, it was sold to Whiskey Pete's Casino in Primm, Nevada, outside Las Vegas, where it is now on display. It's been rumored that the casino has refused offers of $1,000,000 for the famous car.

Specifications:

1934 Ford Deluxe Fordor Sedan
Vehicle Identification Number (VIN) 649198
Model 40, Body style 730
Color: Cordoba gray, Tacoma cream pinstripe
Interior: mohair—olive/tan
Engine: Ford V-8, 85 HP, 221 cubic inch
Transmission: three-speed manual
Tires: Firestone 525/550X17
License plate when stolen: Kansas 3-17832
License plate when recovered: Arkansas 15-368
Weight: 2675 lbs.
Length: 175.9 in.

Sandy Jones with his modern restoration of the death car.

—Courtesy Sandy Jones–The John Dillinger Historical Society

Purchase price: $835 as equipped[1]

Options: Potter trunk, 1933 Arvin Hot Water Heater model 80B, front and rear bumper guards, Greyhound radiator cap, spare wheel lock, and oil bath air cleaner.

Other details: The rear spare tire was a Goodrich 525/550X17 that Clyde had changed somewhere. Early-production 1934 Ford interior door handles were forward with pull strap; standard fuel gauge—not dual gauge. The Potter trunk brackets/skirt were all body color. The dash and garnish molding were mahogany woodgrain. The car had safety glass, and Clyde had changed the gearshift knob to a flat one for easy shifting.

Author's note: Sandy Jones is a longtime friend of the late Marie Barrow Scoma and other members of the Barrow and Parker families. He is head of the John Dillinger Historical Society, a collector of depression-era outlaw memorabilia, a founding member of an Internet discussion and research group called "Partners in Crime," and an expert on automobiles of the period—especially 1930s Ford V-8s. He currently owns a 1933 Pontiac, a 1933 Essex Terraplane 8 once owned by John Dillinger, and a 1934 Ford V-8 restored as an exact duplicate of the Bonnie and Clyde death car. In order to make his Ford as close as possible to the original, Mr. Jones needed access to the death car itself. At his request, in January 1998, Whiskey Pete's Casino allowed Mr. Jones and a friend, Bob Fischer, to completely inspect, photograph, and catalog the original car at Primm, Nevada. Mr. Jones, with his restoration, is pictured above.

Appendix Three

Killings done by (or charged to) Clyde Barrow or other members of the Barrow gang

1. Ed "Big Ed" Crowder—prison farm trusty or "building tender." Killed by Clyde Barrow and Aubrey Skelley at Eastham Prison Farm Camp One sometime in 1931.
2. John N. Bucher—storekeeper, Hillsboro, Texas. Killed by Ted Rogers, a member of Clyde Barrow's "Lake Dallas gang," during the robbery of Bucher's store on the evening of April 30, 1932. Clyde Barrow was driving the getaway car.
3. Eugene C. "Gene" Moore—undersheriff, Atoka County, Oklahoma. Killed by Clyde Barrow or Raymond Hamilton at an outdoor dance pavilion near Stringtown, Oklahoma, on Friday evening, August 5, 1932. Sheriff C. G. Maxwell was seriously wounded at the same time.
4. Howard Hall—storekeeper, Sherman, Texas. Killed October 11, 1932, during the robbery of Little's Market, on the corner of Wells and Vaden streets. The fifty-seven-year-old unarmed meat market clerk was shot three times (once while on the ground) by a twenty- to twenty-five-year-old assailant who escaped. The next day, Clyde Barrow was identified by the other clerk as Hall's killer, from a mug shot sent up from Dallas.
5. Doyle Johnson—employee of Strasburger's Market, Temple, Texas. Killed on the street in front of his house at 606 South Thirteenth Street on Christmas Day, 1932, by W. D. Jones and Clyde Barrow. Johnson was attempting to stop Barrow and Jones

from stealing his car when both men fired at him. Jones' shot appears to have killed him.
6. Malcolm Davis—deputy sheriff, Tarrant County, Texas. Killed on the front porch of Lilly McBride's house at 507 County Avenue in west Dallas by Clyde Barrow. Davis and four other officers were waiting at the house for Odell Chambless, who was wanted for the robbery of the bank at Grapevine, Texas. Due to unrelated circumstances, Clyde Barrow showed up during the stakeout, and a gunfight erupted.
7. J. W. "Wes" Harryman—constable, Newton County, Missouri. Killed at Joplin, Missouri, on Thursday, April 13, 1933, by either Clyde Barrow or W. D. Jones as he and four other officers attempted to raid the garage apartment at Thirty-fourth Street and Oak Ridge Drive where the Barrows were staying.
8. Harry McGinnis—motor car detective, Joplin, Missouri. Mortally wounded a few seconds after Officer Harryman, in the same action at the apartment on the south edge of Joplin described above. While Officer Harryman was pronounced dead at the scene, McGinnis died at St. John's Hospital later that evening.
9. Henry D. Humphrey—town marshal, Alma, Arkansas. Mortally wounded on June 23, 1933, on U.S. 71, just north of Alma, by Buck Barrow and W. D. Jones. Barrow and Jones were involved in a car wreck while fleeing the scene of a grocery store robbery in Fayetteville, Arkansas. Humphrey and A. M "Red" Salyers arrived to investigate, and a gunfight erupted. Humphrey died two and a half

days later at St. John's Hospital in Fort Smith, Arkansas.

10. Major Joseph Crowson ("Major" was his given name, not a rank)—prison guard and high rider, Eastham Prison Farm Camp One. Mortally wounded, January 16, 1934, by Joe Palmer during an escape from the prison farm, engineered by Clyde Barrow and Floyd Hamilton. Clyde was present, fired some shots over the guard's heads, and provided the getaway car. Crowson died eleven days later at Memorial Hospital, Huntsville, Texas.

11. Wade Hampton McNabb—trusty or "building tender," Eastham Prison Farm. Kidnapped at Gladewater, Texas, on March 29, 1934, by Clyde Barrow, Henry Methvin, and Joe Palmer, and killed soon after by Joe Palmer. McNabb was an inmate at Eastham Farm until he was granted a sixty-day furlough on February 24, 1934, said to have been arranged by a lawyer paid by Joe Palmer. While free on leave, McNabb was abducted at Gladewater and taken to some woods north of Waskom, Texas, where Joe Palmer killed him as revenge for beatings he had suffered from McNabb in prison.

12. E. B. Wheeler—Texas State Highway patrolman (motorcycle). Killed on Easter Sunday, April 1, 1934, by Henry Methvin on a dirt road just off Highway 114, five and a half miles northwest of Grapevine, Texas. Wheeler, along with Officer H. D. Murphy, turned off Highway 114 to investigate a car parked on the dirt road. As he got off his motorcycle, he was shot by Henry Methvin and died at the scene.

13. H. D. Murphy—Texas State Highway patrolman (motorcycle). Mortally wounded a few seconds after Officer Wheeler, by Clyde Barrow or Henry Methvin, in the same action described above. After Murphy fell, one of the killers, described by a witness as "the taller of the two men," indicating Methvin, who was almost six feet tall, rolled him over and shot him several more times. Murphy died on the way to the hospital. It was his first day on motorcycle duty.

14. Cal Campbell—constable, Commerce, Oklahoma. Killed April 6, 1934, outside Commerce, Oklahoma, by Clyde Barrow or Henry Methvin. Campbell and Commerce Police Chief Percy Boyd were fired upon as they approached a car parked on a muddy road outside of town. Campbell fired three shots before he was killed. Boyd was wounded and then forced to go with Bonnie Parker, Clyde Barrow, and Henry Methvin as they fled the scene. He was released later that evening near Fort Scott, Kansas, after promising to tell the press that Bonnie didn't smoke cigars.

Appendix Four

Banks known or suspected of being robbed by Clyde Barrow

1. Unknown bank somewhere in the Midwest. Robbed by Clyde Barrow, Ralph Fults, and Raymond Hamilton sometime between March 25 and April 11, 1932. The take was said to have been $33,000, but the location is unknown. (For Ralph Fults' version of the robbery, and the problems involved, see the end of this appendix.)

2. Farmers and Miners Bank, Oronogo, Missouri. Robbed by Clyde Barrow, Frank Hardy, and Hollis Hale, November 30, 1932. One of three occasions when Clyde Barrow was required to fire a weapon during a bank robbery. He returned the fire of a teller who pulled a gun inside the bank and exchanged shots with some townspeople who fired at the bandits as they were driving away. In spite of all the shooting, no one was hit. The take was said to have been around $100.

3. Lucerne State Bank, Lucerne, Indiana. Robbed by Clyde and Buck Barrow on May 12, 1933. Probably the brothers' first attempt at bank robbery together. They broke into the bank during the night and surprised the first two employees to come to work. These men managed to take cover inside the vault and arm themselves, however, so Clyde and Buck fired several shots inside the bank and ran to the car, where Bonnie and Blanche were waiting. During the getaway, they shot up the town, slightly wounded two bystanders, and ran over two pigs. No money was taken.

4. First State Bank, Okabena, Minnesota. Robbed by Clyde and Buck Barrow on May 19, 1933. The Barrow family, in two different documents, claim that Clyde and Buck did this robbery, but three other people were tried and convicted for it. This was the third time that there was an exchange of gunfire associated with a Clyde Barrow bank robbery. Again, no one was hit. The take was given by the local paper as $1,419.

5. First National Bank, Rembrandt, Iowa. Robbed by Clyde Barrow, Raymond Hamilton, Henry Methvin, Hilton Bybee, and Joe Palmer on Tuesday, January 23, 1934. This was the first bank robbery done by the second "Barrow gang," one week after the January 16 Eastham Prison Farm escape. The take was $3,800.

6. Central National Bank, Poteau, Oklahoma. Robbed by Clyde Barrow, Henry Methvin, Raymond Hamilton, and Joe Palmer on Thursday, January 25, 1934. This robbery was done forty-eight hours after—and 500 miles away from—the Rembrandt, Iowa, job, but two sources credit it to the Barrow gang, which at this point was just trying to raise money as quickly as possible. The take was $1,500.

7. State Savings Bank, Knierim, Iowa. Robbed by Clyde Barrow, Henry Methvin, and Raymond Hamilton on February 1, 1934. This was the third bank robbed by the gang in nine days. By this point, the gang had lost two members. Hilton Bybee had left them and been captured in Amarillo, Texas, and Joe Palmer was staying in Joplin, Missouri. The take was $272 from the bank and $35 from a customer.

8. R. P. Henry and Sons Bank, Lancaster, Texas.

Robbed by Clyde Barrow, Henry Methvin, and Raymond Hamilton on February 27, 1934. On this occasion, Clyde Barrow returned $27 to a bank customer rather than take his WPA paycheck. A disagreement about how the money should be divided from this robbery began the final split between Clyde Barrow and Raymond Hamilton. The take was $4,176.

9. First National Bank, Stuart, Iowa. Robbed by Clyde Barrow and Henry Methvin on April 16, 1934. Barrow and Methvin had become separated from Joe Palmer after the Grapevine killings. Bonnie waited in the car. The take was no more than $1,500—probably less.

10. Farmers Trust and Savings Bank branch located at Everly, Iowa. Robbed by Clyde Barrow, Henry Methvin, and Joe Palmer on May 3, 1934. By this time, Palmer had rejoined the gang. This is the last bank robbery done by Clyde Barrow for which we have any evidence. At first, the take was thought to be as much as $2,000, but later checks by the bank found that the gang had missed a good part of the cash on hand. The bank's final loss figure was about $700.

For these ten bank robberies, we have fairly convincing evidence that Clyde Barrow was involved. There are others that some authors credit to Barrow but lack the same kind of evidence. For instance:

First State Bank of Willis, Texas, robbed on July 28, 1932. This is sometimes credited to Clyde Barrow and Raymond Hamilton, who were twenty-three and nineteen years old at the time, even though the two men involved were described as "about 30 years old, heavily whiskered and dressed in overalls and khaki shirts." The men, whoever they were, got $3,575.

Commercial Bank, Alma, Arkansas, robbed in the early hours of June 22, 1933. Clyde Barrow, Buck Barrow, and W. D. Jones were staying in a tourist camp thirteen miles away when this robbery occurred, so some authors assume that it was their work. The robbery included the capture of the town marshal, who was serving as the night watchman, and the physical removal of a 4,000-pound safe containing $3,600 by use of a stolen truck with a winch. The safe was later found unopened with the contents intact, so whoever did it got nothing.

Finally, there is the mystery bank where Clyde Barrow, Ralph Fults, and Raymond Hamilton made their big score sometime around the first of April 1932.

The only account of the robbery was given by Fults to his biographer, John Neal Phillips, fifty years after the fact, and it goes like this:

Fults said that after the three of them decided against robbing the bank at Okabena, Minnesota (see p. 43), they drove south to Lawrence, Kansas. There they checked in to the Eldridge Hotel and began to case the First National Bank at the corner of Eighth and Massachusetts. They watched it for three days, and on the morning of the fourth day they intercepted the bank president at the front door as he came to work and took him inside, along with two other employees who happened to show up. A few minutes later, Raymond Hamilton pulled the car around and the three left with two bags full of money totaling $33,000. They then drove away, without seeing any pursuit, and didn't stop until they reached East St. Louis.[1]

Fults' story is very convincing and his details are accurate. The building occupied by the First National Bank in 1932 stills stands today in downtown Lawrence (it's a restaurant called Tellers), and the old Eldridge Hotel is still there too (also a restaurant), just one block north on Seventh Street. Unfortunately, no record has ever been found of a robbery of the First National or any other bank in Lawrence during the time in question. In 1932 the First National Bank of Lawrence did business out of an impressive three-story marble building and had a capitalization of $300,000. It was probably the largest bank in town—maybe in the county. The odds that it could have been robbed, in the middle of downtown at 8:45 in the morning, of an amount of cash that would have represented just over 10 percent of its assets, and that the event would leave no record in any of the newspapers or other documents of the time, are very long indeed.

Ralph Fults' record for accuracy in the stories he told his biographer is extremely good, and at least three people saw Clyde Barrow or one of the others with a lot of money after they returned to Texas from the road trip, so they almost certainly made a big score somewhere, and the amount of money involved favors a bank job. For all Fults' detail, however, Lawrence, Kansas, seems out of the running and the actual location remains a mystery.

There were other bank robberies planned but never carried out, and probably some that were done that we know nothing about. No one can even begin to guess how many robberies of other, smaller places were done, or the number of stolen cars for which Clyde Barrow was responsible.

Endnotes

INTRODUCTION

1. Jan I. Fortune, *Fugitives: The Story of Clyde Barrow and Bonnie Parker* (Ranger Press, Inc., Dallas, 1934).

2. All stories and other materials pertaining to the Barrow family history have as their source—unless otherwise referenced—notes taken by Jonathan Davis during several years of conversations with Marie Barrow Scoma at her home in Dallas, Texas. These notes were taken with Mrs. Barrow's permission in the knowledge that they might someday be used in a publication. Mrs. Barrow also furnished other family material for Mr. Davis' use. Together, they form the basis for most of the Barrow family material in this volume. Other materials, used to verify Mrs. Barrow's information, or Mrs. Barrow's statements given to others, will be separately cited.

3. The series entitled "The Bloody Barrows" ran in *True Detective* magazine in six installments from June through November 1934.

4. Marie Barrow was a woman of strong opinions, especially where her family and her famous (or infamous) brothers were concerned. She felt that they were unfairly portrayed in every book, newsreel, or movie she saw. Of course, some were worse than others. She was known, on occasion, to take a copy of what she considered the worst offenders and bounce them off the walls of her house, or to say a few well-chosen words to their authors when she met them. Sadly, her feelings about the accuracy of many of the works on Bonnie and Clyde were well founded. Many of the errors that originated in *The Bloody Barrows* and *Fugitives* can be followed through all later treatments, some of which—like the 1967 movie—would also add new ones of their own. The good news, for those of us interested in the true story, is that the level of scholarship and documentation has risen substantially in the last few years. By far the best effort to date—and this was grudgingly admitted by Marie Barrow herself—is the 1996 book by John Neal Phillips, *Running with Bonnie and Clyde*.

5. Marie Barrow's concern that nobody came to the family and asked for information may have been sincere, but the fact is, she and other family members have said repeatedly that the subject was not discussed for years afterward—even among themselves. One of Clyde's younger nephews said that it was never discussed when children were in the room. He finally asked, "Who was Clyde?" He was told that they would tell him when he was older. He was seventeen at the time. Somehow, the idea that the family would have been receptive to requests from authors during this time to "set the record straight" is a little hard to believe. This began to change in the 1980s and 1990s. The two most recent books on Bonnie and Clyde, as well as this one, have had significant Barrow family involvement.

6. Marie Barrow often left the impression that everything in *Fugitives* was made up by Jan Fortune. It has, in fact, been shown to be in error in many places, and must be verified by other sources, but recent research has shown it to be more accurate than previously believed. *Fugitives* is still the starting point for any study of the subject and is repeatedly referenced by all authors.

7. For instance, the *True Detective* series cited above was written by the chief of detectives of the Joplin, Missouri, Police, Ed Portley.

CHAPTER 1

1. These dates for the births of Buck and Nell are the ones the Barrow family insists are correct. Unfortunately, Buck's headstone says "1905–1933." Marie Barrow said that, in the stress and confusion of Clyde's death and funeral, her mother, Cumie, gave the wrong date for Buck's birth to the stonecutters who were preparing the marker. For personal and financial reasons, it had been agreed that the two brothers would be buried side by side and share one marker, so it wasn't bought and engraved until Clyde's death. Most researchers, and the Barrow family, agree that the 1903 date is actually correct for Buck Barrow.

2. L. C. was the only name Clyde's younger brother ever used. As far as the Barrow family members know today, the initials didn't stand for anything. Some of the news items at the time of L. C.'s death give names for the initials, but the family says that they are not correct.

CHAPTER 2

1. The family stories in this chapter come from Marie Barrow's conversations with Jonathan Davis.

CHAPTER 3

1. The information on the effect of the end of World War I on the cotton market in the South and the lives of farmers was taken from a speech given by Charles R. Starbird, attorney for the Commercial Bank, Alma, Arkansas, on his retirement. Fort Smith, Arkansas, 1981. Mr. Starbird was eighty-six years old at the time. His father was an original stockholder when the bank was founded in 1902.

CHAPTER 4

1. Cumie T. Barrow, unfinished manuscript. There is some question about the dates here. If the 1903 date for Buck's birth is correct, as most researchers believe, then the 1920 date in the text represents Buck at seventeen, as his mother's manuscript says. Unfortunately, the manuscript goes on to say that this was "shortly after we moved to Dallas," which was in 1922. If this is true, then Buck would have been nineteen at the time—unless, of course, we are all mistaken and the 1905 date on Buck's tombstone is correct, after all. Sometime in this two-year period, Marvin I. Barrow married Margaret Heneger.

2. Cumie T. Barrow, unfinished manuscript.

CHAPTER 5

1. One of Clyde Barrow's pay stubs, furnished by Sandy Jones, shows wages of $18 for sixty hours' work.

2. According to her cousin, Lela Heslep, the girl's full name was Eleanor Bee Williams. Eleanor had two brothers who worked at Procter and Gamble, so that may be how Clyde met her. This mirror was recently sold in the same auction as Clyde's rifle. For the information about Eleanor Bee Williams, the author would like to thank Buddy Williams and Lela Heslep.

3. John Neal Phillips, *Running with Bonnie and Clyde* (University of Oklahoma Press, Norman, OK, 1996), p. 45.

4. Fortune, *Fugitives*, pp. 23–24.

CHAPTER 6

1. *True Detective* magazine, "The Inside Story of the Bloody Barrows," by Ed Portley, June 1934.

2. Ibid.

3. Cumie T. Barrow, unfinished manuscript.

4. Buck Barrow to Ralph Fults. Phillips, *Running with Bonnie and Clyde*, pp. 101–102.

5. If anything, the Barrow family seemed to feel that Clyde took advantage of his older brother's concern about him. They admit that Buck took the blame for things that were really Clyde's doing. They believed that Buck felt responsible for Clyde's situation and tried repeatedly to get him to mend his ways. This was not reflected in Buck's conversations in prison, however. Cumie T. Barrow, unpublished manuscript. Phillips, *Running with Bonnie and Clyde*, pp. 101–102.

6. Phillips, *Running with Bonnie and Clyde*, p. 46.

7. E. R. Milner, *The Life and Times of Bonnie and Clyde* (Southern Illinois University Press, Carbondale, IL., 1996), p. 11.

8. Robert E. Davis, edited by Eugene Baker, *Blanche Barrow: The Last Victim of Bonnie and Clyde* (Waco, Texas, 2001), p. 8. The information on Blanche's birth is from her birth certificate, published by Mr. Davis.

9. Ibid., p. 62.

10. Marie Barrow, as told to Sandy Jones.

11. The information on Buck's wives comes from his mother's writings. She says Buck's first wife was Margaret Heneger. Less than a year later, however, he fell for another girl, named Pearl Churchley. Margaret divorced him and received custody of their son. Buck and Pearl later married and had a daughter, but then separated. That was Buck's situation when he met Blanche in early 1929. Cumie T. Barrow, unfinished manuscript.

12. Phillips, *Running with Bonnie and Clyde*, pp. 125, 306.

13. Fortune, *Fugitives*, p. 30.

14. Denton (TX) *Record Chronicle*, November 30, 1929.

15. E.R. Milner, *The Life and Times of Bonnie and Clyde*, pp. 11–15. Phillips, *Running with Bonnie and Clyde*, pp. 46–47.

16. Other sources say that Bonnie was there because someone (Clay's daughter or a girlfriend of Bonnie's) had broken an arm in an accident. Bonnie was helping out with the housework either out of the goodness of her heart or because she had been hired to do so (she was out of work at the time), depending on the source (see Phillips, p. 47; Milner, p. 17; and Fortune, p. 57). Marie Barrow always maintained that it was just a social gathering with no injured girl involved.

17. E. R. Milner, *The Life and Times of Bonnie and Clyde*, p. 15. Marie Barrow to Jonathan Davis.

CHAPTER 7

1. Milner, *The Life and Times of Bonnie and Clyde*, p. 16.

2. Fortune, *Fugitives*, p. 36.

3. Phillips, *Running with Bonnie and Clyde*, p. 81.

4. Fortune, *Fugitives*, p. 44.

5. Ibid., p. 43.

6. Phillips, *Running with Bonnie and Clyde*, pp. 82–84, note 63.

7. Fortune, *Fugitives*, p. 47.

8. Milner, *The Life and Times of Bonnie and Clyde*, p. 17.

9. Phillips, *Running with Bonnie and Clyde*, p. 83. Bonnie may have worked at a third cafe also. Ted Hinton says he knew her as a waitress at the "American Cafe," near the post office. Ted Hinton, *Ambush* (Bryan, Texas, 1979), p. 7.

CHAPTER 8

1. Fortune, *Fugitives*, p. 59.

2. Ibid. Milner, *The Life and Times of Bonnie and Clyde*, p. 17.

3. According to the heading on Bonnie's letters to Clyde while he was in jail, the house was located at 1406 Cockrell Street. Fortune, *Fugitives*, p. 61.

4. Fortune, *Fugitives*, pp. 59–60.

5. Phillips, *Running with Bonnie and Clyde*, pp. 47–48. Fortune, *Fugitives*, p. 71.

6. Text of letter provided by Jonathan Davis.

7. Ibid.

8. Ibid.

9. Many authors like to emphasize the fact that Bonnie was small, and she certainly was petite. Marie Barrow, who was over 5 feet, said that, as a fifteen-year-old, she was sent to buy clothes for Bonnie, since she and Bonnie wore the same sizes. There are several pictures of Clyde and Bonnie side by side in which Bonnie reaches to at least the bridge of Clyde's nose. This would make Bonnie about four to five inches shorter than Clyde, who was variously listed as 5'5½" to 5'7". While the 4'10" that some have stated is probably too small, the 5'5" given for Bonnie by the Division of Investigation (later the FBI) is certainly too tall. Most likely, Bonnie was 5 feet to 5'1". Marie Barrow interview. Dept. of Investigation wanted poster #1227, May 21, 1934. Hinton, *Ambush*, p. 11.

10. Fortune, *Fugitives*, p. 56. Marie Barrow interview.

11. Ibid., p. 71.

CHAPTER 9

1. Some may wonder how this escape would be possible from a prison such as Huntsville. The fact is that Buck was not at the main prison location (called "The Walls"). It would have been almost impossible for them to simply walk away from there. Buck (see his letter of February 24, 1930) was at one of the outlying "farms." These were old cotton plantations acquired by the state in the surrounding countryside. The inmates were used as convict labor in the agricultural operations, which were named for the family who had owned them before the state took over. Buck was at Ferguson Farm. Later, he and Clyde would be at Eastham Farm.

2. Marie Barrow interview.

3. Marie Barrow told a story connected with this hand-drawn diagram. Bonnie kept this note with her as a keepsake, and the diagram came into the possession of the Barrow family a few years later. In early 1934, Bonnie left one of her purses at the Barrow service station after she and Clyde paid a visit. When Clyde's mother found the purse and opened it to determine to whom it belonged, Cumie found this note from the Waco jail, written on a piece of tablet paper. Under the diagram of the house where the gun was located, Clyde had added a personal message to Bonnie: "You are the sweetest baby in the world to me—I love you." Marie Barrow interview. Cumie T. Barrow, unfinished manuscript.

4. This account of the jailbreaks of the two Barrow brothers was assembled using the following sources: Milner, *The Life and Times of Bonnie and Clyde*, pp. 19–25. Phillips, *Running with Bonnie and Clyde*, p. 48. Fortune, *Fugitives*, pp. 74–78. *Waco* (TX) *Times-Herald*, March 12, 1930. Marie Barrow interview. Cumie T. Barrow, unfinished manuscript.

CHAPTER 10

1. This car was later found to have been stolen in Joplin, Missouri. *Waco* (TX) *Times-Herald* March 19, 1930.

2. The story of the capture of Clyde and his fellow escapees is found in the Middletown, Ohio, *Journal*, March 18 and 19, 1930. The newspaper only said that Clyde was at large for a few hours. He told the family that he hid under a house. Cumie T. Barrow, unfinished manuscript. Additional material on Barrow's experience in Ohio was provided by Rick Williams, a native of Middletown, who is preparing his own account of the incident.

3. Milner, *The Life and Times of Bonnie and Clyde*, p. 23.

4. For the Waco news coverage, see the *Waco* (TX) *Times-Herald*, March 12–23, 1930.

5. Cumie T. Barrow, unfinished manuscript.

6. Marie Barrow interview.

7. Phillips, *Running with Bonnie and Clyde*, p. 48.

8. Fortune, *Fugitives*, pp. 81–83 (Clyde's letter to Bonnie).

9. Hinton, *Ambush*, p. 11.

CHAPTER 11

1. Phillips, *Running with Bonnie and Clyde*, pp. 3–32. The testimony of Fults and several other men who were in prison with Clyde Barrow, given to John Neal Phillips for his book on Fults' life, is the primary source of information about Clyde's stay at Eastham. Clyde said very little about his experiences to his family or anyone else after he got out. When asked by his family, he would just say that Eastham was "a burning hell." (Marie Barrow interview). Fults' testimony, through Mr. Phillips, will therefore, of necessity, be quoted extensively.

2. Phillips, *Running with Bonnie and Clyde*, pp. 37–38.

3. Ibid., pp. 39–40.

4. Ibid., p. 8.

5. Ibid., p. 41.

6. Ibid., p. 50.

7. Ibid., p. 52.

8. A "building tender" was a convict trusty who was in a position of authority over the inmates in his building. Many used their position to brutalize other prisoners. Phillips, *Running with Bonnie and Clyde*, p. 25.

9. Ibid., p. 53.

10. Ralph Fults' story of the killing of "Big Ed" is found in Phillips, *Running with Bonnie and Clyde*, pp. 53–54. The story Clyde told his family is found in Fortune, *Fugitives*, p. 87.

11. Fortune, *Fugitives*, pp. 88–89. Marie Barrow interview. Marie said that her mother and Blanche saw the prisoners forced to run to keep up with the mounted officers to and from the fields when they visited Buck.

12. Clyde's letters to Bonnie, Fortune, *Fugitives*, pp. 85–86.

13. Elvin "Jack" Barrow's wife's name is omitted at the request of her family.

14. Text of letter supplied by Jonathan Davis.

15. Phillips, *Running with Bonnie and Clyde*, pp. 125, 341n52.

16. Sid Underwood, *Depression Desperado* (Austin, Texas, 1995), pp. 3–5.

17. Marie Barrow interview. Marie Barrow statement to Sandy Jones.

18. Phillips, *Running with Bonnie and Clyde*, p. 51.

19. Ibid. pp. 54-55, 331n57. Marie Barrow interview.

CHAPTER 12

1. While the lot the house sat on was purchased by Nell for her parents, Henry had to have some money to set up the station. One story is that he sued the driver responsible for killing his white horse and won a settlement. He then used the

money to buy a Ford Model T truck (with which he moved the house from the campground) and built the station. Phillips, *Running with Bonnie and Clyde*, p. 44, Marie Barrow statement to Sandy Jones. Eventually, the Barrows owned the lot next to the service station also. Marie Barrow said that Clyde bought it with the idea of opening an auto repair and parts shop. Others say he bought it with the proceeds of a bank robbery. Phillips, *Running with Bonnie and Clyde*, pp. 332n22.

2. Marie Barrow interview.

3. Fortune, *Fugitives*, p. 94. Bonnie's mother remembered the date of Clyde's return as March 17 or 18.

4. Text of letter from Marie Barrow interview. Beginning with *Fugitives* in 1934, most authors have given Worcester, Massachusetts, as the site of Clyde's construction job (some authors just spelled it like it's pronounced: "Wooster"). It is obvious, from his letter, that Clyde planned on getting his mail in Framingham. The job, however, could have been in the Worcester area, since the two towns are only about twenty miles apart.

5. Marie Barrow interview.

6. Phillips, *Running with Bonnie and Clyde*, pp. 55–56.

7. Underwood, *Depression Desperado*, pp. 7–8.

8. Phillips, *Running with Bonnie and Clyde*, p. 57. Underwood says Hamilton had a radio that he played loudly to cover the noise. Underwood, *Depression Desperado*, p. 8.

9. Phillips, *Running with Bonnie and Clyde*, pp. 57–58.

10. Ibid., p. 64. Underwood says that Hamilton had gone to Bay City, Michigan, after breaking out of the McKinney jail but had returned to Dallas by the time of the Simms robbery. Underwood, *Depression Desperado*, p. 8.

11. Phillips, *Running with Bonnie and Clyde*, pp. 59–60.

12. Ibid., p. 67.

13. Ibid., pp. 68–70.

14. Ibid., p. 70.

CHAPTER 13

1. Phillips, *Running with Bonnie and Clyde*, p. 70. In his note on this passage, Phillips says that Hamilton eventually lost most of this money when he had to abandon his car at a roadblock near Wichita Falls, Texas. Hamilton's attitude about Clyde and Fults' plan is ironic in hindsight. Less than two years later, Ray would himself be a prisoner at the same Eastham Farm and would appeal to Clyde Barrow to break him out in a similar raid.

2. Ray Hamilton's biographer, Sid Underwood, makes no mention of the bank robbery and large amount of money involved. He says that Ray went to Michigan about this time (probably after the split with Fults and Barrow), arriving in Bay City on April 12. Underwood, *Depression Desperado*, p. 9. Three other people, however, either heard about the bank job or saw one of the trio with "several thousand dollars" about this time. See Phillips, *Running with Bonnie and Clyde*, p. 332n22.

3. Phillips, *Running with Bonnie and Clyde*, p. 73.

4. Ibid., p. 74.

5. Ralph Fults learned years later that it was Red who had tipped off the law about the Denton bank job. Ibid., p. 333n37.

6. Ibid., pp. 76–78.

7. Ibid., pp. 78–79.

8. Phillips, *Running with Bonnie and Clyde*, p. 86.

9. Ibid., p. 87.

10. In his version of the story, Ralph Fults told author John Neal Phillips that the store he and Clyde attempted to rob was in Kaufman, Texas, and that's the way I have told the story here. Both local newspapers, however, insist that the store was named "H. Block store" and was located in Mabank, Texas, about twenty miles south of Kaufman. In spite of this disputed beginning point, the remaining details are fairly consistent through both versions. JRK

11. As mentioned in the previous note, the narrative in this chapter follows the one in John Neal Phillips' book *Running with Bonnie and Clyde* very closely, for the simple reason that it is the only source to offer a first-person account of the events. Ralph Fults was there with Clyde and Bonnie and told his version of the story to Phillips in the 1980s. Fults' statements have been substantiated by other evidence to the extent that he is considered reliable. That doesn't mean that there are not differing versions and details, however. The local news coverage, for instance, differs from Fults' account in some places. As noted above, both local newspapers say that the burglary took place at the H. Block store in Mabank, Texas, instead of Kaufman. The two towns are about twenty miles apart. There are also several names in the news reports that are different from Fults' version. The overall story, however, agrees with Fults in most other areas. For the local news coverage, see the *Kaufman Herald*, Kaufman, Texas, April 21 and 25, 1932, and *Mabank Weekly Banner*, Mabank, Texas, April 27, 1932.

12. Phillips, *Running with Bonnie and Clyde*, pp. 87–89.

13. Local news coverage says that they got stuck again. *Kaufman* (Texas) *Herald*, April 21, 1932.

14. Phillips, *Running with Bonnie and Clyde*, p. 89.

15. At this writing, the little jail is still there.

16. Phillips, pp. 89–93. *The Kaufman Herald*, Kaufman, Texas, April 21, 1932. *Mabank Weekly Banner*, Mabank, Texas, April 27, 1932.

17. For a detailed account of the Celina robbery, see Phillips, *Running with Bonnie and Clyde*, pp. 95–96, *Daily Courier-Gazette*, McKinney, Texas, April 21–23 1932. *Record Chronicle*, Denton, Texas, April 21–22, 1932.

18. Phillips, *Running with Bonnie and Clyde*, pp. 96–97.

19. *Mabank Weekly Banner*, Mabank, Texas, April 27, 1932.

20. Red, the tough guy, who ran away at Electra, Texas, later turned up in the McKinney jail with Jack and "Fuzz," as well as Ralph Fults. Phillips, *Running with Bonnie and Clyde*, p. 98.

CHAPTER 14

1. Phillips, *Running with Bonnie and Clyde*, pp. 93–95.

2. Fortune, *Fugitives*, p. 102.

3. Ibid., p. 109.

4. Marie Barrow comments to Jonathan Davis.

5. *The Kaufman Herald*, Kaufman, Texas, April 25, 1932. *Mabank Weekly Banner*, Mabank, Texas, April 27, 1932.

6. Fortune, *Fugitives*, pp. 96-97.

7. Ibid., p. 98.

8. Ibid., pp. 99–102. Text supplied courtesy Bob Fischer and Renay Stanard.

9. This may have gone back to 1929, when Clyde, Frank

Clause, and others were burglarizing places in the Hillsboro and Waco area.

10. Phillips, *Running with Bonnie and Clyde*, pp. 100–101.

11. Jack Hammett, interviewed by John Neal Phillips, February 20, 1982. See also Phillips, *Running with Bonnie and Clyde*, pp. 99–100, 109–110.

12. Underwood, *Depression Desperado*, p. 36.

13. Marie Barrow statement to Jonathan Davis.

14. Fortune, *Fugitives*, p. 109.

Chapter 15

1. Underwood, *Depression Desperado*, p. 10.

2. Ibid., p. 31.

3. Marie Barrow statement to Jonathan Davis.

4. Ibid.

5. Blanche Barrow interview by John Neal Phillips. November 18, 1984.

6. Underwood, *Depression Desperado*, p. 11.

7. Marie Barrow, statement to Jonathan Davis.

8. *Dallas* (TX) *Morning News*, July 22, 1932.

9. Ibid., July 28, 1932.

10. Fortune, *Fugitives*, p. 111.

11. Phillips, *Running with Bonnie and Clyde*, p. 102.

12. Underwood, *Depression Desperado*, pp. 11–12. Marie Barrow statement to Jonathan Davis.

13. Ibid., p. 12. Ross Dyer is also mentioned in Cumie T. Barrow's unfinished manuscript.

14. Phillips, *Running with Bonnie and Clyde*, pp. 103–104. Phillips' account is based on personal interviews with two of the people present at the time.

15. Clyde and Raymond were certainly in the group. Underwood includes Dyer, as does Cumie Barrow in her manuscript. Another man, James Acker, was picked up near Durant, Oklahoma, during the search. He had been wounded, but there is no indication he was involved. JRK

See: Underwood, pp. 12–13. Cumie T. Barrow unfinished manuscript. *Atoka* (OK) *Indian Citizen-Democrat*, August 11, 1932.

16. Ralph "Duke" Ellis interview by Art Weinreich.

17. *Atoka* (OK) *Indian Citizen-Democrat*, August 11, 1932. The words "You four" are quoted in the newspaper. We know that Clyde and Ray were in the car and Ross Dyer (alias Everett Milligan) was on the dance floor. The number four may have been referring to a couple of local men—maybe suppling the whiskey—or there may have been a fourth man with Clyde whose identity is unknown.

18. Ibid.

19. Ralph "Duke" Ellis interview by Art Weinreich.

20. *Atoka* (OK) *Indian Citizen-Democrat*, August 11, 1932.

21. Cumie T. Barrow, unfinished manuscript.

22. *Atoka* (OK) *Indian Citizen-Democrat*. August 11, 1932.

23. Ken Butler, "The Barrow Gang's Crimes in Oklahoma," *Oklahombre's Journal* 10 (Winter 1999).

24. Cumie T. Barrow, unfinished manuscript.

25. Butler, "The Barrow Gang's Crimes in Oklahoma," p. 11.

26. Clyde and Raymond were both firing. They really didn't know which one had fired the shot that killed Moore. Fortune, *Fugitives*, p. 120. Cumie T. Barrow, unfinished manuscript.

Chapter 16

1. Cumie T. Barrow, unpublished manuscript.

2. *Atoka*(OK) *Indian Citizen-Democrat*, August 11, 1932.

3. Marie Barrow statement to Jonathan Davis.

4. *Atoka*(OK) *Indian Citizen-Democrat*, August 11, 1932.

5. Fortune, *Fugitives*, p. 117.

6. Bonnie's mother's address given in Phillips, *Running with Bonnie and Clyde*, p. 105.

7. Ibid. The unidentified man was known to the Barrow family only as a friend of Clyde's. Most sources believe the man to have been Raymond Hamilton. JRK

8. Underwood, *Depression Desperado*, p. 15.

9. Phillips, *Running with Bonnie and Clyde*, p. 105.

10. Fortune, *Fugitives*, p. 124.

11. Ibid., p. 123.

12. Phillips, *Running with Bonnie and Clyde*, p. 106.

13. Ibid.

14. Hinton, *Ambush*, p. 22.

15. Phillips, *Running with Bonnie and Clyde*, pp. 106, 338n77.

16. Ibid.

17. Ibid., p. 107.

Chapter 17

1. Marie Barrow conversations with Jonathan Davis.

2. Fortune, *Fugitives*, p. 127.

3. The information about the beginning of the federal involvement with Bonnie and Clyde is from the Official FBI website.

4. Fortune, *Fugitives*, p. 127.

5. Ibid., p. 128.

6. Underwood, *Depression Desperado*, pp. 17–18.

7. The account of the killing of Howard Hall is from the *Sherman* (TX) *Daily Democrat*, October 12–13, 1932.

8. Ibid., May 1, 1977.

9. Fortune, *Fugitives*, p. 129.

10. The first suggestion that a woman was present was made in the "Bloody Barrows" series (*True Detective*, June 1934). It appears later in Hinton, *Ambush*, p. 24, and Treherne, *The Strange History of Bonnie and Clyde*, p. 79, and possibly others. One author, while not involving Bonnie, assumes that Clyde was the killer and even gives the names of the two men with him as Frank Hardy and Hollis Hale. Unfortunately, he gives no basis or sources for this information, so again we are left with only speculation and no hard evidence. Milner, *The Life and Times of Bonnie and Clyde*, p. 47ff.

11. Interview with Walter Enloe: Sherman, Texas, *Sherman Democrat*, May 1, 1977; L. C. Barrow arrest record provided by Barrow family members.

12. Fortune, *Fugitives*, p. 129.

13. Ibid., 130.

14. Ibid.

15. *Carthage* (MO) *Evening Press*, November 30, 1932.

16. Ibid. A few years before, Norton had driven off another bank robber with this same tactic.

17. Ibid. The newspaper only said that the loss was less than $300. Clyde told his family the amount was closer to $100. Fortune, *Fugitives*, p. 131. Whatever the amount, after the split, only a few dollars went to each partner.

18. Ibid. Fortune, *Fugitives*, pp. 130–131.

19. Fortune, *Fugitives*, pp. 131–132.

CHAPTER 18

1. Phillips, *Running with Bonnie and Clyde*, pp. 109–110.

2. Jones, W. D. "Riding with Bonnie and Clyde," *Playboy* 15 no. 11, November 1968, p. 151. Jones, Voluntary Statement B-71.

3. Copy of W. D. Jones application for a social security number, provided by Bob Fischer.

4. This was the story Jones told. The Barrow family said that Jones was the one who asked to go along. Fortune, *Fugitives*, p. 132.

5. Phillips, *Running with Bonnie and Clyde*, p. 338n91.

6. Thirty-six years later, Jones would say that Clyde never liked getting his hands dirty. Jones, "Riding with Bonnie and Clyde," p. 160.

7. *Temple* (TX) *Daily Telegram*, December 27, 1932. Contrary to my version of the shooting, W. D. Jones always maintained that Clyde shot Doyle Johnson. He said that the old pistol Clyde gave him wouldn't even fire. Since Clyde wasn't around to protest, and Jones didn't want to be charged with murder, his position is understandable. Later authors are divided on the issue. The Barrow family always believed that W. D. did it. Almost all accounts say that Clyde was in the driver's seat at the time of the shooting, and the newspaper plainly says that the driver, whom Johnson was choking at the time, fired and missed. The fatal shot clearly came from across the car and was from a different gun (.45, not .38) than the one the driver fired. If this is true, it must have been Jones who fired the fatal shot.

8. Jones, *Riding with Bonnie and Clyde*, p. 160.

CHAPTER 19

1. This statement assumes that Clyde's involvement in the murder of Howard Hall is still unresolved.

2. Fortune, *Fugitives*, p. 134.

3. *Temple* (TX) *Daily Telegram*, December 27, 1932.

4. Phillips, *Running with Bonnie and Clyde*, p. 113.

5. Fortune, *Fugitives*, p. 134.

6. Phillips, *Running with Bonnie and Clyde*, p. 119.

7. Ibid., pp. 119–120.

8. W. D. Jones, in his statement to Dallas County officers in November 1933, said that they had picked up Bonnie's sister Billie, and that she was the one who went in and talked to Maggie Fairris. Jones, Voluntary Statement B-71.

9. This was surely one of Clyde's "whippit guns." It was simply a standard Remington Model 11 semiautomatic shotgun cut down on both ends. The barrel was cut back to about twelve to fourteen inches and the stock cut off just behind the pistol grip. Clyde did this himself with a hacksaw. He then attached a loop to the stock and slung it over his right shoulder. It hung down under his armpit and was covered by the overcoat. He could quickly "whip it out"—hence the name—and he had a five-shot weapon that, in close quarters, was absolutely deadly. It was, however, prone to exactly the kind of malfunction Clyde experienced on this occasion. Over his two-year run, he made many of these weapons. Several examples are known today, in 12, 16, and 20 gauge. At least four of the men killed by Barrow or his associates fell to this weapon.

10. Except where noted, the story of the gunfight at Lillian McBride's house is taken from Phillips, *Running with Bonnie and Clyde*, pp. 115–121. Phillips, in turn, quotes from several Dallas newspapers and other sources. This is one of the many times the author is deeply indebted to Mr. Phillips' excellent research.

CHAPTER 20

1. Sixteen months later, Bonnie and Clyde would be killed in a tan Ford V-8.

2. Author's interview with Roy Ferguson at Oronogo, Missouri, October 23, 2000.

3. The story of the kidnapping of Tom Persell comes from the *Springfield* (MO) *Daily News*, January 27–28, and the *Joplin* (MO) *Globe*, January 27, 1933.

CHAPTER 21

1. Phillips, *Running with Bonnie and Clyde*, p. 124.

2. Marie Barrow interview.

3. Fortune, *Fugitives*, p. 146.

4. Phillips, *Running with Bonnie and Clyde*, p. 341n51.

5. Ibid., p. 101.

6. Ibid., p. 337n44.

7. Ibid., p. 125.

8. At this point (late March 1933), Clyde had definitely been present at the scene of four murders (not counting his killing of "Big Ed" in prison), been an actual shooter in three of them, and may have fired the fatal shots twice. The murder of Howard Hall in Sherman, Texas, is a possible fifth incident, but the evidence is less convincing.

9. Throughout their two-year "career," Bonnie and Clyde ranged over a wide area of the Southwest and Midwest, but they were never out of communication with their families in Dallas for long. In this case, it seems that Buck and Clyde had no problem contacting each other.

10. *True Detective* magazine, "The Bloody Barrows," July 1934.

11. Milner, *The Life and Times of Bonnie and Clyde*, p. 62.

12. Fortune, *Fugitives*, p. 148.

13. Phillips, *Running with Bonnie and Clyde*, p. 129, Marie Barrow interview.

14. *Joplin* (MO) *Globe*, April 18, 1933.

15. Ibid., April 14, 1933.

16. Ibid.

17. Phillips, *Running with Bonnie and Clyde*, pp. 125–126.

18. Marie Barrow interview. Cumie T. Barrow, unfinished manuscript.

19. Ibid.

20. *True Detective* magazine, "The Bloody Barrows," July 1934.

21. Ibid.

22. *Joplin* (MO) *Globe*, April 15, 16, 18, 1933. The "whippit gun" modification was not invented by Clyde Barrow, but he used it extensively. At Neosho, he added a zipper on his pants leg to hold it in place.

23. *True Detective* magazine, "The Bloody Barrows," July 1934.

24. Marie Barrow interview.

25. *True Detectives,* "The Bloody Barrows," July 1934.

26. *Joplin* (MO) *Globe,* April 15, 1933.

27. Ibid.

28. Ibid., April 16, 1933.

29. Fortune, *Fugitives,* p. 149.

30. Phillips, *Running with Bonnie and Clyde,* p. 127.

31. These doors were not the "overhead"-type door we are familiar with but slid from side to side. Author's conversation with Dewayne L. Tuttle, current owner of the property, May 1999.

32. *Joplin* (MO) *Globe,* April 14, 1933.

33. Ibid., April 15, 1933.

34. Ibid.

35. There are two different views as to where Buck was when the shooting started. The original account in 1934 said Buck was upstairs on the couch. Fortune, *Fugitives,* p. 150. W. D. Jones, in his statement to Dallas police, said Buck was waiting when they got back to the garage, and he was the one trying to close the door. W. D. Jones, Voluntary Statement B-71. Officer DeGraff at first identified Buck ("the shorter of the two brothers") as the man with the shotgun but changed to Clyde the next day. *Joplin* (MO) *Globe,* April 15, 16, 1933. There is a third version that says Buck was out back washing the Marmon. This would have made it impossible to get past the officers and into the house to help get everyone out. As stated earlier, the only weak spot in this place Clyde had picked for a hideout was that it had no back door. (Author's personal inspection of the scene and conversation with the present owner, May 1999.)

36. *Joplin* (MO) *Globe,* April 14, 1933. Clyde was indeed hit in this gunfight, but probably not by Kalher's last bullet. Kalher thought he hit the man in the back, while Clyde was hit in the chest by an almost spent round that lodged just under the skin. Fortune, *Fugitives,* p. 151.

37. Phillips, *Running with Bonnie and Clyde,* p. 128.

38. *Joplin* (MO) *Globe,* April 15, 1933.

39. Ibid.

40. Ibid., April 14, 1933.

41. The early version of this story has Blanche screaming hysterically, running down the street with a bunch of cards still clamped in her hand. (Fortune, *Fugitives,* p. 150.) Everyone who knew Blanche, and Blanche herself in later years, denied this. She did go looking for the dog, but the police had stopped firing by that time. The witness statements at the time mentioned a woman walking out to the street, but nothing about screaming or hysterics. In the 1967 movie *Bonnie and Clyde,* Blanche is portrayed just as Jan Fortune wrote it in 1934— frightened out of her mind and running wildly down the street. Blanche sued the movie because of it. Blanche's personal opinion of the movie, given to Marie Barrow and author John Neal Phillips, was that "they made me look like a screaming horse's ass." (Marie Barrow statement to Sandy Jones).

42. Cumie T. Barrow, unfinished manuscript.

43. *Joplin* (MO) *Globe,* April 14, 1933.

44. Ibid., April 14, 15, 1933.

45. Ibid., April 15, 1933.

46. Ibid., April 14, 1933.

47. Phillips, *Running with Bonnie and Clyde,* p. 131.

CHAPTER 22

1. Phillips, *Running with Bonnie and Clyde,* p. 342n99. Fortune, *Fugitives,* p. 161.

2. Phillips, *Running with Bonnie and Clyde,* p. 133.

3. Ibid.

4. Except where mentioned in the notes above, the story of the Darby and Stone kidnapping comes from *Ruston* (LA) *Daily Leader,* April 27–29, 1933.

5. Cumie T. Barrow, unfinished manuscript.

6. The Ford had Indiana plates (625-096) issued to Carl Porter of Waveland. Logansport (IN) *Pharos Tribune,* May 12, 1933.

7. This account of the attempted robbery of the Lucerne State Bank was taken from the Logansport (IN) *Pharos Tribune,* May 12, 13, 1933.

8. Fortune, *Fugitives,* pp. 163–164.

9. The account of the Okabena, Minnesota, robbery is from *Okabena Press,* May 25, 1933. Copies of the newspapers courtesy Brian Beerman.

10. Cumie T. Barrow, unfinished manuscript. Fortune, *Fugitives,* p. 163.

11. The Strains' convictions are found in *Jackson* (MN) *Republic,* September 22, 1933, and the *Okabena* (MN) *Press,* February 27, 1936.

12. Cumie T. Barrow, unfinished manuscript. Fortune, *Fugitives,* p. 156.

13. The account of the visit at Commerce, Texas, is given in Fortune, *Fugitives,* pp. 156–167.

CHAPTER 23

1. When Jones was finally picked up by the law, he claimed to be almost a slave to Barrow. He denied ever being a party to any killing. There is, however, abundant evidence that he was a shooter in six gunfights and almost certainly killed at least one person and probably others during that time.

2. Cumie T. Barrow, unpublished manuscript. Their belief that Jones could just drop out of sight and not be connected with Bonnie and Clyde was probably based on the fact that all the news coverage referred to the third man as "unidentified." This would remain the case even after Jones really did leave them. Unfortunately for Jones, however, his face was featured in several of the pictures from the film recovered at Joplin, and his identification was a top priority. At this time, there was a lively discussion among several police departments as to who this fellow might be, and numerous requests for copies of the pictures were coming into the Joplin Police Department. Copies of these requests were provided the author by Lt. Jim Hounschell of the Joplin Police Department. Jones' identification was only a matter of time, no matter what he did.

3. *Amarillo* (TX) *Daily News,* June 12, 1933.

4. Fortune, *Fugitives,* p. 168.

5. Mrs. Cartwright eventually lost her thumb due to the wound. *Amarillo* (TX) *Daily News,* June 12, 1933.

6. Details of this incident from Gladys Cartrwright interview by Marty Black, Wellington, Texas, April 3-4, 2003. *Amarillo* (TX) *Daily News,* June 12, 1933. Some details from Fortune, *Fugitives,* pp. 168–171, and W. D. Jones, Voluntary Statement B-71.

7. Most other authors either state specifically or imply that Clyde drove directly from the bridge at Erick, Oklahoma, to the motel in Fort Smith, Arkansas, where Bonnie was finally seen by a doctor—a distance of about 300 miles. However, the Amarillo newspaper account and Jones' statement quoted above, plus the date of the theft of the car in their possession when they arrived in Fort Smith (*Fort Smith Southwest American*, June 26, 1933) make it clear that they arrived in Fort Smith four days after the wreck at Wellington and not a few hours later, as has been commonly stated.

CHAPTER 24

1. This street is now called Midland Boulevard. It turns into North Eleventh and is actually the part of U.S. 64, which runs through the city.

2. Interview with Ida Dennis. *Fort Smith (AR) Southwest Times Record*, October 5, 1975.

3. Phillips, *Running with Bonnie and Clyde*, p. 137.

4. In the interview with Mrs. Ida Dennis in note 2 above, Hazel is said to be a "teenager." In a telephone interview with the author (Summer 1999), Hazel Dennis Green's son and husband said that she was born in 1909—therefore twenty-four years old at the time—and had worked as a dietitian in a hospital.

5. Fortune, *Fugitives*, p. 173.

6. Interview with Ida Dennis. See note 2 above.

7. Cumie T. Barrow, unfinished manuscript.

8. Jeffery S. King, *The Life and Death of Pretty Boy Floyd* (Kent State University Press, Kent, Ohio, 1998), pp. 12–23.

9. Cumie T. Barrow, unpublished manuscript.

10. King, *The Life and Death of Pretty Boy Floyd*, p. 138.

11. One of Pretty Boy's biographers states that Bonnie and Clyde had sent word that they admired him and wanted to work with him on a bank job. He says that Floyd never met Clyde Barrow and never considered working with him. "Those two give all of us a bad name," Floyd is said to have told his relatives. Even though Floyd told his kinfolks to have nothing to do with Bonnie and Clyde, on at least one occasion, two of Floyd's brothers are said to have helped them out when they came through the area, on the run from police. Michael Wallis, *Pretty Boy* (St. Martin Press, New York, 1992), p. 327.

12. King, *The Life and Death of Pretty Boy Floyd*, pp. 101–103.

13. Ibid., pp. 106–107.

14. Robert Unger, *The Union Station Massacre* (Andrew McMeel Publishing, Kansas City, 1997), pp. 36–43.

15. Clyde, of course, did exactly that—put both mothers and other family members in danger—on the many occasions that they met him out in the country over the two years he was on the run, but he seemed to think that this was a different situation.

16. Fortune, *Fugitives*, p. 174.

17. Hinton, *Ambush*, p. 54.

18. There is some confusion as to the exact date of Clyde's trip to Dallas. Both accounts cited in notes 16 and 17 above give the date as "Sunday, June 19th." That is not possible, since June 19, 1933, was a Monday. My guess is that Clyde made the trip on Sunday the 18th and was back in Fort Smith by midmorning on Monday the 19th, but the whole thing could have happened twenty-four hours later.

19. Most authors and other researchers have been mistaken as to the location of the bank that was robbed in Alma on June 22, 1933. There is a building on the east side of Fayetteville Avenue and closer to the railroad tracks that says "Commercial Bank" on a pillar out front and in a mosaic at the entrance. This was indeed the home of the Commercial Bank until early 1930, but it was actually the second bank established in town. As a result of the many bank failures brought on by the depression, the Commercial Bank and the older institution, the Bank of Alma (established in 1902), merged several months after the stock market crash in October 1929, simply for survival. The resulting business was called "The Commercial Bank of Alma" and took over the larger Bank of Alma building one block south and on the west side of the street. The old Commercial Bank building was taken over by two sisters named Miller and at the time of the 1933 robbery was probably the only ladies' dry goods store with a walk-in vault. Both buildings still stand in downtown Alma. This information comes from a speech given by Charles R. Starbird, attorney for the Commercial Bank, Alma, Arkansas, on his retirement. Speech by C.R. Starbird, Fort Smith, Arkansas, 1981. Mr. Starbird was eighty-six years old at the time. Mr. Starbird became attorney for the bank in 1939 on the death of his father, Charles A. Starbird, who was also an attorney, a county judge, an original stockholder and founder of the Bank of Alma, and the author's great-grandfather.

20. *Fort Smith (AR) Times Record*, June 22, 1933, *Fort Smith (AR) Southwest American*, June 23, 1933. At the time of the robbery, there were no real suspects. When the presence of the "Barrow gang" became known, three days later, there was naturally some speculation that they were responsible, but local authorities didn't seem to give the theory much credence at the time and actually continued to pick up other suspects. Even so, several later authors credit Clyde and Buck with the job. The Barrows always denied the robbery, and their family say they would never have pulled their next robbery if they had $3,600 in their pockets (Fortune, *Fugitives*, p. 176). In fact, the safe was eventually recovered and the contents found intact (author's interview with Walter Patton Jr., summer 1995), so nobody got the money. No one was ever charged with the robbery.

21. *Van Buren (AR) Press Argus*, July 7, 1933.

22. *Fort Smith (AR) Southwest American*, June 26, 1933.

23. *Fayetteville (AR) Daily Democrat*, June 24, 1933. Phillip Steele, *The Family Story of Bonnie and Clyde* (Pelican Publishing Company, Gretna, LA, 2000), pp. 96–99.

24. James R. Knight, "Incident at Alma: The Barrow Gang in Northwest Arkansas." *Arkansas Historical Quarterly* 51 no. 4 (Winter 1997), p. 405.

25. All other accounts state that Salyers had only a pistol. For confirmation of the .30-30 in the fight, see *Fort Smith Times Record*, June 24, 1933, p. 3. Salyers owned a Winchester .30-30 (Model 1894, Sn# 929294) that he consistently claimed was the gun he used in the shootout. About 1960, he sold the rifle to Frank Parker of Alma. Marshal Humphrey's pistol, after an interesting journey, is now in the possession of the Alma Police Department.

26. Almost all other authors claim that the lawmen had set up a roadblock or at least shouted a warning to Wilson: Milner, *The Life and Times of Bonnie and Clyde*, p. 85, and

Miriam Allen deFord, *The Real Bonnie and Clyde* (New York, Ace Books Inc., 1968), p. 83. Deputy Salyers, in his only interview with the press, is quoted as saying that they had already passed Wilson and did not recognize the bandit car when it went by them. This was recorded within twenty-four hours of the event. *Fort Smith Times Record,* June 24, 1933.

27. The exact site was identified by Warren Blaylock of Alma, who saw it as a twelve-year-old boy. He lives today within a quarter-mile and walked over the ground with the author. Blaylock interview by author, March 1996.

28. The number-four buck shot is mentioned in *Van Buren* (AR) *Press Argus,* July 7, 1933.

29. This was the weapon referred to in the press simply as "a machine gun." It was heard firing by several people, and a number of empty shell casings and as many as 800 rounds of 30-06 ammunition were found at the site. *Fort Smith* (AR) *Times Record,* June 24, 1933.

30. The position of the cars, as well as the reconstruction of the gunfight which followed the wreck, is based on Salyer's account cited in note 26 above and other articles in both Fort Smith papers June 24 and following; the author's interview with Velma Humphrey, the marshal's daughter (summer 1995); an article by W. D. Jones, "Riding with Bonnie and Clyde," *Playboy,* November 1968, plus his Voluntary Statement B-71; and logical deductions from the few known facts. The author has also personally examined all the weapons used except the BAR. The license number, given in the phone call from Fayetteville police, appears in *Fort Smith Times Record,* June 24, 1933. Marvin I. Barrow, in an interview with Salyers and Crawford County Sheriff Albert Maxey, said that he shot the marshal. *Fort Smith Times Record,* July 26, 1933. Velma Humphrey said that her father, in the hospital, told her and the rest of the family, "As soon as I stepped out on the running board, he shot me." W. D. Jones, in his 1968 *Playboy* article, said that Salyers (whom he mistakenly thought only had a pistol) hit the horn button and took off two of his fingertips. This agrees with *Times Record,* June 24, 1933, which stated that Salyers' car, when recovered a few hours later, had a blood-stained driving wheel that had been hit by a bullet. Thirty-five years later, Jones was still impressed with Salyers' marksmanship. "That man could shoot," he said; Jones, *Riding with Bonnie and Clyde,* p. 165; B. C. Ames, as quoted in *Fort Smith Times Record,* June 24, 1933.

31. *Fort Smith* (AR) *Southwest American,* June 24, 1933. Author interview with William S. Farris, late 1995, early 1996.

32. He found one of Clyde's "whippit guns," a sawed-off Remington Model 11 .12-gauge shotgun, a .45 automatic with U.S. government markings, two coats, one pair of dark glasses, six license plates, a large siren, and 800 rounds of ammunition. *Fort Smith* (AR) *Times Record,* June 24, 1933.

33. The Loftons' story appears several times in both Fort Smith papers beginning June 24, 1933. In *Fort Smith Times Record,* July 31, 1933, Mark Lofton identified Buck as the one who "did the talking" when their car was taken. Mrs. Brewer's identification as a witness is in *Southwest American,* June 26, 1933.

34. Salyers' phone call had alerted the sheriff's department. Velma Humphrey, the marshal's daughter, on her way home from her job in Fort Smith, crossed the bridge into Van Buren just before 7:00 P.M. and saw her uncle, Dave Biggerstaff, standing at the foot of the bridge with a shotgun. She was still talking to him when the ambulance containing her father went past. Velma Humphrey interview.

35. *Fort Smith* (AR) *Southwest American,* June 24, 1933.

36. Jones, Voluntary Statement B-71; Marvin Barrow statement to Sheriff Albert Maxey, *Southwest American,* July 30, 1933.

37. *Fort Smith* (AR) *Southwest American,* June 26, 1933. *Fort Smith* (AR) *Times Record,* June 26, 1933.

38. Fortune, *Fugitives,* p. 180. In this passage, Fortune has Billie Mace, Bonnie's sister, telling in some detail about the move to the woods. Unfortunately, she also insists that Clyde wouldn't move Bonnie on Friday night but waited until Saturday evening the 24th. This is contradicted by both Fort Smith newspapers cited above and by the fact that, by Saturday evening—when Billie said they left—Sebastian County Sheriff John Williams had already discovered they had stayed at the motel, contacted the sheriff in Wellington, Texas, and suspected that the Barrows were involved. *Fort Smith* (AR) *Times Record,* June 26, 1933, Letter from Ed Portley, chief of detectives, Joplin, Missouri, to John B. Williams, sheriff, Sebastian County, Arkansas, June 26, 1933. In Buck Barrow's statement to Sheriff Maxey cited in note 36 above, he confirms the move to eastern Oklahoma before the attack on Mrs. Rogers.

39. *Fort Smith* (AR) *Southwest American,* June 26, 1933, Crawford County wanted poster issued by Sheriff Albert Maxey. Letter from Georgia Cagle to Art Weinreich. Mrs. Cagle, as a young girl, knew Clara Rogers and described how her injuries affected her for years afterwards. Copy of letter provided by Art Weinreich.

40. *Fort Smith* (AR) *Times Record,* June 26, 1933.

41. Clyde's mother states that the selection of Dr. Field's car was no accident. Clyde targeted the doctor's car in hopes he could get the medical bag as well. With Bonnie's condition still serious, they put it to good use. Cumie T. Barrow, unfinished manuscript.

42. Phillips, *Running with Bonnie and Clyde,* p. 139.

43. The story of Dr. Fields' car and medical bag is found in *Enid* (OK) *Morning News,* July 27, 1933. Until the bag was recovered at the site of the Platte City gunfight, the authorities thought drug addicts had stolen the car for the medical bag.

44. The story of the overalls chase is in the *Fort Smith* (AR) *Southwest American,* June 28, 1933. Even though, in retrospect, this seems like a comic episode, it was deadly serious. Since the use of the machine gun in the Alma fight, Crawford, Sebastian, and Washington county officials had all rushed to provide automatic weapons for their officers. This may have been the first time the officers had them available, and had the shopkeeper or his friend made one wrong move, they could have been just as dead as Marshal Humphrey. The Keystone Cops characterization was first used by John Treherne in *The Strange History of Bonnie and Clyde.* He is the only other author who mentions the story, but he places it in his account as if it happened before Buck and W. D. got back to the motel, not four days later.

45. Phillips, *Running with Bonnie and Clyde,* p. 139.

Chapter 25

1. *Enid* (OK) *Morning News,* July 9, 1933.
2. Phillips, *Running with Bonnie and Clyde,* p. 139.

Phillips' information here is from W. D. Jones' statement to the Dallas Sheriff Department. Jones says they got forty-six pistols and only mentions "several rifles" and several cases of ammunition. Whatever the actual number, it was a huge haul.

3. The way the Browning automatic rifle is built, Clyde could cut the barrel back as far as the gas tube that runs beneath the barrel and not affect the functioning of the weapon. The stock, however, has a metal recoil tube inside it, so only an inch or two could be cut off there—unlike the shotguns Clyde cut down. The result was certainly a more compact weapon, but one still too large to be used with ease inside a car. This was demonstrated to the author by Sandy Jones, a collector who owns exact replicas of both a "scattergun" and a 1934 Ford.

4. Jones, "Riding with Bonnie and Clyde," *Playboy*, November 1968, p. 162.

5. Fortune, *Fugitives*, p. 183.

6. The account of the Fort Dodge gas station robberies is from the *Fort Dodge* (IA) *Messenger*, July 18, 1933. Buck Barrow was identified a week later by Anderson and Chevalier when they viewed him in the Perry, Iowa, hospital after the Dexter fight. *Fort Dodge* (IA) *Messenger*, July 25, 1933.

7. Phillips, *Running with Bonnie and Clyde*, p. 140.

8. Delbert Crabtree, as quoted in *Kansas City* (MO) *Star*, September 17, 1978.

9. Phillips, *Running with Bonnie and Clyde*, p. 140–141.

10. Ibid., p. 141.

11. Ibid., pp. 141–142.

12. Ibid., pp. 142–143.

13. Kermit Crawford interview by John Neal Phillips, April 19, 1983.

14. Ibid.

15. Cumie T. Barrow, unfinished manuscript.

16. Phillips, *Running with Bonnie and Clyde*, p. 143.

17. Ibid., pp. 143–145. Crawford interview.

18. Ibid., p. 145. *Enid* (OK) *Morning News*, July 27, 1933.

19. Fortune, *Fugitives*, p. 189.

CHAPTER 26

1. Buck Barrow's statement to his brother Clyde, as recalled by Blanche Barrow in 1984 interview.

2. Crawford interview. Fortune, *Fugitives*, pp. 188–189.

3. Phillips, *Running with Bonnie and Clyde*, p. 145.

4. Ibid., pp. 146–147.

5. *Perry* (IA) *Daily Chief*, July 24, 1933.

6. Phillips, *Running with Bonnie and Clyde*, pp. 148–149.

7. Ibid., p. 149.

8. Ibid., pp. 149–150.

9. Fortune, *Fugitives*, pp. 190–191.

10. Phillips, *Running with Bonnie and Clyde*, p. 150.

11. In spite of his reputation as a cold-blooded killer, there is a good chance that this first volley of automatic weapons fired by Clyde was intended to go right where it did—over the lawmen's head. Several times, before and after Dexter, Clyde fired just to scare or intimidate when he could have easily killed instead. Several people later commented that if the Barrow's aim had been better, they could have "mowed down the whole line." *Dallas Center* (IA) *Times*, August 3, 1933. Of course, there is also the possibility that Clyde was trying his best from the start and fired high in the heat of the moment.

12. Dr. Keller was near Riley when he was hit, and several bullets cut the brush around him. Dr. Keller later said, "Three or four bullets hit this little sapling by me. The trees weren't big enough to hide behind—never are when you're being shot at." *Des Moines* (IA) *Sunday Register*, March 17, 1968.

13. Phillips, *Running with Bonnie and Clyde*, pp. 150–151. Jones, Voluntary Statement B-71.

14. Ibid., pp. 151–152. Fortune, *Fugitives*, pp. 192–193.

15. Ibid., p. 152.

16. Ibid., pp. 152–153. Fortune, *Fugitives*, p. 197.

17. Ibid., pp. 154–155.

18. Later, the lawmen found that Buck's pistol, a .45 automatic, had ammunition in the magazine but Buck had been unable to chamber a round, so the pistol wouldn't have fired. *Des Moines* (IA) *Sunday Register*, March 17, 1968.

19. Ibid., p. 155.

20. The story of Buck and Blanche's trip to Dexter and the examination by the doctors is from a letter written by Dr. Keith Chapler forty-one years later to Alanna Nash, a writer in Louisville, KY. Chapler letter courtesy of Sandy Jones.

21. Chapler letter. Medical bulletin issued by Drs. Chapler and Osborn as given in the *Perry* (IA) *Daily Chief*, July 25, 1933.

22. Jones, Voluntary Statement B-71.

23. Ibid., *Perry* (IA) *Daily Chief*, July 24, 1933. Valley Fellers got his Plymouth back but had to pay a $15 towing charge.

CHAPTER 27

1. *Perry* (IA) *Daily Chief*, July 26, 1933.

2. Ibid., July 25, 1933.

3. Ibid.

4. For the statement in Fortune claiming that Buck was there, see Fortune, *Fugitives*, p. 179. For Buck's denial to Sheriff Maxey, see *Ft. Smith* (AR) *Southwest American*, July 30, 1933.

5. In Hinton, *Ambush*, p. 39, Ted Hinton states that he and Bob Alcorn went to Joplin the day after the shooting in April when two officers were killed. There, he says, they viewed the pictures left behind by the gang and positively identified W. D. Jones (April 14, 1933). In spite of this statement, there is no evidence that W. D. Jones' identity was known to any law enforcement agency involved in any of the incidents during the rest of that summer, that is, the Ruston, Louisiana, kidnapping, the Wellington, Texas, wreck, or the Alma, Platte City, or Dexter gunfights. The third man is always listed as "unidentified" and great effort was put forth to find his real name. Either Hinton is mistaken or the Dallas authorities kept the information to themselves until mid-November, when Jones was captured in Houston.

6. Phillips, *Running with Bonnie and Clyde*, pp. 305–306.

7. *Fort Smith* (AR) *Southwest American*, July 29, 1933.

8. These were the same two witnesses who, one month earlier, had "positively" identified Clyde as the machine gunner.

9. Ibid., July 30, 1933.

10. Knight, *Incident at Alma*, p. 424.

11. Ibid.

12. Bud Russell, "The Clyde Barrow–Bonnie Parker Harboring Case," unpublished manuscript provided by Robert Russell. In this manuscript, Russell says that the armory robbery was on August 20, 1933, at Plattsville, Illinois, and that

they got three BARs and several .45 automatics. While robbery of an armory would be the natural thing for Barrow to do, no evidence has been found for this particular incident.

13. Jones, Voluntary Statement B-71. Jones, *Playboy*, "Riding with Bonnie and Clyde," November 1968.

14. Marie Barrow, statement to Jonathan Davis.

15. Bud Russell, "The Clyde Barrow–Bonnie Parker Harboring Case," unpublished manuscript.

16. Jones, *Playboy*, "Riding with Bonnie and Clyde," November 1968.

CHAPTER 28

1. Fortune, *Fugitives*, p. 205.

2. Marie Barrow, conversations with Jonathan Davis.

3. Fortune, *Fugitives*, p. 207.

4. Ibid., p. 209.

5. Marie Barrow, conversations with Jonathan Davis.

6. Fortune, *Fugitives*, pp. 210–211.

7. Marie Barrow, conversation with Jonathan Davis.

8. Phillips, *Running with Bonnie and Clyde*, pp. 162–163.

9. Cumie T. Barrow, unfinished manuscript.

10. Phillips, *Running with Bonnie and Clyde*, p. 163. Fortune, *Fugitives*, p. 212.

11. Hamilton, Floyd, *Public Enemy Number One* (Acclaimed Books, Dallas, TX, 1978), p. 25. Floyd Hamilton said that what Clyde saw was a tin can nailed to a fence post by an informant as a reference point for the lawmen.

12. Hinton, *Ambush*, p. 105.

13. Phillips, *Running with Bonnie and Clyde*, p. 167.

14. Cumie T. Barrow, unfinished manuscript.

15. Fortune, *Fugitives*, p. 213.

16. Depending on whom you believe, the car was a 1931 or 1932 four-cylinder coupe—Hinton, *Ambush*, p. 107. Phillips, *Running with Bonnie and Clyde*, pp. 164.

17. Fortune, *Fugitives*, pp. 214–215. Phillips, *Running with Bonnie and Clyde*, pp. 166–167.

18. Phillips, *Running with Bonnie and Clyde*, p. 165.

19. Jones says that he was working for a vegetable peddler in Houston and a boy who knew him turned him in to police. Jones, *Playboy*, "Riding with Bonnie and Clyde," November 1968, p. 165.

20. *Dallas* (TX) *Morning News*, November 24, 1933.

21. Ibid.

22. Ibid., November 23, 1933.

23. Hinton, *Ambush*, pp. 103–104.

24. Author's conversation with John Neal Phillips, March 2001.

CHAPTER 29

1. This quote is from Bonnie Parker's poem originally titled "The End of the Line" but better known as "The Story of Bonnie and Clyde."

2. This information is found in several sources and was confirmed to the author by Barrow family members. For Ted Hinton's version of the threats, and his reaction to them, see Hinton, *Ambush*, pp. 113–114. See also Fortune, *Fugitives*, pp. 215–217. Marie Barrow believed that Clyde also had a strong opinion about the identity of the informer, but she doubted

that he was angry enough to take revenge. Phillips, *Running with Bonnie and Clyde*, p. 167.

3. Fortune, *Fugitives*, pp. 140–141.

4. If, in fact, Clyde actually considered murdering the sheriff and the deputies, which Marie Barrow doubted, he was talked out of it by either his sister Nell (Fortune, *Fugitives*, pp. 216–217), or Floyd Hamilton (Phillips, *Running with Bonnie and Clyde*, p. 167).

5. Underwood, *Depression Desperado*, p. 32.

6. Ray received 263 years for various crimes, and a three-year suspended sentence was reinstated, making a total of 266 years. Phillips, *Running with Bonnie and Clyde*, pp. 160, 347n3.

7. Underwood, *Depression Desperado*, p. 41.

8. Phillips, *Running with Bonnie and Clyde*, p. 168.

9. Mullins later said that the trusty's name was Fred Yost. Lee Simmons, *Assignment Huntsville* (University of Texas Press, Austin, TX, 1957), p. 125. Floyd Hamilton and Ralph Fults both said that the trusty was Aubrey Skelly, the same building tender who helped Clyde kill "Big Ed" several years before. Phillips, *Running with Bonnie and Clyde*, p. 168, and Ralph Fults, conversations with John Phillips.

10. Phillips, *Running with Bonnie and Clyde*, p. 167. Ralph Fults, conversations with John Phillips. Jack Hammett, interview by John Phillips, February 20, 1982.

11. Ibid., pp. 159–160.

12. Ibid.

13. Ralph Fults, conversations with John Phillips.

14. Patrick M. McConal, *Over the Wall* (Eakin Press, Austin, TX, 2000), p. 92.

15. Floyd Hamilton much later claimed that Clyde was "too yellow" to plant the guns himself. Phillips, *Running with Bonnie and Clyde*, p. 168, 349n42. In fact, Clyde was afraid that Mullins might have sold him out to the authorities and set up an ambush. He had just been set up six weeks before and so was understandably suspicious. Simmons, *Assignment Huntsville*, p. 167.

16. McConal, *Over the Wall*, pp. 92–93.

17. Ibid., pp. 84–86.

18. *State of Texas vs. Henry Methvin*, no. 831, Fall term, 1930.

19. Jack Hammett, interviewed by John Neal Phillips February 20, 1982. Hammett, a friend and sometime partner of Clyde Barrow and Ralph Fults, knew Methvin at Eastham.

20. McConal, *Over the Wall*, pp. 64–68.

21. Phillips, *Running with Bonnie and Clyde*, p. 172.

22. Simmons, *Assignment Huntsville*, p. 121.

23. Underwood, *Depression Desperado*, p. 43. An alternative version says that the guns were hidden in a woodpile and not brought into the prison at all. Hugh Kennedy, who saw the whole thing, takes the middle ground. He says that Hamilton pulled his gun from a woodpile, but that Palmer had his gun on his person. I tend to believe that both guns were together, and, if one was brought in, both were. JRK

24. McConal, *Over the Wall*, p. 94.

25. Ibid. "Major" was his given name, not a rank. He was just a guard assigned a special duty.

26. Simmons, *Assignment Huntsville*, p. 115.

27. Crowson later said that he heard Palmer also say, "Don't you boys try to do anything," before he fired (McConal, *Over the Wall*, p. 99). Many believe that Palmer shot Crowson

as payback for beatings he had received from the guard. Whatever his motivation, there is no doubt that Palmer shot Crowson, and he never denied the shooting.

28. McConal, *Over the Wall*, pp. 94–97. An alternative version of the shooting of Crowson and Bozeman says that Palmer did it all. Floyd Hamilton, Ray's older brother, claimed that the magazine fell out of Ray's pistol before he could shoot. (Phillips, *Running with Bonnie and Clyde*, p. 170). Hugh Kennedy, who saw it happen, and Ray Hamilton's biographer both say that Ray shot Bozeman (Underwood, *Depression Desperado*, p. 43).

29. Simmons, *Assignment Huntsville*, p. 166.

30. McConal, *Over the Wall*, p. 97.

31. Phillips, *Running with Bonnie and Clyde*, p. 171.

32. Marie Barrow believed that only Raymond Hamilton was part of the original plan and that Methvin and Bybee were just last-minute additions who happened to be around at the time. The statements of both Ralph Fults and Jack Hammett to John Neal Phillips and the statement of Joe Palmer to Lee Simmons shortly before Palmer's execution all indicate that Henry Methvin and Hilton Bybee were part of the plan from the start. Whether this was known by Mullins—or even Clyde—is a valid question. If Clyde knew he was going to have to transport four men in addition to himself, Bonnie, and Mullins, why didn't he bring two cars? The extra men did seem to be a genuine surprise that caused an argument.

33. McConal, *Over the Wall*, p. 98.

34. Ibid.

35. Ibid., p. 100.

36. Ibid., p. 98.

37. Ibid., pp. 103–104.

38. Bud Russell, "The Clyde Barrow–Bonnie Parker Harboring Case," unpublished manuscript.

39. Cumie T. Barrow, unfinished manuscript.

Chapter 30

1. Some sources say that Raymond Hamilton was on the hook for the whole amount (Underwood, *Depression Desperado*, p. 41). Joe Palmer, who was part of the break, said that each of the four escapees promised $250 a piece. (Simmons, *Assignment Huntsville*, p. 165).

2. This happened February 2, 1934. *Storm Lake* (IA) *Pilot-Tribune*, February 1, 1934.

3. *Storm Lake* (IA) *Register*, January 23, 1934. *Storm Lake* (IA) *Pilot-Tribune*, January 25, February 1, 1934.

4. Simmons, *Assignment Huntsville*, p. 165.

5. Ibid.

6. Phillips, *Running with Bonnie and Clyde*, p. 172. Bybee was captured seven days after the Rembrandt job at Amarillo, Texas.

7. Cumie T. Barrow, unfinished manuscript. Mrs. Barrow says that they robbed a filling station and took a 1933 Dodge. In view of the witnesses at the bank job in Poteau, Oklahoma, the next day, she was mistaken about the make of the car.

8. Simmons, *Assignment Huntsville*, p. 166.

9. There is a photograph of Clyde Barrow and Henry Methvin, both dressed almost exactly as this man was described, taken in early February 1934. Phillips, *Running with Bonnie and Clyde*, p. 184.

10. The story of the Poteau, Oklahoma, robbery is found in the *Fort Smith* (AR) *Southwest American*, January 26, 1934. In addition to the descriptions and modus operandi matching the Barrow gang, this robbery is attributed to them by Clyde's mother in her unfinished manuscript and by Jimmy Mullins in his testimony at the harboring trial in early 1935. Bud Russell, unpublished manuscript, p. 13.

11. This story was told to John Neal Phillips by Ralph Fults. Phillips, *Running with Bonnie and Clyde*, p. 172. Phillips tells the story as if everything happened in a few days. In fact, it was two months before Joe Palmer's plan was finally carried out.

12. Phillips, *Running with Bonnie and Clyde*, p. 172.

13. Simmons, *Assignment Huntsville*, p. 167.

14. Phillips, *Running with Bonnie and Clyde*, p. 173.

15. *Des Moines* (IA) *Sunday Register*, March 17, 1968. The 1934 Iowa plates—13-1234—were not used in the Knierim robbery but would be used in a later robbery at Everly, Iowa, and finally be found in the death car at Gibsland, Louisiana. Additional information provided by Mike Woltz of Des Moines, Iowa.

16. The account of the Knierim, Iowa, bank robbery appears in the *Fort Dodge* (IA) *Messenger*, February 1–6, 1934.

17. Ibid., February 6, 1934. All the normal skepticism about eyewitness testimony and identification from photos applies here as well, but nothing in the description of the number and makeup of the suspects (three men and one woman) is inconsistent with what we know about the gang at that point.

18. *Methvin vs. Oklahoma*, A-9060. Although Clyde Barrow would later claim that Raymond Hamilton was "yellow" because he hid in the floorboard during this gunfight, afraid of getting shot, at least one of the lawmen would later testify that three men inside the car were shooting with rifles. Unless Clyde and Henry persuaded their hostage, Mr. Gunn, to join in the shooting, that means that Raymond was not hiding the whole time.

19. Cumie T. Barrow, unfinished manuscript.

20. Gene O'Dare was, at the time, doing ninety-nine years for helping Raymond rob the Carmine State Bank.

21. Phillips, *Running with Bonnie and Clyde*, p. 173. Floyd Hamilton interview with John Neal Phillips, July 18, 1981.

22. *Eastland* (TX) *Telegram*, February 20, 21, March 20, 1934.

23. Underwood, *Depression Desperado*, p. 47.

24. Ibid., p. 48.

25. The account of the R. P. Henry and Sons bank robbery is taken from Phillips, *Running with Bonnie and Clyde*, pp. 175–176.

26. Underwood, *Depression Desperado*, p. 48.

27. Phillips, *Running with Bonnie and Clyde*, p. 178.

28. Floyd Hamilton, *Public Enemy Number One* (Acclaimed Books, Dallas, TX, 1978), p. 34.

29. Phillips, *Running with Bonnie and Clyde*, p. 173. Fortune, *Fugitives*, p. 227.

30. Underwood, *Depression Desperado*, p. 49.

31. Hamilton, *Public Enemy Number One*, p. 34.

Chapter 31

1. That deputy was Bob Alcorn. Ted Hinton would later say that he was also working full time on Clyde from the time of

the Sowers ambush. Hinton did join the small group in time to be in on the final ambush, but the evidence points to his join-ing sometime in April 1934. Both Alcorn and Hinton were acquainted with the Barrow family—Hinton more so with Bonnie Parker—and were probably the only law officers who could identify Bonnie and Clyde on sight. See Phillips, *Running with Bonnie and Clyde*, pp. 202–203, and especially p. 335n21.

2. Simmons, *Assignment Huntsville*, p. 118. Phillips, *Running with Bonnie and Clyde*, p. 180.

3. This was actually Mrs. Ferguson's second time as gov-ernor. She also served from 1925 to 1927.

4. Simmons, *Assignment Huntsville*, pp. 126–127.

5. Information provided by Harrison Hamer, grandson of Harrison Lester Hamer and grandnephew of Frank Hamer.

6. Phillips, *Running with Bonnie and Clyde*, p. 201.

7. Ibid. Depending on whom you believe, Hamer either resigned in protest or was asked to resign for previous insubor-dination.

8. At least two other Texas Rangers were said to have been offered the job before Simmons went to Hamer. See Phillips, *Running with Bonnie and Clyde*, p. 354n3

9. Simmons, *Assignment Huntsville*, p. 128.

10. Phillips, *Running with Bonnie and Clyde*, p. 202.

11. Ibid.

12. There is some dispute about the dates involved. Hamer later said that he and Alcorn were in Bienville Parish by February 19 (Phillips, p. 202). Henry Methvin's mother and John Joyner, the go-between, testified that it was about the first of March (*Methvin vs. Oklahoma*, A-9060).

13. Phillips, *Running with Bonnie and Clyde*, p. 202. *Methvin vs. Oklahoma*, A-9060.

14. Joe Palmer thought that it was probably Henry's father, Ivy Methvin, who set everything up. He thought Henry liked Clyde too much to give him up. Simmons, *Assignment Huntsville*, p. 166.

15. *Methvin vs. Oklahoma*, A-9060. Lee Simmons seems to have expressed two different opinions on the subject. In a let-ter to Governor Ferguson on August 11, 1934, he states that he didn't think Henry knew about the pardon deal. In anoth-er letter, dated two days later, however, he states that Henry "gave to the authorities of Louisiana valuable information that led to the apprehension and capture" of Bonnie and Clyde. In the same letter, Simmons and Hamer both recommend not only a pardon for Henry, but the payment of a $500 reward. It's difficult to see how, if all of this is true, Henry did not know. Simmons, *Assignment Huntsville*, pp. 143–144.

CHAPTER 32

1. Phillips, *Running with Bonnie and Clyde*, p. 180. Simmons, *Assignment Huntsville*, p. 166.

2. Even after Bonnie's name began to be printed along with Clyde's, it was always in the order "Clyde Barrow and Bonnie Parker." Bonnie did get top billing in the *True Detective* series "The Inside Story of Bonnie Parker and the Bloody Barrows," but in *Fugitives*, the book supposedly from the family, except for page one, the caption at the top of every page is "The Story of Clyde and Bonnie."

3. Simmons, *Assignment Huntsville*, p. 166.

4. Ibid., pp. 165, 167.

5. *Marshall* (TX) *Evening Messenger*, April 5, 1934.

6. Ibid., April 3, 1934.

7. Ibid., April 4, 1934.

8. Ibid., April 5, 1934. Phillips, *Running with Bonnie and Clyde*, p. 172. After the murder, police interviewed Tom Cagle, a current inmate at Eastham named in the note as McNabb's "partner." He was reported to have mentioned one convict who might have done it, a prisoner who had been out of jail about three months, which would have fit Joe Palmer, but no name was given in the paper. McNabb's sister also said that he had mentioned one man who had threatened him while still at Eastham, but, again, no name is given.

9. As mentioned before, between January 25 and 30 seems the only time available for the trip to Houston. Before then, Palmer didn't have the money from the bank jobs to pay the lawyer. After that, he was separated from Clyde and the gang until after the furlough was granted.

10. Phillips, *Running with Bonnie and Clyde*, p. 172.

11. Underwood, *Depression Desperado*, p. 50.

12. Ibid., p. 51.

13. Phillips, *Running with Bonnie and Clyde*, p. 180.

14. Underwood, *Depression Desperado*, pp. 53–54.

15. Fortune, *Fugitives*, p. 229.

16. Ibid., p. 230.

17. *Dallas* (TX) *Morning News*, April 2, 1934.

18. Fortune, *Fugitives*, pp. 231–232. Phillips, *Running with Bonnie and Clyde*, p. 182.

19. This story, about the meeting of the two cars, is from Barrow family sources who wish to remain anonymous. The same sources maintain that the meeting itself was a plot to lure Raymond Hamilton. They say that word of the meeting had been passed to Hamilton, and that Clyde planned to kill him when he arrived. If so, the policemen who died may have saved Ray Hamilton's life.

20. *Dallas* (TX) *Morning News*, April 2, 1934.

21. Phillips, *Running with Bonnie and Clyde*, pp. 183, 351n21. In this passage, Phillips quotes from the *Dallas Evening Journal* as well as the *Dallas Morning News*.

22. Fortune, *Fugitives*, p. 236.

23. *Dallas* (TX) *Morning News*, April 2, 1934.

24. Fortune, *Fugitives*, p. 233.

25. Hamilton, *Public Enemy Number One*, p. 37.

26. Phillips, *Running with Bonnie and Clyde*, p. 185.

27. Fortune, *Fugitives*, pp. 232–233. It also seems that the kind of language supposedly used on Henry Methvin was not unusual for either Clyde or Bonnie. They probably watched their language around their mothers, but several people with whom they came in contact—either witnesses to robberies or hostages who had to ride with them for some distance—commented on the amount of profanity or "hard language" that was used.

28. Phillips, *Running with Bonnie and Clyde*, p. 184.

29. Ibid., p. 203.

CHAPTER 33

1. Hinton, *Ambush*, pp. 138–139.

2. Underwood, *Depression Desperado*, p. 58

3. *Miami* (OK) *Daily News-Record*, April 6, 1934.

4. Ibid., April 6, 8, 1934. Two years later, Boyd seems to have changed his story. At Henry Methvin's appeal of his death sentence, Boyd testified that the shooting "commenced from the car." *Methvin vs. Oklahoma*, #9060.

5. Ibid. Here again, Boyd changed his testimony. At Methvin's appeal, Boyd said that only one man jumped out of the car and did the shooting.

6. Ibid., April 8, 1934.

7. Ibid. Boyd told reporters that Clyde threatened to kill the people if they didn't get his car out of the ditch.

8. *Methvin vs. Oklahoma*, #9060.

9. *Miami (OK) Daily News-Record*, April 8, 1934.

10. Ibid., April 6, 1934. Despite the fact that Clyde knew full well that only one man had been shot (and Boyd later said that Barrow didn't know for sure that Campbell was dead until later), this is the exact quote that Mr. Butterfield gave to the police within a few hours of the event.

11. Ibid.

12. The warrant issued for the murder of Cal Campbell initially named "Clyde Barrow, Bonnie Parker, and John Doe, whose true name is unknown." This was amended to add Henry Methvin's name as the "John Doe" on September 12, 1934—just in time to arrest him in Shreveport, Louisiana.

13. *Miami (OK) Daily News-Record*, April 8, 1934.

14. Ibid. In addition to Oklahoma, Missouri, and Kansas, Texas authorities were notified to guard the crossings on the Red River in case they turned south.

15. Ibid. Boyd said that when Clyde heard the airplane, he said, "There's a bug up there," and got out to look for it.

16. Ibid., April 8, 1934. Phillips, *Running with Bonnie and Clyde*, p. 188. In spite of the sentiment offered by Clyde, Percy Boyd said that they joked about the shooting all afternoon.

17. Ibid. Phillips, *Running with Bonnie and Clyde*, p. 187.

18. Ibid. Boyd said that they seemed to have plenty of money and didn't bother to take $25 that he had on him at the time.

19. Ibid. This picture of Bonnie is one of the group of pictures developed by the *Joplin Globe* photography staff for the Joplin Police Department. They were on a roll of film found at the apartment in Joplin where two policemen were killed in April 1933. In another picture from the same roll, taken at the same time, you will see Bonnie pretending to "hold up" Clyde with a sawed-off shotgun. If you look closely, you can see the same cigar that Bonnie posed with between the fingers of Clyde's left hand. For the two pictures, see Steele, *The Family Story of Bonnie and Clyde*, pp. 74-75.

20. Ibid., Phillips, *Running with Bonnie and Clyde*, p. 187.

21. Fortune, *Fugitives*, p. 235.

Chapter 34

1. The original of this letter is on display at the Ford Museum, Dearborn, Michigan. Copy of the original provided to the author by Bob Fischer.

2. Phillips, *Running with Bonnie and Clyde*, p. 194. Bonnie and Clyde read newspapers and magazines constantly, to keep up with the press coverage they were getting. While they complained that much of it was inaccurate or sensationalized, they enjoyed seeing their names in print. It's easy to believe that Clyde would have written a letter like the one to Ford, just for the publicity, but the objective evidence all points to the letter being the work of someone else.

3. The account of the robbery of the First National Bank of Stuart, Iowa, is from the *Stuart (IA) Herald*, April 20, 1934.

4. Fortune, *Fugitives*, pp. 235–238. On page 234, Fortune says that the date of this family meeting was April 17, 1934. There is no doubt that they were 700 miles away, in Stuart, Iowa, robbing the First National Bank, thirty-six hours earlier. It's possible, with Clyde's driving style, for them to have made the trip, so I have put the family meeting on the day after the Stuart robbery, as *Fugitives* claims. It's also very possible that *Fugitives* is wrong about the date of the family meeting. There are many instances in Ms. Fortune's book where dates are incorrect. It is therefore possible that this family meeting came a few days before the Stuart robbery instead of one day after it. JRK

5. Simmons, *Assignment Huntsville*, p. 165.

6. Underwood, *Depression Desperado*, pp. 73–74.

7. Text of the letter from Phillips, *Running with Bonnie and Clyde*, pp. 189–190. Additional information from Underwood, *Depression Desperado*, pp. 64–65.

8. A copy of the original handwritten letter, from which this text is derived, was furnished the author by Bob Fischer.

9. For the text of this letter, see Hinton, *Ambush*, pp. 155–156.

10. Simmons, *Assignment Huntsville*, p. 166.

Chapter 35

1. The Warrens' address is from Phillips, *Running with Bonnie and Clyde*, p. 193. The details of the car are from Sandy Jones and Bob Fischer, *It's Death to Bonnie and Clyde*, Appendix 1. The author's information comes from an original limited edition of the work. It was later edited and published in the journal of the *Oklahombres*.

2. King, *The Life and Death of Pretty Boy Floyd*, pp. 90–91.

3. This occurred during the robbery of the Farmers and Miners Bank at Oronogo, Missouri, on November 30, 1932. Clyde exchanged a few shots with the teller inside the bank and with some townspeople during the getaway. No one was hurt. There was some shooting associated with the robbery of the bank at Lucerne, Indiana, and also Okabena, Minnesota, which the Barrow family says that Clyde and Buck did, even though others were convicted of the crime.

4. *Spencer (IA) News-Herald*, May 4, 11, 1934.

5. Ibid., May 11, 1934.

6. Ibid.

7. Simmons, *Assignment Huntsville*, p. 165.

8. Fortune, *Fugitives*, pp. 239, 240.

9. Ibid., p. 241.

10. Phillips, *Running with Bonnie and Clyde*, p. 216

11. Text of "The End of the Line" furnished by Bob Fischer.

12. Phillips, *Running with Bonnie and Clyde*, p. 195. Fortune, *Fugitives*, pp. 239–241.

13. Ibid., 195–196.

Chapter 36

1. *State of Texas vs. Henry Methvin*, no. 821, District Court of Refugio County, Fall Term, 1930.

2. Henry Methvin's relationship with Clyde Barrow is still something of a mystery after all these years. Joe Palmer, who had known them both through a lot of hard times, believed that Henry thought very highly of Clyde and would not have turned him in. When it came down to it, though, Henry almost certainly participated in the plan to ambush his friend in return for a pardon from the state of Texas. Henry was a more physically imposing man than Clyde; Henry, his brothers, and most of the other male Methvins were almost six feet tall or more, and Henry had shown many times that he was capable of violence. To this day, however, Henry's relatives say that he was afraid of Clyde Barrow. Henry seems to have admired Clyde but feared him at the same time. Henry surely realized how deadly it would be to cross him. Some Methvin family members feel that Henry saw himself as "riding the tiger" and looking for a way to get off. What finally happened in Bienville Parish, Louisiana, on May 23, 1934, seems to have been a demonstration of the fact that, in hard times, when lives are at stake, families look out for their own. Information about Henry Methvin was provided by Methvin family members who wish to remain anonymous.

3. The information on Henry Methvin's family was provided by Methvin family members and the Methvin Family Genealogy Forum.

4. Methvin family members.

5. LaVohn Cole Neal and Mildred Cole Lyons quoted in *Remembering Bonnie and Clyde* (Turquoise Film/Video Productions Inc., St. Louis, MO, 1994). Videotape.

6. Phillips, *Running with Bonnie and Clyde*, p. 188. In spite of the testimony of several witnesses, it should be noted here that the Barrow family never believed that Bonnie and Clyde used the Cole place as a hideout. They said it was much too isolated—with only one way in and one way out—for Clyde ever to let himself be caught there.

7. These two stories of home visits by Bonnie and Clyde are from the author's interview with Clemie Booker Methvin, age ninety-one, July 29, 2001. In these two instances, Clemie was an eyewitness.

8. Clemie Methvin interview. As indicated in the text, Clemie did not hear the story of the pregnancy from Bonnie herself, but from her sister-in-law, Emma, and other women who were in a position to hear it directly. Clemie's knowledge of the story at least shows that it was in circulation among people who knew Bonnie personally, perhaps for a few weeks before Bonnie's death.

9. Marie Barrow, statement to Jonathan Davis and Sandy Jones.

10. Phillips, *Running with Bonnie and Clyde*, pp. 203–204.

11. Ibid., p. 204.

12. Ibid., p. 197. Also p. 353n78. For an alternative version of the Majestic Cafe incident, see Hinton, *Ambush*, pp. 158–159. In this passage, Hinton tells essentially the same story about the Majestic Cafe but sets it on Saturday night, the 19th.

13. Ibid. For Ted Hinton's version, see Hinton, *Ambush*, pp. 163–167.

14. Ivy T. Methvin is often referred to by other authors as "Old Man Methvin," suggesting a decrepit senior citizen. In fact, in May 1934, Ivy Methvin was forty-nine years old—a year younger than Frank Hamer. Two accounts of the ambush

of Bonnie and Clyde are attributed to members of the posse—Frank Hamer and Ted Hinton. Neither of these accounts suggests that any of the Methvin family were anything but unwilling participants in the ambush, forced by the lawmen to help against their will. While it can be understood that the lawmen felt an obligation to protect their sources, other witnesses, official documents, and court records show that Henry Methvin, his father and mother, and John Joyner were, by their own admission, involved in the plan for almost three months before the outlaw couple were killed.

15. Phillips, *Running with Bonnie and Clyde*, p. 204.

16. LaVohn Cole Neal, quoted in *Remembering Bonnie and Clyde*, videotape. There is no way to know exactly when Ivy Methvin arrived at the ambush site, or when the disabled log truck was put in position. The first time we can definitely place Ivy at the scene is the encounter mentioned here with the school bus driver and his passengers at about 7:45 A.M. on Wednesday morning, about ninety minutes before the ambush. He may have been there from the first, or he may have just arrived. In any case, in spite of Hamer and Hinton's statements to the contrary, Ivy Methvin was not only present at the scene of the ambush but was standing by his truck, not handcuffed to a tree.

17. Phillips, *Running with Bonnie and Clyde*, pp. 204–205.

18. Alice Brock, quoted in *Remembering Bonnie and Clyde*, videotape.

19. Phillips, *Running with Bonnie and Clyde*, pp. 197 and 209.

20. Ibid., p. 205. Phillips says that each posse member had a BAR. That statement is disputed by several other sources. There were at least two other kinds of rifles present, in addition to the Monitor and one or two BARs. Some sources say that Hamer fired a .35 Remington. The Monitor is on display at the Texas Ranger Museum at Waco, Texas.

21. Ibid., pp. 205–206. Phillips, along with many other authors, says that the log truck was coming from the opposite direction (south to north). Buddy Goldston, driving the truck, said they were behind the gray car, going in the same direction. Buddy Goldston, quoted in *Remembering Bonnie and Clyde*, videotape. Goldston said, "When they [the gray Ford] stopped on top of the hill, I was intending to pass them, but I never got to the top of the hill before they went to shootin'." It's possible that Goldston's truck was the log truck mentioned and the other sources simply have the direction from which it came wrong. It's also possible that there were actually two vehicles, one coming from each direction.

22. Ibid., p. 205.

23. Prentis Oakley, statement to H. M. Parnell, quoted in *Remembering Bonnie and Clyde*, videotape.

24. Information about the rifle Oakley used is from Sandy Jones, a researcher who has interviewed the present owner. The position of the other four shots in Oakley's volley is from Jones and Fischer, *It's Death to Bonnie and Clyde*.

25. Buddy Goldston, quoted in *Remembering Bonnie and Clyde*, videotape.

26. In a book published thirteen years after Frank Hamer's death, there is a dramatic scene where Hamer steps out in plain view and demands, "Stick 'em up!" He is eye to eye with Bonnie and Clyde as both pick up weapons whereupon Hamer kills them both. While exciting, it bears little resemblance to

the facts as reported by eyewitnesses. John H. Jenkins and H. Gordon Frost, *"I'm Frank Hamer"* (The Pemberton Press, 1968), p. 232.

27. Jones and Fischer, *It's Death to Bonnie and Clyde.* This may be one of the most surprising findings of recent research, since previous authors have only mentioned shots fired into the left side and rear of the car. The holes in the right side, above the passenger window, appear in photos taken of the car at Arcadia, Louisiana, within a few hours of the ambush. Although Bob Alcorn is quoted in the *Dallas* (TX) *Morning News,* May 24, 1934, as saying that he fired into the right side, the most logical member of the ambush to have administered this coup de grâce would be Frank Hamer. Not only was he the last in line, and therefore closest to the car when it finally stopped, but, of all the posse members, he was the most consummate professional. The size and grouping of the holes is consistent with Hamer's Monitor rifle. There is no wound to Bonnie's face from the right listed in Dr. Wade's report, but in at least one picture of Bonnie, taken before any cleanup was attempted by the undertaker, a small entry wound can be seen in her right cheek, along with the large exit wound in the left.

28. Phillips, *Running with Bonnie and Clyde,* p. 206.

29. Hinton, *Ambush,* pp. 169–170, and Phillips, *Running with Bonnie and Clyde,* pp. 206 and especially p. 356n42.

30. Jones and Fischer, *It's Death for Bonnie and Clyde.* Jones and Fischer were allowed, by the current owners, to spend over an hour with the death car. Jones inspected it—inside and out. Their comments represent the latest and most thorough examination of the car itself and its forensic evidence.

31. Information on bullet wounds from a transcript of Dr. J. L. Wade's coroner's report found in Carroll Y. Rich, *The Death and Autopsy of Bonnie and Clyde* (Carroll Y. Rich, 1990) pp. 14–15. Transcript provided by Bob Fischer.

32. Phillips, *Running with Bonnie and Clyde,* p. 207.

33. Ibid. Joe Palmer later said that the Colt .45 double action was bought for Commerce, Oklahoma, police chief Percy Boyd. He had lost his sidearm when Bonnie, Clyde, and Henry Methvin had taken Boyd for a ride after the Commerce shooting. Bonnie and Clyde thought he was a brave man and promised to replace his pistol. Simmons, *Assignment Huntsville,* p. 166.

34. Ibid. Among the stolen license plates was one set—1934 Iowa 13-1234—that would tie Bonnie and Clyde to several bank robberies in western Iowa, committed from February through early May.

CHAPTER 37

1. Phillips, *Running with Bonnie and Clyde,* p. 207.

2. Buddy Goldston, *Remembering Bonnie and Clyde,* videotape.

3. Ibid.

4. Hinton, *Ambush,* p. 178.

5. Phillips, *Running with Bonnie and Clyde,* p. 209.

6. One of the witnesses described it as "a little ol' T model wrecker." Buddy Goldston, *Remembering Bonnie and Clyde,* videotape.

7. Ibid., Alice Brock quoted.

8. Ibid., Mildred Cole Lyons quoted.

9. Hinton, *Ambush,* p. 182.

10. Phillips, *Running with Bonnie and Clyde,* p. 132.

11. Rich, *The Death and Autopsy of Bonnie and Clyde,* p. 18.

12. Phillips, *Running with Bonnie and Clyde,* p. 210.

13. In the years following their death, there have been repeated references to "the Autopsy of Bonnie and Clyde." In fact, Dr. Wade lacked the time, the equipment, and the inclination to perform a standard autopsy on either body. What he did was simply an external examination, listing identifying marks (Clyde had two toes missing), tattoos (Bonnie had one; Clyde had four), scars (the scarring from the burns Bonnie suffered in the Wellington wreck eleven months before were evident on her right leg), and finally, listing the bullet wounds. For Clyde, he lists seventeen separate wounds, plus "several shots entering the left shoulder joint." For Bonnie, he lists twenty-six wounds, including three head or face shots. These numbers indicate "hits." Other sources list more "wounds," possibly by counting entry and exit wounds separately and therefore counting holes instead of bullet hits.

There is no mention of any diseases, or, in Bonnie's case, pregnancy. If the story circulating among the Methvin women was true, and Bonnie was "expecting" about the same time as Clemie Methvin (late December–early January), she could only have been eight to ten weeks pregnant. Even in a woman as small as Bonnie, Dr. Wade may not have been able to confirm that without an internal examination. Carroll Rich, who provides the best transcript of Dr. Wade's almost illegible notes, goes on to say that Dr. Wade not only ruled out Bonnie being pregnant but also found evidence of gonorrhea in both bodies (Rich, *The Death and Autopsy of Bonnie and Clyde,* p. 18). Carroll Rich, in a conversation with the author, said that Dr. Wade made these statements to him privately, in the late 1960s. No such statement appears in his notes made at the time.

The Barrow family believed that Bonnie was physically unable to have children. Marie Barrow, statement to Sandy Jones.

14. Phillips, *Running with Bonnie and Clyde,* p. 213.

15. Fortune, *Fugitives,* p. 246.

16. Marie Barrow, statement to Jonathan Davis.

17. Phillips, *Running with Bonnie and Clyde,* pp. 212, 214.

18. Ibid., p. 213. Rich, *The Death and Autopsy of Bonnie and Clyde,* p. 17.

19. Ibid.

20. Ibid.

21. Rich, *The Death and Autopsy of Bonnie and Clyde,* p. 17.

22. Ibid.

23. Phillips, *Running with Bonnie and Clyde,* p. 212.

24. Ibid., pp. 213–214. After it was all over, Conger's Furniture Store claimed that they sustained $500 in damages. Rich, *The Death and Autopsy of Bonnie and Clyde,* p. 18.

25. Ibid., p. 215.

26. Ibid., p. 216.

27. Ibid., pp. 216–217. Phillips, *Running with Bonnie and Clyde,* pp. 190–191. Fortune, *Fugitives,* p. 255.

28. Sparkman-Holts-Brand Funeral Home record book on display at Dallas Historical Society, September 2001.

29. Simmons, *Assignment Huntsville,* pp. 165–167. Phillips, *Running with Bonnie and Clyde,* p. 217.

30. Fortune, *Fugitives,* pp. 253–254.

31. Phillips, *Running with Bonnie and Clyde,* p. 217.

32. Hinton, *Ambush*, p. 190.

33. Phillips, *Running with Bonnie and Clyde*, p. 218.

34. In "The Story of Bonnie and Clyde," there is this stanza:
A newsboy once said to his buddy:
"I wish old Clyde would get jumped;
In these awful hard times
We'd make a few dimes
If five or six cops would get bumped."

35. Phillips, *Running with Bonnie and Clyde*, pp. 218–219.

36. During Bonnie and Clyde's career, the younger members of their families, who were still in school, were often taunted by students and teachers alike with questions such as "Well, have they killed that brother of yours yet?" Years later, Clyde's younger brother, L. C., was once pulled over for a minor traffic offense in Dallas. The policeman, after checking his driver's license, said, "Oh, you're one of those bad-ass Barrow boys!" This was twenty-five years after Clyde was dead and buried, so it's doubtful that the officer was old enough to remember it himself. Nonetheless, memories were long in the Dallas law enforcement community. Information from Barrow family members who wish to remain anonymous.

CHAPTER 38

1. Hamilton, *Public Enemy Number One*, p. 60.

2. Unless otherwise noted, the information presented here is from "The Clyde Barrow–Bonnie Parker Harboring Case," an unpublished manuscript by Bud Russell, transfer agent for the Texas Prison System. It is used by permission of Robert H. Russell.

3. Marie Barrow Scoma statement to Sandy Jones as well as others. Bonnie's shoes were size three and a half. Marie Barrow Scoma statement in *Remembering Bonnie and Clyde* video.

EPILOGUE

1. Information supplied by Barrow family members.

2. Barrow family members. *Dallas* (TX) *Times Herald*, September 17, 1938.

3. Barrow family members.

4. Ibid.

5. Ibid. Dallas (TX) *Morning News*, September 4, 1979.

6. Steele, *The Family Story of Bonnie and Clyde. Dallas* (TX) *Morning News*, February 7, 1999.

7. Davis, *Blanche Barrow: The Last Victim of Bonnie and Clyde*, p. 17.

8. Phillips, *Running with Bonnie and Clyde*, p. 306. Ken Holmes Jr., "On the Road to Gibsland," Barrow-Parker newsletter, May 1998.

9. *Dallas* (TX) *Morning News*, May 7, 1932.

10. The information on the life of Ralph Fults is taken from various pages of his excellent biography by John Neal Phillips, *Running with Bonnie and Clyde*.

11. McConal, *Over the Wall*, p. 145ff.

12. Phillips, *Running with Bonnie and Clyde*, pp. 308–309. Hamilton, *Public Enemy Number One*, various pages.

13. *Dallas* (TX) *Morning News*, November 24, 1933.

14. Ralph Fults in conversation with Floyd Hamilton and John Neal Phillips. July 18, 1981. Notes supplied by Mr. Phillips.

15. Phillips, *Running with Bonnie and Clyde*, p. 309.

16. William Daniel Jones police records, Houston, Texas. Provided by Joe Bauske.

17. Court records, Ottawa County, Oklahoma, concerning *State vs. Clyde Barrow, Bonnie Parker, and John Doe, whose true name is unknown—Henry Methvin*. Signed by John H. Venable, October 3, 1934.

18. Henry Methvin's Oklahoma prison record #32834. Copy provided by Mike Koch.

19. Clemie Booker Methvin interview.

20. McConal, *Over the Wall*, pp. 152, 161–162.

21. Ibid., p. 115.

22. Ibid., pp. 115–116.

23. Phillips, *Running with Bonnie and Clyde*, p. 308.

24. Information provided by the Dallas Historical Society. Research by John Neal Phillips.

25. Ibid.

26. Phillips, *Running with Bonnie and Clyde*, p. 309. Hinton, *Ambush*, back endpaper.

27. Information provided by the Dallas Historical Society. Research by John Neal Phillips.

28. Ibid.

29. Phillips, *Running with Bonnie and Clyde*, p. 312, plus additional research by Phillips for the Dallas Historical Society.

30. Dallas Historical Society research by John Neal Phillips.

31. Ibid., pp. 319–320.

32. "Boots" Hinton, conversation with author.

33. Gatewood, *Decker*, p. 368. Dallas Historical Society, research by John Neal Phillips.

34. Whitehead, "The Murder of Cal Campbell," *Oklahombres*, Spring 1997, vol. 8, no 3.

35. Clemie Methvin interview.

36. Ibid.

37. Phillips, *Running with Bonnie and Clyde*, p. 310.

38. Clemie Methvin interview.

39. Ibid.

40. Phillips, *Running with Bonnie and Clyde*, p. 313. *Boston* (MA) *Daily Record*, October 4, 1937.

APPENDIX TWO

1. Author Carroll Y. Rich gives slightly different numbers for a couple of items about the death car. He says the actual purchase price was $785.92 and gives the Kansas tag number as 3-17198. Mr. Jones says the tag number came from Mrs. Warren herself by way of Marie Barrow. As for the price, it's quite possible that Jess Warren negotiated a $50 discount from the list price. Rich, *The Death Car of Bonnie and Clyde*, p. 1.

APPENDIX FOUR

1. Phillips, *Running with Bonnie and Clyde*, pp. 67–70.

Bibliography

Public Documents

Crawford County, Arkansas wanted poster, issued by Sheriff Albert Maxey, late June 1933.

Department of Investigation wanted poster #1227, May 21, 1934.

Department of Investigation wanted poster #1211, October 24, 1933.

Hill County, Texas, wanted poster for Frank Albert Clause and Clyde Champion Barrow, May 1932.

Jones, William Daniel, Voluntary Statement B-71, Dallas County Sheriff's Department, November 18, 1933.

Methvin, Henry, vs. State of Texas, No. 831, District Court of Refugio County, Fall Term, 1930, vs. State of Oklahoma. A-9060.

Court record, Ottawa County, Oklahoma. Petition to have the name "Henry Methvin" replace the name "John Doe"on the arrest warrant for Clyde Barrow and Bonnie Parker, October 3, 1934.

Oklahoma Prison Record #32834, copy provided by Mike Koch.

Books and Articles

Butler, Ken. "The Barrow Gang's Crimes in Oklahoma." *Oklahombre's Journal* (Winter 1999).

Davis, Robert E., edited by Eugene Baker. *Blanche Barrow: The Last Victim of Bonnie and Clyde.* Waco, Texas: Texian Press, 2001.

deFord, Miriam Allen. *The Real Bonnie and Clyde.* New York: Ace Books, Inc., 1968.

Fortune, Jan I. *Fugitives: The Story of Clyde Barrow and Bonnie Parker, as Told by Bonnie's Mother (Emma Krause Parker) and Clyde's Sister (Nell Barrow Cowan).* Dallas, TX: The Ranger Press, 1934.

Gatewood, Jim. *Decker: A Biography of Sheriff Bill Decker of Dallas County, 1898–1970.* Garland, TX: Mullaney Corp., 1999.

Hamilton, Floyd. *Public Enemy Number One.* Dallas, TX: Acclaimed Books, 1978.

Helmer, William, with Rick Mattix. *Public Enemies: America's Criminal Past, 1919–1940.* New York: Checkmark Books, 1998.

Hinton, Ted, as told to Larry Grove. *Ambush: The Real Story of Bonnie and Clyde.* Austin, TX: Shoal Creek, 1979.

Holmes, Ken. "On the Road to Gibsland. Barrow-Parker Newsletter." May 1998.

Jenkins, John H., and H. Gordon Frost. *I'm Frank Hamer: The Life of a Texas Peace Officer.* Austin, TX: Pemberton Press, 1968.

Jones, William Daniel. "Riding with Bonnie and Clyde." New York: *Playboy,* vol. 15 no. 11, November 1968.

King, Jeffery S. *The Life and Death of Pretty Boy Floyd.* Kent, OH: Kent State University Press, 1998.

Knight, James R. "Incident at Alma: The Barrow Gang in Northwest Arkansas." *Arkansas Historical Quarterly* 51, no. 4 (Winter 1997).

McConal, Patrick M. *Over the Wall.* Austin, TX: Eakin Press, 2000.

Milner, E.R. *The Life and Times of Bonnie and Clyde.* Carbondale, IL: Southern Illinois University Press, 1996.

Phillips, John Neal. *Running with Bonnie and Clyde.* Norman, OK: University of Oklahoma Press, 1996.

Portley, Ed, as told to C. F. Waers. "The Inside Story of Bonnie Parker and The Bloody Barrows." *True*

Detective 22, nos. 3 through 8 (six-part series), June–November 1934.

"Remembering Bonnie and Clyde." Turquoise Film/Video Productions, Inc., St. Louis, MO: 1994. Videotape.

Rich, Carroll Y. "The Death and Autopsy of Bonnie and Clyde." Carroll Y. Rich, 1990.

———. "The Death Car of Bonnie and Clyde." Carroll Y. Rich, 1990.

Steele, Phillip W., with Marie Barrow Scoma. *The Family Story of Bonnie and Clyde.* Gretna, LA: Pelican Publishing Co., 2000.

Treherne, John. *The Strange History of Bonnie and Clyde.* London: Jonathan Cape Ltd., 1984.

Underwood, Sid. *Depression Desperado: The Chronicle of Raymond Hamilton.* Austin, TX: Eakin Press, 1995.

Unger, Robert. *The Union Station Massacre: The Original Sin of J. Edgar Hoover's FBI.* Kansas City, MO: Andrews McMeel, 1997.

Wallis, Michael. *Pretty Boy.* New York: St. Martin Press, 1992.

Webb, Walter Prescott. *The Texas Rangers: A Century of Frontier Defense.* Austin, TX: University of Texas Press, 2000.

Whitehead, Terry. "The Murder of Cal Campbell." *Oklahombres Journal* 8, no. 3 (Spring 1997).

Newspapers

Amarillo Daily News (Texas).
Daily Courier-Gazette (McKinney, Texas).
Daily Democrat (Fayetteville, Arkansas).
Daily Leader (Ruston, Louisiana).
Daily News-Record (Miami, Oklahoma).
Daily Telegram (Temple, Texas).
Dallas Center Times (Dallas Center, Iowa).
Dallas Morning News (Texas).
Dallas Times Herald (Texas).
Des Moines Sunday Register (Iowa).
Evening Press (Carthage, Missouri).
Fort Smith Times-Record (Arkansas).
Globe (Joplin, Missouri).
Herald (Stuart, Iowa).
Indian Citizen-Democrat (Atoka, Oklahoma).
Jackson Republic (Minnesota).
Kansas City Star (Missouri).
Kaufman Herald (Texas).
Mabank Weekly Banner (Texas).
Marshall Evening Messenger (Texas).
Messenger (Fort Dodge, Iowa).
Middletown Journal (Ohio).
Morning News (Enid, Oklahoma).
News-Herald (Spencer, Iowa).
Okabena Press (Minnesota).
Perry Daily Chief (Iowa).
Pharos Tribune (Logansport, Indiana)
Pilot-Tribune (Storm Lake, Iowa).
Press Argus (Van Buren, Arkanas).
Record Chronicle (Denton, Texas).
Register (Storm Lake, Iowa).
Sherman Daily Democrat (Texas).
Southwest American (Fort Smith, Arkansas).
Southwest Times Record (Fort Smith, Arkansas).
Springfield Daily News (Missouri).
Telegram (Eastland, Texas).
Waco Times-Herald (Texas).

Unpublished Papers and Letters

Barrow, Cumie T. Unfinished manuscript. Copy provided by Jonathan Davis.

Cagle, Georgia. Letter to Art Weinreich. Copy provided by Mr. Weinreich.

Chapler, Keith. Dexter, Iowa. Letter written to Alanna Nash. Copy provided by Sandy Jones.

Davis, Jonathan, Dallas, Texas. Unpublished manuscript based on interviews and conversations with Marie Barrow Scoma. Copy provided by Mr. Davis.

Phillips, John Neal. Research done for the Bonnie and Clyde Exhibit, Texas State Fair, September 2001. Notes provided by Mr. Phillips.

Jones, Sandy, and Bob Fischer. "It's Death to Bonnie and Clyde." Original, unpublished version, 1998.

Portley, Ed. Letter to Sebastian County, Arkansas, Sheriff John Williams, June 26, 1933.

Russell, Bud. "The Clyde Barrow–Bonnie Parker Harboring Case." Unpublished manuscript. Copy provided by Robert Russell.

Starbird, Charles R. Alma, Arkansas. Tape of speech at his retirement dinner. Fort Smith, Arkansas, 1981.

Interviews

Barrow, Blanche. Dallas, Texas. Interview by John Neal Phillips, November 18, 1984. Notes provided by Mr. Phillips.

Blaylock, Warren. Alma, Arkansas. Interviewed by author, March 1996.

Cartwright, Gladys. Wellington, Texas. Interviewed by Marty Black, April 3–4, 2003.

Crawford, Kermit. Platte City, Missouri. Interviewed by John Neal Phillips, April 19, 1983. Notes provided by Mr. Phillips.

Ellis, Ralph "Duke." Stringtown, Oklahoma. Interviewed by Art Weinreich. Text provided by Mr. Weinreich.

Farris, William S. West Lafayette, Indiana. Interviewed by author, January 1996.

Ferguson, Roy. Oronogo, Missouri. Interviewed by author, October 23, 2000.

Green, Bill. Fort Smith, Arkansas. Phone interview by author, July 1999.

Hamer, Harrison. Fort Worth, Texas. Interviewed by author, December 10, 2001.

Hamilton, Floyd. Dallas, Texas. Interviewed by John Neal Phillips, July 18, 1981. Notes provided by Mr. Phillips.

Hammett, Jack. Interviewed by John Neal Phillips, February 20, 1982. Notes provided by Mr. Phillips.

Hinton, S. J. "Boots." Dallas, Texas. Conversations with the author, September 2001.

Humphrey, Velma. Fort Smith, Arkansas. Interviewed by author, July 1995.

Knight, Hilda M. Alma, Arkansas. Author's mother and eyewitness to the getaway from the Alma, Arkansas, shooting of Marshal Henry Humphrey.

Methvin, Clemie Booker. (Location withheld by request.) Interviewed by author, July 29, 2001.

Patton, Walter, Jr. Alma, Arkansas. Interviewed by author, June 1995.

Scoma, Marie Barrow. Dallas, Texas. Interviewed by Jonathan Davis many times over a period of several years. Notes and manuscript provided by Mr. Davis.

Tuttle, Dewayne L. Joplin, Missouri. Interviewed by author, May 1999. Mr. Tuttle is the present owner of the apartment where the Joplin shooting took place.

Index

JAMES R. KNIGHT was born in 1945 in Alma, Arkansas, site of one of the Barrow Gang's shootouts. He is a 1967 graduate of Harding University, a veteran of the U.S. Air Force, and, for the past thirty years, has been a pilot for Federal Express. He is currently a DC-10 captain. In 1998 he published an article on the Barrow Gang's killing of the local city marshal in his hometown. In 2000 he began work on this updated biography of Bonnie and Clyde, working with Dallas historian Jonathan Davis. Knight and his wife, Judy, have three children and two grandchildren, and live in Franklin, Tennessee.

JONATHAN DAVIS was born in Evansville, Indiana. Davis became acquainted with Marie Barrow in 1993 in connection with their mutual involvement on a documentary concerning Bonnie and Clyde. He worked with her on several projects over the last five and a half years of her life. Davis has been involved with different Barrow-related productions, including several television programs and an off-Broadway play. He currently resides in Dallas, Texas.

Printed in August 2019
by Rotomail Italia S.p.A., Vignate (MI) - Italy